The Ethnic Experience in the United States

Edited by Grace Peña Delgado
and Troy R. Johnson
California State University—Long Beach

KENDALL/HUNT PUBLISHING COMPANY
4050 Westmark Drive Dubuque, Iowa 52002

ISBN 0-7575-2008-1

Printed in the United States of America
10 9 8 7 6 5 4 3 2 1

Contents

History

Native American Studies

African American Studies

Chicano and Latino Studies

Asian American Studies

Culture

Native American Studies

African American Studies

Chicano and Latino Studies

Asian American Studies

Contemporary Issues

Native American Studies

African American Studies

Chicano and Latino Studies

Asian American Studies

Section 1

History

Native American Perspectives on the United States

Troy R. Johnson

As an introduction I must first clarify the term "Native American" as used throughout this article. Prior to European contact there were some eight hundred indigenous groups that we now call "tribes" or "nations." These groups were not related by birth, culture, religion, or for the most part by shared languages. Each group had its own name that translated to something similar to *first people, river people, forest people, mountain people, desert people, real people,* or simply *the people.* Names that we are familiar with today such as Mohawk or Apache were assigned by other native groups, and tribal names such as Gros Ventre or Nez Perce were of French origin. The term Native American came into use because "native" seemed to incorporate the concept of these people being native to the United States, and the word "American" honored the cartographer Amerigo Vespucci. It was Vespucci who recognized that the land discovered by Columbus in 1492 was not Asia, but indeed, a separate continent. The German cartographer Martin Waldseemuller printed the first map of the "new world" using the name Amerigo after having read a record of Vespucci's travel. Other names or terms such as American Indian are equally faulty in that they incorporate the Amerigo distinction as well as the word "Indian," which was first used by Columbus to describe the inhabitants of Guanahani (present-day San Salvador) when he mistakenly thought that he had reached the East Indies and thus called the inhabitants "los Indois," or Indians. From this Spanish term came the French Indien, the German Indianer, and the English Indian as the general name for the native inhabitants. With this brief history in mind, I use the terms Native American tribe, Native nation, or Native people in this article with respect for their particular culture, name, and history.

Today, there are over 562 federally recognized Indian nations and over 100 non-federally recognized Indian nations in the United States. These nations, just as their ancestors, are not related and their histories are not the same. Thus there is no single "Native American," and there is no singular "Native American perspective" on the United States. This article, then, will present the most commonly expressed and accepted viewpoint arrived at after years of research and conversation with Native People from across the United States.

The Native American view of the people who would come to explore, exploit, settle, found, and develop the United States began prior to actual contact. The views were developed as the results of dreams, visions, and events that shaped the understanding of the world for many Native People.

The White Man's Foot

Long before European contact the great Iroquois visionary Iagoo told of the coming of these strange people. Henry Wadsworth Longfellow recorded the vision of Iagoo in his poem "The White Man's Foot." Iagoo said that he had seen, Longfellow said: "water bigger than the big-sea-water. . . . Bitter so that none could drink it. . . . O'er it . . . came a great canoe with pinions [giant bird wings], . . . bigger than a grove of pine-trees, taller than the tallest treetops! . . . In it, said [Iagoo], came a people . . . painted white were all their faces and with hair their chins were covered! . . . The Great Spirit, the Creator, sends them hither on his errand [said Iagoo]. . . . Wheresoe'er they move, before them swarms the stinging fly . . . swarms the bee, the honey-maker; wheresoe'er they tread, beneath them springs a flower unknown among us, springs the White-man's Foot in blossom. . . . I beheld, too, in that vision all the secrets of the future. . . . I beheld the westward marches of the unknown, crowded nations. All the land was full of people, restless, struggling, toiling, striving, speaking many tongues. . . . In the woodlands rang their axes, smoked their towns in all the valleys. Over all the lakes and rivers rushed their great canoes of thunder. Then a darker, drearier vision passed before me, vague and cloud-like. I beheld our nation scattered, all forgetful of my counsel, weakened, warring with each other: [I] saw the remnants of our people sweeping westward, wild and woeful, like the cloud-rack of a tempest, like the withered leaves of Autumn!" In his vision Iagoo had seen the coming of the Europeans in large ships, the spreading of the new nation westward, and the scattering of the Indian nations. The vision of the scattering of Native nations, thousands of years old, and the development of the United States, given to Iagoo years before actual contact, was fulfilled in less than three hundred years.

Seven Cities of Gold

The Native Americans of the American Southwest did not see a European until 1530 and their view of what would become the United States developed as the result of direct contact rather than through a vision. The protagonists were a Moroccan by the name of Estevanico and his fellow explorers.

Estevanico was a member of the 1527 Cabeza de Vaca expedition intent on exploring and conquering the unknown lands of present-day Florida. De Vaca's party consisted of three hundred poorly trained men who demanded access to Indian women and tortured or enslaved Indian men. The Indians retaliated and de Vaca's party sustained many casualties. The survivors made crude canoes and set sail into the Gulf of Mexico, hoping to reach Mexico. Only eight men survived after the boats capsized on the Texas coast near present-day Galveston. The Native People treated the survivors friendly at first, but later enslaved them. Only four of the eighty survivors lived through the enslavement, Estevanico being one of the four.

In 1534, Estevanico and his companions escaped inland and lived among Indian tribes who were impressed by their basic medical skills and revered them as medicine men. Their reputation as healers preceded them as they traveled westward. Estevanico was particularly respected because of his dark skin and because he assumed the dress of a medicine man. He carried a medicine rattle, a feathered and beaded gourd given to him by a chief, and wore Indian beadwork and feathered clothing. Out of respect and possibly fear, the Native People took turns guiding the travelers through each of their respective lands. In July 1536 Estevanico's group reached their goal, Mexico City, not, however, before creating a story of having seen seven cities of gold in the lands of the Pueblo Indians.

The Viceroy of Mexico, hearing of the discovery, saw an opportunity for riches based on Estevanico's report and in February 1539, Estevanico led a small, advanced party northward on foot. Estevanico traveled ahead of the larger party, sending runners back daily with promises of the rich country ahead. When Estevanico arrived at Hawikuh, a Zuni pueblo, the Zunis met him with distrust. The medicine gourd that Estevanico carried was trimmed with owl feathers, a bird that symbolized death to the Zuni. Estevanico demanded gold, food, and access to the Zuni women. The Zuni men responded by attacking Estevanico and his men, killing them all, but not before a runner escaped carrying the message that the seven cities of gold had been found.

The Spanish conquistador Francisco de Coronado led the most famous journey ever made in search of treasures in the New World. Seeking the now-fabled seven cities of gold, his expedition of 1,400 men and 1,500 animals found only poor Indian villages, but established Spain's later claim to the entire American Southwest. Moving northward out of Mexico, Coronado and his advance party of Spanish cavalry came upon the Zuni pueblo of Hawikuh, in western New Mexico. Coronado made the same demands on the Zuni as had Estevanico. A Zuni medicine man drew a line of sacred corn pollen in the sand and forbade the Spanish to cross into the Zuni village. Coronado and his men, mounted on horses and armed with guns, metal spears, and swords, attacked and laid waste to the pueblo and its inhabitants. This established an enduring legacy of Europeans as evil, warlike, and hungry for access to Indian women that would be repeated time and time again in the development of the United States.

The California Experience: People of Peace and Prosperity

It can be accurately stated that hundreds of thousands of Native People inhabitated the present-day state of California long before European contact. The actual numbers vary with a general consensus of 330,000 even though 1,000,000 is probably closer to an accurate accounting. If one had the ability to return to those days and travel this land they would see hundreds, if not thousands of prosperous and peaceful villages made up of patrilineal (male-centered) families. Some villages were small with one hundred or fewer inhabitants. Other villages were large with populations numbering in the thousands. Leadership within the villages lacked any hierarchical structure and was without formal chiefs of councils. Villages were governed by a head-man who was a social leader whose prestige was based on the accumulation and display of wealth. As trade, gift-giving and reciprocity were widely practiced by the indigenous people, the accumulation of wealth (trade goods) was extremely important. As native peoples traveled from place to place and entered the territory of another village it was expected that they would bring with them both gifts and trade goods. A runner would precede the visit advising the host of the trade goods being brought so that ample and equal quality goods would be available. In order to ensure a sufficient amount of goods it was not uncommon that a village leader might have more than one wife to assist him in the collection of goods and the hosting of the visiting group. Warfare on a large scale was rare. Murder or trespassing did lead to brief conflicts however most disagreements were settled by the payment in the form of trade goods and perhaps the performance so some form of labor over a period of time. Bow and arrow, deer hide sling, and spear were the only weapons used and fatalities were usually low.

The Portuguese-born explorer Juan Cabrillo was the first European to explore California. Sailing under the Spanish flag in 1542, Cabrillo hoped to find the Northwest Passage; instead, he made land-fall on the California coast and claimed the new land for Spain. In 1579, an Englishman, Sir Francis Drake, arrived in California. After spending five weeks among the California natives he and his crew departed. Before leaving however, members of his crew passed European diseases among the Native People. Claiming the territory based on "right of discovery," Cabrillo claimed the land for the English Crown. Thus, within the first forty years of European influence in California, two countries had claimed the land, and neither had acknowledged the rights of the Native People who had flourished there for thousands of years.

The relationship between the Spanish and the Indians was not one of peaceful coexistence. Rather, the history of California Indians is the story of an attempt to survive a series of invasions and the hardships that ensued. The Native People based their view of Europeans on their contact experience and religious belief. The Europeans came onto their lands uninvited, brought livestock that destroyed their food crops, and most devastating they frequently sexually assaulted Indian women. When husbands or fathers attempted to intervene they were killed. Records of mission priests and letters to seniors in Spain are filled with statements that indicate that "the most difficulty in our endeavor for conversion is wrought by the abuse of Indian women by the soldiers and men of the presidio who go to great distance to capture and have their way with young women."

Spain's regarded the indigenous people participants in a form of economic, military, and religious relationship. Indian People were regarded by the Spanish government as subjects of the Crown "by right of discovery," and human beings capable of receiving the sacraments of Christianity." To achieve this goal it was essential that California Indians be removed from their village environment and be resettled in missions they would become Catholic converts and citizens of the King. Additionally, the missions of California were not solely religious institutions. They were, on the contrary, instruments designed to bring about a total destruction of Indian culture and to be profitable through the hide and tallow trade to the Spanish treasury.

The opposition to the harsh labor conditions, separation of families, and the exploitive and un-ending physical coercion that characterized mission life resulted in several well documented forms of Indian resistance. Indian people within the missions feigned conversion in order to receive kinder treatment while they continued to secretly worship their creator as well as conduct native dances and rituals out of sight and hearing of the mission community. By far the most frequent form of mission Indian resistance was fugitivism or running away. This was extremely difficult however because their villages had been decimated by the Spanish in quest for new subjects to be brought into the mission system. More importantly, many Native People Indians viewed the padres as powerful witches who could be put to death. Consequently, several assassinations occurred. In 1801 at Mission San Miguel in the year of 1801 three padres were poisoned, one of whom died. In 1804 a San Diego Padre was poisoned by his personal cook. In 1812 Costanoan Indians at Mission Santa Cruz killed a padre for introducing a new instrument of torture. The Ipai and Tipai of San Diego launched two assaults against the missionaries and their military escorts within five weeks of their arrival in 1769. In another revolt they destroyed Mission San Diego and killed the local padre in 1775. The last great mission Indian revolt occurred in 1824 when Chumash Indians violently overthrew mission control at Santa Barbara.

The cultural and physical damage had been done however. At the end of the mission period the California Indian population had dropped to 100,000 to be followed by the Mexican period, lowering the population to approximately 33,000 and the American period that propelled the genocide down to fewer than 10,000. Today there are over 600,000 Indian people representing over 100 tribes living in California demonstrating the amazing resilience of California Indian people. The People entered the new century filled with optimism.

The Colonial Period

As the European population in the New World increased and moved toward the formation of the United States, so too did the Native American perspective of these new neighbors. In the Chesapeake Bay area of presentday Virginia the contact was between the Jamestown settlers and the powerful Powhatan Confederacy.

In the Chesapeake Bay area of present-day Virginia, European entrepreneurs founded the Jamestown colony in 1607. These businessmen intended to become rich by the discovery of gold and silver just as the Spanish had in the Caribbean and South America. The founders did not intend to work themselves or to import a labor force. Their plan was to emulate the Spanish and use forced labor (of Native People) to become wealthy. This dream died quickly as it was soon discovered that there was no mineral wealth to be extracted in the area. The reorganization of the Jamestown colony and the cash crop tobacco provided a second chance at riches.

The Powhatan Confederacy, under the leadership of the Pamunkey Indian Chief Powhatan, was the immediate eastern neighbor of the Jamestown colony. This Algonquian confederacy consisted of some two hundred villages and about 2,400 warriors, all of whom paid tribute to Powhatan in the form of deer skins, beaver furs, or agricultural products.

The presence of such a formidable number of Indian warriors caused great fear for the Jamestown colony leaders, as they were fighting a battle for survival with the foreign environment that they faced in the New World. The harsh climate, lack of food supplies, and exposure to germs to which they had no immunity caused large numbers of deaths. They rightly realized that an alliance with the neighboring Powhatan Confederacy was both necessary and beneficial. The Powhatans could provide them with food and teach them survival skills in the New World while providing a strong security force against possible attacks by other Native groups. Born of necessity, the Europeans moved toward a positive relationship with Powhatan and his confederacy. A positive attitude toward the Native People grew out of that alliance.

For Powhatan and his people the colonists posed a new challenge. The colonists brought with them technology and materials that made life easier for them. Guns and powder increased the number of animals that they could kill. Broadcloth, sewing thread, needles, and metal pots and pans all made life easier for the Indian people. At first the colonists did not ask for much: food for survival, advice on what crops would grow and when and where to plant, and the use of land on which to build and farm. The Powhatans accepted the colonists' gifts and in a relationship of reciprocity they granted the settlers the use (not ownership) of the small portion of land that they desired.

It can be said, then, that a positive view of the European colonists by the Native People existed and was balanced by a positive view of the Native People by the colonists. This did not last long, however. The colonists understood that they were purchasing the lands by the gifts that they gave the Powhatans. The Powhatans had no sense of ownership of the land in the sense that it could be bought or sold. As soil fertility was reduced by overplanting of tobacco crops, the colonists began to put more pressure on Powhatan for additional land. The colonists soon found it easier to break into the Powhatan's food caches (storage) than to plant, tend, and harvest their own foodstuffs, and European diseases took large death tolls among the Native People. Soon the accommodating relationship between the two groups was strained beyond repair. Warfare erupted in 1622 and again in 1644. Captain John Smith praised God for the warfare and stated that the wars, now known as the Powhatan Wars, gave the colonists an excuse to kill all Indians, not just the Powhatans but also any Indian with whom they came into contact.

The Powhatan Indians now viewed the colonists as liars, thieves, murderers, and people who could not be trusted. This attitude spread to Native nations far beyond the Powhatan Confederacy as tribes not associated in any way with the Powhatan Confederacy suffered relentless attacks by colonists pushing westward. Meanwhile, in the Northeast (present-day Connecticut) a similar scenario played out in the Puritan massacre of the Pequot Indians at Mystic River. A perspective of fear, distrust, trepidation, and apprehension solidified among Native People east of the Mississippi River, from Canada south to the Gulf of Mexico, as the colonists' "new world" began to be transformed by violence into what we now call the United States.

United States Domination during the Reservation Era

Troy R. Johnson

The reservation era, the period when Native Americans were forcibly confined to small, government-controlled areas in the western United States, began for most tribal groups during the period 1867 to 1884. Puritans, however, established the earliest reservation in the "new world" in 1638. Under an agreement between the Quinnipiac Nation and the Puritans, the Quinnipiac retained 1,200 acres of their original lands near present-day New Haven, Connecticut and were made subject to the jurisdiction of an English magistrate or agent. As with the later western reservations, the Quinnipiac people could not sell or leave their lands without being subject to harsh punishments including death. Though circumstances have changed over the ensuing years, many Native People still live on Indian reservations today.

The reservation era has been identified as a great pulverizing agent on the part of the U.S. government for suppression of culture, language, religion, and the detribalization of the Native People. Beginning with the Little Arkansas Council in October 1865, Indian people were relocated onto reservations where they fell under the watchful eyes of military personnel and government Indian agents. These representatives of the government often spent more time cheating Indian people out of food and other treaty annuities than they did seeing to the well-being of the Native People.

Indian people were forced onto reservations as the result of the overpowering technology of rapid communication by the new telegraph, invented in 1838, massive troop movements made possible by the expanding railroad networks, and the superiority of firepower as the industrial Northeast manufactured rifles, pistols, and cannons by the thousands. Scorched-earth policies and relentless winter campaigns brought suffering and death to Indian people who clung tenaciously to their traditional ways of life. Still, the Native People resisted the taking of their lands and forced concentration on reservations. Great leaders arose whose names are recorded in legend, books, oral history, song, and tradition. Leaders such as Crazy Horse, Sitting Bull, Geronimo, Satank, Satanta, Gall, Cochise, and Manuleto counseled resistance and fought against the surrendering of Indian lands. Ultimately Western technology prevailed and in 1884 the last reservation, the Northern Cheyenne Reservation, was created in the Tongue River Agency in Montana. The western Apache, the last of the resistive tribes, was conquered in 1885 and forced onto an assigned reservation. The government's goal of detribalization and Americanization could now begin in earnest.

The tribal structure was central to the life of Native People, and was viewed as a threat to "civilized" Americans. Whether matrilineal or patrilineal, most Native People viewed the tribal structure as an extended kinship group and participated in an egalitarian lifestyle where reciprocity, the act of obligatory exchange, was a key to survival. Parents, grandparents, brothers, sisters, aunts, and uncles all shared in a communal lifestyle that was anathema to the Western worldview.

Native People and tribal life-ways specifically were regarded as threatening to the immigrants who were moving west in large numbers and were purchasing or homesteading former Indian lands. Settlers expected the new national government to protect whatever land rights existed and to destroy any remaining vestiges of Indian nations that might threaten white hegemony. The concentration of Indians on restricted reservations would limit their mobility and permit their forced detribalization. Indian agents were instructed to destroy any remaining vestiges of tribal government, language, religion, or culture. Recognized tribal leaders were ignored by Indian agents who appointed new "chiefs." Treaty annuities were distributed through these newly appointed leaders, thus usurping the authority of traditional leaders. The responsibility of Indian men was supplanted further as government cattle replaced the buffalo hunt and the roles of village crier, village police, war leader, and social leader were rendered obsolete. The practice of native religions such as the Sun Dance and Ghost Dance were forbidden and Christian missionaries divided up the reservations and attempted to convert Indian people to an American religion. Much to the credit of Native People, however, these changes were not internalized. Although it appeared to many Indian agents and to Christian evangelists that traditional forms of government, Native religions, and cultural practices were abandoned or destroyed, a large body of evidence now exists that indicates that Native People retained their traditional beliefs and lifeways in secret and out-of-sight of the Indian agents. Tribal members, many of whom were Native women, memorized songs, dances, and ceremonies that survived the reservation era to be resurfaced and revitalized in later years.

A key component to the detribalization and Americanization of the Native American was the removal of Indian children from the Indian family and tribal environment to be educated in a Western model. In 1877 Congress appropriated $20,000 for the express purpose of the reeducation of Indian children, to "kill the Indian and save the child." By 1900 the funding reached approximately $3 million. The idea was not new to the 1800s, however. From colonial times it had been felt that civilization and assimilation of the Indian person required an American education. President Thomas Jefferson believed that education was the key to preparing Indians for assimilation. It was not until the nineteenth century that a concerted effort was made and enforced by the U.S. government. The off-reservation boarding school based on the Carlisle Indian School would become the model program.

In 1879 Army Captain Richard H. Pratt founded the Carlisle Indian School at Carlisle Barracks, Pennsylvania as a demonstration project to convince the government and the general public that Indians could be educated. Carlisle became the model for off-reservation boarding schools. The number of students enrolled in day schools on reservations and off-reservation boarding schools increased. From an enrollment of 3,598 in 1877, over 20,000 Indian students were enrolled in 148 boarding schools and 225 day schools by the close of the nineteenth century.

Indian parents were demoralized and terrorized by the threat of their children being kidnapped by Indian agents and army soldiers and being taken to remote boarding schools, some as distant as eight hundred miles from their homes. Attendance was made mandatory, however. In 1891 Congress authorized the Commissioner of Indian Affairs "to make and enforce by proper means" rules and regulations to ensure that Indian children attended the schools. Native People resisted by sequestering their children in mountain hideaways or by taking them deep into reservations where agents often pursued them on horseback and lassoed them like animals, bound them hand and foot, threw them into wagons, and hauled them like freight to train terminals where they were then shipped off to distant schools.

In the Southwestern United States pressure to enroll children in boarding schools began in earnest in 1887 when the first government school was established at Keams Canyon. According to the Indian agent E. H. Plummer, the Keams Canyon School was in dismal condition. The school was crowded and the buildings were poorly maintained. Plummer himself feared that disease would spread and death among the children would occur. As a result, many Hopi parents refused to send their children to a school so far away to learn the white man's ways.

When parents resisted, the government attempted to bribe or force them into sending their children to school. In January 1894, with two feet of snow on the ground and the temperature 17 degrees below zero, agent Plummer told the superintendent of the Keams Canyon School to stop issuing treaty annuity goods and to cease all work on houses and wells for the village of Second Mesa until the families agreed to send their children to the school. The government also resorted to force. In December 1890 soldiers entered the village of Oraibi and through coercion and force secured 104 children for the Keams Canyon School. The scene was repeated in 1894 at the Hopi village on Second Mesa.

The removal and education of children was fiercely resisted by Indian people, perhaps none more strongly than the Hopi. Finally, in January 1895, as an example to resistant families the government arrested nineteen Hopi Indian men and sentenced them to confinement on Alcatraz Island because they had hidden their children and would not allow them to be taken to the boarding school. The prisoners were released in September 1895.

When Indian children arrived at the boarding schools both boys and girls had their hair cut short and were given new American names. For most Indian people the cutting off of the hair represented a condition of mourning and was associated with death. For Indian children in boarding schools this represented a life-and-death battle to retain their religion, language, and cultural identity. Many Indian children were required to select an Anglo name from lists that they could not possibly read or understand. Other children were simply assigned new names. Traditional clothing was taken away and miniature copies of military uniforms with high collars, stiff shirts, and leather boots were given to the boys and long cotton dresses and hard leather shoes were given to the girls.

The goals of the boarding schools were numerous. First and foremost was the belief that Indian children should be removed from parental and tribal influences. Accordingly, the children were sent to distant boarding schools, some as far as eight hundred miles from their families. A summer program called the "outing" program was added to the boarding school program and placed Indian children on farms and ranches near the boarding school. This prevented the child's return to the reservation during the summer months. The federal government paid the host family $50 a year per student for upkeep and any money generated by the labor of the student was claimed by the boarding school. As a result of the distant schools and the outing program, Indian children typically were separated from their family for periods ranging from four to eight years. At Carlisle Indian School, Indian children who had completed their schooling were "outed" to non-Indian families for a three-year period.

A second goal of the boarding schools was to destroy the cultural heritage of the individual Indian. For Native girls this meant that they were to be transformed into a government version of the ideal American woman. They were instructed in the skills of housekeeping, laundry, cooking, ironing, and the use of sewing machines; skills that had no relationship to life on a reservation.

Indian boys were felt to be more unmanageable than girls because of an "inherited spirit of independence." Accordingly, the training for Native boys was organized in a military fashion and followed a strict time schedule.

Treatment at the boarding school varied but most children endured harsh discipline, particularly if they were caught speaking their native language, performing a traditional ceremony, or practicing their native religion. Corporal punishment, solitary confinement, and withholding of rations were common punishments used to control Native students who insisted on retaining and practicing traditional ways.

Not all Indian children enrolled in boarding schools were there as the result of threats and kidnapping, nor were all experiences reported as being brutal. During the Great Depression years, 1929–1940, some Indian families simply could not provide for their children. The boarding schools were seen as a place where their children would be fed, clothed, and boarded. Some Indian families delivered their children in order to save them from starvation or death by exposure. Life at the boarding schools varied from one school to another as well. As more books are being written by Indian adults who underwent the boarding school experience it has become clear that some, not a large number, found the experience preferable to life on the stark, depressing reservations where they found little hope for a productive future. Traditional life had been destroyed and some Native children found in the boarding schools a new hope for a future in the "new world order" being forced upon them.

For most Indian children the "new hope" proved to be more illusionary than real. Indian boys and girls were taught skills in the boarding schools that had little or no relationship to tribal or reservation life. Indian children who attempted to return to their families could no longer speak their native languages. Skills necessary for survival in a tribal or reservation setting had been crushed. The children were poorly trained for the non-Indian world as well. Some Indian boys found work on farms and ranches. To the disappointment of boarding school administrators most returned to the reservations and attempted to reestablish themselves within the tribal culture. A small number of Native girls found work for the Bureau of Indian Affairs, but most met only with discrimination and unemployment.

As mentioned earlier, all boarding school students were required to speak the English language, or at least the American version of the English language. To speak the Native tongue brought swift and certain punishment. Though this had disastrous results on children who would no longer be able to speak with or understand their own family members, this misguided government program had a long-term unintended effect, the benefit of which was not perceived by the federal government. Indian children, soon to be Indian adults, would now have a *lingua franca,* a common language. This had never existed in the past. Over five hundred Native nations spoke over three hundred languages or dialects. Now Indian people from different tribal groups could speak in a common tongue of shared sufferings, lies, deceits, mistreatment, and land thefts by the federal government. Additionally, in the boarding schools Indian boys and girls from different Indian nations came into contact with each other for the first time. Romances and liaisons emerged and marriages crossed tribal boundaries in large numbers for the first time in their history. The children of the boarding school children would be tribally mixed-blood children, with reading, writing, and speaking the English language forced upon them in the boarding schools. These "Americanized" Indian children would fill the ranks and lead the activism that would emerge among Native People in the late 1950s, 1960s, and 1970s, a subject to be addressed in a later chapter.

The next step in the government's plan to Americanize and assimilate Indian people into the general U.S. population came with the passage of the Dawes General Allotment Act of 1887. The act is more generally known as the Allotment Act. The intent of the Act was to abolish reservations and to allot land to individual Indian people as private property, and was the single most devastating development during this period because it worked to undermine tribal self-sufficiency and tribal sovereignty.

As more and more settlers moved west under the national ideology of "manifest destiny," new lands were needed. Pressure mounted to abolish Indian reservations. Allotment, a thinly disguised way to break up tribal land holdings, was the answer. The chief provisions of the Allotment Act provided that each Indian family head would receive a grant of 160 acres of reservation land, in fee simple title. Each single Indian person over eighteen years and each orphan under eighteen years of age received 80 acres, and each other single person under eighteen received 40 acres of former reservation land. The key to the Allotment Act was that all land remaining after the allotment to Native People would revert to the federal government and the government would in turn offer this "surplus" land for sale.

Proponents of the Allotment Act claimed that they had the endorsement of Indian rights associations across the country. Allotment would break up communal holdings, they said, and instill the American ethos of individual ambition in the individual Indian. The overarching goal of the "friends of the Indian," those who supported allotment, was to substitute white civilization for Indian culture. Individual land holding would break up extended families and further undermine traditional leadership patterns.

Not all non-Indians were blind to the intent of the Allotment Act. U.S. Senator Henry M. Teller warned that within forty years Indians would be homeless, separated from their fee simple titles to allotment homesteads. Teller called the bill "a bill to despoil the Indians of their lands and to make them vagabonds on the face of the earth." Attacking those who promoted allotment, Teller charged that allotment was not in the best interest of Native People but rather "was in the interests of the land-grabbing speculators." The minority report of the House Indian Affairs Committee in 1880, going further even than Senator Teller, stated that "The real aim of this bill is to get at the Indian lands and open them up to settlement. The provisions for the apparent benefit of the Indian are but the pretext to get at his lands and occupy them. . . . If this were done in the name of greed," the Committee wrote, "it would be bad enough; but to do it in the name of humanity, and under the cloak of an ardent desire to promote the Indian's welfare by making him like ourselves whether he will or not, is infinitely worse."

The Allotment Act was passed into law even though there was little or no support of the concept of allotment by Indian people. In 1888 Congress ratified five agreements with different Indian nations providing for the allotment and sale of what the federal government now described as surplus reservation lands. In 1889 eight such laws were passed. By 1891 it was apparent that Senator Teller's fears were well founded. Between 1889 and 1891 an estimated 104,314,349 acres of Indian reservation lands had been reduced by 12,000,000 acres. In the first nine months of 1891 an additional 8,000,000 acres of former reservation lands passed into non-Indian hands. In 1906 the Burke Act was passed, removing restrictions that had been contained in the Allotment Act requiring a twenty-five year period before individual allotments could be sold. Oil speculators and timber companies bought up individual allotments. Minor Indian children who possessed allotment lands were declared wards of non-Indians so that oil could be extracted from their allotments or fertile farmlands could be exploited. Through these methods the total of Indian land holdings was cut from 138,000,000 acres in 1887 to 48,000,000 acres in 1934. Many Indian people did become landless persons as forecasted by Senator Teller, and Native People living on the remaining allotted reservation lands increasingly experienced extreme poverty, despondency, and despair.

Over the ensuing years, and as a result of the passage of the Allotment Act, other problems regarding Indians lands have emerged. Indian people who were successful in "holding on" to their allotted land either passed their land on to heirs or died intestate and their allotments were divided among the remaining heirs. Through the passage of time, the original 160, 80, or 40 acres have been subdivided among successive generations to a point where original allotments are now measured in acres, feet, or even inches, commonly called fractionalized lands. In some cases these small parcels are of little profitable use to any one person alone. The federal government, however, bears a fiduciary relationship with Indian people under the trust relationship established in the 1881 court case *Cherokee Nation* v. *Georgia* and has combined small parcels and leased these and larger Indian lands to non-Indian entrepreneurs for the purpose of pasturage, farming, and mineral extraction. The royalties from the use of the Indian lands, however small, are to be held in trust for Native landowners. The failure of the U.S. government to fulfill its financial obligation and trust responsibility has most recently come to light. Beginning in 1998, the Native American Rights Fund, located in Boulder, Colorado, has pursued a court case regarding the failure of the government to live up to its constitutional responsibility regarding the Indian trust responsibility. In January 2000 the U.S. Justice Department reported that the Department of Interior, charged with overseeing and fulfilling the trust responsibility, cannot account for over $2 billion in missing trust fund moneys belonging to Native People. Records have disappeared over the years, and as the investigation was underway additional records were shredded despite a judge's orders not to do so. The Secretary of the Interior was held in contempt of court for obstructing the ongoing investigation. The Native American Rights Fund has challenged the monetary sum as far less than the amount rightfully owed to the Native People, and the investigation continues as this book is being written.

Indian Interpretations and Responses to the Reservation System

Troy R. Johnson

Despite the onerous government policies of detribalization, allotment, and assimilation, Native People did not willingly surrender their traditional religions, cultures, and traditions. Though it may have appeared to Indian agents, military officers, government officials, and "friends of the Indians" that Indian people had abandoned their life-ways and adopted that of the dominant society, the fact is that most of the traditional ways were retained. Native People might, for instance, attend a Christian worship service of some Western denomination, or appear to no longer practice their native religion. Most often out of sight of "white eyes," Native People retained their strong ties in their sacred beliefs and cultural practices. Specifically, in the western United States, many tribes continued to participate in a rapidly spreading religion known as the Ghost Dance.

On January 1, 1889 a Paiute visionary by the name of Wovoka announced that he had received a message from the Creator. The Creator instructed Wovoka to tell the people that they must be good and love one another. Indian people were to cooperate with the white people and live in peace without warfare until the time that the Creator would remove all white people from the earth.

Wovoka was given a number of powers that included five songs for weather control, invulnerability to weapons, political responsibility, and prophecies. He was also given a sacred dance that he was to teach to his people. The dance was known to the Northern Paiute as *nanigukwa,* "dance in a circle." The dance was to be performed for four successive nights and the last night they were to keep up the dance until the morning of the fifth day. The people were instructed to do the new dance every six weeks. If the people obeyed these instructions they would be reunited with family and friends in the other world, where there would be no sickness, old age, or death. The white people would be removed from the earth.

Word of the new religion spread quickly among Indian people of the Great Basin and Plains regions. Indian people representing over thirty tribes traveled great distances to visit Wovoka and to learn more of his teachings, often returning home filled with messages of hope for their people. Many Indian people who had undergone severe cultural and physical attacks eagerly accepted the teachings of Wovoka. The U.S. Army's scorched-earth military policy instituted by Generals Sherman and Sheridan, the destruction of the buffalo, confinement on reservations, and epidemics of strange and lethal diseases set the stage for the acceptance of Wovoka's message of revitalization.

As the religious movement spread, it took on features unique to individual tribes. When the Ghost Dance reached the Lakota they added the wearing of a Ghost Dance shirt to the religion. The Ghost Dance shirt, it was believed, would repel the white man's bullets. Non-Indians became alarmed by reports of what they perceived to be warriors performing a new war dance that was supposed to result in the disappearance of whites and the return of the buffalo. In their eyes, the wearing of the Ghost Dance shirt transformed Wovoka's religious movement into a warrior movement. Government agents and missionaries opposed the Ghost Dance and in 1890 the army outlawed the practice of the Ghost Dance on Indian reservations. Tensions intensified between the Lakota and the soldiers as Indian people left the reservations without permission to hunt and to participate in the Ghost Dance ritual out of sight of the army. Sitting Bull, a great Lakota spiritual leader, was killed by Indian police in December 1890 when it was believed that he intended to join the Ghost Dancers. Two weeks later, on December 29, 1890, remnants of Custer's Seventh Cavalry massacred more than two hundred men, women, and children of Big Foot's band of Miniconjou Sioux at Wounded Knee in South Dakota. It was incorrectly believed that Big Foot was en route to join Ghost Dancers who had left the Cheyenne River Reservation to carry out the teachings of Wovoka.

The massacre at Wounded Knee was just one of a number of such atrocities carried out against Native People. It was one of the last in a series of attempts by the U.S. federal government to crush Native nationalism and to exterminate Indian people. The Chivington massacre of 1864 was one such event and has been recognized as "one of the worst massacres of the wars for the West."

Beginning in the mid-1850s, the Cheyenne Indian people were under increasing pressure to surrender their homelands brought about by the expanding mining frontier that now included their traditional lands in Colorado Territory. The general increase in traffic brought about by miners, homesteaders, and ranchers was destroying the Cheyenne way of life. Ultimately the Cheyenne were removed to an area they shared with the Arapaho Nation called the Sand Creek Reserve that was described as the "most dry and desolate region" in the territory. To control the Indians and to ensure that they did not interfere with westward expansion, the federal government constructed Fort Lyon on the reserve.

The Indian people found the Sand Creek Reserve impossible to live on. The reserve could not support life and the bison that they depended on for food, shelter, and clothing were increasingly hard to find. As a result, and out of desperation, Cheyenne and Arapaho hunters left the San Creek Reserve in order to provide sustenance for their families. Colorado Governor John Evans considered the Indian hunters who left the reserve as being in a state of war and sent word that they were to return to their reservation or "suffer the consequences."

In response to Governor Evans's mandate, Black Kettle led five hundred Cheyenne back to the San Creek Reserve where they set up their village as instructed. On November 29, 1864, Colonel John M. Chivington, a former Methodist minister, led nine hundred men of the First Colorado Volunteer Regiment to the reserve and attacked Black Kettle's village. In the resulting carnage, the soldiers (known as the "bloodless First") butchered some 270 Indian people, mostly women and children. Soldiers cut off body parts from men, women, and children and displayed them to cheering audiences in Denver, Colorado. A congressional investigation found that the Cheyenne "were mutilated in the most horrible manner." The investigation also found that Black Kettle had raised an American flag and a white peace flag as he had been instructed to do. The commissioner of Indian affairs stated that Chivington and his troops had participated in a massacre in which Indian people were "butchered in cold blood by troops in the service of the United States." Among the statements attributed to Chivington are "all Indians should be killed and scalped, including infants. Nits make lice!", "Damn any man who sympathizes with Indians!", and "I have come to kill Indians, and believe it is right and honorable to use any means under God's heaven to kill Indians." The Indian response to the Chivington massacre and similar atrocities culminated in a battle at a place called "Greasy Grass."

In the mid 1800s, the numerous Indian nations who hunted and lived on the Great Plains were under increasing pressure to abandon their traditional ways of life, to abandon the hunt, and to acquiesce to the government's demands that they be confined to reservations which were in actuality nothing more than early "prisoner-of-war camps." Great Indian leaders such as Crazy Horse (Brule Sioux), Sitting Bull (Hunkpapa Sioux), and Gall (Hunkpapa Sioux), however, refused to give up the way of their grandfathers, to break their ties to the place of their creation, to put down the bow and pick up the plow. Disparate Indian nations would unite at Greasy Grass in a last attempt to stop the assault on Native nationalism.

In the spring of 1876, General Philip Sheridan initiated a campaign that was intended to either exterminate or capture the remaining Indian people who refused to be confined to reservations. Using a now-common military tactic of maneuvering three forces in concert to surround the enemy, Sheridan joined with General Alfred Terry and Colonel John Gibbon to surround a large group of resistant Indians in an encampment on a river called the Little Bighorn. Serving under General Terry was an impetuous former Civil War general, George Armstrong Custer. Now a colonel, Custer had been recently court-martialed and removed from the army for one year. Returned to active duty, Custer was anxious to restore his military reputation and some say to pursue a political career, possibly for the presidency of the United States.

Anxious to score a major military victory against the Indians, Custer moved on his own to attack the concentrated Indian force at Little Big Horn. Custer was most likely unaware of the size of the combined Indian encampment until he had divided his own troop into three divisions and committed them to the attack. On June 25, 1876, Custer directed Major Marcus A. Reno to begin the attack with 112 men. One division of 125 men under the leadership of Captain Frederick W. Benteen was ordered to move to the south in order to prevent any escape by the Indians in that direction. Custer, now commanding some two hundred soldiers, ascended a bluff overlooking the Little Big Horn River and commenced an attack on an Indian force now estimated to be in excess of 1,500 warriors. Colonel Gibbon's final admonition to Custer had been "Now Custer, don't be greedy, but wait for us" to which Custer replied. "I will not." Custer's failure to heed Gibbon's warning resulted in the death of some 215 men including himself, his brother Captain Thomas W. Custer, his brother Boston Custer, his nephew Autie Reed, and his brother-in-law Captain James Calhoun, all of whom were in the final charge led by Colonel George Armstrong Custer.

The battle quickly became known as the Custer massacre although the attack was planned and initiated by the U.S. Army. Coming as it did in 1876, during the centennial anniversary of American independence, the American public was righteously outraged and demanded that the Indian nations be punished. Heavy military reinforcements poured onto the Great Plains where they pursued the Native People relentlessly. The government troops carried out a scorched-earth policy that included winter campaigns and unrelenting pursuit. Unable to rest, care for their wounded, or provide for their families the mighty nations succumbed to military pressure. On May 6, 1877, Crazy Horse, leading more than 1,100 Sioux, surrendered at Camp Robinson, Nebraska. Sitting Bull and some four hundred Hunkpapa Sioux escaped into Canada and in July 1881 he and forty-three families surrendered to the U.S. Army. The last of the great nations agreed to submit to the reservation way of life.

Confinement on reservations and other assimilationist programs such as the allotment program received strong support from the public and so called "friends" of the Indians. Many non-Indian people believed that these policies represented the only alternative to Indian extinction. The truth was that Indian people were suffering untold hardships while whites were securing vast quantities of Indian land. Native People were living in grinding poverty, Indian health and education were in an abominable state, and government policies were not working.

In 1869 Congress appointed a Board of Indian Commissioners to investigate mismanagement in the Bureau of Indian Affairs and address widespread corruption on Indian reservations. Helen Hunt Jackson's 1881 expose *A Century of Dishonor* brought these conditions to public view and made people aware of broken treaties and other unfulfilled promises. Jackson's book spurred the formation of organizations such as the Indian Rights Association, founded in 1882, that worked to protect the rights and interests of Indian people. Members of the association met in annual conferences at a plush New York resort on Lake Mohonk and discussed "what was best for the Indian." The most far-reaching effect, however, was a major study of conditions on Indian reservations commissioned by the federal government and conducted by the Institute for Government Research. The study, titled *The Problem of Indian Administration,* but more commonly called "the Meriam report," was conducted in 1926 and highlighted the disastrous conditions affecting Indian people as a result of a succession of failed government policies. These conditions included high infant death rates, high mortality rates for the entire population, appalling housing conditions, low incomes, poor health, and inadequate education.

The report was an extremely detailed document describing and analyzing the entire spectrum of Indian life and the problems of governmental administration of Indian affairs. It brought these problems into sharp focus and in so doing set the stage for sweeping changes in federal Indian policies including the enactment of the Indian Reorganization Act (IRA) six years later.

The Meriam report recommended an end to the government policy of allotment of Indian land and stated that "the object of work with or for the Indian people should fit them to either merge into the social and economic life of the prevailing civilization as developed by the whites" or that Indian people should be allowed "to live in the presence of the white civilization at least in accordance with a minimum standard of health and decency." The authors of the report recognized that many Native People wished to maintain a separate culture even though in many cases the U.S. government had destroyed the basic economic underpinnings of the old culture. The report recognized that the allotment of Indian lands had done nothing for Native People other than divest them of their lands and acknowledged that government policies enacted for the education of Native People was largely ineffective. Last, and not surprising, the report stated, "the government had historically failed to appropriate sufficient funds to permit the Indian service to employ adequate personnel, properly qualified, for the task before it." The Meriam report recommended a new approach to Indian affairs that would allow Indian people to reach a level of self-support. The answer to the problems faced by Indian people was a new government policy embodied in the Indian Reorganization Act (IRA) that encouraged Indian nations to abandon their traditional forms of organization and adopt a governmental structure that mirrored the U.S. form. Rather than having tribal elders consult together, a tribal chairman would be elected along with a vice chairman, treasurer, and associated officials. Traditional elders felt abandoned by this approach as they lost their leadership positions and attendant prestige to younger, mixed-blood Indians who appointed family members to key positions. The federal government recognized only the IRA governmental structure and would respond only to requests and inquiries from that body. A generational and blood gap quickly developed on many Indian reservations. The federal government had finally found a wedge to drive between the traditionalists, as represented by the elders, and the more modern mixed-blood government body.

The Freedmen's Bureau

W. E. Burghardt Du Bois

The problem of the twentieth century is the problem of the color line; the relation of the darker to the lighter races of men in Asia and Africa, in America and the islands of the sea. It was a phase of this problem that caused the Civil War; and however much they who marched south and north in 1861 may have fixed on the technical points of union and local autonomy as a shibboleth, all nevertheless knew, as we know, that the question of Negro slavery was the deeper cause of the conflict. Curious it was, too, how this deeper question ever forced itself to the surface, despite effort and disclaimer. No sooner had Northern armies touched Southern soil than this old question, newly guised, sprang from the earth,—What shall be done with slaves? Peremptory military commands, this way and that, could not answer the query; the Emancipation Proclamation seemed but to broaden and intensify the difficulties; and so at last there arose in the South a government of men called the Freedmen's Bureau, which lasted, legally, from 1865 to 1872, but in a sense from 1861 to 1876, and which sought to settle the Negro problems in the United States of America.

It is the aim of this essay to study the Freedmen's Bureau,—the occasion of its rise, the character of its work, and its final success and failure,—not only as a part of American history, but above all as one of the most singular and interesting of the attempts made by a great nation to grapple with vast problems of race and social condition.

No sooner had the armies, east and west, penetrated Virginia and Tennessee than fugitive slaves appeared within their lines. They came at night, when the flickering camp fires of the blue hosts shone like vast unsteady stars along the black horizon: old men, and thin, with gray and tufted hair; women with frightened eyes, dragging whimpering, hungry children; men and girls, stalwart and gaunt,—a horde of starving vagabonds, homeless, helpless, and pitiable in their dark distress. Two methods of treating these newcomers seemed equally logical to opposite sorts of minds. Said some, "We have nothing to do with slaves." "Hereafter," commanded Halleck, "no slaves should be allowed to come into your lines at all; if any come without your knowledge, when owners call for them, deliver them." But others said, "We take grain and fowl; why not slaves?" Whereupon Fremont, as early as August, 1861, declared the slaves of Missouri rebels free. Such radical action was quickly countermanded, but at the same time the opposite policy could not be enforced; some of the black refugees declared themselves freemen, others showed their masters had deserted them, and still others were captured with forts and plantations. Evidently, too, slaves were a source of strength to the Confederacy, and were being used as laborers and producers. "They constitute a military resource," wrote the Secretary of War, late in 1861; "and being such, that they should not be turned over to the enemy is too plain to discuss." So the tone of the army chiefs changed, Congress forbade the rendition of fugitives, and Butler's "contrabands" were welcomed as military laborers. This complicated rather than solved the problem; for now the scattering fugitives became a steady stream, which flowed faster as the armies marched.

Then the long-headed man, with care-chiseled face, who sat in the White House, saw the inevitable, and emancipated the slaves of rebels on New Year's, 1863. A month later Congress called earnestly for the Negro soldiers whom the act of July, 1862, had half grudgingly allowed to enlist. Thus the barriers were leveled, and the deed was done. The stream of fugitives swelled to a flood, and anxious officers kept inquiring: "What must be done with slaves arriving almost daily? Am I to find food and shelter for women and children?"

It was a Pierce of Boston who pointed out the way, and thus became in a sense the founder of the Freedmen's Bureau. Being specially detailed from the ranks to care for the freedmen at Fortress Monroe, he afterward founded the celebrated Port Royal experiment and started the Freedmen's Aid Societies. Thus, under the timid Treasury officials and bold army officers, Pierce's plan widened and developed. At first, the able-bodied men were enlisted as soldiers or hired as laborers, the women and children were herded into central camps under guard, and "superintendents of contrabands" multiplied here and there. Centres of massed freedmen arose at Fortress Monroe, Va., Washington, D. C., Beaufort and Port Royal, S. C., New Orleans, La., Vicksburg and Corinth, Miss., Columbus, Ky., Cairo, Ill., and elsewhere, and the army chaplains found here new and fruitful fields.

Then came the Freedmen's Aid Societies, born of the touching appeals for relief and help from these centres of distress. There was the American Missionary Association, sprung from the Amistad, and now full grown for work, the various church organizations, the National Freedmen's Relief Association, the American Freedmen's Union, the Western Freedmen's Aid Commission,—in all fifty or more active organizations, which sent clothes, money, school-books, and teachers southward. All they did was needed, for the destitution of the freedmen was often reported as "too appalling for belief," and the situation was growing daily worse rather than better.

And daily, too, it seemed more plain that this was no ordinary matter of temporary relief, but a national crisis; for here loomed a labor problem of vast dimensions. Masses of Negroes stood idle, or, if they worked spasmodically, were never sure of pay; and if perchance they received pay, squandered the new thing thoughtlessly. In these and in other ways were camp life and the new liberty demoralizing the freedmen. The broader economic organization thus clearly demanded sprang up here and there as accident and local conditions determined. Here again Pierce's Port Royal plan of leased plantations and guided workmen pointed out the rough way. In Washington, the military governor, at the urgent appeal of the superintendent, opened confiscated estates to the cultivation of the fugitives, and there in the shadow of the dome gathered black farm villages. General Dix gave over estates to the freedmen of Fortress Monroe, and so on through the South. The government and the benevolent societies furnished the means of cultivation, and the Negro turned again slowly to work. The systems of control, thus started, rapidly grew, here and there, into strange little governments, like that of General Banks in Louisiana, with its 90,000 black subjects, its 50,000 guided laborers, and its annual budget of $100,000 and more. It made out 4000 pay rolls, registered all freedmen, inquired into grievances and redressed them, laid and collected taxes, and established a system of public schools. So too Colonel Eaton, the superintendent of Tennessee and Arkansas, ruled over 100,000, leased and cultivated 7000 acres of cotton land, and furnished food for 10,000 paupers. In South Carolina was General Saxton, with his deep interest in black folk. He succeeded Pierce and the Treasury officials, and sold forfeited estates, leased abandoned plantations, encouraged schools, and received from Sherman, after the terribly picturesque march to the sea, thousands of the wretched camp followers.

Three characteristic things one might have seen in Sherman's raid through Georgia, which threw the new situation in deep and shadowy relief: the Conqueror, the Conquered, and the Negro. Some see all significance in the grim front of the destroyer, and some in the bitter sufferers of the lost cause. But to me neither soldier nor fugitive speaks with so deep a meaning as that dark and human cloud that clung like remorse on the rear of those swift columns, swelling at times to half their size, almost engulfing and choking them. In vain were they ordered back, in vain were bridges hewn from beneath their feet; on they trudged and writhed and surged, until they rolled into Savannah, a starved and naked horde of tens of thousands. There too came the characteristic military remedy: "The islands from Charleston south, the abandoned ricefields along the rivers for thirty miles back from the sea, and the country bordering the St. John's River, Florida, are reserved and set apart for the settlement of Negroes now made free by act of war." So read the celebrated field order.

All these experiments, orders, and systems were bound to attract and perplex the government and the nation. Directly after the Emancipation Proclamation, Representative Eliot had introduced a bill creating a Bureau of Emancipation, but it was never reported. The following June, a committee of inquiry, appointed by the Secretary of War, reported in favor of a temporary bureau for the "improvement, protection, and employment of refugee freedmen," on much the same lines as were afterward followed. Petitions came in to President Lincoln from distinguished citizens and organizations, strongly urging a comprehensive and unified plan of dealing with the freedmen, under a bureau which should be "charged with the study of plans and execution of measures for easily guiding, and in every way judiciously and humanely aiding, the passage of our emancipated and yet to be emancipated blacks from the old condition of forced labor to their new state of voluntary industry."

Some half-hearted steps were early taken by the government to put both freedmen and abandoned estates under the supervision of the Treasury officials. Laws of 1863 and 1864 directed them to take charge of and lease abandoned lands for periods not exceeding twelve months, and to "provide in such leases or otherwise for the employment and general welfare" of the freedmen. Most of the army officers looked upon this as a welcome relief from perplexing "Negro affairs;" but the Treasury hesitated and blundered, and although it leased large quantities of land and employed many Negroes, especially along the Mississippi, yet it left the virtual control of the laborers and their relations to their neighbors in the hands of the army.

In March, 1864, Congress at last turned its attention to the subject, and the House passed a bill, by a majority of two, establishing a Bureau for Freedmen in the War Department. Senator Sumner, who had charge of the bill in the Senate, argued that freedmen and abandoned lands ought to be under the same department, and reported a substitute for the House bill, attaching the Bureau to the Treasury Department. This bill passed, but too late for action in the House. The debate wandered over the whole policy of the administration and the general question of slavery, without touching very closely the specific merits of the measure in hand.

Meantime the election took place, and the administration, returning from the country with a vote of renewed confidence, addressed itself to the matter more seriously. A conference between the houses agreed upon a carefully drawn measure which contained the chief provisions of Charles Sumner's bill, but made the proposed organization a department independent of both the War and Treasury officials. The bill was conservative, giving the new department "general superintendence of all freedmen." It was to "establish regulations" for them, protect them, lease them lands, adjust their wages, and appear in civil and military courts as their "next friend." There were many limitations attached to the powers thus granted, and the organization was made permanent. Nevertheless, the Senate defeated the bill, and a new conference committee was appointed. This committee reported a new bill, February 28, which was whirled through just as the session closed, and which became the act of 1865 establishing in the War Department a "Bureau of Refugees, Freedmen, and Abandoned Lands."

This last compromise was a hasty bit of legislation, vague and uncertain in outline. A Bureau was created, "to continue during the present War of Rebellion, and for one year thereafter," to which was given "the supervision and management of all abandoned lands, and the control of all subjects relating to refugees and freedmen," under "such rules and regulations as may be presented by the head of the Bureau and approved by the President." A commissioner, appointed by the President and Senate, was to control the Bureau, with an office force not exceeding ten clerks. The President might also appoint commissioners in the seceded states, and to all these offices military officials might be detailed at regular pay. The Secretary of War could issue rations, clothing, and fuel to the destitute, and all abandoned property was placed in the hands of the Bureau for eventual lease and sale to ex-slaves in forty-acre parcels.

Thus did the United States government definitely assume charge of the emancipated Negro as the ward of the nation. It was a tremendous undertaking. Here, at a stroke of the pen, was erected a government of millions of men,—and not ordinary men, either, but black men emasculated by a peculiarly complete system of slavery, centuries old; and now, suddenly, violently, they come into a new birthright, at a time of war and passion, in the midst of the stricken, embittered population of their former masters. Any man might well have hesitated to assume charge of such a work, with vast responsibilities, indefinite powers, and limited resources. Probably no one but a soldier would have answered such a call promptly; and indeed no one but a soldier could be called, for Congress had appropriated no money for salaries and expenses.

Less than a month after the weary emancipator passed to his rest, his successor assigned Major General Oliver O. Howard to duty as commissioner of the new Bureau. He was a Maine man, then only thirty-five years of age. He had marched with Sherman to the sea, had fought well at Gettysburg, and had but a year before been assigned to the command of the Department of Tennessee. An honest and sincere men, with rather too much faith in human nature, little aptitude for systematic business and intricate detail, he was nevertheless conservative, hard-working, and, above all, acquainted at first-hand with much of the work before him. And of that work it has been truly said, "No approximately correct history of civilization can ever be written which does not throw out in bold relief, as one of the great landmarks of political and social progress, the organization and administration of the Freedmen's Bureau."

On May 12, 1865, Howard was appointed, and he assumed the duties of his office promptly on the 15th, and began examining the field of work. A curious mess he looked upon: little despotisms, communistic experiments, slavery, peonage, business speculations, organized charity, unorganized almsgiving,—all reeling on under the guise of helping the freedman, and all enshrined in the smoke and blood of war and the cursing and silence of angry men. On May 19 the new government—for a government it really was—issued its constitution; commissioners were to be appointed in each of the seceded states, who were to take charge of "all subjects relating to refugees and freedmen," and all relief and rations were to be given by their consent alone. The Bureau invited continued cooperation with benevolent societies, and declared, "It will be the object of all commissioners to introduce practicable systems of compensated labor," and to establish schools. Forthwith nine assistant commissioners were appointed. They were to hasten to their fields of work; seek gradually to close relief establishments, and make the destitute self-supporting; act as courts of law where there were no courts, or where Negroes were not recognized in them as free; establish the institution of marriage among ex-slaves, and keep records; see that freedmen were free to choose their employers, and help in making fair contracts for them; and finally, the circular said, "Simple good faith, for which we hope on all hands for those concerned in the passing away of slavery, will especially relieve the assistant commissioners in the discharge of their duties toward the freedmen, as well as promote the general welfare."

No sooner was the work thus started, and the general system and local organization in some measure begun, than two grave difficulties appeared which changed largely the theory and outcome of Bureau work. First, there were the abandoned lands of the South. It had long been the more or less definitely expressed theory of the North that all the chief problems of emancipation might be settled by establishing the slaves on the forfeited lands of their masters,—a sort of poetic justice, said some. But this poetry done into solemn prose meant either wholesale confiscation of private property in the South, or vast appropriations. Now Congress had not appropriated a cent, and no sooner did the proclamations of general amnesty appear than the 800,000 acres of abandoned lands in the hands of the Freedmen's Bureau melted quickly away. The second difficulty lay in perfecting the local organization of the Bureau throughout the wide field of work. Making a new machine and sending out officials of duly ascertained fitness for a great work of social reform is no child's task; but this task was even harder, for a new central organization had to be fitted on a heterogeneous and confused but already existing system of relief and control of ex-slaves; and the agents available for this work must be sought for in an army still busy with war operations,—men in the very nature of the case ill fitted for delicate social work,—or among the questionable camp followers of an invading host. Thus, after a year's work, vigorously as it was pushed, the problem looked even more difficult to grasp and solve than at the beginning. Nevertheless, three things that year's work did, well worth the doing: it relieved a vast amount of physical suffering; it transported 7000 fugitives from congested centres back to the farm; and, best of all, it inaugurated the crusade of the New England schoolma'am.

The annals of this Ninth Crusade are yet to be written, the tale of a mission that seemed to our age far more quixotic than the quest of St. Louis seemed to his. Behind the mists of ruin and rapine waved the calico dresses of women who dared, and after the hoarse mouthings of the field guns rang the rhythm of the alphabet. Rich and poor they were, serious and curious. Bereaved now of a father, now of a brother, now of more than these, they came seeking a life work in planting New England schoolhouses among the white and black of the South. They did their work well. In that first year they taught 100,000 souls, and more.

Evidently, Congress must soon legislate again on the hastily organized Bureau, which had so quickly grown into wide significance and vast possibilities. An institution such as that was well-nigh as difficult to end as to begin. Early in 1866 Congress took up the matter, when Senator Trumbull, of Illinois, introduced a bill to extend the Bureau and enlarge its powers. This measure received, at the hands of Congress, far more thorough discussion and attention than its predecessor. The war cloud had thinned enough to allow a clearer conception of the work of emancipation. The champions of the bill argued that the strengthening of the Freedmen's Bureau was still a military necessity; that it was needed for the proper carrying out of the Thirteenth Amendment, and was a work of sheer justice to the ex-slave, at a trifling cost to the government. The opponents of the measure declared that the war was over, and the necessity for war measures past; that the Bureau, by reason of its extraordinary powers, was clearly unconstitutional in time of peace, and was destined to irritate the South and pauperize the freedmen, at a final cost of possibly hundreds of millions. Two of these arguments were unanswered, and indeed unanswerable: the one that the extraordinary powers of the Bureau threatened the civil rights of all citizens; and the other that the government must have power to do what manifestly must be done, and that present abandonment of the freedmen meant their practical enslavement. The bill which finally passed enlarged and made permanent the Freedmen's Bureau. It was promptly vetoed by President Johnson, as "unconstitutional," "unnecessary," and "extrajudicial," and failed of passage over the veto. Meantime, however, the breach between Congress and the President began to broaden, and a modified form of the lost bill was finally passed over the President's second veto, July 16.

The act of 1866 gave the Freedmen's Bureau its final form,—the form by which it will be known to posterity and judged of men. It extended the existence of the Bureau to July, 1868; it authorized additional assistant commissioners, the retention of army officers mustered out of regular service, the sale of certain forfeited lands to freedmen on nominal terms, the sale of Confederate public property for Negro schools, and a wider field of judicial interpretation and cognizance. The government of the unreconstructed South was thus put very largely in the hands of the Freedmen's Bureau, especially as in many cases the departmental military commander was now made also assistant commissioner. It was thus that the Freedmen's Bureau became a full-fledged government of men. It made laws, executed them and interpreted them; it laid and collected taxes, defined and punished crime, maintained and used military force, and dictated such measures as it thought necessary and proper for the accomplishment of its varied ends. Naturally, all these powers were not exercised continuously nor to their fullest extent; and yet, as General Howard has said, "scarcely any subject that has to be legislated upon in civil society failed, at one time or another, to demand the action of this singular Bureau."

To understand and criticise intelligently so vast a work, one must not forget an instant the drift of things in the later sixties: Lee had surrendered, Lincoln was dead, and Johnson and Congress were at loggerheads; the Thirteenth Amendment was adopted, the Fourteenth pending, and the Fifteenth declared in force in 1870. Guerrilla raiding, the ever present flickering after-flame of war, was spending its force against the Negroes, and all the Southern land was awakening as from some wild dream to poverty and social revolution. In a time of perfect calm, amid willing neighbors and streaming wealth, the social uplifting of 4,000,000 slaves to an assured and self-sustaining place in the body politic and economic would have been an herculean task; but when to the inherent difficulties of so delicate and nice a social operation were added the spite and hate of conflict, the Hell of War; when suspicion and cruelty were rife, and gaunt Hunger wept beside Bereavement,—in such a case, the work of any instrument of social regeneration was in large part foredoomed to failure. The very name of the Bureau stood for a thing in the South which for two centuries and better men had refused even to argue,—that life amid free Negroes was simply unthinkable, the maddest of experiments. The agents which the Bureau could command varied all the way from unselfish philanthropists to narrow-minded busybodies and thieves; and even though it be true that the average was far better than the worst, it was the one fly that helped to spoil the ointment. Then, amid all this crouched the freed slave, bewildered between friend and foe. He had emerged from slavery: not the worst slavery in the world, not a slavery that made all life unbearable,—rather, a slavery that had here and there much of kindliness, fidelity, and happiness,—but withal slavery, which, so far as human aspiration and desert were concerned, classed the black man and the ox together. And the Negro knew full well that, whatever their deeper convictions may have been, Southern men had fought with desperate energy to perpetuate this slavery, under which the black masses, with half-articulate thought, had writhed and shivered. They welcomed freedom with a cry. They fled to the friends that had freed them. They shrank from the master who still strove for their chains. So the cleft between the white and black South grew. Idle to say it never should have been; it was as inevitable as its results were pitiable. Curiously incongruous elements were left arrayed against each other: the North, the government, the carpetbagger, and the slave, here; and there, all the South that was white, whether gentleman or vagabond, honest man or rascal, lawless murderer or martyr to duty.

Thus it is doubly difficult to write of this period calmly, so intense was the feeling, so mighty the human passions, that swayed and blinded men. Amid it all two figures ever stand to typify that day to coming men: the one a gray-haired gentleman, whose fathers had quit themselves like men, whose sons lay in nameless graves, who bowed to the evil of slavery because its abolition boded untold ill to all; who stood at last, in the evening of life, a blighted, ruined form, with hate in his eyes. And the other, a form hovering dark and mother-like, her awful face black with the mists of centuries, had aforetime bent in love over her white master's cradle, rocked his sons and daughters to sleep, and closed in death the sunken eyes of his wife to the world; ay, too, had laid herself low to his lust and borne a tawny man child to the world, only to see her dark boy's limbs scattered to the winds by midnight marauders riding after Damned Niggers. These were the saddest sights of that woeful day; and no man clasped the hands of these two passing figures of the present-past; but hating they went to their long home, and hating their children's children live to-day.

Here, then, was the field of work for the Freedmen's Bureau; and since, with some hesitation, it was continued by the act of 1868 till 1869, let us look upon four years of its work as a whole. There were, in 1868, 900 Bureau officials scattered from Washington to Texas, ruling, directly and indirectly, many millions of men. And the deeds of these rulers fall mainly under seven heads,—the relief of physical suffering, the overseeing of the beginnings of free labor, the buying and selling of land, the establishment of schools, the paying of bounties, the administration of justice, and the financiering of all these activities. Up to June, 1869, over half a million patients had been treated by Bureau physicians and surgeons, and sixty hospitals and asylums had been in operation. In fifty months of work 21,000,000 free rations were distributed at a cost of over $4,000,000,—beginning at the rate of 30,000 rations a day in 1865, and discontinuing in 1869. Next came the difficult question of labor. First, 30,000 black men were transported from the refuges and relief stations back to the farms, back to the critical trial of a new way of working. Plain, simple instructions went out from Washington,—the freedom of laborers to choose employers, no fixed rates of wages, no peonage or forced labor. So far so good; but where local agents differed toto coelo in capacity and character, where the personnel was continually changing, the outcome was varied. The largest element of success lay in the fact that the majority of the freedmen were willing, often eager, to work. So contracts were written,—50,000 in a single state,—laborers advised, wages guaranteed, and employers supplied. In truth, the organization became a vast labor bureau; not perfect, indeed,—notably defective here and there,—but on the whole, considering the situation, successful beyond the dreams of thoughtful men. The two great obstacles which confronted the officers at every turn were the tyrant and the idler: the slaveholder, who believed slavery was right, and was determined to perpetuate it under another name; and the freedman, who regarded freedom as perpetual rest. These were the Devil and the Deep Sea.

In the work of establishing the Negroes as peasant proprietors the Bureau was severely handicapped, as I have shown. Nevertheless, something was done. Abandoned lands were leased so long as they remained in the hands of the Bureau, and a total revenue of $400,000 derived from black tenants. Some other lands to which the nation had gained title were sold, and public lands were opened for the settlement of the few blacks who had tools and capital. The vision of landowning, however, the righteous and reasonable ambition for forty acres and a mule which filled the freedmen's dreams, was doomed in most cases to disappointment. And those men of marvelous hind-sight, who to-day are seeking to preach the Negro back to the soil, know well, or ought to know, that it was here, in 1865, that the finest opportunity of binding the black peasant to the soil was lost. Yet, with help and striving, the Negro gained some land, and by 1874, in the one state of Georgia, owned near 350,000 acres.

The greatest success of the Freedmen's Bureau lay in the planting of the free school among Negroes, and the idea of free elementary education among all classes in the South. It not only called the schoolmistress through the benevolent agencies, and built them schoolhouses, but it helped discover and support such apostles of human development as Edmund Ware, Erastus Cravath, and Samuel Armstrong. State superintendents of education were appointed, and by 1870 150,000 children were in school.

The opposition to Negro education was bitter in the South, for the South believed an educated Negro to be a dangerous Negro. And the South was not wholly wrong; for education among all kinds of men always has had, and always will have, an element of danger and revolution, of dissatisfaction and discontent. Nevertheless, men strive to know. It was some inkling of this paradox, even in the unquiet days of the Bureau, that allayed an opposition to human training, which still to-day lies smouldering, but not flaming. Fisk, Atlanta, Howard, and Hampton were founded in these days, and nearly $6,000,000 was expended in five years for educational work, $750,000 of which came from the freedmen themselves.

Such contributions, together with the buying of land and various other enterprises, showed that the ex-slave was handling some free capital already. The chief initial source of this was labor in the army, and his pay and bounty as a soldier. Payments to Negro soldiers were at first complicated by the ignorance of the recipients, and the fact that the quotas of colored regiments from Northern states were largely filled by recruits from the South, unknown to their fellow soldiers. Consequently, payments were accompanied by such frauds that Congress, by joint resolution in 1867, put the whole matter in the hands of the Freedmen's Bureau. In two years $6,000,000 was thus distributed to 5000 claimants, and in the end the sum exceeded $8,000,000. Even in this system, fraud was frequent; but still the work put needed capital in the hands of practical paupers, and some, at least, was well spent.

The most perplexing and least successful part of the Bureau's work lay in the exercise of its judicial functions. In a distracted land where slavery had hardly fallen, to keep the strong from wanton abuse of the weak, and the weak from gloating insolently over the half-shorn strength of the strong, was a thankless, hopeless task. The former masters of the land were peremptorily ordered about, seized and imprisoned, and punished over and again, with scant courtesy from army officers. The former slaves were intimidated, beaten, raped, and butchered by angry and revengeful men. Bureau courts tended to become centres simply for punishing whites, while the regular civil courts tended to become solely institutions for perpetuating the slavery of blacks. Almost every law and method ingenuity could devise was employed by the legislatures to reduce the Negroes to serfdom,—to make them the slaves of the state, if not of individual owners; while the Bureau officials too often were found striving to put the "bottom rail on top," and give the freedmen a power and independence which they could not yet use. It is all well enough for us of another generation to wax wise with advice to those who bore the burden in the heat of the day. It is full easy now to see that the man who lost home, fortune, and family at a stroke, and saw his land ruled by "mules and niggers," was really benefited by the passing of slavery. It is not difficult now to say to the young freedman, cheated and cuffed about, who has seen his father's head beaten to a jelly and his own mother namelessly assaulted, that the meek shall inherit the earth. Above all, nothing is more convenient than to heap on the Freedmen's Bureau all the evils of that evil day, and damn it utterly for every mistake and blunder that was made.

All this is easy, but it is neither sensible nor just. Some one had blundered, but that was long before Oliver Howard was born; there was criminal aggression and heedless neglect, but without some system of control there would have been far more than there was. Had that control been from within, the Negro would have been reenslaved, to all intents and purposes. Coming as the control did from without, perfect men and methods would have bettered all things; and even with imperfect agents and questionable methods, the work accomplished was not undeserving of much commendation. The regular Bureau court consisted of one representative of the employer, one of the Negro, and one of the Bureau. If the Bureau could have maintained a perfectly judicial attitude, this arrangement would have been ideal, and must in time have gained confidence; but the nature of its other activities and the character of its personnel prejudiced the Bureau in favor of the black litigants, and led without doubt to much injustice and annoyance. On the other hand, to leave the Negro in the hands of Southern courts was impossible.

What the Freedmen's Bureau cost the nation is difficult to determine accurately. Its methods of bookkeeping were not good, and the whole system of its work and records partook of the hurry and turmoil of the time. General Howard himself disbursed some $15,000,000 during his incumbency; but this includes the bounties paid colored soldiers, which perhaps should not be counted as an expense of the Bureau. In bounties, prize money, and all other expenses, the Bureau disbursed over $20,000,000 before all of its departments were finally closed. To this ought to be added the large expenses of the various departments of Negro affairs before 1865; but these are hardly extricable from war expenditures, nor can we estimate with any accuracy the contributions of benevolent societies during all these years.

Such was the work of the Freedmen's Bureau. To sum it up in brief, we may say: it set going a system of free labor; it established the black peasant proprietor; it secured the recognition of black freemen before courts of law; it founded the free public school in the South. On the other hand, it failed to establish good will between ex-masters and freedmen; to guard its work wholly from paternalistic methods that discouraged self-reliance; to make Negroes landholders in any considerable numbers. Its successes were the result of hard work, supplemented by the aid of philanthropists and the eager striving of black men. Its failures were the result of bad local agents, inherent difficulties of the work, and national neglect. The Freedmen's Bureau expired by limitation in 1869, save its educational and bounty departments. The educational work came to an end in 1872, and General Howard's connection with the Bureau ceased at that time. The work of paying bounties was transferred to the adjutant general's office, where it was continued three or four years longer.

Such an institution, from its wide powers, great responsibilities, large control of moneys, and generally conspicuous position, was naturally open to repeated and bitter attacks. It sustained a searching congressional investigation at the instance of Fernando Wood in 1870. It was, with blunt discourtesy, transferred from Howard's control, in his absence, to the supervision of Secretary of War Belknap in 1872, on the

Secretary's recommendation. Finally, in consequence of grave intimations of wrong-doing made by the Secretary and his subordinates, General Howard was court-martialed in 1874. In each of these trials, and in other attacks, the commissioner of the Freedmen's Bureau was exonerated from any willful misdoing, and his work heartily commended. Nevertheless, many unpleasant things were brought to light: the methods of transacting the business of the Bureau were faulty; several cases of defalcation among officials in the field were proven, and further frauds hinted at; there were some business transactions which savored of dangerous speculation, if not dishonesty; and, above all, the smirch of the Freedmen's Bank, which, while legally distinct from, was morally and practically a part of the Bureau, will ever blacken the record of this great institution. Not even ten additional years of slavery could have done as much to throttle the thrift of the freedmen as the mismanagement and bankruptcy of the savings bank chartered by the nation for their especial aid. Yet it is but fair to say that the perfect honesty of purpose and unselfish devotion of General Howard have passed untarnished through the fire of criticism. Not so with all his subordinates, although in the case of the great majority of these there were shown bravery and devotion to duty, even though sometimes linked to narrowness and incompetency.

The most bitter attacks on the Freedmen's Bureau were aimed not so much at its conduct or policy under the law as at the necessity for any such organization at all. Such attacks came naturally from the border states and the South, and they were summed up by Senator Davis, of Kentucky, when he moved to entitle the act of 1866 a bill "to promote strife and conflict between the white and black races . . . by a grant of unconstitutional power." The argument was of tremendous strength, but its very strength was its weakness. For, argued the plain common sense of the nation, if it is unconstitutional, unpracticable, and futile for the nation to stand guardian over its helpless wards, then there is left but one alternative: to make those wards their own guardians by arming them with the ballot. The alternative offered the nation then was not between full and restricted Negro suffrage; else every sensible man, black and white, would easily have chosen the latter. It was rather a choice between suffrage and slavery, after endless blood and gold had flowed to sweep human bondage away. Not a single Southern legislature stood ready to admit a Negro, under any conditions, to the polls; not a single Southern legislature believed free Negro labor was possible without a system of restrictions that took all its freedom away; there was scarcely a white man in the South who did not honestly regard emancipation as a crime, and its practical nullification as a duty. In such a situation, the granting of the ballot to the black man was a necessity, the very least a guilty nation could grant a wronged race. Had the opposition to government guardianship of Negroes been less bitter, and the attachment to the slave system less strong, the social seer can well imagine a far better policy: a permanent Freedmen's Bureau, with a national system of Negro schools; a carefully supervised employment and labor office; a system of impartial protection before the regular courts; and such institutions for social betterment as savings banks, land and building associations, and social settlements. All this vast expenditure of money and brains might have formed a great school of prospective citizenship, and solved in a way we have not yet solved the most perplexing and persistent of the Negro problems.

That such an institution was unthinkable in 1870 was due in part to certain acts of the Freedmen's Bureau itself. It came to regard its work as merely temporary, and Negro suffrage as a final answer to all present perplexities. The political ambition of many of its agents and proteges led it far afield into questionable activities, until the South, nursing its own deep prejudices, came easily to ignore all the good deeds of the Bureau, and hate its very name with perfect hatred. So the Freedmen's Bureau died, and its child was the Fifteenth Amendment.

The passing of a great human institution before its work is done, like the untimely passing of a single soul, but leaves a legacy of striving for other men. The legacy of the Freedmen's Bureau is the heavy heritage of this generation. Today, when new and vaster problems are destined to strain every fibre of the national mind and soul, would it not be well to count this legacy honestly and carefully? For this much all men know: despite compromise, struggle, war, and struggle, the Negro is not free. In the backwoods of the Gulf states, for miles and miles, he may not leave the plantation of his birth; in well-nigh the whole rural South the black farmers are peons, bound by law and custom to an economic slavery, from which the only escape is death or the penitentiary. In the most cultured sections and cities of the South the Negroes are a segregated servile caste, with restricted rights and privileges. Before the courts, both in law and custom, they stand on a different and peculiar basis. Taxation without representation is the rule of their political life. And the result of all this is, and in nature must have been, lawlessness and crime. That is the large legacy of the Freedmen's Bureau, the work it did not do because it could not.

I have seen a land right merry with the sun; where children sing, and rolling hills lie like passioned women, wanton with harvest. And there in the King's Highway sat and sits a figure, veiled and bowed, by which the traveler's footsteps hasten as they go. On the tainted air broods fear. Three centuries' thought has been the raising and unveiling of that bowed human heart, and now, behold, my fellows, a century new for the duty and the deed. The problem of the twentieth century is the problem of the color line.

Of the Training of Black Men

W. E. Burghardt Du Bois

From the shimmering swirl of waters where many, many thoughts ago the slave-ship first saw the square tower of Jamestown have flowed down to our day three streams of thinking: one from the larger world here and over-seas, saying, the multiplying of human wants in culture lands calls for the world-wide co-operation of men in satisfying them. Hence arises a new human unity, pulling the ends of earth nearer, and all men, black, yellow, and white. The larger humanity strives to feel in this contact of living nations and sleeping hordes a thrill of new life in the world, crying, If the contact of Life and Sleep be Death, shame on such Life. To be sure, behind this thought lurks the afterthought of force and dominion,—the making of brown men to delve when the temptation of beads and red calico cloys.

The second thought streaming from the death-ship and the curving river is the thought of the older South: the sincere and passionate belief that somewhere between men and cattle God created a tertium quid, and called it a Negro,—a clownish, simple creature, at times even lovable within its limitations, but straitly foreordained to walk within the Veil. To be sure, behind the thought lurks the afterthought,—some of them with favoring chance might become men, but in sheer self-defense we dare not let them, and build about them walls so high, and hang between them and the light a veil so thick, that they shall not even think of breaking through.

And last of all there trickles down that third and darker thought, the thought of the things themselves, the confused half-conscious mutter of men who are black and whitened, crying Liberty, Freedom, Opportunity—vouchsafe to us, O boastful World, the chance of living men! To be sure, behind the thought lurks the afterthought: suppose, after all, the World is right and we are less than men? Suppose this mad impulse within is all wrong, some mock mirage from the untrue?

So here we stand among thoughts of human unity, even through conquest and slavery; the inferiority of black men, even if forced by fraud; a shriek in the night for the freedom of men who themselves are not yet sure of their right to demand it. This is the tangle of thought and afterthought wherein we are called to solve the problem of training men for life.

Behind all its curiousness, so attractive alike to sage and dilettante, lie its dim dangers, throwing across us shadows at once grotesque and awful. Plain it is to us that what the world seeks through desert and wild we have within our threshold;—a stalwart laboring force, suited to the semi-tropics; if, deaf to the voice of the Zeitgeist, we refuse to use and develop these men, we risk poverty and loss. If, on the other hand, seized by the brutal afterthought, we debauch the race thus caught in our talons, selfishly sucking their blood and brains in the future as in the past, what shall save us from national decadence? Only that saner selfishness which, Education teaches men, can find the rights of all in the whirl of work.

Again, we may decry the color prejudice of the South, yet it remains a heavy fact. Such curious kinks of the human mind exist and must be reckoned with soberly. They cannot be laughed away, nor always successfully stormed at, nor easily abolished by act of legislature. And yet they cannot be encouraged by being let alone. They must be recognized as facts, but unpleasant facts; things that stand in the way of civilization and religion and common decency. They can be met in but one way: by the breadth and broadening of human reason, by catholicity of taste and culture. And so, too, the native ambition and aspiration of men, even though they be black, backward, and ungraceful, must not lightly be dealt with. To stimulate wildly weak and untrained minds is to play with mighty fires; to flout their striving idly is to welcome a harvest of brutish crime and shameless lethargy in our very laps. The guiding of thought and the deft coordination of deed is at once the path of honor and humanity.

And so, in this great question of reconciling three vast and partially contradictory streams of thought, the one panacea of Education leaps to the lips of all; such human training as will best use the labor of all men without enslaving or brutalizing; such training as will give us poise to encourage the prejudices that bulwark society, and stamp out those that in sheer barbarity deafen us to the wail of prisoned souls within the Veil, and the mounting fury of shackled men.

But when we have vaguely said Education will set this tangle straight, what have we uttered but a truism? Training for life teaches living; but what training for the profitable living together of black men and white? Two hundred years ago our task would have seemed easier. Then Dr. Johnson blandly assured us that education was needed solely for the embellishments of life, and was useless for ordinary vermin. To-day we have climbed to heights where we would open at least the outer courts of knowledge to all, display its treasures to many, and select the few to whom its mystery of Truth is revealed, not wholly by truth or the accidents of the stock market, but at least in part according to deftness and aim, talent and character. This programme, however, we are sorely puzzled in carrying out through that part of the land where the blight of slavery fell hardest, and where we are dealing with two backward peoples. To make here in human education that ever necessary combination of the permanent and the contingent—of the ideal and the practical in workable equilibrium—has been there, as it ever must be in every age and place, a matter of infinite experiment and frequent mistakes.

In rough approximation we may point out four varying decades of work in Southern education since the Civil War. From the close of the war until 1876 was the period of uncertain groping and temporary relief. There were army schools, mission schools, and schools of the Freedmen's Bureau in chaotic disarrangement, seeking system and cooperation. Then followed ten years of constructive definite effort toward the building of complete school systems in the South. Normal schools and colleges were founded for the freedmen, and teachers trained there to man the public schools. There was the inevitable tendency of war to underestimate the prejudice of the master and the ignorance of the slave, and all seemed clear sailing out of the wreckage of the storm. Meantime, starting in this decade yet especially developing from 1885 to 1895, began the industrial revolution of the South. The land saw glimpses of a new destiny and the stirring of new ideals. The educational system striving to complete itself saw new obstacles and a field of work ever broader and deeper. The Negro colleges, hurriedly founded, were inadequately equipped, illogically distributed, and of varying efficiency and grade; the normal and high schools were doing little more than common school work, and the common schools were training but a third of the children who ought to be in them, and training these too often poorly. At the same time the white South, by reason of its sudden conversion from the slavery ideal, by so much the more became set and strengthened in its racial prejudice, and crystallized it into harsh law and harsher custom; while the marvelous pushing forward of the poor white daily threatened to take even bread and butter from the mouths of the heavily handicapped sons of the freedmen. In the midst, then, of the larger problem of Negro education sprang up the more practical question of work, the inevitable economic quandary that faces a people in the transition from slavery to freedom, and especially those who make that change amid hate and prejudice, lawlessness and ruthless competition.

The industrial school springing to notice in this decade, but coming to full recognition in the decade beginning with 1895, was the proffered answer to this combined educational and economic crisis, and an answer of singular wisdom and timeliness. From the very first in nearly all the schools some attention had been given to training in handiwork, but now was this training first raised to a dignity that brought it in direct touch with the South's magnificent industrial development, and given an emphasis which reminded black folk that before the Temple of Knowledge swing the Gates of Toil.

Yet after all they are but gates, and when turning our eyes from the temporary and the contingent in the Negro problem to the broader question of the permanent uplifting and civilization of black men in America, we have a right to inquire, as this enthusiasm for material advancement mounts to its height, if after all the industrial school is the final and sufficient answer in the training of the Negro race; and to ask gently, but in all sincerity, the ever recurring query of the ages, Is not life more than meat, and the body more than raiment? And men ask this to-day all the more eagerly because of sinister signs in recent educational movements. The tendency is here born of slavery and quickened to renewed life by the crazy imperialism of the day, to regard human beings as among the material resources of a land to be trained with an eye single to future dividends. Race prejudices, which keep brown and black men in their "places," we are coming to regard as useful allies with such a theory, no matter how much they may dull the ambition and sicken the hearts of struggling human beings. And above all, we daily hear that an education that encourages aspiration, that sets the loftiest of ideals and seeks as an end culture and character than breadwinning, is the privilege of white men and the danger and delusion of black.

Especially has criticism been directed against the former educational efforts to aid the Negro. In the four periods I have mentioned, we find first boundless, planless enthusiasm and sacrifice; then the preparation of teachers for a vast public school system; then the launching and expansion of that school system amid increasing difficulties; and finally the training of workmen for the new and growing industries. This development has been sharply ridiculed as a logical anomaly and flat reversal of nature. Soothly we have been told that first industrial and manual training should have taught the Negro to work, then simple schools should have taught him to read and write, and finally, after years, high and normal schools could have completed the system, as intelligence and wealth demanded.

That a system logically so complete was historically impossible, it needs but a little thought to prove. Progress in human affairs is more often a pull than a push, surging forward of the exceptional man, and the lifting of his duller brethren slowly and painfully to his vantage ground. Thus it was no accident that gave birth to universities centuries before the common schools, that made fair Harvard the first flower of our wilderness. So in the South: the mass of the freedmen at the end of the war lacked the intelligence so necessary to modern workingmen. They must first have the common school to teach them to read, write, and cipher. The white teachers who flocked South went to establish such a common school system. They had no idea of founding colleges; they themselves at first would have laughed at the idea. But they faced, as all men since them have faced, that central paradox of the South, the social separation of the races. Then it was the sudden volcanic rupture of nearly all relations between black and white, in work and government and family life. Since then a new adjustment of relations in economic and political affairs has grown up,—an adjustment subtle and difficult to grasp, yet singularly ingenious, which leaves still that frightful chasm at the color line across which men pass at their peril. Thus, then and now, there stand in the South two separate worlds; and separate not simply in the higher realms of social intercourse, but also in church and school, on railway and street car, in hotels and theatres, in streets and city sections, in books and newspapers, in asylums and jails, in hospitals and graveyards. There is still enough of contact for large economic and group cooperation, but the separation is so thorough and deep, that it absolutely precludes for the present between the races anything like that sympathetic and effective group training and leadership of the one by the other, such as the American Negro and all backward peoples must have for effectual progress.

This the missionaries of '68 soon saw; and if effective industrial and trade schools were impractical before the establishment of a common school system, just as certainly no adequate common schools could be founded until there were teachers to teach them. Southern whites would not teach them; Northern whites in sufficient numbers could not be had.

If the Negro was to learn, he must teach himself, and the most effective help that could be given him was the establishment of schools to train Negro teachers. This conclusion was slowly but surely reached by every student of the situation until simultaneously, in widely separated regions, without consultation or systematic plan, there arose a series of institutions designed to furnish teachers for the untaught. Above the sneers of critics at the obvious defects of this procedure must ever stand its one crushing rejoinder: in a single generation they put thirty thousand black teachers in the South; they wiped out the illiteracy of the majority of the black people of the land, and they made Tuskegee possible.

Such higher training schools tended naturally to deepen broader development: at first they were common and grammar schools, then some became high schools. And finally, by 1900, some thirty-four had one year or more of studies of college grade. This development was reached with different degrees of speed in different institutions: Hampton is still a high school, while Fisk University started her college in 1871, and Spelman Seminary about 1896. In all cases the aim was identical: to maintain the standards of the lower training by giving teachers and leaders the best practicable training; and above all to furnish the black world with adequate standards of human culture and lofty ideals of life. It was not enough that the teachers of teachers should be trained in technical normal methods; they must also, so far as possible, be broad-minded, cultured men and women, to scatter civilization among a people whose ignorance was not simply of letters, but of life itself.

It can thus be seen that the work of education in the South began with higher institutions of training, which threw off as their foliage common schools, and later industrial schools, and at the same time strove to shoot their roots ever deeper toward college and university training. That this was an inevitable and necessary development, sooner or later, goes without saying; but there has been, and still is, a question in many minds if the natural growth was not forced, and if the higher training was not either overdone or done with cheap and unsound methods. Among white Southerners this feeling is widespread and positive. A prominent Southern journal voiced this in a recent editorial:

"The experiment that has been made to give the colored students classical training has not been satisfactory. Even though many were able to pursue the course, most of them did so in a parrot-like way, learning what was taught, but not seeming to appropriate the truth and import of their instruction, and graduating without sensible aim or valuable occupation for their future. The whole scheme has proved a waste of time, efforts, and the money of the state."

While most far-minded men would recognize this as extreme and overdrawn, still without doubt many are asking, Are there a sufficient number of Negroes ready for college training to warrant the undertaking? Are not too many students prematurely forced into this work? Does it not have the effect of dissatisfying the young Negro with his environment? And do these graduates succeed in real life? Such natural questions cannot be evaded, nor on the other hand must a nation naturally skeptical as to Negro ability assume an unfavorable answer without careful inquiry and patient openness to conviction. We must not forget that most Americans answer all queries regarding the Negro a priori, and that the least that human courtesy can do is to listen to evidence.

The advocates of the higher education of the Negro would be the last to deny the incompleteness and glaring defects of the present system: too many institutions have attempted to do college work, the work in some cases has not been thoroughly done, and quantity rather than quality has sometimes been sought. But all this can be said of higher education throughout the land: it is the almost inevitable incident of educational growth, and leaves the deeper question of the legitimate demand for the higher training of Negroes untouched. And this latter question can be settled in but one way—by a first-hand study of the facts. If we leave out of view all institutions which have not actually graduated students from a course higher than that of a New England high school, even though they be called colleges; if then we take the thirty-four remaining institutions, we may clear up many misapprehensions by asking searchingly, what kind of institutions are they, what do they teach, and what sort of men do they graduate?

And first we may say that this type of college, including Atlanta, Fisk and Howard, Wilberforce and Lincoln, Biddle, Shaw, and the rest, is peculiar, almost unique. Through the shining trees that whisper before me as I write, I catch glimpses of a boulder of New England granite, covering a grave, which graduates of Atlanta University have placed there:—

> "IN GRATEFUL MEMORY OF THEIR FORMER TEACHER AND FRIEND AND OF THE UNSELFISH LIFE HE LIVED, AND THE NOBLE WORK HE WROUGHT; THAT THEY, THEIR CHILDREN, AND THEIR CHIL- DREN'S CHILDREN MIGHT BE BLESSED."

This was the gift of New England to the freed Negro: not alms, but a friend; not cash, but character. It was not and is not money these seething millions want, but love and sympathy, the pulse of hearts beating with red blood; a gift which to-day only their own kindred and race can bring to the masses, but which once saintly souls brought to their favored children in the crusade of the sixties, that finest thing in American history, and one of the few things untainted by sordid greed and cheap vainglory. The teachers in these institutions came not to keep the Negroes in their place, but to raise them out of their places where the filth of slavery had wallowed them. The colleges they founded were social settlements; homes where the best of the sons of the freedmen came in close and sympathetic touch with the best traditions of New England. They lived and ate together, studies and worked, hoped and harkened in the dawning light. In actual formal content their curriculum was doubtless old-fashioned, but in educational power it was supreme, for it was the contact of living souls.

From such schools about two thousand Negroes have gone forth with the bachelor's degree. The number in itself is enough to put at rest the argument that too large a proportion of Negroes are receiving higher training. If the ratio to population of all Negro students throughout the land, in both college and secondary training, be counted, Commissioner Harris assures us "it must be increased to five times its present average" to equal the average of the land.

Fifty years ago the ability of Negro students in any appreciable numbers to master a modern college course would have been difficult to prove. To-day it is proved by the fact that four hundred Negroes, many of whom have been reported as brilliant students, have received the bachelor's degree from Harvard, Yale, Oberlin, and seventy other leading colleges. Here we have, then, nearly twenty-five hundred Negro graduates, of whom the crucial query must be made. How far did their training fit them for life? It is of course extremely difficult to collect satisfactory data on such a point,—difficult to reach the men, to get trustworthy testimony, and to gauge that testimony by any generally acceptable criterion of success. In 1900, the Conference at Atlanta University undertook to study these graduates, and published the results. First they sought to know what these graduates were doing, and succeeded in getting answers from nearly two thirds of the living. The direct testimony was in almost all cases corroborated by the reports of the colleges where they graduated, so that in the main the reports were worthy of credence. Fifty-three per cent of these graduates were teachers,—presidents of institutions, heads of normal schools, principals of city school systems, and the like. Seventeen per cent were clergymen; another seventeen per cent were in the professions, chiefly as physicians. Over six per cent were merchants, farmers, and artisans, and four per cent were in the government civil service. Granting even that a considerable proportion of the third unheard from are unsuccessful, this is a record of usefulness. Personally I know many hundreds of these graduates and have corresponded with more than a thousand; through others I have followed carefully the life-work of scores; I have taught some of them and some of the pupils whom they have taught, lived in homes which they have builded, and looked at life through their eyes. Comparing them as a class with my fellow students in New England and in Europe, I cannot hesitate in saying that nowhere have I met men and women with a broader spirit of helpfulness, with deeper devotion to their life-work, or with more consecrated determination to succeed in the face of bitter difficulties than among Negro college-bred men. They have, to be sure, their proportion of ne'er-do-weels, their pedants and lettered fools, but they have a surprisingly small proportion of them; they have not that culture of manner which we instinctively associate with university men, forgetting that in reality it is the heritage from cultured homes, and that no people a generation removed from slavery can escape a certain unpleasant rawness and gaucherie, despite the best of training.

With all their larger vision and deeper sensibility, these men have usually been conservative, careful leaders. They have seldom been agitators, have withstood the temptation to head the mob, and have worked steadily and faithfully in a thousand communities in the South. As teachers they have given the South a commendable system of city schools and large numbers of private normal schools and academies. Colored college-bred men have worked side by side with white college graduates at Hampton; almost from the beginning the backbone of Tuskegee's teaching force has been formed of graduates from Fisk and Atlanta. And to-day the institute is filled with college graduates, from the energetic wife of the principal down to the teacher of agriculture, including nearly half of the executive council and a majority of the heads of departments. In the professions, college men are slowly but surely leavening the Negro church, are healing and preventing the devastations of disease, and beginning to furnish legal protection for the liberty and property of the toiling masses. All this is needful work. Who would do it if Negroes did not? How could Negroes do it if they were not trained carefully for it? If white people need colleges to furnish teachers, ministers, lawyers, and doctors, do black people need nothing of the sort?

If it be true that there are an appreciable number of Negro youth in the land capable by character and talent to receive that higher training, the end of which is culture, and if the two and a half thousand who have had something of this training in the past have in the main proved themselves useful to their race and generation, the question then comes, What place in the future development of the South might the Negro college and college-bred man to occupy? That the present social separation and acute race sensitiveness must eventually yield to the influences of culture as the South grows civilized is clear. But such transformation calls for singular wisdom and patience. If, while the healing of this vast sore is progressing, the races are to live for many years side by side, united in economic effort, obeying a common government, sensitive to mutual thought and feeling, yet subtly and silently separate in many matters of deeper human intimacy—if this unusual and dangerous development is to progress amid peace and order, mutual respect and growing intelligence, it will call for social surgery at once the delicatest and nicest in modern history. It will demand broad-minded, upright men both white and black, and in its final accomplishment American civilization will triumph. So far as white men are concerned, this fact is to-day being recognized in the South, and a happy renaissance of university education seems imminent. But the very voices that cry Hail! to this good work are, strange to relate, largely silent or antagonistic to the higher education of the Negro.

Strange to relate! for this is certain, no secure civilization can be built in the South with the Negro as an ignorant, turbulent proletariat. Suppose we seek to remedy this by making them laborers and nothing more: they are not fools, they have tasted of the Tree of Life, and they will not cease to think, will not cease attempting to read the riddle of the world. By taking away their best equipped teachers and leaders, by slamming the door of opportunity in the faces of their bolder and brighter minds, will you make them satisfied with their lot? or will you not rather transfer their leading from the hands of men taught to think to the hands of untrained demagogues? We ought not to forget that despite the pressure of poverty, and despite the active discouragement and even ridicule of friends, the demand for higher training steadily increases among Negro youth: there were, in the years from 1875 to 1880, twenty-two Negro graduates from Northern colleges; from 1885 to 1895 there were forty-three, and from 1895 to 1900, nearly 100 graduates. From Southern Negro colleges there were, in the same three periods, 143, 413, and over 500 graduates. Here, then, is the plain thirst for training; by refusing to give this Talented Tenth the key to knowledge can any sane man imagine that they will lightly lay aside their yearning and contentedly become hewers of wood and drawers of water?

No. The dangerously clear logic of the Negro's position will more and more loudly assert itself in that day when increasing wealth and more intricate social organization preclude the South from being, as it so largely is, simply an armed camp for intimidating black folk. Such waste of energy cannot be spared if the South is to catch up with civilization. And as the black third of the land grows in thrift and skill, unless skillfully guided in its larger philosophy, it must more and more brood over the red past and the creeping, crooked present, until it grasps a gospel of revolt and revenge and throws its new-found energies athwart the current of advance. Even to-day the masses of the Negroes see all too clearly the anomalies of their position and the moral crookedness of yours. You may marshal strong indictments against them, but their counter-cries, lacking though they be in formal logic, have burning truths within them which you may not wholly ignore, O Southern Gentlemen! If you deplore their presence here, they ask, Who brought us? When you shriek, Deliver us from the vision of intermarriage, they answer, that legal marriage is infinitely better than systematic concubinage and prostitution. And if in just fury you accuse their vagabonds of violating women, they also in fury quite as just may wail: the rape which your gentlemen have done against helpless black women in defiance of your own laws is written on the foreheads of two millions of mulattoes, and written in ineffaceable blood. And finally, when you fasten crime upon this race as its peculiar trait, they answer that slavery was the arch-crime, and lynching and lawlessness its twin abortion; that color and race are not crimes, and yet they it is which in this land receive most unceasing condemnation, North, East, South, and West.

I will not say such arguments are wholly justified—I will not insist that there is no other side to the shield; but I do say that of the nine millions of Negroes in this nation, there is scarcely one out of the cradle to whom these arguments do not daily present themselves in the guise of terrible truth. I insist that the question of the future is how best to keep these millions from brooding over the wrongs of the past and the difficulties of the present, so that all their energies may be bent toward a cheerful striving and cooperation with their white neighbors toward a larger, juster, and fuller future. That one wise method of doing this lies in the closer knitting of the Negro to the great industrial possibilities of the South is a great truth. And this the common schools and the manual training and trade schools are working to accomplish. But these alone are not enough. The foundations of knowledge in this race, as in others, must be sunk deep in the college and university if we would build a solid, permanent structure. Internal problems of social advance must inevitably come,—problems of work and wages, of families and homes, of morals and the true valuing of the things of life; and all these and other inevitable problems of civilization the Negro must meet and solve largely for himself, by reason of his isolation; and can there be any possible solution other than by study and thought and an appeal to the rich experience of the past? Is there not, with such a group and in such a crisis, infinitely more danger to be apprehended from half-trained minds and shallow thinking than from over-education and over-refinement? Surely we have wit enough to found a Negro college so manned and equipped as to steer successfully between the dilettante and the fool. We shall hardly induce black men to believe that if their bellies be full it matters little about their brains. They already dimly perceive that the paths of peace winding between honest toil and dignified manhood call for the guidance of skilled thinkers, the loving, reverent comradeship between the black lowly and black men emancipated by training and culture.

The function of the Negro college then is clear: it must maintain the standards of popular education, it must seek the social regeneration of the Negro, and it must help in the solution of problems of race contact and cooperation. And finally, beyond all this, it must develop men. Above our modern socialism, and out of the worship of the mass, must persist and evolve that higher individualism which the centres of culture protect; there must come a loftier respect for the sovereign human soul that seeks to know itself and the world about it; that seeks a freedom for expansion and self-development; that will love and hate and labor in its own way, untrammeled alike by old and new. Such souls aforetime have inspired and guided worlds, and if we be not wholly bewitched by our Rhine-gold, they shall again. Herein the longing of black men must have respect: the rich and bitter depth of their experience, the unknown treasures of their inner life, the strange rendings of nature they have seen, may give the world new points of view and make their loving, living, and doing precious to all human hearts. And to themselves in these the days that try their souls the chance to soar in the dim blue air above the smoke is to their finer spirits boon and guerdon for what they lose on earth by being black.

I sit with Shakespeare and he winces not. Across the color line I move arm in arm with Balzac and Dumas, where smiling men and welcoming women glide in glided halls. From out the caves of Evening that swing between the strong-limbed earth and the tracery of the stars, I summon Aristotle and Aurelius and what soul I will, and they come all graciously with no scorn nor condescension. So, wed with Truth, I dwell above the Veil. Is this the life you grudge us, O knightly America? Is this the life you long to change into the dull red hideousness of Georgia? Are you so afraid lest peering from this high Pisgah, between Philistine and Amalekite, we sight the Promised Land?

The Talented Tenth

W. E. Burghardt Du Bois

The Negro race, like all races, is going to be saved by its exceptional men. The problem of education, then, among Negroes must first of all deal with the Talented Tenth; it is the problem of developing the Best of this race that they may guide the Mass away from the contamination and death of the Worst, in their own and other races. Now the training of men is a difficult and intricate task. Its technique is a matter for educational experts, but its object is for the vision of seers. If we make money the object of man-training, we shall develop money-makers but not necessarily men; if we make technical skill the object of education, we may possess artisans but not, in nature, men. Men we shall have only as we make manhood the object of the work of the schools—intelligence, broad sympathy, knowledge of the world that was and is, and of the relation of men to it—this is the curriculum of that Higher Education which must underlie true life. On this foundation we may build bread winning, skill of hand and quickness of brain, with never a fear lest the child and man mistake the means of living for the object of life.

If this be true—and who can deny it—three tasks lay before me; first to show from the past that the Talented Tenth as they have risen among American Negroes have been worthy of leadership; secondly to show how these men may be educated and developed; and thirdly to show their relation to the Negro problem.

You misjudge us because you do not know us. From the very first it has been the educated and intelligent of the Negro people that have led and elevated the mass, and the sole obstacles that nullified and retarded their efforts were slavery and race prejudice; for what is slavery but the legalized survival of the unfit and the nullification of the work of natural internal leadership? Negro leadership therefore sought from the first to rid the race of this awful incubus that it might make way for natural selection and the survival of the fittest. In colonial days came Phillis Wheatley and Paul Cuffe striving against the bars of prejudice; and Benjamin Banneker, the almanac maker, voiced their longings when he said to Thomas Jefferson, "I freely and cheerfully acknowledge that I am of the African race and in colour which is natural to them, of the deepest dye; and it is under a sense of the most profound gratitude to the Supreme Ruler of the Universe, that I now confess to you that I am not under that state of tyrannical thraldom and inhuman captivity to which too many of my brethren are doomed, but that I have abundantly tasted of the fruition of those blessings which proceed from that free and unequalled liberty with which you are favored, and which I hope you will willingly allow, you have mercifully received from the immediate hand of that Being from whom proceedeth every good and perfect gift.

"Suffer me to recall to your mind that time, in which the arms of the British crown were exerted with every powerful effort, in order to reduce you to a state of servitude; look back, I entreat you, on the variety of dangers to which you were exposed; reflect on that period in which every human aid appeared unavailable, and in which even hope and fortitude wore the aspect of inability to the conflict, and you cannot but be led to a serious and grateful sense of your miraculous and providential preservation, you cannot but acknowledge, that the present freedom and tranquility which you enjoy, you have mercifully received, and that a peculiar blessing of heaven.

"This, sir, was a time when you clearly saw into the injustice of a state of Slavery, and in which you had just apprehensions of the horrors of its condition. It was then that your abhorrence thereof was so excited, that you publicly held forth this true and invaluable doctrine, which is worthy to be recorded and remembered in all succeeding ages: 'We hold these truths to be self evident, that all men are created equal; that they are endowed with certain inalienable rights, and that among these are life, liberty and the pursuit of happiness.'"

Then came Dr. James Derham, who could tell even the learned Dr. Rush something of medicine, and Lemuel Haynes, to whom Middlebury College gave an honorary A. M. in 1804. These and others we may call the Revolutionary group of distinguished Negroes – they were persons of marked ability, leaders of a Talented Tenth, standing conspicuously among the best of their time. They strove by word and deed to save the color line from becoming the line between the bond and free, but all they could do was nullified by Eli Whitney and the Curse of Gold. So they passed into forgetfulness.

But their spirit did not wholly die; here and there in the early part of the century came other exceptional men. Some were natural sons of unnatural fathers and were given often a liberal training and thus a race of educated mulattoes sprang up to plead for black men's rights. There was Ira Aldridge, whom all Europe loved to honor; there was that Voice crying in the Wilderness, David Walker, and saying:

"I declare it does appear to me as though some nations think God is asleep, or that He made the Africans for nothing else but to dig their mines and work their farms, or they cannot believe history sacred or profane. I ask every man who has a heart, and is blessed with the privilege of believing—Is not God a God of justice to all his creatures? Do you say he is? Then if he gives peace and tranquility to tyrants and permits them to keep our fathers, our mothers, ourselves and our children in eternal ignorance and wretchedness to support them and their families, would he be to us a God of Justice? I ask, O, ye Christians, who hold us and our children in the most abject ignorance and degradation that ever a people were afflicted with since the world began—I say if God gives you peace and tranquility, and suffers you thus to go on afflicting us, and our children, who have never given you the least provocation – would He be to us a God of Justice? If you will allow that we are men, who feel for each other, does not the blood of our fathers and of us, their children, cry aloud to the Lord of Sabaoth against you for the cruelties and murders with which you have and do continue to afflict us?"

This was the wild voice that first aroused Southern legislators in 1829 to the terrors of abolitionism.

In 1831 there met that first Negro convention in Philadelphia, at which the world gaped curiously but which bravely attacked the problems of race and slavery, crying out against persecution and declaring that "Laws as cruel in themselves as they were unconstitutional and unjust, have in many places been enacted against our poor, unfriended and unoffending brethren (without a shadow of provocation on our part), at whose bare recital the very savage draws himself up for fear of contagion—looks noble and prides himself because he bears not tile name of Christian." Side by side this free Negro movement, and the movement for abolition, strove until they merged in to one strong stream. Too little notice has been taken of the work which the Talented Tenth among Negroes took in the great abolition crusade. From the very day that a Philadelphia colored man became tile first subscriber to Garrison's "Liberator," to the day when Negro soldiers made the Emancipation Proclamation possible, black leaders worked shoulder to shoulder with white men in a movement, the success of which would have been impossible without them. There was Purvis and Remond, Pennington and Highland Garnett, Sojourner Truth and Alexander Crummel, and above all, Frederick Douglass—what would the abolition movement have been without them? They stood as living examples of the possibilities of the Negro race, their own hard experiences and well wrought culture said silently more than all the drawn periods of orators—they were the men who made American slavery impossible. As Maria Weston Chapman once said, from the school of anti-slavery agitation, "a throng of authors, editors, lawyers, orators and accomplished gentlemen of color have taken their degree! It has equally implanted hopes and aspirations, noble thoughts, and sublime purposes, in the hearts of both races. It has prepared the white man for the freedom of the black man, and it has made the black man scorn the thought of enslavement, as does a white man, as far as its influence has extended. Strengthen that noble influence! Before its organization, the country only saw here and there in slavery some faithful Cudjoe or Dinah, whose strong natures blossomed even in bondage, like a fine plant beneath a heavy stone. Now, under the elevating and cherishing influence of the

American Anti-slavery Society, the colored race, like the white, furnishes Corinthian capitals for the noblest temples."

Where were these black abolitionists trained? Some, like Frederick Douglass, were self-trained, but yet trained liberally; others, like Alexander Crummell and McCune Smith, graduated from famous foreign universities. Most of them rose up through the colored schools of New York and Philadelphia and Boston, taught by college-bred men like Russworm, of Dartmouth, and college-bred white men like Neau and Benezet.

After emancipation came a new group of educated and gifted leaders: Langston, Bruce and Elliot, Greener, Williams and Payne. Through political organization, historical and polemic writing and moral regeneration, thee men strove to uplift their people. It is the fashion of to-day to sneer at them and to say that with freedom Negro leadership should have begun at the plow and not in the Senate—a foolish and mischievous lie; two hundred and fifty years that black serf toiled at the plow and yet that toiling was in vain till the Senate passed the war amendments; and two hundred and fifty years more the half-free serf of to-day may toil at his plow, but unless he have political rights and righteously guarded civic status, he will still remain the poverty-stricken and ignorant plaything of rascals, that he now is. This all sane men know even if they dare not say it.

And so we come to the present—a day of cowardice and vacillation, of strident wide-voiced wrong and faint hearted compromise; of double-faced dallying with Truth and Right. Who are to-day guiding the work of the Negro people? The "exceptions" of course. And yet so sure as this Talented Tenth is pointed out, the blind worshippers of the Average cry out in the alarm: "These are exceptions, look here at death, disease and crime—these are the happy rule." Of course they are the rule, because a silly nation made them the rule: Because for three long centuries this people lynched Negroes who dared to be brave, raped black women who dared to be virtuous, crushed dark-hued youth who dared to be ambitious, and encouraged and made to flourish servility and lewdness and apathy. But nor even this was able to crush all manhood and chastity and aspiration from black folk. A saving remnant continually survives and persists, continually aspires, continually shows itself in thrift and ability and character. Exceptional it is to be sure, but this is its chiefest promise; it shows the capability of Negro blood, the promise of black men. Do Americans ever stop to reflect that there are in this land a million men of Negro blood, well-educated, owners of homes, against the honor of whose womanhood no breath was ever raised, whose men occupy positions of trust and usefulness, and who, judged by any standard, have reached the full measure of the best type of modern European culture? Is it fair, is it decent, is it Christian to ignore these facts of the Negro problem, to belittle such aspiration, to nullify such leadership and seek to crush these people back into the mass out of which by toil and travail, they and their fathers have raised themselves?

Can the masses of the Negro people be in any possible way more quickly raised than by the effort and example of this aristocracy of talent and character? Was there ever a nation on God's fair earth civilized from the bottom upward? Never; it is, ever was and ever will be from the top downward that culture filters. The Talented Tenth rises and pulls all that are worth the saving up to their vantage ground. This is the history of human progress; and the two historic mistakes which have hindered that progress were the thinking first that no more could ever rise save the few already risen; or second, that it would better the uprisen to pull the risen down.

How then shall the leaders of a struggling people be trained and the hands of the risen few strengthened? There can be but one answer: The best and most capable of their youth must be schooled in the colleges and universities of the land. We will not quarrel as to just what the university of the Negro should teach or how it should teach it—I willingly admit that each sould and each race-soul needs its own peculiar curriculum. But this is true: A university is a human invention for the transmission of knowledge and culture from generation to generation, through the training of quick minds and pure hearts, and for this work no other human invention will suffice, not even trade and industrial schools.

All men cannot go to college but some men must; every isolated group or nation must have its yeast, must have for the talented few centers of training where men are not so mystified and befuddled by the hard and necessary toil of earning a living, as to have no aims higher than their bellies, and no God greater than Gold. This is true training, and thus in the beginning were the favored sons of the freedmen trained. Out of tile colleges of the North came, after the blood of war, Ware, Cravath, Chase, Andrews, Bumstead and Spence to build the foundations of knowledge and civilization in the black South. Where ought they to have begun to build? At the bottom, of course, quibbles the mole with his eyes in the earth. Aye! truly at the bottom, at the very bottom; at the bottom of knowledge, down in the very depths of knowledge there where the roots of justice strike into the lowest soil of Truth. And so they did begin; they founded colleges, and up from the colleges shot normal schools, and out from the normal schools went teachers, and around the normal teachers clustered other teachers to teach the public schools; the college trained in Greek and Latin and mathematics, 2,000 men; and these men trained full 50,000 others in morals and manners, and they in turn taught thrift and the alphabet to nine millions of men, who to-day hold $300,000,000 of property. It was a miracle - the most wonderful peace-battle of the 19th century, and yet to-day men smile at it, and in fine superiority tell us that it was all a strange mistake; that a proper way to found a system of education is first to gather the children and buy them spelling books and hoes; afterward men may look about for teachers, if haply they may find them; or again they would teach men Work, but as for Life—why, what has Work to do with Life, they ask vacantly.

Was the work of these college founders successful; did it stand the test of time? Did the college graduates, with all their fine theories of life, really live? Are they useful men helping to civilize and elevate their less fortunate fellows? Let us see. Omitting all institutions which have not actually graduated students from a college course, there are to-day in the United States thirty-four institutions giving something above high school training to Negroes and designed especially for this race.

Three of these were established in border States before the War; thirteen were planted by the Freedmen's Bureau in the years 1864-1869; nine were established between 1870 and 1880 by various church bodies; five were established after 1881 by Negro churches, and four are state institutions supported by United States' agricultural funds. In most cases the college departments are small adjuncts to high and common schoolwork. As a matter of fact six institutions—Atlanta, Fisk, Howard, Shaw, Wilberforce and Leland, are the important Negro colleges so far as actual work and number of students are concerned. In all these institutions, seven hundred and fifty Negro college students are enrolled. In grade the best of these colleges are about a year behind the smaller New England colleges and a typical curriculum is that of Atlanta University. Here students from the grammar grades, after a three years' high school course, take a college course of 136 weeks. One-fourth of this time is given to Latin and Greek; one-fifth, to English and modern languages; one-sixth, to history and social science; one-seventh, to natural science; one-eighth to mathematics, and one-eighth to philosophy and pedagogy.

In addition to these students in the South, Negroes have attended Northern colleges for many years. As early as 1826 one was graduated from Bowdoin College, and from that time till to-day nearly every year has seen elsewhere, other such graduates. They have, of course, met much color prejudice. Fifty years ago very few colleges would admit them at all. Even to-day no Negro has ever been admitted to Princeton, and at some other leading institutions they are rather endured than encouraged. Oberlin was the great pioneer in tile work of blotting out the color line in colleges, and has more Negro graduates by far than any other Northern college.

The total number of Negro college graduates up to 1899, (several of the graduates of that year not being reported), was as follows:

	Negro Colleges	**White Colleges**
Before '76	137	75
'75–80	143	22
'80–85	250	31
'85–90	413	43
'90–95	465	66
'95–99	475	88
Class Unknown	57	64
Total	1,914	390

Of these graduates 2,079 were men and 252 were women; 50 per cent. of Northern-born college men come South to work among the masses of their people, at a sacrifice which few people realize; nearly 90 per cent. of the Southern-born graduates instead of seeking that personal freedom and broader intellectual atmosphere which their training has led them, in some degree, to conceive, stay and labor and wait in the midst of their black neighbors and relatives.

The most interesting question, and in many respects the crucial question, to be asked concerning college-bred Negroes, is: Do they earn a living? It has been intimated more than once that the higher training of Negroes has resulted in sending into the world of work, men who could find nothing to do suitable to their talents. Now and then there comes a rumor of a colored college man working at menial service etc. Fortunately, returns as to occupations of college-bred Negroes, gathered by the Atlanta conference, are quite full—nearly sixty per cent of the total number of graduates.

This enables us to reach fairly certain conclusions as to the occupations of all college-bred Negroes. Of 1,312 persons reported, there were:

Teachers, 53.4%
Clergymen, 16.8%
Physicians, etc., 6.3%
Students, 5.6%
Lawyers, 4.7%
In Govt. Service, 4.0%
In Business, 3.6%
Farmers and Artisans, 2.7%
Editors, Secretaries and Clerks, 2.4%
Miscellaneous, .5

Over half are teachers, a sixth are preachers, another sixth are students and professional men; over 6 per cent. are farmers, artisans and merchants, and 4 per cent. are in government service. In detail the occupations are as follows:

Occupations of College-Bred Men

701 Teachers:
- Presidents and Deans, 19
- Teacher of Music, 7
- Professors, Principals and Teachers, 675

221 Clergymen:
- Bishop, 1
- Chaplains U.S. Army, 2
- Missionaries, 9
- Presiding Elders, 12
- Preachers, 197

83 Physicians:
- Doctors of Medicine, 76
- Druggists, 4
- Dentists, 3

74 Students

62 Lawyers

53 in Civil Service:
- U.S. Minister Plenipotentiary, 1
- U.S. Consul, 1
- U.S. Deputy Collector, 1
- U.S. Gauger, 1
- U.S. Postmasters, 2
- U.S. Clerks, 44
- State Civil Service, 2
- City Civil Service, 1

47 Business Men:
- Merchants, etc., 30
- Managers, 13
- Real Estate Dealers, 4

26 Farmers

22 Clerks and Secretaries:
- Secretary of National Societies, 7
- Clerks, etc., 15

9 Artisans

9 Editors

5 Miscellaneous

These figures illustrate vividly the function of the college-bred Negro. He is, as he ought to be, the group leader, the man who sets the ideals of the community where he lives, directs its thoughts and heads its social movements. It need hardly be argued that the Negro people need social leadership more than most groups; that they have no traditions to fall back upon, no long established customs, no strong family ties, no well defined social classes. All these things must be slowly and painfully evolved. The preacher was, even before the war, the group leader of the Negroes, and the church their greatest social institution. Naturally this preacher was ignorant and often immoral, and the problem of replacing the older type by better educated men has been a difficult one. Both by direct work and by direct influence on other preachers, and on congregations, the college-bred preacher has an opportunity for reformatory work and moral inspiration, the value of which cannot be overestimated.

It has, however, been in the furnishing of teachers that the Negro college has found its peculiar function. Few persons realize how vast a work, how mighty a revolution has been thus accomplished. To furnish five millions and more of ignorant people with teachers of their own race and blood, in one generation, was not only a very difficult undertaking, but very important one, in that, it placed before the eyes of almost every Negro child an attainable ideal. It brought the masses of the blacks in contact with modern civilization, made black men the leaders of their communities and trainers of the new generation. In this work college-bred Negroes were first teachers, and then teachers of teachers. And here it is that the broad culture of college work has been of peculiar value. Knowledge of life and its wider meaning, has been the point of the Negro's deepest ignorance, and the sending out of teachers whose training has not been simply for bread winning, but also for human culture, has been of inestimable value in the training of these men.

In earlier years the two occupations of preacher and teacher were practically the only ones open to the black college graduate. Of later years a larger diversity of life among his people, has opened new avenues of employment. Nor have these college men been paupers and spendthrifts; 557 college-bred Negroes owned in 1899, $1,342,862.50 worth of real estate (assessed value), or $2,411 per family. The real value of the total accumulations of the whole group is perhaps about $10,000,000 or $5,000 a piece. Pitiful is it not beside the fortunes of oil kings and steel trusts, but after all is the fortune of the millionaire the only stamp of true and successful living? Alas! It is, with many and there's the rub.

The problem of training the Negro is to-day immensely complicated by the fact that the whole question of the efficiency and appropriateness of our present systems of education, for any kind of child, is a matter of active debate, in which final settlement seems still afar off. Consequently it often happens that persons arguing for or against certain systems of education for Negroes, have these controversies in mind and miss the real question at issue. The main question, so far as the Southern Negro is concerned, is: What under the present circumstance, must a system of education do in order to raise the Negro as quickly as possible in the scale of civilization? The answer to this question seems to me clear: It must strengthen the Negro's character, increase his knowledge and teach him to earn a living. Now it goes without saying that it is hard to do all these things simultaneously or suddenly and that at the same time it will not do to give all the attention to one and neglect the others; we could give black boys trades, but that alone will not civilize a race of ex-slaves; we might simply increase their knowledge of the world, but this would not necessarily make them wish to use this knowledge honestly; we might seek to strengthen character and purpose, but to what end if this people have nothing to eat or to wear? A system of education is not one thing, nor does it have a single definite object, nor is it a mere matter of schools. Education is that whole system of human training within and without the school house walls, which molds and develops men. If then we start out to train an ignorant and unskilled people with a heritage of bad habits, our system of training must set before itself two great aims—the one dealing with knowledge and character, the other part seeking to give the child the technical knowledge necessary for him to earn a living under the present circumstances. These objects are accomplished in part by the opening of the common schools on the one, and of the industrial schools on the other. But only in part, for there must also be trained those who are to teach these schools—men and women of knowledge and culture and technical skill who understand modern civilization, and have the training and aptitude to impart it to the children under them. There must be teachers, and teachers of teachers, and to attempt to establish any sort of a system of common and industrial school training, without *first* (and I say *first* advisedly) without *first* providing for the higher training of the very best teachers, is simply throwing your money to the winds. School houses do not teach themselves - piles of brick and mortar and machinery do not send out men. It is the trained, living human soul, cultivated and strengthened by long study and thought, that breathes the real breath of life into boys and girls and makes them human, whether they be black or white, Greek, Russian or American. Nothing, in these latter days, has so dampened the faith of thinking Negroes in recent educational movements, as the fact that such movements have been accompanied by ridicule and denouncement and decrying of those very institutions of higher training which made the Negro public school possible, and make Negro industrial schools thinkable. It was : Fisk, Atlanta, Howard and Straight, those colleges born of the faith and sacrifice of the abolitionists, that placed in the black schools of the South the 30,000 teachers and more, which some, who depreciate the work of these higher schools, are using to teach their own new experiments. If Hampton, Tuskegee and the hundred other industrial schools prove in the future to be as successful as they deserve to be, then their success in training black artisans for the South, will be due primarily to the white colleges of the North and the black colleges of the south, which trained the teachers who to-day conduct these institutions. There was a time when the American people believed pretty devoutly that a log of wood with a boy at one end and Mark Hopkins at the other, represented the highest ideal of human training. But in these eager days it would seem that we have changed all that and think it necessary to add a couple of saw-mills and a hammer to this outfit, and, at a pinch, to dispense with the services of Mark Hopkins.

I would not deny, or for a moment seem to deny, the paramount necessity of teaching the Negro to work, and to work steadily and skillfully; or seem to depreciate in the slightest degree the important part industrial schools must play in the accomplishment of these ends, but I do say, and insist upon it, that it is industrialism drunk with its vision of success, to imagine that its own work can be accomplished without providing for the training of broadly cultured men and women to teach its own teachers, and to teach the teachers of the public schools.

But I have already said that human education is not simply a matter of schools; it is much more a matter of family and group life - the training of one's home, of one's daily companions, of one's social class. Now the black boy of the South moves in a black world - a world with its own leaders, its own thoughts, its own ideals. In this world he gets by far the larger part of his life training, and through the eyes of this dark world he peers into the veiled world beyond. Who guides and determines the education which he receives in his world? His teachers here are the group-leaders of the Negro people—the physicians and clergymen, the trained fathers and mothers, the influential and forceful men about him of all kinds; here it is, if at all, that the culture of the surrounding world trickles through and is handed on by the graduates of the higher schools. Can such culture training of group leaders be neglected? Can we afford to ignore it? Do you think that if the leaders of thought among Negroes are not trained and educated thinkers, that they will have no leaders? On the contrary a hundred half-trained demagogues will still hold the places they so largely occupy now, and hundreds of vociferous busy-bodies will multiply. You have no choice; either you must help furnish this race from within its own ranks with thoughtful men of trained leadership, or you must suffer the evil consequences of a headless misguided rabble.

I am an earnest advocate of manual training and trade teaching for black boys, and for white boys, too. I believe that next to the founding of Negro colleges the most valuable addition to Negro education since the war, has been industrial training for black boys. Nevertheless, I insist that the object of all true education is not to make men carpenters, it is to make carpenters men; there are two means of making the carpenter a man, each equally important: the first is to give the group and community in which he works, liberally trained teachers and leaders to teach him and his family what life means; the second is to give him sufficient intelligence and technical skill to make him an efficient workman; the first object demands the Negro college and college-bred men—not a quantity of such colleges, but a few of excellent quality; not too many college-bred men, but enough to leaven the lump, to inspire the masses, to raise the Talented Tenth to leadership; the second object demands a good system of common schools, well-taught, conveniently located and properly equipped.

The Sixth Atlanta Conference truly said in 1901: " We call the attention of the Nation to the fact that less than one million of the three million Negro children of school age, are at present regularly attending school, and these attend a session which lasts only a few months.

"We are to-day deliberately rearing millions of our citizens in ignorance, and at the same time limiting the rights of citizenship by educationl qualification. This is unjust. Half the black youth of the land have no opportunities open to them for learning to read, write and cipher. In the discussion as to the proper training of Negro children after they leave the public schools, we have forgotten that they are not yet decently provided with public schools.

"Propositions are beginning to be made in the South to reduce the already meagre school facilities of Negroes. We congratulate the South on resisting, as much as it has, this pressure, and on the many millions it has spent on Negro education. But it is only fair to point out that Negro taxes and the Negroes' share of the income from indirect taxes and endowments have fully repaid this expenditure, so that the Negro public school system has not in all probability cost the white taxpayers a single cent since the war.

"This is not fair. Negro schools should be a public burden, since they are a public benefit. The Negro has a right to demand good common school training at the hands of the States and the Nation since by their fault he is not in position to pay for this himself."

What is the chief need for the building up of the Negro public school in the South? The Negro race in the South needs teachers to-day above all else. This is the concurrent testimony of all who know the situation. For the supply of this great demand two things are needed - institutions of higher education and money for school houses and salaries. It is usually assumed that a hundred or more institutions for Negro training are to-day turning out so many teachers and college-bred men that the race is threatened with an over-supply. This is sheer nonsense. There are to-day less than 3,000 living Negro college graduates in the United States, and less than 1,000 Negroes in college. Moreover, in the 164 schools for Negroes, 95 per cent. of their students are doing elementary and secondary work, work which should be done in the public schools. Over half the remaining 2,157 students are taking high school studies. The mass of so-called "normal" schools for the Negro, are simply doing elementary common school work, or, at most, high school work, with a little instruction in methods. The Negro colleges and the post-graduate courses at other institutions are the only agencies for the broader and more careful training of teachers. The work of these institutions is hampered for lack of funds. It is getting increasingly difficult to get funds for training teachers in the best modern methods, and yet all over the south, from State Superintendents, county officials, city boards and school principals comes the wail, "We need TEACHERS!" and teachers must be trained. As the fairest minded of all white Southerners, Atticus G. Haygood, once said: "The defects of colored teachers are so great as to create an urgent necessity for training better ones. Their excellencies and their successes are sufficient to justify the best hopes of success in the effort, and to vindicate the judgment of those who make large investments of money and service, to give to colored students opportunity for thoroughly preparing themselves for the work of teaching children of their people."

The truth of this has been strikingly shown in the marked improvement of white teachers in the South. Twenty years ago the rank and file of white public school teachers were not as good as the Negro teachers. But they, by scholarships and good salaries, have been encouraged to thorough normal and collegiate preparation, while the Negro teachers have been discouraged by starvation wages and the idea that any training will do for a black teacher. If carpenters are needed it is well and good to train men as carpenters. But to train men as carpenters, and then set them to teaching is wasteful and criminal; and to train men as teachers and then refuse them living wages, unless they become carpenters, is rank nonsense.

The United States Commissioner of Education says in his report for 1900: "For comparison between the white and colored enrollment in secondary and higher education, I have added together the enrollment in high schools and secondary schools, with the attendance on colleges and universities, not being sure of the actual grade of work done in the colleges and universities. The work done in the secondary schools is reported in such detail in this office, that there can be no doubt of its grade."

He then makes the following comparisons of persons in every million enrolled in secondary and higher education:

	Whole Country	**Negroes**
1880	4,362	1,289
1900	10,743	2,061

And he concludes: "While the number in colored high schools and colleges had increased somewhat faster than the population, it had not kept pace with the average of the whole country, for it had fallen from 30 per cent. to 24 per cent. of the average quota. Of all colored pupils, one (1) in one hundred was engaged in secondary and higher work, and that ration has continued substantially for the past twenty years. If the ratio of colored population in secondary and higher education is to be equal to the average for the whole country, it must be increased to five times its present average." And if this be true of the secondary and higher education, it is safe to say that the Negro has not one-tenth his quota in college studies. How baseless, therefore, is the charge of too much training! We need Negro teachers for the Negro common schools, and we need first-class normal schools and colleges to train them. This is the work of higher Negro education and it must be done.

Further than this, after being provided with group leaders of civilization, and a foundation of intelligence in the public schools, the carpenter, in order to be a man, needs technical skill. This calls for trade schools. Now trade schools are not nearly such simple things as people once thought. The original idea was that the "Industrial" school was to furnish education, practically free, to those willing to work for it; it was to "do" things—i.e.: become a center of productive industry, it was to be partially, if not wholly, self-supporting, and it was to teach trades. Admirable as were some of the ideas underlying this scheme, the whole thing simply would not work in practice; it was found that if you were to use time and material to teach trades thoroughly, you could not at the same time keep the industries on a commercial basis and make them pay. Many schools started out to do this on a large scale and went into virtual bankruptcy. Moreover, it was found also that it was possible to teach a boy a trade mechanically, without giving him the full educative benefit of the process, and, vice versa, that there was a distinctive educative value in teaching a boy to use his ands and eyes in carrying out certain physical processes, even though he did not actually learn a trade. It has happened, therefore, in the last decade, that a noticeable change has come over the industrial schools. In the first place the idea of commercially remunerative industry in a school is being pushed rapidly to the background. There are still schools with shops and farms that bring an income, and schools that use student labor partially for the erection of their buildings and the furnishing of equipment. It is coming to be seen, however, in the education of the Negro, as clearly as it has been seen in the education of the youths the world over, that it is the *boy* and not the material product, that is the true object of education. Consequently the object of the industrial school came to be the thorough training of boys regardless of the cost of the training, so long as it was thoroughly well done.

Even at this point, however, the difficulties were not surmounted. In the first place modern industry has taken great strides since the war, and the teaching of trades is no longer a simple matter. Machinery and long processes of work have greatly changed the work of the carpenter, the ironworker and the shoemaker. A really efficient workman must be to-day an intelligent man who has had good technical training in addition to thorough common school, and perhaps even higher training. To meet this situation the industrial schools began a further development; they established distinct Trade Schools for the thorough training of better class artisans, and at the same time they sought to preserve for the purposes of general education, such of the simpler processes of elementary trade learning as were best suited therefor. In this differentiation of the Trade School and manual training, the best of the industrial schools simply followed the plain trend of the present educational epoch. A prominent educator tells us that, in Sweden, "In the beginning the economic conception was generally adopted, and everywhere manual training was looked upon as a means of preparing the children of the common people to earn their living. But gradually it came to be recognized that manual training has a more elevated purpose, and one, indeed, more useful in the deeper meaning of the term. It came to be considered as an educative process for the complete moral, physical and intellectual development of the child."

Thus, again, in the manning of trade schools and manual training schools we are thrown back upon the higher training as its source and chief support. There was a time when any aged and wornout carpenter could teach in a trade school. But not so to-day. Indeed the demand for college-bred men by a school like Tuskegee, ought to make Mr. Booker T. Washington the firmest friend of higher training. Here he has as helpers the son of a Negro senator, trained in Greek and the humanities, and graduated at Harvard; the son of a Negro congressman and lawyer, trained in Latin and mathematics, and graduated at Oberlin; he has as his wife, a woman who read Virgil and Homer in the same class room with me; he has as college chaplain, a classical graduate of Atlanta University; as teacher of science, a graduate of Fisk; as teacher of history, a graduate of Smith,—indeed some thirty of his chief teachers are college graduates, and instead of studying French grammars in the midst of weeds, or buying pianos for dirty cabins, they are at Mr. Washington's right hand helping him in a noble work. And yet one of the effects of Mr. Washington's propaganda has been to throw doubt upon the expediency of such training for Negroes, as these persons have had.

Men of America, the problem is plain before you. Here is a race transplanted through the criminal foolishness of your fathers. Whether you like it or not the millions are here, and here they will remain. If you do not lift them up, they will pull you down. Education and work are the levers to uplift a people. Work alone will not do it unless inspired by the right ideals and guided by intelligence. Education must not simply teach work—it must teach Life. The Talented Tenth of the Negro race must be made leaders of thought and missionaries of culture among their people. No others can do this work and Negro colleges must train men for it. The Negro race, like all other races, is going to be saved by its exceptional men.

Treaty of Guadalupe Hidalgo February 2, 1848

N. P. Trist, Luis P. Cuevas, Bernardo Couto, Migl. Atristain

Treaty of peace, friendship, limits, and settlement between the United States of America and the United Mexican States Concluded at Guadalupe Hidalgo, February 2, 1848; ratification advised by senate, with amendments, March 10, 1848; ratified by President, March 16, 1848; ratifications exchanged at queretaro, May 30, 1848; proclaimed, July 4, 1848.

In the Name of Almighty God

The United States of America and the United Mexican States animated by a sincere desire to put an end to the calamities of the war which unhappily exists between the two Republics and to establish Upon a solid basis relations of peace and friendship, which shall confer reciprocal benefits upon the citizens of both, and assure the concord, harmony, and mutual confidence wherein the two people should live, as good neighbors have for that purpose appointed their respective plenipotentiaries, that is to say: The President of the United States has appointed Nicholas P. Trist, a citizen of the United States, and the President of the Mexican Republic has appointed Don Luis Gonzaga Cuevas, Don Bernardo Couto, and Don Miguel Atristain, citizens of the said Republic; Who, after a reciprocal communication of their respective full powers, have, under the protection of Almighty God, the author of peace, arranged, agreed upon, and signed the following: Treaty of Peace, Friendship, Limits, and Settlement between the United States of America and the Mexican Republic.

Article I

There shall be firm and universal peace between the United States of America and the Mexican Republic, and between their respective countries, territories, cities, towns, and people, without exception of places or persons.

Article II

Immediately upon the signature of this treaty, a convention shall be entered into between a commissioner or commissioners appointed by the General-in-chief of the forces of the United States, and such as may be appointed by the Mexican Government, to the end that a provisional suspension of hostilities shall take place, and that, in the places occupied by the said forces, constitutional order may be reestablished, as regards the political, administrative, and judicial branches, so far as this shall be permitted by the circumstances of military occupation.

Article III

Immediately upon the ratification of the present treaty by the Government of the United States, orders shall be transmitted to the commanders of their land and naval forces, requiring the latter (provided this treaty shall then have been ratified by the Government of the Mexican Republic, and the ratifications exchanged) immediately to desist from blockading any Mexican ports and requiring the former (under the same condition) to commence, at the earliest moment practicable, withdrawing all troops of the United States then in the interior of the Mexican Republic, to points that shall be selected by common agreement, at a distance from the seaports not exceeding thirty leagues; and such evacuation of the interior of the Republic shall be completed with the least possible delay; the Mexican Government hereby binding itself to afford every facility in its power for rendering the same convenient to the troops, on their march and in their new positions, and for promoting a good understanding between them and the inhabitants. In like manner orders shall be despatched to the persons in charge of the custom houses at all ports occupied by the forces of the United States, requiring them (under the same condition) immediately to deliver possession of the same to the persons authorized by the Mexican Government to receive it, together with all bonds and evidences of debt for duties on importations and on exportations, not yet fallen due. Moreover, a faithful and exact account shall be made out, showing the entire amount of all duties on imports and on exports, collected at such customhouses, or elsewhere in Mexico, by authority of the United States, from and after the day of ratification of this treaty by the Government of the Mexican Republic; and also an account of the cost of collection; and such entire amount, deducting only the cost of collection, shall be delivered to the Mexican Government, at the city of Mexico, within three months after the exchange of ratifications.

The evacuation of the capital of the Mexican Republic by the troops of the United States, in virtue of the above stipulation, shall be completed in one month after the orders there stipulated for shall have been received by the commander of said troops, or sooner if possible.

Article IV

Immediately after the exchange of ratifications of the present treaty all castles, forts, territories, places, and possessions, which have been taken or occupied by the forces of the United States during the present war, within the limits of the Mexican Republic, as about to be established by the following article, shall be definitely restored to the said Republic, together with all the artillery, arms, apparatus of war, munitions, and other public property, which were in the said castles and forts when captured, and which shall remain there at the time when this treaty shall be duly ratified by the Government of the Mexican Republic. To this end, immediately upon the signature of this treaty, orders shall be despatched to the American officers commanding such castles and forts, securing against the removal or destruction of any such artillery, arms, apparatus of war, munitions, or other public property. The city of Mexico, within the inner line of intrenchments surrounding the said city, is comprehended in the above stipulation, as regards the restoration of artillery, apparatus of war, & c.

The final evacuation of the territory of the Mexican Republic, by the forces of the United States, shall be completed in three months from the said exchange of ratifications, or sooner if possible; the Mexican Government hereby engaging, as in the foregoing article to use all means in its power for facilitating such evacuation, and rendering it convenient to the troops, and for promoting a good understanding between them and the inhabitants.

If, however, the ratification of this treaty by both parties should not take place in time to allow the embarcation of the troops of the United States to be completed before the commencement of the sickly season, at the Mexican ports on the Gulf of Mexico, in such case a friendly arrangement shall be entered into between the General-in-Chief of the said troops and the Mexican Government, whereby healthy and otherwise suitable places, at a distance from the ports not exceeding thirty leagues, shall be designated for the residence of such troops as may not yet have embarked, until the return of the healthy season. And the space of time here referred to as, comprehending the sickly season shall be understood to extend from the first day of May to the first day of November.

All prisoners of war taken on either side, on land or on sea, shall be restored as soon as practicable after the exchange of ratifications of this treaty. It is also agreed that if any Mexicans should now be held as captives by any savage tribe within the limits of the United States, as about to be established by the following article, the Government of the said United States will exact the release of such captives and cause them to be restored to their country.

Article V

The boundary line between the two Republics shall commence in the Gulf of Mexico, three leagues from land, opposite the mouth of the Rio Grande, otherwise called Rio Bravo del Norte, or Opposite the mouth of its deepest branch, if it should have more than one branch emptying directly into the sea; from thence up the middle of that river, following the deepest channel, where it has more than one, to the point where it strikes the southern boundary of New Mexico; thence, westwardly, along the whole southern boundary of New Mexico (which runs north of the town called Paso) to its western termination; thence, northward, along the western line of New Mexico, until it intersects the first branch of the river Gila; (or if it should not intersect any branch of that river, then to the point on the said line nearest to such branch, and thence in a direct line to the same); thence down the middle of the said branch and of the said river, until it empties into the Rio Colorado; thence across the Rio Colorado, following the division line between Upper and Lower California, to the Pacific Ocean.

The southern and western limits of New Mexico, mentioned in the article, are those laid down in the map entitled "Map of the United Mexican States, as organized and defined by various acts of the Congress of said republic, and constructed according to the best authorities. Revised edition. Published at New York, in 1847, by J. Disturnell," of which map a copy is added to this treaty, bearing the signatures and seals of the undersigned Plenipotentiaries. And, in order to preclude all difficulty in tracing upon the ground the limit separating Upper from Lower California, it is agreed that the said limit shall consist of a straight line drawn from the middle of the Rio Gila, where it unites with the Colorado, to a point on the coast of the Pacific Ocean, distant one marine league due south of the southernmost point of the port of San Diego, according to the plan of said port made in the year 1782 by Don Juan Pantoja, second sailing-master of the Spanish fleet, and published at Madrid in the year 1802, in the atlas to the voyage of the schooners Sutil and Mexicana; of which plan a copy is hereunto added, signed and sealed by the respective Plenipotentiaries.

In order to designate the boundary line with due precision, upon authoritative maps, and to establish upon the ground land-marks which shall show the limits of both republics, as described in the present article, the two Governments shall each appoint a commissioner and a surveyor, who, before the expiration of one year from the date of the exchange of ratifications of this treaty, shall meet at the port of San Diego, and proceed to run and mark the said boundary in its whole course to the mouth of the Rio Bravo del Norte. They shall keep journals and make out plans of their operations; and the result agreed upon by them shall be deemed a part of this treaty, and shall have the same force as if it were inserted therein. The two Governments will amicably agree regarding what may be necessary to these persons, and also as to their respective escorts, should such be necessary.

The boundary line established by this article shall be religiously respected by each of the two republics, and no change shall ever be made therein, except by the express and free consent of both nations, lawfully given by the General Government of each, in conformity with its own constitution.

Article VI

The vessels and citizens of the United States shall, in all time, have a free and uninterrupted passage by the Gulf of California, and by the river Colorado below its confluence with the Gila, to and from their possessions situated north of the boundary line defined in the preceding article; it being understood that this passage is to be by navigating the Gulf of California and the river Colorado, and not by land, without the express consent of the Mexican Government.

If, by the examinations which may be made, it should be ascertained to be practicable and advantageous to construct a road, canal, or railway, which should in whole or in part run upon the river Gila, or upon its right or its left bank, within the space of one marine league from either margin of the river, the Governments of both republics will form an agreement regarding its construction, in order that it may serve equally for the use and advantage of both countries.

Article VII

The river Gila, and the part of the Rio Bravo del Norte lying below the southern boundary of New Mexico, being, agreeably to the fifth article, divided in the middle between the two republics, the navigation of the Gila and of the Bravo below said boundary shall be free and common to the vessels and citizens of both countries; and neither shall, without the consent of the other, construct any work that may impede or interrupt, in whole or in part, the exercise of this right; not even for the purpose of favoring new methods of navigation. Nor shall any tax or contribution, under any denomination or title, be levied upon vessels or persons navigating the same or upon merchandise or effects transported thereon, except in the case of landing upon one of their shores. If, for the purpose of making the said rivers navigable, or for maintaining them in such state, it should be necessary or advantageous to establish any tax or contribution, this shall not be done without the consent of both Governments.

The stipulations contained in the present article shall not impair the territorial rights of either republic within its established limits.

Article VIII

Mexicans now established in territories previously belonging to Mexico, and which remain for the future within the limits of the United States, as defined by the present treaty, shall be free to continue where they now reside, or to remove at any time to the Mexican Republic, retaining the property which they possess in the said territories, or disposing thereof, and removing the proceeds wherever they please, without their being subjected, on this account, to any contribution, tax, or charge whatever.

Those who shall prefer to remain in the said territories may either retain the title and rights of Mexican citizens, or acquire those of citizens of the United States. But they shall be under the obligation to make their election within one year from the date of the exchange of ratifications of this treaty; and those who shall remain in the said territories after the expiration of that year, without having declared their intention to retain the character of Mexicans, shall be considered to have elected to become citizens of the United States.

In the said territories, property of every kind, now belonging to Mexicans not established there, shall be inviolably respected. The present owners, the heirs of these, and all Mexicans who may hereafter acquire said property by contract, shall enjoy with respect to it guarantees equally ample as if the same belonged to citizens of the United States.

Article IX

The Mexicans who, in the territories aforesaid, shall not preserve the character of citizens of the Mexican Republic, conformably with what is stipulated in the preceding article, shall be incorporated into the Union of the United States, and be admitted at the proper time (to be judged of by the Congress of the United States) to the enjoyment of all the rights of citizens of the United States, according to the principles of the Constitution; and in the mean time, shall be maintained and protected in the free enjoyment of their liberty and property, and secured in the free exercise of their religion without; restriction.

Article X

[Stricken out]

Article XI

Considering that a great part of the territories, which, by the present treaty, are to be comprehended for the future within the limits of the United States, is now occupied by savage tribes, who will hereafter be under the exclusive control of the Government of the United States, and whose incursions within the territory of Mexico would be prejudicial in the extreme, it is solemnly agreed that all such incursions shall be forcibly restrained by the Government of the United States whensoever this may be necessary; and that when they cannot be prevented, they shall be punished by the said Government, and satisfaction for the same shall be exactedall in the same way, and with equal diligence and energy, as if the same incursions were meditated or committed within its own territory, against its own citizens.

It shall not be lawful, under any pretext whatever, for any inhabitant of the United States to purchase or acquire any Mexican, or any foreigner residing in Mexico, who may have been captured by Indians inhabiting the territory of either of the two republics; nor to purchase or acquire horses, mules, cattle, or property of any kind, stolen within Mexican territory by such Indians.

And in the event of any person or persons, captured within Mexican territory by Indians, being carried into the territory of the United States, the Government of the latter engages and binds itself, in the most solemn manner, so soon as it shall know of such captives being within its territory, and shall be able so to do, through the faithful exercise of its influence and power, to rescue them and return them to their country, or deliver them to the agent or representative of the Mexican Government.

The Mexican authorities will, as far as practicable, give to the Government of the United States notice of such captures; and its agents shall pay the expenses incurred in the maintenance and transmission of the rescued captives; who, in the mean time, shall be treated with the utmost hospitality by the American authorities at the place where they may be. But if the Government of the United States, before receiving such notice from Mexico, should obtain intelligence, through any other channel, of the existence of Mexican captives within its territory, it will proceed forthwith to effect their release and delivery to the Mexican agent, as above stipulated.

For the purpose of giving to these stipulations the fullest possible efficacy, thereby affording the security and redress demanded by their true spirit and intent, the Government of the United States will now and hereafter pass, without unnecessary delay, and always vigilantly enforce, such laws as the nature of the subject may require. And, finally, the sacredness of this obligation shall never be lost sight of by the said Government, when providing for the removal of the Indians from any portion of the said territories, or for its being settled by citizens of the United States; but, on the contrary, special care shall then be taken not to place its Indian occupants under the necessity of seeking new homes, by committing those invasions which the United States have solemnly obliged themselves to restrain.

Article XII

In consideration of the extension acquired by the boundaries of the United States, as defined in the fifth article of the present treaty, the Government of the United States engages to pay to that of the Mexican Republic the sum of fifteen millions of dollars.

Immediately after the treaty shall have been duly ratified by the Government of the Mexican Republic, the sum of three millions of dollars shall be paid to the said Government by that of the United States, at the city of Mexico, in the gold or silver coin of Mexico. The remaining twelve millions of dollars shall be paid at the same place, and in the same coin, in annual installments of three millions of dollars each, together with interest on the same at the rate of six per centum per annum. This interest shall begin to run upon the whole sum of twelve millions from the day of the ratification of the present treaty by—the Mexican Government, and the first of the installments shall be paid-at the expiration of one year from the same day. Together with each annual installment, as it falls due, the whole interest accruing on such installment from the beginning shall also be paid.

Article XIII

The United States engage, moreover, to assume and pay to the claimants all the amounts now due them, and those hereafter to become due, by reason of the claims already liquidated and decided against the Mexican Republic, under the conventions between the two republics severally concluded on the eleventh day of April, eighteen hundred and thirty-nine, and on the thirtieth day of January, eighteen hundred and forty-three; so that the Mexican Republic shall be absolutely exempt, for the future, from all expense whatever on account of the said claims.

Article XIV

The United States do furthermore discharge the Mexican Republic from all claims of citizens of the United States, not heretofore decided against the Mexican Government, which may have arisen previously to the date of the signature of this treaty; which discharge shall be final and perpetual, whether the said claims be rejected or be allowed by the board of commissioners provided for in the following article, and whatever shall be the total amount of those allowed.

Article XV

The United States, exonerating Mexico from all demands on account of the claims of their citizens mentioned in the preceding article, and considering them entirely and forever canceled, whatever their amount may be, undertake to make satisfaction for the same, to an amount not exceeding three and one-quarter millions of dollars. To ascertain the validity and amount of those claims, a board of commissioners shall be established by the Government of the United States, whose awards shall be final and conclusive; provided that, in deciding upon the validity of each claim, the boa shall be guided and governed by the principles and rules of decision prescribed by the first and fifth articles of the unratified convention, concluded at the city of Mexico on the twentieth day of November, one thousand eight hundred and forty-three; and in no case shall an award be made in favour of any claim not embraced by these principles and rules.

If, in the opinion of the said board of commissioners or of the claimants, any books, records, or documents, in the possession or power of the Government of the Mexican Republic, shall be deemed necessary to the just decision of any claim, the commissioners, or the claimants through them, shall, within such period as Congress may designate, make an application in writing for the same, addressed to the Mexican Minister of Foreign Affairs, to be transmitted by the Secretary of State of the United States; and the Mexican Government engages, at the earliest possible moment after the receipt of such demand, to cause any of the books, records, or documents so specified, which shall be in their possession or power (or authenticated copies or extracts of the same), to be transmitted to the said Secretary of State, who shall immediately deliver them over to the said board of commissioners; provided that no such application shall be made by or at the instance of any claimant, until the facts which it is expected to prove by such books, records, or documents, shall have been stated under oath or affirmation.

Article XVI

Each of the contracting parties reserves to itself the entire right to fortify whatever point within its territory it may judge proper so to fortify for its security.

Article XVII

The treaty of amity, commerce, and navigation, concluded at the city of Mexico, on the fifth day of April, A.D. 1831, between the United States of America and the United Mexican States, except the additional article, and except so far as the stipulations of the said treaty may be incompatible with any stipulation contained in the present treaty, is hereby revived for the period of eight years from the day of the exchange of ratifications of this treaty, with the same force and virtue as if incorporated therein; it being understood that each of the contracting parties reserves to itself the right, at any time after the said period of eight years shall have expired, to terminate the same by giving one year's notice of such intention to the other party.

Article XVIII

All supplies whatever for troops of the United States in Mexico, arriving at ports in the occupation of such troops previous to the final evacuation thereof, although subsequently to the restoration of the custom-houses at such ports, shall be entirely exempt from duties and charges of any kind; the Government of the United States hereby engaging and pledging its faith to establish and vigilantly to enforce, all possible guards for securing the revenue of Mexico, by preventing the importation, under cover of this stipulation, of any articles other than such, both in kind and in quantity, as shall really be wanted for the use and consumption of the forces of the United States during the time they may remain in Mexico. To this end it shall be the duty of all officers and agents of the United States to denounce to the Mexican authorities at the respective ports any attempts at a fraudulent abuse of this stipulation, which they may know of, or may have reason to suspect, and to give to such authorities all the aid in their power with regard thereto; and every such attempt, when duly proved and established by sentence of a competent tribunal, They shall be punished by the confiscation of the property so attempted to be fraudulently introduced.

Article XIX

With respect to all merchandise, effects, and property whatsoever, imported into ports of Mexico, whilst in the occupation of the forces of the United States, whether by citizens of either republic, or by citizens or subjects of any neutral nation, the following rules shall be observed:

1. All such merchandise, effects, and property, if imported previously to the restoration of the custom-houses to the Mexican authorities, as stipulated for in the third article of this treaty, shall be exempt from confiscation, although the importation of the same be prohibited by the Mexican tariff.
2. The same perfect exemption shall be enjoyed by all such merchandise, effects, and property, imported subsequently to the restoration of the custom-houses, and previously to the sixty days fixed in the following article for the coming into force of the Mexican tariff at such ports respectively; the said merchandise, effects, and property being, however, at the time of their importation, subject to the payment of duties, as provided for in the said following article.
3. All merchandise, effects, and property described in the two rules foregoing shall, during their continuance at the place of importation, and upon their leaving such place for the interior, be exempt from all duty, tax, or imposts of every kind, under whatsoever title or denomination. Nor shall they be there subject to any charge whatsoever upon the sale thereof.
4. All merchandise, effects, and property, described in the first and second rules, which shall have been removed to any place in the interior, whilst such place was in the occupation of the forces of the United States, shall, during their continuance therein, be exempt from all tax upon the sale or consumption thereof, and from every kind of impost or contribution, under whatsoever title or denomination.
5. But if any merchandise, effects, or property, described in the first and second rules, shall be removed to any place not occupied at the time by the forces of the United States, they shall, upon their introduction into such place, or upon their sale or consumption there, be subject to the same duties which, under the Mexican laws, they would be required to pay in such cases if they had been imported in time of peace, through the maritime custom-houses, and had there paid the duties conformably with the Mexican tariff.
6. The owners of all merchandise, effects, or property, described in the first and second rules, and existing in any port of Mexico, shall have the right to reship the same, exempt from all tax, impost, or contribution whatever.

With respect to the metals, or other property, exported from any Mexican port whilst in the occupation of the forces of the United States, and previously to the restoration of the custom-house at such port, no person shall be required by the Mexican authorities, whether general or state, to pay any tax, duty, or contribution upon any such exportation, or in any manner to account for the same to the said authorities.

Article XX

Through consideration for the interests of commerce generally, it is agreed, that if less than sixty days should elapse between the date of the signature of this treaty and the restoration of the custom houses, conformably with the stipulation in the third article, in such case all merchandise, effects and property whatsoever, arriving at the Mexican ports after the restoration of the said custom-houses, and previously to the expiration of sixty days after the day of signature of this treaty, shall be admitted to entry; and no other duties shall be levied thereon than the duties established by the tariff found in force at such custom-houses at the time of the restoration of the same. And to all such merchandise, effects, and property, the rules established by the preceding article shall apply.

Article XXI

If unhappily any disagreement should hereafter arise between the Governments of the two republics, whether with respect to the interpretation of any stipulation in this treaty, or with respect to any other particular concerning the political or commercial relations of the two nations, the said Governments, in the name of those nations, do promise to each other that they will endeavour, in the most sincere and earnest manner, to settle the differences so arising, and to preserve the state of peace and friendship in which the two countries are now placing themselves, using, for this end, mutual representations and pacific negotiations. And if, by these means, they should not be enabled to come to an agreement, a resort shall not, on this account, be had to reprisals, aggression, or hostility of any kind, by the one republic against the other, until the Government of that which deems itself aggrieved shall have maturely considered, in the spirit of peace and good neighbourship, whether it would not be better that such difference should be settled by the arbitration of commissioners appointed on each side, or by that of a friendly nation. And should such course be proposed by either party, it shall be acceded to by the other, unless deemed by it altogether incompatible with the nature of the difference, or the circumstances of the case.

Article XXII

If (which is not to be expected, and which God forbid) war should unhappily break out between the two republics, they do now, with a view to such calamity, solemnly pledge themselves to each other and to the world to observe the following rules; absolutely where the nature of the subject permits, and as closely as possible in all cases where such absolute observance shall be impossible:

1. The merchants of either republic then residing in the other shall be allowed to remain twelve months (for those dwelling in the interior), and six months (for those dwelling at the seaports) to collect their debts and settle their affairs; during which periods they shall enjoy the same protection, and be on the same footing, in all respects, as the citizens or subjects of the most friendly nations; and, at the expiration thereof, or at any time before, they shall have full liberty to depart, carrying off all their effects without molestation or hindrance, conforming therein to the same laws which the citizens or subjects of the most friendly nations are required to conform to. Upon the entrance of the armies of either nation into the territories of the other, women and children, ecclesiastics, scholars of every faculty, cultivators of the earth, merchants, artisans, manufacturers, and fishermen, unarmed and inhabiting unfortified towns, villages, or places, and in general all persons whose occupations are for the common subsistence and benefit of mankind, shall be allowed to continue their respective employments, unmolested in their persons. Nor shall their houses or goods be burnt or otherwise destroyed, nor their cattle taken, nor their fields wasted, by the armed force into whose power, by the events of war, they may happen to fall; but if the necessity arise to take anything from them for the use of such armed force, the same shall be paid for at an equitable price. All churches, hospitals, schools, colleges, libraries, and other establishments for charitable and beneficent purposes, shall be respected, and all persons connected with the same protected in the discharge of their duties, and the pursuit of their vocations.
2. In order that the fate of prisoners of war may be alleviated all such practices as those of sending them into distant, inclement or unwholesome districts, or crowding them into close and noxious places, shall be studiously avoided. They shall not be confined in dungeons, prison ships, or prisons; nor be put in irons, or bound or otherwise restrained in the use of their limbs. The officers shall enjoy liberty on their paroles, within convenient districts, and have comfortable quarters; and the common soldiers shall be dispose (in cantonments, open and extensive enough for air and exercise and lodged in barracks as roomy and good as are provided by the party in whose power they are for its own troops. But if any office shall break his parole by leaving the district so assigned him, o any other prisoner shall escape from the limits of his cantonment after they shall have been designated to him, such individual, officer, or other prisoner, shall forfeit so much of the benefit of this article as provides for his liberty on parole or in cantonment. And if any officer so breaking his parole or any common soldier so escaping from the limits assigned him, shall afterwards be found in arms previously to his being regularly exchanged, the person so offending shall be dealt with according to the established laws of war. The officers shall be daily furnished, by the party in whose power they are, with as many rations, and of the same articles, as are allowed either in kind or by commutation, to officers of equal rank in its own army; and all others shall be daily furnished with such ration as is allowed to a common soldier in its own service; the

value of all which supplies shall, at the close of the war, or at periods to be agreed upon between the respective commanders, be paid by the other party, on a mutual adjustment of accounts for the subsistence of prisoners; and such accounts shall not be mingled with or set off against any others, nor the balance due on them withheld, as a compensation or reprisal for any cause whatever, real or pretended Each party shall be allowed to keep a commissary of prisoners, appointed by itself, with every cantonment of prisoners, in possession of the other; which commissary shall see the prisoners as often a he pleases; shall be allowed to receive, exempt from all duties a taxes, and to distribute, whatever comforts may be sent to them by their friends; and shall be free to transmit his reports in open letters to the party by whom he is employed. And it is declared that neither the pretense that war dissolves all treaties, nor any other whatever, shall be considered as annulling or suspending the solemn covenant contained in this article. On the contrary, the state of war is precisely that for which it is provided; and, during which, its stipulations are to be as sacredly observed as the most acknowledged obligations under the law of nature or nations.

Article XXIII

This treaty shall be **ratified by the President of the United States of America, by and with the advice and consent of the Senate thereof;** and by the President of the Mexican Republic, with the previous approbation of its general Congress; and the ratifications shall be exchanged in the City of Washington, or at the seat of Government of Mexico, in four months from the date of the signature hereof, or sooner if practicable. In faith whereof we, the respective Plenipotentiaries, have signed this treaty of peace, friendship, limits, and settlement, and have hereunto affixed our seals respectively. Done in quintuplicate, at the city of Guadalupe Hidalgo, on the second day of February, in the year of our Lord one thousand eight hundred and forty-eight.

Empire and the Origins of 20th-Century Migration from Mexico to the United States

Gilbert G. González and Raúl Fernandez

The [the migrant] is forced to seek better conditions north of the border by the slow but relentless pressure of United States' agricultural, financial, and oil corporate interests on the entire economic and social evolution of the Mexican nation.

Ernesto Galarza, 1949[1]

Preamble

In this article we show how the twentieth-century appearance of a Chicano minority population in the United States originated from the subordination of the nation of Mexico to U.S. economic and political interests. We argue that, far from being marginal to the course of modern U.S. history, the Chicano minority, an immigrant people, stands at the center both of that history and of a process of imperial expansionism that originated in the last three decades of the nineteenth century and that continues today.

Several challenges to conventional interpretations of Mexican migration and the Chicano experience derive from this approach. This century-long exodus of Mexicans to the United States has often been perceived as an "American" problem, affecting welfare, education, culture, crime, drug abuse, and public budgets, to be solved by get-tough measures, such as California's Proposition 187, and softer policies, such as those of immigrant rights agencies. In contrast, we take the position that migration signifies a Mexican national crisis, reflecting Mexico's economic subordination to the United States and the limitations placed upon its national sovereignty by that domination. A century of mass border crossings displays the breaking apart of the social fabric of the Mexican nation and its resettlement in enclaves across the United States as a national minority.

The social and political repercussions of this subordination have been enormous. More than a century of domination by the United States increasingly undermined the social and political cohesion of Mexico, causing dislocation to its domestic agriculture and industry as well as migration to the United States-Mexico border and into the United States itself. In his 1911 classic exposé, *Barbarous Mexico,* John Kenneth Turner addressed the dismantling of the Mexican nation. "The partnership of Díaz and American capital," he argued, "has wrecked Mexico as a national entity. The United States government, as long as it represents American capital . . . will have a deciding voice in Mexican affairs."[2] Washington preferred economic domination by U.S. corporations to the direct annexation of Mexico. As John Mason Hart has persuasively demonstrated, U.S. capital realized that policy objective and established its supremacy in Mexico by the late nineteenth century.[3] Mexico became the first foreign country to fall under the imperial umbrella of the United States.

The practice of territorial conquest and expansion in pursuit of, or as a consequence of, commercial developments is very old; from the Romans to the Aztecs to nineteenth-century Great Britain, this characteristic has been shared by most imperial powers. Over the last century, however, the United States, along with other global powers, developed an empire of a new type, a transnational mode of economic domination similar to but in important respects different from previous imperial regimes.

While the United States throughout its history has engaged in numerous acts of territorial aggression and conquest—like other historical centers of power—its particular mode of empire building and maintenance emerged when the growth of large corporations and financial institutions became directly involved in alliance with local elites, in the formally independent economies and politics of other countries. Simultaneously, these large conglomerates of finance and production came to dominate the government of United States, using the power of the state to jockey for position with other world powers. This practice of empire construction and management was aptly captured by U.S. Secretary of State John Foster Dulles in the 1950s: "[T]here [are] two ways of dominating a foreign nation," he remarked, "invading it militarily or controlling it financially."[4] In the case of Mexico, U.S. policy preferred financial over military control.

Mexico and the U.S. Model of Empire Building

A transnational mode of imperial hegemony has defined U.S. relations with the rest of the world throughout the twentieth century. Mexico provided the first testing ground. The United States initiated new mechanisms of empire in the late 1870s when it became the senior partner in an alliance with the local Mexican elite personified in the figure of dictator Porfirio Díaz. Using threats of military intervention, U.S. capital interests invested heavily in the construction of railroads in Mexico. These initial intrusions were quickly followed by massive investments in mining, cattle farming, and cotton production. After Mexico, the United States moved swiftly to establish economic control and political influence southward. The United States launched the War of 1898 for a variety of motives: to insure that no sovereign and independent nation appeared in Cuba upon the defeat of the Spanish empire; to establish a military presence guaranteeing the security of its investments; and to establish strategic outposts to secure and control commerce and investments in the Caribbean and East Asia. U.S. political leaders defended the war with rhetoric of supporting the underdog, a rationale to allay public unease over war and manipulate public opinion. The War of 1898 was followed quickly by the U.S.-supported secession of the province of Panama from Colombia, ensuring U.S. control of interoceanic trade. At the same time, large U.S. investments in Mexico and Cuba took place via the company town model in agriculture, railroad construction, and mining.[5]

Beginning at the turn of the century, investment by U.S.-based corporations in Latin America, in cooperation with archaic land-based elites and bolstered by the U.S. military and the threat of annexation, transformed the hemisphere into a series of neocolonial republics. Mexico became something of a laboratory for the imperial experiments; few events of significance in the history of twentieth-century Mexico were not decisively influenced by the power of U.S. economic, political, and, as a last recourse, military power.[6] A few examples will suffice: The United States played a determining role in the outcome of the 1910 Mexican Revolution; after World War II the United States provided the money, propaganda, and logistics to control the labor and social movements in which the ideas of socialism were taking root, not only in Mexico but throughout Latin America;[7] in the 1990s the United States established NAFTA to secure further its investments in Mexico and to restrict access for investment there by competitors. The freedom and security of U.S. capital thus remained a constant in U.S. policy toward Mexico in the twentieth century.

This establishment of U.S. imperial hegemony over Mexico and other Latin America nations has long been acknowledged in Latin America as central to local histories and identity. From the 1880s to the 1930s, major Mexican and Latin American thinkers, including Jose Vasconcelos, Jose Martí, Jose Enrique Rodó, and Eugenio María de Hostos, placed U.S. presence in Latin America as central to their essays on Latin America's future. The profound awareness of the United States that pervades the lives, history, politics, and economics of Latin American countries is not matched by a parallel knowledge in the United States of its southern neighbors. In the academy, official U.S. historiography dates national emergence onto the global scene to World War I, privileging U.S. activity in Europe over decades of investment, interference, and invasions into Mexico and other southern neighbors. As a subset of official U.S. history, the study of the Chicano national minority has largely been constructed in an atmosphere in which "race matters," and culture, too, but empire does not. Insofar as the U.S. transnational mode of hegemony is acknowledged, it is not seen as essential or even related to understanding the origins and development of the Chicano national minority.[8]

The Push-Pull Thesis: The "Official" Line on Mexican Migration

Since the first decade of the twentieth century, academic studies of Mexican migration to the United States established one basic theoretical construct—the push-pull thesis, modeled upon conventional supply and demand economics. The thesis reduces the causes of migration to sets of conditions within the sending country and the host country, conditions that *function independently* of each other. In one country, a push (supply), usually attributed to poverty, unemployment, or political unrest, motivates people to consider a significant move; in the other country, a pull (demand), usually a shortage of labor, operates to attract the disaffected. In tandem, they synergistically lead to transnational migration.

Following the political militancy and cultural nationalism of the late 1960s, numerous studies focused on the origins of the Mexican population in the United States. These stemmed from the interest not only of Chicano activists but also of academics attracted to the issues raised by the regional political rebellion. As the Chicano Studies research agenda matured, immigration, particularly in the 1900–1930 period, gained a central place in many studies. The original push-pull thesis, as enunciated by the U.S. Industrial Commission on Immigration in 1901 and repeated by Victor S. Clark in 1908 and by Manuel Gamio and Paul S. Taylor in the early 1930s, became an article of faith among a new generation of academics destined to dominate the field to the end of the century.[9]

Many academics simply made the 1910 Revolution the principal push factor operating in the 1900–1930 era.[10] Consequently, when the UCLA Mexican American Study Project turned its attention to immigration in the late 1960s, the theoretical scenario had been set: "The Mexican revolutionary period beginning in 1909–1910 spurred the first substantial and permanent migration to the United States," the report's authors wrote. "By liberating masses of people from social as well as geographic immobility, [the Revolution] served to activate a latent migration potential of vast dimensions."[11]

To be sure, different research projects often emphasized particular conditions that modified the form in which push-pull ostensibly manifested. There *were* variations on the theme. A number of authors viewed the policies of Díaz as similar to European elites' expropriation of peasants' lands and the simultaneous de-peasanting of the countryside. Some saw the extension of railroads throughout Mexico as the key element that made migration possible. For others, the devastation of the Mexican Revolution and its aftermath precipitated the early twentieth-century migrations. A survey of the more significant studies of the last twenty years reveals a collage of factors that propel migration; seldom is the "push" viewed as the result of one factor alone. Currently, most students of Mexican migration and border studies agree that a complex of "push" factors, such as low wages, unemployment, poverty, and political oppression have operated at various times to create the conditions leading to Mexican migration over the course of the twentieth century.[12] The "pull" factors—high wages and labor demand in the United States—are taken as a given.

Around 1970 the push-pull thesis came under critical scrutiny, resulting in refinement but not substantial overhaul. Condemned as a neoclassical artifact, the thesis was ostensibly supplanted by a set of theoretical approaches to explain Mexican migration. The new paradigms—social capital theory, segmented market theory, new economics theory, and world systems theory—challenged push-pull. The first three of these contended that the old economic categories—wages, poverty, surplus population, and unemployment—inadequately explain the "push" of Mexican migration, particularly the long-term trends appearing since roughly 1970. World systems theory, on the other hand, contended that global capitalism reaching into the remotest corners of Mexico uprooted peasants from the land and caused unemployment; both conditions drive migration. In spite of the claim that these approaches go beyond the limitations of the push-pull paradigm, we shall argue below that the basic premises of push-pull have not been completely uprooted by these modifications.

Most analysts of migration seem to view the "push" factors, such as Porfirian policies, the 1910 revolution, low wages, and surplus population, as operating independently of the economic power of the United States. Implicit in the argument is the contention that an autonomous modernization process, not unlike what occurred in Europe, led to Mexican migration to the United States. In short, older versions and modern variations of push-pull inherently assume that Mexican migration—from 1900 to the present—followed from independently stimulated economic progress in Mexico. Largely absent in discussions of migration are two questions: Is it appropriate to conflate all migrations into a single "one size fits all" paradigm? And, if the forces of supply and demand work to eliminate economic *disequilibria*, why has there been an apparent permanent *disequilibrium* that no amount of migration from Mexico (or modernization therein) has been able to root out and that remains in effect more than a century after it began?[13]

Recent "Refinements" to Push-Pull

Recent research by sociologists has pointed out that migration continued unabated since the 1960s when economic conditions in Mexico were relatively good. Studies analyzed noneconomic factors and questioned whether these factors affected the decision to migrate. Framed in such a perspective, emphasis swung to the role of "agency," or the independent decision making of the migrants as they "negotiated" their migratory treks. Social capital theory configured transnational migrant networks linking communities divided by national borders. Migrants summoned motivations, constructed pathways, and provided the resources that propelled migrations over the long term. Theoretically, a culture of migration establishes a social network across borders that feeds migrations. Migration, in other words, exists autonomously above the economic and political life of Mexico. As migrants cross the border, they allegedly define the border on their own terms, reconfiguring sociopolitical spaces. Ultimately, recent sociological models have celebrated migration as "transnational resistance" to internationalized economic and political imperatives.[14]

According to this perspective, migration evolved into an institutionalized "self-feeding process" with a life of its own. Tautological in essence, migration is explained by migration; migrants migrate because, as "historical actors," they have voluntarily chosen to create a culture of migration. Nevertheless, the question of origins, of the factors that send the first migration and lead to subsequent migrations, is left, by default, to push-pull. The original sin, push-pull, prompts the first migrations, but, once the sin is committed, the migration assumes a *self-generating* state. The only true national and/or transnational factor of significance in this theory is the migration itself. Rational choices made by migrants, to acquire commodities or reestablish community, cultural lifestyle, and family ties, motivate migrations. Such analyses relegate international economic relations to the margins and ignore the economic domination that we address here; instead, they home in on the "independent" decision making of migrants.[15]

A second theoretical design arising from the critique of push-pull, the segmented labor market model, emphasizes an economic aspect of the receiving country, precisely the structured dependence of modernized, "post-industrial" forms of production upon the continued flow of cheap immigrant labor. An insatiable thirst for cheap labor drives migration. Adherents to this position contend that the old push conditions—wage differentials, surplus population, and so forth—are secondary if not irrelevant. However, while the push side of the equation evaporates, the pull side—that is, the demand for labor in the receiving country—functions as before. Note that both the social capital theory and the segmented labor market theory view the two economically interconnected countries as *economically independent of each other* and ignore transnational financial *domination* with respect to the process of migration. Like the original push-pull theory, these revisions separate the process of migration into two interacting but independent operations.[16]

A third model, new economics theory, contends that migration is explained "by measures of risk and the need for access to capital" rather than by the workings of the labor market.[17] According to Douglas Massey, "Considerable work suggests that the acquisition of housing, the purchase of land, and the establishment of small businesses constitute the primary motivations for international labor migration."[18] Here the push argument seems to have been supplanted by factors other than wages; however, this theoretical model, like social capital theory, stands well within the old model. New economics theorists argue that the sending country fails to supply needed capital, land, and business opportunities. These contentions fit into the push-pull model as it was first articulated nearly a century ago: The host country has something that the sending country lacks; hence, people migrate to satisfy a felt need, and a neoclassical equilibrium is established (or should be established).

In these critiques of push-pull theory, basic assumptions replicate the old model. For one, migrants have a felt need that Mexico cannot meet—thus, a push. Secondly, the United States has the conditions and wherewithal to satisfy migrants' yearnings—therefore, a pull. Lastly, the national economies of Mexico and the United States are interactive (often described as "interdependent") but without domination exerted by either party.[19]

Finally, the world systems model causally links global capitalism with migrations. In this view, direct foreign investments generate economic development in sending countries, which removes natives from farming lands or causes unemployment in traditional occupations, creating a body of migrants within the country. Saskia Sassen, perhaps the best-known world systems theoretician of migration, rightly points out how foreign investment in export agriculture modernizes production, which simultaneously upsets traditional farming practices, removes small farmers from the Mexican countryside, and resettles them in cities. Some migrate to the northern states where foreign-owned assembly plants advertise employment. Ultimately, that same surplus labor migrates to the United States where immigrant labor is in constant demand.[20]

While a thorough discussion of world systems theory is beyond the purview of this article, our basic differences with world systems theory as applied to Mexican migration to the United States stem from 1) the emphasis on direct investments, 2) the implicit argument that modernization via foreign financing equals the development experienced by Europe in the nineteenth century, and 3) the exclusive attention to the post-1960 period. First, direct investments are only one type of foreign capital that has affected the national economy of Mexico. Other types of capital have had serious consequences for the economy and society as well. For example, U.S. government lending programs, private philanthropic organizations like the Rockefeller Foundation and others, as well as economic development programs (loans) run by the International Monetary Fund (IMF), the World Bank, and the trade policies of the World Trade Organization, have had a decided impact on the economy and society of Mexico. Second, world systems theory implicitly parallels notions of the great nineteenth-century European migrations, which occurred via an indigenous capitalist modernization and consequent de-peasanting of the land. In the case of Mexico, we contend that foreign economic incursions led to a colonial status, resulting in neither indigenous, capitalist-driven modernization nor dependent modernization, but rather one under foreign control that removes peasants from the land to other parts of Mexico and to the United States. Third, regarding the proposition that the post-1960s migrations are distinct from those of earlier decades, we argue that U.S. economic domination over Mexico has remained more or less constant over the course of the twentieth century. While world systems theory does point to the significance of foreign investments in the removal of people from the countryside and their migration to cities and northern assembly plants, the model holds that the roots of migration derive from global capital, or direct foreign investment, which "modernizes" the Mexican economy. Accordingly, Mexico and the United States are sovereign nations as in the first versions of the push-pull thesis, each in its own way subject to the nuances of global capital and interdependent in the process. The theory ignores government-to-government lending programs, bank capital, massive foreign debt, and empire; the "world system" is all one massive capitalist system covering the entire globe, in which issues of inequality and domination become obscured.

In social capital theory, the segmented labor model, new economic theory, and world systems theory, the core premise of push-pull—the imbalance of independent conditions in sending and host countries—still obtains in spite of critiques. A real alternative requires a reconceptualization of migration within the context of empire.

Economic Conquest: Porfirian Mexico, 1876–1910

A critical examination of the push side of the thesis requires that we analyze the economic policies carried out by the Mexican government in the 1880–1910 period and their social consequences. It is necessary to take another look at four processes: first, the building of Mexico's railroads by U.S. companies; second, the investment of U.S. capital in mining and smelting; third, the effects of the above modernization projects on Mexico's agriculture; and fourth, the displacement of large segments of Mexico's peasant population as a consequence of the foreign-induced modernization.

We will show that foreign monopolistic economic interests—not the much vaunted *cientificos*—were the principal architects of the policies implemented by the Porfirio Díaz administrations and that these policies resulted in the subjection of Mexico to domination of a new type: a transnational mode of economic colonialism. While Porfirian policies forcibly removed peasants from ancestral village lands, it is wrong to assume that these were policies wholly designed in Mexico City. Like the construction of railroads, oil exploration and exploitation, mining, and agricultural investments by foreign capital, the removal of peasants from village lands emanated from the integration and exploitation of Mexican natural resources into foreign, primarily U.S., industrial production.

Not only Mexico but all of Latin America fell under the gaze of U.S. foreign policy at the end of the nineteenth century. The United States saw Mexico as the doorway to Latin America's riches, but only if it remained under U.S. economic tutelage. U.S. policy essentially followed the dictum of no less a patron of imperialism than Cecil Rhodes, who envisioned Mexico as the material fountain of empire. "Mexico," he once observed, "is the treasure house from which will come the gold, silver, copper, and precious stones that will build the empires of tomorrow, and will make the future cities of the world veritable Jerusalems."[21] The United States changed the plural "empires" to the singular "empire."

The 1865 victory of the Northern armies in the U.S. Civil War failed to deter the cry for "all of Mexico" that lingered in the minds of adventurous entrepreneurs and their supporters in the United States. In 1868 a spate of articles in the *New York Herald* and other metropolitan newspapers called upon the United States to establish "a protectorate over Mexico." Voices of opposition to such a policy were heard; not all were enthralled by the easy victories of 1848 and the imagined expansion to the isthmus. Anti-annexationists responded with an economic alternative free of any humanitarian impulses. William S. Rosecrans, speculator and promoter of Mexican railroads, while serving as minister to Mexico, anticipated future U.S. policy toward Mexico in his response to the newspaper articles. Rosecrans urged that Americans abandon the notion of "all of Mexico." "Pushing American enterprise up to, and within Mexico wherever it can profitably go," he claimed, "will give us advantages which force and money alone would hardly procure. It would give us a peaceful conquest of the country."[22]

A number of Rosecrans's contemporaries engaged the discussion as to whether U.S. economic interests required annexation. One prominent American investor, Edward Lee Plumb, wrote, "If we have their trade and development meanwhile we need not hasten the greater event [annexation]." Former President U.S. Grant, himself an investor in Mexico's railroads, leaned toward the Rosecrans position. According to David M. Pletcher, "Grant's fragmentary writings about Mexico . . . suggest that in the last years of his life he developed toward that country an ideology of economic imperialism closely similar to that of other promoters."[23] Former U.S. commercial attaché Chester Lloyd Jones reiterated this approach decades later in *Mexico and Its Reconstruction* (1921):

> The economic advantage that would result to the United States from annexation as contrasted to that which may follow independence and friendship is doubtful. Mexican trade, both import and export, is already almost inevitably American and investments will be increasingly so. . . . A friendly, strong, and independent Mexico will bring greater economic advantages than annexation that certain classes of Mexicans fear and some citizens of the United States desire.[24]

However, when Jones set down his policy recommendations, Mexico was well on the way to being "an economic satellite of the United States."[25]

U.S. capital first conquered the Mexican railroad system (which, for all practical purposes, was an extension of the American system), then the mining and petroleum industries, and, concurrently, trade between the two countries. The social consequences reverberated throughout Mexico in the form of mass removal of people from village lands, the ruin of artisans and craftsmen, the creation of a modern working class subject to the business cycle, and the appearance of a migratory surplus population. That migratory population first appeared within Mexico in both a rural-to-urban movement and a south-to-north movement; as the tide of U.S. investments grew, the migratory distances increased and crossed over to the United States.

Mexico began to build its railroads during the administration of Benito Juárez (1867–1872), who granted a concession to a British company to build between Mexico

City and Veracruz. His successor, Sebastián Lerdo de Tejada, continued the Juárez policies but refused to allow railroad lines to be built toward the north for fear that they might become a military advantage to the United States. Following a period of political instability, military strongman Porfirio Díaz took over Mexico's government in 1876. Díaz inaugurated the period of economic liberalism—forerunner of the current NAFTA-style neoliberalism—by selling railroad concessions to large U.S. railroad companies in the northern states. Within three years, concessions and $32 million in subsidies to U.S. corporations provided for the construction of five railroads in Mexico. Extending 2,500 miles from south to north, these lines provided a route to the interior of Mexico from which mineral ores and agricultural products were transported to the United States.[26]

These developments occurred simultaneously with the development of railroads in the southwestern United States by the same corporate interests. By 1902 U.S. investments in Mexican railroads amounted to $281 million with the northern states of Sonora, Coahuila, and Chihuahua the main recipients. Fully 80 percent of all investments in railroads in Mexico emanated from the United States.[27] By 1910 U.S. corporate capital had largely financed the building of 15,000 miles of track, providing a basic infrastructure that would insure the transport of raw materials northward and technology south.

By the dawn of the twentieth century the United States controlled the Mexican economy. According to U.S. Consul-General Andrew D. Barlow, 1,117 U.S.-based companies and individuals had invested $500 million in Mexico. Railroads were the cornerstone of the modernization process, initiated, designed, and constructed by foreign capital. Railroads enabled myriad economic activities, principally those under foreign control, including mining, export of agricultural products, and oil production. In 1902 Walter E. Weyl observed that railroads "permitted the opening up of mines" and stimulated "agriculture, and manufacturing by establishing foreign markets."[28] While foreign investments entered Mexico "at an astonishing rate," Mexican national markets for raw materials like copper were practically nonexistent or, in the case of coffee, sugar, and henequen, severely limited. Consequently, both U.S. enterprises and those owned by Mexicans marketed their commodities primarily in foreign outlets. Railroads were indispensable for the increased export of raw materials and agricultural products and the import of tools, machinery, and other products supporting the modernized sectors of the economy.

Before 1880, for example, copper was processed through the centuries-old patio method for deriving precious metals from ore. "Railroads," commented Marvin Bernstein, "aided mining from their very inception."[29] This aid, however, worked to the detriment of established miners using archaic techniques. According to mining engineer H. A. C. Jenison, writing in the *Engineering and Mining Journal-Press* in 1921, railroads "made the more remote regions accessible, made the transportation of heavy machinery possible, and the shipment of low-grade ores to smelters profitable." Consequently, about one-sixth of rail mileage was "mineral railroad," but conversely "most railroads counted upon mineral shipments."[30]

Under the stimulus of terms largely favorable to corporate investors rather than smaller individual stakeholders, U.S. capital thus assumed nearly complete control of railroads, oil, agriculture, and mining, as well as substantial control of Mexico's finances, communication (telegraphs, telephones), and urban transport. Mexico had passed into the hands of foreign economic interests. As historian Robert G. Cleland wrote in 1927:

> large numbers of foreign companies, most of them which were American, entered Mexico. As the foreigner became interested in the industry, the Mexican gradually withdrew; little by little the important properties passed out of his control, until by 1912, of a total investment in the mining business estimated at $323,600,000, he could lay claim to less than $15,000,000.[31]

American investors held $223 million, and of the total invested in Mexico, nearly 68 percent originated from foreign sources. Foreign capital's power multiplied through its control of key areas of the economy. Every review of the evidence came to the same general conclusion: "Foreign investment [almost entirely of U.S. origin] was on the order of two-thirds of the total for the decade of 1900–1910; foreign ownership by 1910 has been estimated at half the national wealth."[32] For all practical purposes, the regional elites—the *comprador caciques*—and their representatives serving as the Mexican government provided the midlevel managing agency for foreign capital.

Internal Migration: The First Step Toward Emigration

Even as the railroads made the export of agricultural products to the United States and Europe a lucrative possibility, Mexican wealth remained concentrated in the semifeudal hacienda. Enrichment without social change encouraged *hacendados* to transfer production from subsistence to cash crops for export. Coffee, fruits, henequen, hides, cattle, sugar, cotton, and other goods entered the international marketplace. For good measure, the large exporters received favorable transit rates that discriminated against domestic traders and forced the latter to produce for local consumption or not at all.[33] Hacienda export production, developed by and dependent upon railroads, was equally significant for the effects upon the peasantry. The economic spur of the railroad promoted land expropriation laws, under the aegis of liberal land reform, and effected the legalized transfer of free peasant village holdings to nearby haciendas. Based on the locations of recorded violent peasant rebellions contesting land seizures between 1880 to 1910, the majority of land expropriations during the Díaz era occurred along or near planned or operating railway routes. These activities, however, were entirely dependent upon the effects of rail transport and production geared to foreign markets. Evidence points to similar patterns in other parts of Mexico. For example, in the northern state of Sonora, sales of empty public land to speculators "faithfully mirror the history of the Sonora railroad."[34]

Interestingly, the railroads, which had little effect upon industrial development, strengthened the precapitalist economic form, the hacienda. However, the hacienda, originally organized for self-sufficiency, engaged in cash crop production on an extended scale to the detriment of staple crops, causing shortages of basic foodstuffs. Corn production fell by 50 percent between 1877 and 1910, and bean production declined by 75 percent, forcing the nation to rely on costly imported staples. At the same time, exports of raw materials, like henequen, coffee, sugar, hides, oil, and ores, grew at an annual rate of 6.5 percent.[35] In 1910 Mexico was exporting a quarter of a million pounds of henequen a year, supplying Midwestern farmers with twine for binding hay. While Mexico's foreign trade grew "tenfold between the mid-1870s and 1910," the average Mexican's diet fell below the levels of the pre-Díaz period as prices for staples rose much faster than wages.[36] The state-sponsored expropriations—the mass removal of hundreds of thousands of peasants from former village subsistence holdings—was the first phase toward the transnational migration that would occur a few years later.

The first victims of Mexico's modernization—that is, economic conquest—were the peasants. By 1910, 90 percent of the central plateau's villages owned no communal land; meanwhile, the haciendas "owned over half of the nation's territory."[37] The army of dispossessed moved from village to town and city and, as the northern mining districts opened up, from south to north. No wonder that over the course of the Porfiriato the village-to-city migration would lead to a dramatic population growth in the provincial capitals, 89 percent, which outstripped the national increase of 61 percent.[38] The most dramatic increase occurred in the nation's capital, where migrating peasants began to settle in substantial numbers. According to Michael Johns, "Railroads and expanding haciendas threw so many off their lands in the 1880s and 1890s that nearly half of the city's five hundred thousand residents . . . were peasants."[39] Daily, the new arrivals searched for quarters as best they could, cramming into overcrowded lodgings. An estimated 25,000 homeless moved into *mesones,* a form of nightly shelter for transients. Men, women, and children could be found sleeping on mats in single rooms, huddled against the cold. Others lived in more permanent quarters, tenements or *vecindades,* which, while not as inhospitable as the *mesones,* were nonetheless overflowing. John Kenneth Turner estimated that at least 100,000 "residents" were without stable shelter.[40]

From this pool, the city's aristocracy and foreign (mainly American) businesspeople selected their domestic servants: drivers, cooks, babysitters, housecleaners, and laundresses. Some 65,000 in 1910 accounted for 30 percent of the capital's workforce.[41] This growing labor pool eventually supplied other regions as well. Labor recruiters working for textile manufacturers, henequen plantations, railroads, mines, and oil operations also targeted displaced peasants. Many ended up in Yucatan henequen estates as virtual slaves, working alongside thousands of Yaqui Indians forcibly removed from their Sonoran homelands to make room for land speculators and railroad builders.[42] As railroads expanded their radius of operations and as ownership of mines shifted from small prospectors to Americans, the search for labor became a key element in the modernization process. The northern trade routes from the central region, which normally occupied 60,000 pack mules, underwent a profound change with the advent of railroads. Early Latin Americanists noted this change. Frank Tannenbaum wrote that in the past the "surplus crop was . . . loaded upon the backs of pack mules or in some instances on the backs of men and carried to the nearest trading center, often days of travel away. More recently it has been delivered to the nearest railroad station."[43] Walter E. Weyl confirmed the gradual displacement in his study:

> the muleteer is now relegated to a lesser sphere of activity and a lower position in the national economy. The driver of the mule car is slowly giving way to the trained motorman, and before long the vast army of *cargadores,* or porters, will go the way which in other cities has been trod by the *lenadores* and *aguadores*—"the hewers of wood and drawers of water."[44]

Others besides mule packers were cast aside as wagon drivers, weavers, shoemakers, tanners, soapmakers, and others found that they could not compete against the new enterprises and imported goods; they too joined the army of dispossessed and unemployed, the burgeoning migrant labor pool.[45]

In a 1908 study for the U.S. Bureau of Labor, Victor Clark noted that underemployment and unemployment interacted with the internal demand for labor to cause a northward migration from the central plateau of Mexico along the railroad routes:

> The railroads that enter Mexico from the United States run for several hundred miles from the border through a desert and very sparsely settled country, but all of them ultimately tap more populous and fertile regions. Along the northern portion of their routes resident labor is so scarce that workers are brought from the south as section hands and for new construction. This has carried the central Mexican villager a thousand miles from his home and to within a few miles of the border, and American employers, with a gold wage, have had little difficulty in attracting him across that not very formidable dividing line.

Clark later noted that, "Like the railways, the mines have had to import labor from the south; and they have steadily lost labor to the United States." Clark interviewed one mining operator who in one year brought 8,000 miners from the south to work in Chihuahua. On the whole, continued Clark, "there is a constant movement of labor northward inside of Mexico itself to supply the growing demands of the less developed states, and this supply is ultimately absorbed by the still more exigent demand . . . of the border States and Territories of the United States."[46]

In his review of the Porfiriato, Mexican historian Moisés González Navarro wrote that this "human displacement from the countryside" was a "phenomenon seen for the first time."[47] Approximately 300,000 persons left the south to settle in the north primarily during the last decade of the Porfiriato, a massive and permanent shift in the nation's population generated by foreign-controlled modernization.[48] One mining engineer lamented that "The call for labor is greater than can be supplied by the native population."[49] Another remarked that "The increase in number of mining operations in recent years has been so great as to make the securing of an adequate supply of labor a difficult problem."[50] At mid-century, scattered mines operated by small contingents of laborers had toiled intermittently, often in a "hand to mouth affair," but by the century's end some 140,000 worked the mines and smelters, and most of these were internal migrants.[51] Another 30,000 to 40,000 were employed annually on the railroads in the 1880s and 1890s. It is no wonder the population growth in the north surpassed that of any other area of Mexico.[52]

Along the rail routes, cities like Torreon and Gomez Palacio expanded enormously, as did ports like Guaymas and Tampico, due to the transport of people and/or export of goods. In 1883 Torreon was classified as a *rancheria,* a collection of ranches. By 1910 it had earned the title "city" with a population of over 43,000. Nuevo Laredo grew from 1,283 in 1877 to 9,000 in 1910; Nogales, which could not claim anything more than desert and some tents, blossomed into a thriving border port of 4,000 within two years after the train passed through. Ciudad Lerdo offers a reverse example of the power of the railroads to determine population placement. In 1900 the city had contained 24,000 inhabitants, but, when the railroad bypassed it, the population declined to fewer than 12,000.[53]

The growth of the city was the other side of the demographic shift from the central plateau to the north. In the case of the north, population growth was most pronounced in the mining areas. Company towns like Cananea, El Boleo, Nacozari, Navojoa, Copola, Concordia, Santa Eulalia, Santa Rosalia, Batopilas, and Esperanzas sprang from virtual wilderness into thriving mining camps within a few years. American employers believed that company housing—albeit segregated, with Americans living apart from the Mexican labor force—was necessary to attract and control labor.[54] Cananea offers a representative example of localized change. A mining engineer reviewing the Greene Consolidated mining operations in 1906 wrote, "La Cananea presents a wonderful contrast to its earlier appearance. . . . [W]here eight years ago there were no persons other than a few warring prospectors . . . is now a camp of 25,000 persons with all the necessities and most of the comforts of civilization."[55] The Cananea operations required the labor of 5,500 regular men, with 8,000 to 9,000 listed as employees.

The Esperanza mining region in Coahuila experienced a similar profound change. In five years the area had grown from several villages to a population of 10,000, the mines employing 2,000. Batopilas, in Chihuahua, grew from 300 to 4,000, employing 900 miners. Mulegè, a port near the copper boomtown of El Boleo in Baja California, demonstrates the secondary effects that mining had on the region. The small port grew from 1,500 in 1880 to 14,000 in 1910. Similarly, Nogales, Hermosillo, El Paso, and other cities that depended on mine-driven commerce paralleled the growth in the mining enterprises themselves.

The reconfiguration of the centuries-old demographic pattern in Mexico comprised the first step in migrations to the United States. Crucially, the economic forces that propelled the population shifts were not indigenous to Mexico. Rather, they emanated from large-scale foreign corporate enterprises operating under the protection of the U.S. government's foreign policy.

Migration and Emigration

"In the southern section of the Western division, immigration from Mexico has become an important factor," stated the 1911 *Report* of the U.S. Immigration Commission. Indeed, even before the launching of the full-scale battles of the 1910 revolution (which were not to occur until 1913 to 1915), emigration had become a part of Mexican life. According to available statistics, Mexican labor began to enter the United States in sizable numbers after 1905, partly as a result of the south-to-north internal migrations in Mexico. Later migrations occurred in response to the economic depression in the United States that caused a slowdown of mining, motivating a northward migration. Data on Mexican migration shows that the numbers declined between 1905 and 1907 from 2,600 to 1,400. However, the numbers rose steeply in 1908 to 10,638, reaching 16,251 in 1909 and 18,691 in 1910. But these figures tell only part of the story. In 1911 the Immigration Bureau noted that at least 50,000 Mexicans without documentation crossed the border annually. The cyclic pattern of migration of superfluous labor from Mexico had begun to take root.

The argument made for the push of the Mexican Revolution does not answer why the migrations, documented and undocumented, appeared before the onset of the revolution or why the migrations slowed during the revolution but increased in the 1920s, well after the fighting had terminated.[56] It is entirely probable, even without the 1910 civil war, that emigration would have moved in the same upward direction. This is precisely what happened from the 1940s forward without the violence of war. The war probably exacerbated a preexisting condition rather than created it.

Moreover, the argument that the railroads as a transportation system inspired migration cannot withstand scrutiny. If railroads *per se* fostered the mass movement, then why did the migrations begin a quarter of a century *after* trains began running from Mexico City to the U.S. border? Furthermore, if wages were the stimulant, then emigration should have occurred earlier rather than in the middle of the first decade of the twentieth century, since wages were always lower in Mexico than in the United States. (This was particularly true during the depression of the 1930s.)

Abundant evidence suggests that the hacendado class provided a major impetus to emigrate since the hacendados perceived the dispossessed peasants as a potential political hazard and therefore financed migration journeys. In El Paso, Victor Clark interviewed several young migrants and was surprised to find evidence of lending by "patrons" in support of emigration, "sometimes a political officer—in one case a judge—and sometimes a merchant, possibly also a landowner."[57] Years later, Paul S. Taylor also found evidence of lending to the unemployed. In Jalisco, Taylor noted,

"Anyone with money engaged in the business of assisting persons to migrate," and "hacendados prefer to let the workers get away so they won't congregate in pueblos and ask for land."[58] Clearly, there are serious problems with the conventional mode of analysis. The usual push arguments and the recent modifications simply cannot hold up to the evidence.

The Ebb and Flow of Migration, 1950–1970

Data on migration indicate that the flows are cyclical as well as long-term in nature. The original push-pull thesis and its newer versions cannot explain what accounts for this pattern. A constant (i.e., a steady disparity in the level of income and wages, or migrant networks, or the like) cannot logically account for variations in the pace of migration. Rather, one must turn again to concrete historical developments to explain those changes.

Despite the upheaval of the 1910 revolution, U.S. investment in the 1920s either retained its position garnered during the Díaz years or increased in significance.[59] With the coming of the global depression that began in the early 1930s, economic activity by U.S. companies at home and abroad diminished. The evidence shows that migration from Mexico declined after 1930 following the 1910–1930 upward trend. The slowdown in migration lasted until the early 1950s when it picked up again. Seeking the causes of this rebound, we once again turn to the pattern of U.S. economic activity in Mexico.

Beginning in the early 1940s, U.S. investments in Mexico began to rise once again in new forms. In Mexico, the depression of the 1930s brought to power what would become the future Partido Revolucionario Institucional (PRI) under its paternalistic leading figure, Lázaro Cárdenas. Like Franklin D. Roosevelt's New Deal, the Cárdenas government used the economic power of the state as never before in Mexico to maintain and protect the free market/private property social contract.

Under the Partido Revolucionario Mexicano (forerunner of the PRI), foreign investment flowed once again: It tripled from 1940 to 1950, and doubled again by 1958.[60] But the profile of the investment was different. Guided by the governing party, the national government instituted in 1934 a major public finance and development institution, the Nacional Financiera, which became the pillar of the economy. Nacional Financiera invested heavily in works of irrigation, highways, and electric power. Of the decades from 1940 to 1970, a period of rapid economic growth in Mexico, it has been said that "[n]o financial institution in Mexico has contributed more to the economic growth of that country than Nacional Financiera."[61]

Beginning in the early 1940s, U.S.-based banks and financial institutions began to invest in Mexico through loans to the Nacional Financiera. Some of the lending institutions included the U.S. Export-Import Bank, the Bank of America, the Chase Manhattan Bank, and eventually the International Bank for Reconstruction and

Development (World Bank). Between 1942 and 1959 more than $900 million (mostly of U.S. origin) had been invested in major works of infrastructure in Mexico by way of the Nacional Financiera.[62] By 1953 foreign loans accounted for the single largest—about one-third—source of equity funds available to the institution.[63] This allowed U.S. capital to maximize its leverage over decision making while minimizing risks: U.S. financial institutions were in the driver's seat of the economic policies of the Nacional Financiera.

The investments financed by the Nacional Financiera had a tremendous impact both on Mexico's economy and on migration to the United States. A significant proportion of the investment went into major irrigation projects, the most important of which were located in the northern border states. The irrigation projects began in the early 1940s and included the Falcón Dam on the Rio Grande and the Rio Fuerte Irrigation Project in the state of Sonora. A tremendous increase in agricultural production followed. For example, cotton production in areas like the Mexicali Valley made Mexico the largest cotton exporter in the world.[64] Cotton production itself developed under the close control, through credit and marketing channels, of a U.S. agribusiness giant, Anderson Clayton (AC).

Mexican growers did not sell their product in the international market but through Anderson Clayton (and other U.S. companies), which monopolized the harvest and provided credit, seed, and fertilizers to the producers (much as AC had done in California's San Joaquin Valley in the 1930s). This company also managed cotton production in the countries with which Mexico competed in the world market: Brazil and the United States. In the late 1960s such control enabled AC to engage in cotton "dumping," reminding the Mexican government who was boss.[65] The opening up of irrigated lands in Sinaloa and Sonora allowed also for the production of "winter vegetables" beginning in the late 1940s, creating additional pockets of U.S. agribusiness control. The Pan-American Highway—another Nacional Financiera project—facilitated the marketing of Mexican vegetables in the United States. Thus, the export of tomatoes from Mexico's northeast increased from less than a million pounds in 1942 to 14 million in 1944.[66] The denationalized character of this production was evident as other U.S. corporations joined AC in effectively taking over Mexico's agribusiness, from production and the sale of machinery and fertilizers to the processing and merchandising of agricultural goods. The method of political control that John Foster Dulles described was complete: Mexico was borrowing money from U.S. banks to develop irrigation projects and transportation, thereby making possible the growth of U.S.-controlled agriculture in the northern tier of Mexican states.

With the growth of agriculture came population shifts, continuing the pattern begun in the late nineteenth century. Outside of the tourist-driven economies of Acapulco and Quintana Roo, only three Mexican states, all border states, showed an astonishing rate of growth of 45 percent or above in the 1950–1960 period (Baja California 232 percent, Tamaulipas 61 percent, and Sonora 45 percent).[67] Between 1950 and 1960 the total population of the eight major *municipios* of the Mexican border (Tijuana, Mexicali, Nogales, Ciudad Juárez, Piedras Negras, Nuevo Laredo, Reynosa, and Matamoros) increased by 83 percent, from less than 900,000 to 1.5 million. By 1970 the population had reached a total of 2.3 million. Between 1960 and 1969 the population rose by 45 percent in the northern border states (Baja California, Sonora, Chihuahua, Coahuila, Nuevo Leon, and Tamaulipas) in contrast with a figure of 31 percent for the nation as a whole. In 1970 fully 29 percent of the border population came from other parts of the country.[68]

Between 1950 and 1970 further ties developed across the Mexico-United States border. Subordination to U.S. corporations and the U.S. government provided the opportunity to construct a giant agribusiness economy on both sides of the border that relied on the ready supply of cheap labor from the interior of Mexico. An evident consequence of this relationship was one of the most spectacular mass movements of people in the history of humanity. The northward migration of people from all corners of Mexico to its north and, for many, eventually to the United States was motivated by the same general force, *the economic dislocation caused by U.S. capital—not an amorphous "global" capital—in Mexico,* the pace of the movement modulated in a cyclical manner by the relative intensity of U.S. economic intrusion. This movement turned the border area into a highly urbanized region. Simultaneously, migration constantly propelled the growth of the Chicano minority in the United States in a variety of forms: regulated and unregulated, legal and illegal, cyclical and long-term.

The Current Cycle, 1970–2000

As in the post-World War II period, U.S. investments in Mexico between 1970 and 2000 shifted away from mining and railroads toward industrial manufacturing. U.S. corporations made their way through direct purchase into the most dynamic sectors of local industry, especially in the 1960s. This trend occurred most notably in consumer durables, chemicals, electronics, department stores, hotels and restaurants, and the food industry, whereby United Fruit (later known as Dole), Heinz, Del Monte, and General Foods became very visible; 225 subsidiaries of U.S.-based corporations operated in the manufacturing sector.[69] U.S. investment in manufacturing concentrated around Mexico City, which accounted for 50 percent of the total manufacturing production of the country in 1975. Although this geographical concentration shifted, in the meantime Mexico's dependence on foreign loans increased. Between 1950 and 1972 the foreign debt grew at an average annual rate of 23 percent, reaching $11 billion by the latter year.

A chronic balance-of-payments problem, resulting from Mexico's reliance on the export of primary commodities and on foreign loans, made the situation worse. Beginning in the late 1960s, Mexico's hardly independent government had no choice but to accept lenders' terms. At the behest of international creditors, economic policies once again resulted in massive economic and demographic dislocation, contributing to a further increase of migration into Mexico's northern region, which became not only highly urbanized but acquired a new role as a major staging area for further migration to the United States.

In 1967 Mexico took a giant step in the complete abdication of its economic sovereignty when it established the Border Industrial Program along its northern border, beginning the transformation of the entire area into a gigantic assembly operation. The sad story of the maquiladora program in all its sordid details has been told elsewhere.[70] Suffice it to say that the maquilas, like a narcotic drug, made Mexico even more dependent while failing to solve its unemployment problems or help the country to become self-sufficient, developed, and modern.

For the purposes of our argument, the maquiladora program made the border states of Mexico, and specifically its border cities, into magnets for poverty-stricken, unemployed masses seeking work in the growing assembly plant industry. The maquiladoras have turned Mexico's northern border into an enclave with few links to the rest of the economy. Into the border area flowed duty-free manufacturing inputs to be assembled into final products for entry into the United States or export to other countries. The northern tier of Mexico has become a direct appendage of U.S. manufacturing, replicating the examples of railroads and mining in the Mexican economy during the early 1900s.

Simultaneous with the development of the maquiladora program, other significant changes affected Mexican agriculture. Between 1940 and the late 1960s, Mexico's countryside provided the basic food staples to its growing urban population. However, pressure from international lenders and agribusiness multinationals caused Mexico's central government to eliminate subsidies to small agricultural producers, who then began to abandon their farm plots to join the migration streams. Into the breach moved the United States, which turned the same agricultural lands into mechanized farms, producing commodities for export to the United States. In the 1970s the rate of growth of basic staples like corn, beans, and wheat began to fall behind population growth. To cover the precipitous decline in staple food production, a problem not seen since the Porfiriato, the country was forced to import basic food supplies.[71] However, imports have not fed Mexico's people satisfactorily. Infectious diseases and other illnesses linked to malnutrition and economic underdevelopment became rampant by the late 1980s.[72]

The 1990s witnessed the signing of the North American Free Trade Agreement (NAFTA), the most recent and devastating example of how U.S. domination over Mexico continues to misdevelop and tear apart the socioeconomic integrity of that society. The U.S. government and major corporate interests promoted NAFTA as a weapon in their trade competition with Europe and Japan. Under the "free trade" slogan, the proposed treaty would ostensibly serve two purposes. First, it would enable U.S. enterprises willing and able to invest in Mexico to take advantage of that country's cheaper wages. Mexico was to become a platform for the export of manufactured commodities to the United States and world markets. Major U.S. corporations, in particular automobile manufacturers, stood to benefit greatly from this scheme. Second, the treaty would, in effect, simultaneously deny to other economic powers the advantage of operating in and exporting from Mexico. Briefly put, the United States sought to create with Mexico (and Canada) an economic bloc to compete against Europe and Japan.

In its quest, the United States could count upon the leadership of Mexico's governing party, the PRI, and President Carlos Salinas. Under his leadership, Mexico undertook a set of wide-ranging measures to make NAFTA a reality. First, to demonstrate resolute support for market-oriented policies and attract foreign capital, the Mexican government broke up numerous government enterprises and laid off thousands of employees. Hundreds of state companies and institutions were sold or "privatized." The government enacted laws to "flexibilize" the labor market, restricting wage increases, curtailing vacation and sick-leave time, extending the work-week, and increasing management powers over the firing and hiring of temporary workers (known in the United States as downsizing). The elimination of trade protection meant that by 1993 nearly 50 percent of Mexico's textile firms and 30 percent of leather manufacturing firms had gone bankrupt. By the time of the signing of the treaty, Mexico's population had become severely polarized in terms of wealth and income.[73]

The actual signing of NAFTA revealed that Mexico was only as strong a bargainer as the weakest of the 535 U.S. parliamentarians. U.S. President Bill Clinton succeeded in obtaining a majority vote in Congress only by guaranteeing a multitude of senators and representatives protection for their districts against any competition that might result from NAFTA. For example, a Texas congressman agreed to vote in favor of NAFTA only after Clinton promised that the Pentagon would add two more cargo planes to a production order previously awarded to his district. A Florida representative voted for the treaty only after the State Department agreed to seek the extradition of an individual residing in Mexico who was accused of a crime in the United States. A lawmaker from Georgia opted for the treaty in exchange for promises by the Agriculture Department that limits would be imposed upon increasing imports of peanut butter from Canada. Even small U.S. producers of brooms were protected from Mexican competition. Throughout the entire humiliating process, not a peep was heard from the Salinas government. In the end, "free trade" meant that Mexico would be completely open to U.S. goods, but U.S. producers were safely guarded against Mexico's products.

Rather than a free trade agreement, NAFTA could be better described as a "free investment" agreement. During the 1980s, tariffs levied by Mexico against the United States had steadily declined. NAFTA codified these changes, and, more importantly, it opened up investment opportunities in Mexico, protected against nationalizations, and eliminated all restrictions against U.S. ventures in Mexico. Of course, the "free investment" part would be limited under a section of the treaty entitled "rules of origin." These rules defined as domestic any inputs originating in Canada, the United States, and Mexico. Other imputs (for example, those from Japan) were classified as "foreign," and any products assembled with them became liable to export limits. In other words, after NAFTA it became more difficult for Japanese or European investors to ship products into Mexico for assembly and export to the United States.

NAFTA was never envisioned as a development policy for Mexico. All announced plans, forecasts, and decisions by U.S. multinationals relied on the low wages prevalent in Mexico as the key variable involved. Further displacement of peasants, massive migration, and the destruction of what remains of domestic Mexican agriculture will follow on the heels of NAFTA's complete opening to competition with the large U.S. agribusiness consortiums. Under NAFTA, Mexico has agreed to subject all land to privatization—that is, sale and speculation. For example, it returned Indian lands to the same juridical status that gave rise to Mexico's famed agrarian revolt over ninety years ago.[74]

Almost to the day of the first anniversary of the signing of NAFTA, the newly installed administration of Ernesto Zedillo faced a catastrophic devaluation of the national currency. Mexico's image changed from an investor's paradise to a disheveled financial hulk, a virtual economic protectorate of the United States. The United States set up conditions for a bailout that were, according to newspaper reports, too sensitive even to be published in Mexico. Eventually it became known that the U.S. plan required Mexico to hand over all revenues from its oil sales and gave to U.S. banks the right to supervise and enforce further privatizations and measures of austerity. Everything was now up for sale: bridges, airports, toll roads, ports, telephones, and so on. In the meantime, thousands of farmers, business people, and consumers went broke because they could not pay bills, meet debts, or finance mortgages. Contemporary estimates indicate that in the first two months of 1995 nearly 600,000 jobs were lost. A whopping 30 percent of Mexico's labor force, 11 million people, were reported unemployed in mid-1995.[75]

The U.S. embassy in Mexico, demonstrating U.S. resolve to remain committed to its plans for Mexico, referred positively to rising unemployment and bankruptcies as the "Darwinian effects" of NAFTA. Embassy officials praised its "stabilizing" effects upon the economy and called it the "bright spot" in the Mexican catastrophe. Taking advantage of the plummeting wage levels in Mexico relative to the dollar, the United States benefited enormously as 250 companies set up shop in the border area in the first three months of 1995. Apparently, Mexico should have been grateful that, in exchange for millions of unemployed and thousands ruined, a handful of Mexicans—a new generation of migrants—obtained jobs toiling in border cities for a miserable wage assembling products for reshipment to the United States. In the long run, the devastating effects of NAFTA upon Mexico's remaining agricultural production and urban manufacturing will throw onto the migration highways an even larger number of people desperately looking to make a living, thereby enlarging at a faster pace the mass of Mexican migrants in the United States. NAFTA is a particularly telling example of the unity of push and pull, as well as the role of U.S. domination in dismembering Mexico and creating a Chicano national minority in the United States.

Conclusion: A Network of Domination

Under NAFTA, steadily dropping manufacturing employment (outside of the maquila sector) points to the deindustrialization of Mexico. While manufacturing employment stood at 2,557,000 in 1981, it fell to 2,325,000 in 1993 and to 2,208,750 by 1997, a 13 percent drop from 1981. This brought with it lower living standards, as many workers moved from permanent to lower wage contingency work that lacked benefits and union protection. The destruction of Mexico's industrial base is particularly pronounced in the area of capital goods. Between 1995 and 1997 alone, following the peso debacle, 36 percent of the nation's 1,100 capital goods plants closed down. In all, 17,000 enterprises of all kinds went bankrupt shortly after the crisis exploded. Meanwhile, employment opportunities in the lowest paying categories ballooned by 60 percent, dragging 5 million people to the official category of "extreme poverty." Manufacturing production has been reduced to the maquiladora sector, situated largely in the northern confines of the country, and to an increasingly concentrated manufacturing system dominated by a few U.S. industrial giants involved in production for export.[76]

The debacle in national industry has also materialized in agriculture with catastrophic consequences. According to a Mexican analyst, the opening of agricultural markets by the NAFTA treaty has led to the rapid ruin of what remained of Mexico's production of basic staples and to the dumping of cheap U.S. corn, wheat, and beans into Mexico. One hundred years of U.S. empire building has produced what 300 years of Spanish rule could not accomplish: the complete inability of the Mexican nation to produce enough to feed its own people. The migratory consequences are staggering: Millions will be forced to leave Mexico's countryside in the next decade.[77]

The demographic impact of this transformation of Mexico's economy has already caused a dramatic shift in the nation's population distribution. Since the 1960s the northern *municipios* feature one of the fastest growing populations in the world. There appears no end in sight. The population there, which topped 4 million in 1995, is expected to double by 2010 and more than triple by 2020. Ciudad Juárez, for example, has grown fivefold since 1970, reaching one million. According to the Associated Press, each day "an estimated 600 new people arrive from Mexico's poor provinces hoping for work" in Ciudad Juárez—or nearly 220,000 new arrivals a year. Internal migrants in desperate straits will later surface as international migrants confronting the dangers of the militarized border.[78]

Today, this process intensifies the Mexicanization in the many barrios across the United States, forging a distinct demographic form in which immigrants either outnumber the second generation or reach a level of parity not seen since the 1930s. Migrants are the fastest growing sector of the Chicano population; approximately 40 percent were born in Mexico, up from 17 percent four decades ago.[79] Had it not been for the Great Depression and World War II, the migratory movement of the 1900 to

1930 period would have proceeded without respite. That interruption made possible a distinctive Mexican American generation and later the Chicano generation. However, once migration resumed its previous pace, a cultural pattern that first surfaced in the 1920s reappeared in the 1960s. We foresee this Mexicanization overwhelming the older enclaves, remaking older barrios into immigrant centers, and thus reshaping the Chicano version of ethnic politics forged in the 1960s.

If there were any doubts about the false dichotomy between push and pull factors in the case of Mexico, the maquila program, NAFTA, and the agricultural collapse have erased them. For the most part, historians and social scientists have chosen not to scrutinize push-pull in this manner. Rather, social science perspectives have, in head-in-sand fashion, chosen to focus away from these "macro" factors toward the agency of migrants who, having constructed networks of migration, are regarded as the self-generators of migration. To be sure, Mexican immigrants have taken active roles and made significant choices in the construction of their lives, families, and communities. But it defies the evidence to insist that the explanation for Mexican migration to the United States lies within the immigrants' subjectivity. A simpler and more powerful explanation for Mexican migration northward to the United States, and the consequent development of the Chicano national minority, focuses on the 100 years of economic domination by centers of transnational economic power in the United States. Bit by bit, this tighter and tighter network of domination has succeeded in disarticulating the Mexican economy, destroying its domestic industry and local agricultural production, creating demographic dislocation, and, in the process, turning an increasing portion of its population into a nomadic mass of migrant workers who eventually emerge as the Chicano national minority. The rise of the Chicano national minority is not an event marginal to U.S. history. Quite the opposite, it has been central to the construction of the U.S. neocolonial empire.

Epilogue

In an earlier article we challenged the widespread view that contemporary Chicano history originated in the aftermath of the 1848 conquest.[80] By focusing on economic transformations, we questioned the conventional periodization of Chicano history and argued that the nineteenth- and twentieth-century Spanish-speaking populations of the southwestern United States were largely two different populations. A focus on the War of 1848—the presumed starting point of Chicano history—obscures the relationship between the establishment of U.S. hegemony over Mexico, which came decades later, and the development of the Chicano national minority in the United States in the twentieth century.

We must distinguish the annexation of 1848 and the ensuing institutional integration of Mexican territory into the United States from the economic conquest of the late nineteenth and early twentieth centuries. Rather than the commonly held belief that the Mexican-American War of 1848 led to the construction of the Chicano minority, this study proposes that the origins of the Chicano population evolved from the economic empire established by corporate capitalist interests with the backing of the U.S. State Department. The political and economic repercussions of 1848 had virtually ended by the last decade of the nineteenth century. Furthermore, at no time did the 1848 annexation cause continuous internal migration, the mass population concentration along the border, the bracero program, low-wage maquila plants, Mexico's agricultural crisis, and, more importantly, a century of migrations to the United States. Those historical chapters, derived from the economic subordination of Mexico, forged the modern Chicano national minority.

Notes

1 Ernesto Galarza, "Program For Action," *Common Ground,* 10 (1949).

2 John Kenneth Turner, *Barbarous Mexico* (Chicago, 1911), 256–257.

3 John Mason Hart, *Revolutionary Mexico: The Coming Process of the Mexican Revolution* (Berkeley, 1997), chapters 5–7.

4 As quoted in the *Ottawa (Canada) Monitor,* Sept. 1995.

5 See, for example, Jonathan C. Brown, *Oil and Revolution in Mexico* (Berkeley, 1993); William E. French, *A Peaceful and Working People: Manners, Morals, and Class Formation in Northern Mexico* (Albuquerque, 1996); G. M. Joseph, *Revolution From Without: Yucatan, Mexico, and the United States, 1880–1924* (Durham, N.C., 1988); Ramon Eduardo Ruiz, *The People of Sonora and Yankee Capitalists* (Tucson, 1988); Mark Wasserman, *Capitalists, Caciques, and Revolution: The Native Elite and Foreign Enterprise in Chihuahua, Mexico, 1854–1911* (Chapel Hill, N.C., 1984).

6 There are a number of studies that look at the characteristics of the cooperation between Mexico's elites and powerful U.S. monopolies that descended upon Mexico at the end of the nineteenth century. In addition to those listed in note 5, see Robert Freeman Smith, *The United States and Revolutionary Nationalism in Mexico, 1916–1922* (Chicago, 1972), and Hart, *Revolutionary Mexico,* chapters 5 and 6.

7 See, for example, Clarence Clendenen, *The United States and Pancho Villa: A Study in Unconventional Diplomacy* (Ithaca, N.Y., 1961); Friedrich Katz, *The Secret War in Mexico: Europe, the United States and the Mexican Revolution* (Chicago, 1981); Gregg Andrews, *Shoulder to Shoulder? The American Federation of Labor, the United States, and the Mexican Revolution* (Berkeley, 1991); and Hart, *Revolutionary Mexico.*

8 Gilbert G. González, *Mexican Consulates and Labor Organizing: Imperial Politics in the American Southwest* (Austin, Tex., 1999).

9 See Mario Barrera, *Race and Class in the American Southwest: A Theory of Racial Inequality* (Notre Dame, Ind., 1979), 68–69; U.S. Industrial Commission, *Reports of the Industrial Commission on Immigration,* 15 (Washington, D.C., 1901), lxxxix. The report's conclusions about the cause of migration were based on the testimony of a former commissioner of immigration of the port of New York. As a witness before the U.S. Industrial Commission, he stated that "Those people who come for settlement in this country have a desire and feel the ability in themselves to expand, to look out for larger and better fields for their activity than they can find at home." *Ibid.,* 183. See also Victor S. Clark, *Mexican Labor in the United States,* Department of Commerce and Labor, Bureau of Labor Bulletin No. 78 (Washington, D. C., 1908), 505; Manuel Gamio, *Migration and Immigration to the United States: A Study of Adjustment* (Chicago, 1930), 171; and Paul S. Taylor, *A Spanish-Mexican Peasant Community, Arandas in Jalisco, Mexico* (Berkeley, 1933), 40.

10 For a summary of sociological critiques of push-pull theories, see Alejandro Portes and Robert L. Bach, *Latin Journey: Cuban and Mexican Immigrants in the United States* (Berkeley, 1985); Stephen Castles and Mark J. Miller, *The Age of Migration: International Population Movements in the Modern World* (New York, 1993); Ewa Morawska, "The Sociology and Historiography of Immigration," in Virginia Yans-McLaughlin, ed., *Immigration Reconsidered: History, Sociology, and Politics* (New York, 1990), 192.

11 Leo Grebler, Joan W. Moore, Ralph C. Guzman, and Jeffrey Lionel Berlant, *The Mexican American People: The Nation's Second Largest Minority* (New York, 1970), 63.

12 The examples of push-pull are many; the following are but a few: Leo R. Chavez, "Defining and Demographically Characterizing the Southern Border of the U.S.," in John R. Weeks and Roberto Ham-Chande, eds., *Demographic Dynamics of the U.S.-Mexico Border* (El Paso, Tex., 1992); Douglas S. Massey, Rafael Alarcón, Jorge Durand, and Humberto González, *Return to Aztlan: The Social Process of International Migrations From Western Mexico* (Berkeley, 1987), 108; Mark Reisler, *By the Sweat of Their Brows: Mexican Immigrant Labor in the United States, 1900–1940* (Westport, Conn., 1976), 14; Arthur F. Corwin and Lawrence A. Cardoso, "Vamos al Norte: Causes of Mass Migration to the United States," in Arthur F. Corwin, ed., *Immigrants and Immigrants: Perspectives on Mexican Labor Migration to the United States* (Westport, Conn., 1978), 39; David Maciel and Maria Herrera Sobek, "Introduction," in David Maciel and Maria Herrera Sobek, eds., *Culture Across Borders: Mexican Immigration and Popular Culture* (Tucson, 1998), 4; Camille Guerin-Gonzales, *Mexican Workers and the American Dreams: Immigration, Repatriation, and California Farm Labor, 1900–1939* (New Brunswick, N.J., 1994), 27–30; George J. Sánchez, *Becoming Mexican American: Ethnicity, Culture, and Identity in Chicano Los Angeles, 1900–1945* (New York, 1993), 20, 39; Richard Griswold del Castillo and Arnoldo de León, *North to Aztlan: A History of Mexican Americans in*

the United States (New York, 1996), 60–61; Antonio Rios-Bustamante, ed., *Mexican Immigrant Workers in the United States* (Los Angeles, 1981); Frank D. Bean, Rodolfo de la Garza, Bryan Roberts, and Sidney Weintraub, eds., *At the Crossroads: Mexico and U.S. Immigration Policy* (New York, 1997).

13 There are a few exceptions. Barrera's *Race and Class in the Southwest* briefly pointed out that the push-pull notions were difficult to separate. Alejandro Portes also points to weaknesses in "From South of the Border: Hispanic Minorities in the United States," in Yans-Mclaughlin, ed., *Immigration Reconsidered.* Portes generally identifies the role of U.S. expansion and intervention in Mexico, which he lumps with "postcolonial" societies. Upon closer examination, he appears to be referring to the territorial acquisition following the Mexican-American War of 1846. He specifically places the origin of the northward migration on the activities of labor recruiters, not on the social dislocations caused by U.S. investments. Interestingly, Saskia Sassen also emphasizes the "emergence of a multinational labor market" consequent to the "internationalization of capital." She writes that investments by U.S. railroad and agricultural corporations and the Border Industrial Program "are all processes which created a labor market." The U.S.-Mexican border artificially divides this "labor market"; hence, migration responds to the international labor marketplace. Saskia Sassen, "U.S. Immigration Policy Toward Mexico in a Global Economy," in David Gutiérrez, *Between Two Worlds: Mexican Immigrants in the United States* (Wilmington, Del., 1996).

14 See the special issue of the *Journal of American History,* 86 (1999), edited by David Thelen, titled "Rethinking History and the Nation-State," 427–697.

15 See, for example, Nestor Rodriguez, "The Battle for the Border: Notes on Autonomous Migration, Transnational Communities, and the State" in Susanne Jonas and Suzie Dod Thomas, eds., *Immigration: A Civil Rights Issue for the Americas* (Wilmington, Del., 1999); for a variation on this theme, see David M. Reimers, *Still the Golden Door: The Third World Comes to America* (New York, 1985), 128–129; Vicki Ruiz, *From Out of the Shadows: Mexican Women in Twentieth-Century America* (New York, 1998), 163; Pierrette Hondagneu-Sotelo, *Gendered Transitions: Mexican Experiences of Migration* (Berkeley, 1994); Douglas Massey, "The Social Organization of Mexican Migration to the United States," in David Jacobson, ed., *The Immigration Reader: American in Multidisciplinary Perspective* (New York, 1998), 213–214; and David Jacobson, "Introduction" in *ibid.,* 11. Jacobson writes that "Mexican migration reflects the earlier development of social networks that sustain it."

16 See, for example, Wayne Cornelius, "The Structural Embeddedness of Demand for Mexican Immigrant Labor: New Evidence from California," in Marcelo M. Suarez-Orozco, ed., *Crossings: Mexican Immigration in Interdisciplinary Perspective* (Cambridge, Mass., 1998), 141–142, and Robert Smith, "Commentary," in *ibid.*

17 Douglas S. Massey and Kristin E. Espinosa, "What's Driving Mexico-U.S. Migration? A Theoretical, Empirical, and Policy Analysis," *American Journal of Sociology,* 102 (1997), 953.

18 *Ibid.*, 954.

19 See Reimers, *Still the Golden Door;* Frank D. Bean, W. Parker Frisbie, Edward Telles, and B. Lindsay Lowell, "The Economic Impact of Undocumented Workers in the Southwest of the United States," in Weeks and Ham-Chande, eds., *Demographic Dynamics.*

20 Saskia Sassen, "Foreign Investment: A Neglected Variable," in Jacobsen, ed., *The Immigration Reader,* Sassen, *Globalization and Its Discontents. Essays on the New Mobility of People and Money* (New York, 1998), chapter 6.

21 Quoted in P. Harvey Middleton, *Industrial Mexico: Facts and Figures* (New York, 1919), frontispiece; for a slightly different version, see Alfred Tischendorf, *Great Britain in Mexico in the Era of Porfirio Díaz* (Durham, N.C., 1961), 75.

22 David M. Pletcher, *Rails, Mines, and Progress: Seven American Promoters in Mexico, 1867–1911* (Ithaca, N.Y., 1958), 38.

23 *Ibid.*, 38, 79–80.

24 Chester Lloyd Jones, *Mexico and Its Reconstruction* (New York, 1921), 299, 310. Mexican elites anticipated the policy design. One-time Mexican representative in Washington, Matias Romero, proposed an economic conquest in an 1864 speech before a gathering of New York City's prominent citizens. Guests included the largest capitalists; names like Aspinwall, Astor, Fish, and Clews filled the list. Romero advised: "The United States are the best situated to avail themselves of the immense wealth of Mexico. . . . We are willing to grant to the United States every commercial facility. . . . This will give to the United States all possible advantages that could be derived from annexation, without any of its inconveniences." Matias Romero, *Mexico and the United States* (New York, 1898), 385.

25 Pletcher, *Rails, Mines, and Progress,* 3.

26 Ruiz, *The People of Sonora,* 14–15; Wasserman, *Capitalists, Caciques, and Revolution,* 108–109.

27 In his authoritative 1921 review of Mexican railroads, Fred Wilbur Powell stated that "Mexican railroad development was *the result of foreign capital and enterprise,* attracted by national franchises or 'concessions' and encouraged by subsidies" (emphasis added). Fred Wilbur Powell, *The Railroads of Mexico* (Boston, 1921), 1.

28 Walter E. Weyl, *Labor Conditions in Mexico,* Bulletin of the U.S. Department of Labor, No. 38 (Jan. 1902), 52.

29 Marvin D. Bernstein, *The Mining Industry in Mexico, 1890–1950* (New York, 1964), 35.

30 *Ibid.*, 33. Booster advertising that offered sure bets on Mexican investments cajoled American investors. Railroads, it was said, guaranteed lucrative profits and vast wealth; they awaited only the enlightened administration of the American investor. David M. Pletcher, "The Development of the Railroads in Sonora," *Inter-American Economic Affairs,* 1 (1948), 1–2. One pamphlet published by the U.S. government announced that "the opening up of new mining districts is largely due to Americans, both through the improved mining meth-

ods and through the development of railroads built by our capital." International Bureau of the American Republics, *Mexico: Geographical Sketch, Natural Resources, Laws, Economic Conditions, Actual Development, Prospects of Future Growth* (Washington, D.C., 1904), 233.

31 Robert G. Cleland, "The Mining Industry of Mexico: A Historical Sketch," *Mining and Scientific Press* (July 2, Nov. 5, 1921), [part 1] 13; Wasserman, *Capitalists, Caciques, and Revolution,* 76.

32 John Sheahan, *Patterns of Development in Latin America* (Princeton, N.J., 1987), 297; Joseph, *Revolution From Without,* 30, 51, 62; Wasserman, *Capitalists, Caciques, and Revolution,* 46.

33 John Coatsworth, *Growth Against Development: The Economic Impact of Railroads in Porfirian Mexico* (DeKalb, III., 1981), 123–124.

34 *Ibid.,* 158, 170. John Mason Hart makes this same point: "In the midst of land seizures associated with the planning of the new railroad system, peasant uprisings ranged from Chihuahua in the north to Oaxaca in the south." Hart, *Revolutionary Mexico,* 41, 170. See also French, *A Peaceful and Working People,* 37–47; Ruiz, *The People of Sonora,* 16–17; Wasserman, *Capitalists, Caciques, and Revolution,* 109.

35 Coatsworth, *Growth Against Development,* 145.

36 Michael Johns, *The City of Mexico in the Age of Díaz* (Austin, Tex., 1997), 14.

37 Roger D. Hansen, *The Politics of Mexican Development* (Baltimore, 1971), 27; Nathan L. Whetten, *Rural Mexico* (Chicago, 1948), 89.

38 Moisés González Navarro, *El Porfiriato: La Vida Social* (Mexico City, 1957), 20.

39 Johns, *The City of Mexico,* 64.

40 Turner, *Barbarous Mexico,* 116.

41 Johns, *The City of Mexico,* 30.

42 Evelyn Hu-Dehart, "Pacification of the Yaquis in the Late Porfiriato: Development and Implications," *Hispanic American Historical Review,* 54 (1974), 77.

43 Frank Tannenbaum, *The Mexican Agrarian Revolution* (Washington, D.C., 1929), 126.

44 Weyl, *Labor Conditions in Mexico,* 91.

45 See Rodney D. Anderson, *Outcasts in Their Own Land: Mexican Industrial Workers, 1906–1911* (De Kalb, III., 1976), 48–50. Anderson writes that "the artisans added to the growing numbers of rural people forced off their lands by enclosure."

46 Clark, *Mexican Labor in the United States,* 470–471. See also French, *A Peaceful and Working People,* 42–43.

47 González Navarro, *El Porfiriato,* xvii, 25.

48 Friedrich Katz, "The Liberal Republic and the Porfiriato, 1867–1910," in Leslie Bethell, ed., *Mexico Since Independence* (New York, 1991), 89.

49 E. A. H. Tays, "Present Labor Conditions in Mexico," *The Engineering and Mining Journal,* 84 (1907), 622.

50 Allen H. Rogers, "Character and Habits of Mexican Miners," *The Engineering and Mining Journal,* 85 (1908), 700.

51 See Cleland, "The Mining Industry of Mexico," [part 2] 640.

52 J. Fred Rippy, *Latin America and the Industrial Age* (New York, 1947). Jonathan Brown, "Foreign and Native-Born Workers in Porfirian Mexico," *American Historical Review,* 98 (1993), 798.

53 González Navarro, *El Porfiriato,* 23.

54 Rogers, "Character and Habits of Mexican Miners," 701. See also Brown, *Oil and Revolution in Mexico,* 80–81. Brown writes that the Veracruz state population increased by 280,000 between 1890 and 1910, the oil boom years cited by personages like Edward Doheny, who developed the Veracruz area oil explorations.

55 Dwight E. Woodbridge, "La Cananea Mining Camp," *The Engineering and Mining Journal,* 82 (1906), 623. This citation also applies to the following paragraph.

56 See French, *A Peaceful and Working People;* Brown, *Oil and Revolution in Mexico;* Wasserman, *Capitalists, Caciques, and Revolution;* Ruiz, *The People of Sonora;* Smith, *The United States and Revolutionary Nationalism in Mexico.*

57 Clark, *Mexican Labor in the United States,* 472.

58 Taylor, *A Spanish-Mexican Peasant Community,* 44.

59 Smith, *The United States and Revolutionary Nationalism,* 34.

60 Howard F. Cline, *Mexico: Revolution to Evolution, 1940–1960* (New York, 1963), 244.

61 Benjamin Higgins, *Economic Development: Problems, Principles, and Policies* (New York, 1968), 643.

62 Cline, *Mexico,* 245.

63 Higgins, *Economic Development,* 645.

64 W. Whitney Hicks, "Agricultural Development in Northern Mexico, 1940–1960," *Land Economics,* 53 (Nov. 1967), 396.

65 Raúl A. Fernandez, *The United States-Mexico Border: A Politico-Economic Profile* (Notre Dame, Ind., 1977), 108.

66 *Ibid.,* 123.

67 Raúl A. Fernandez, *The Mexican American Border Region: Issues and Trends* (Notre Dame, Ind., 1989), 61. It is interesting to note that during the cotton boom years (1940–1960), the border *municipios* where cotton was the main agricultural product (Mexicali, Juárez, Reynosa, and Matamoros) registered the highest rates of population growth. On the other hand, during the years of the cotton crisis (1960–1970), the same municipalities suffered a sharp drop in their populations.

68 *Ibid.,* 108.

69 See *ibid.* and Fernandez, *The United States-Mexico Border.*

70 Fernandez, *The United States-Mexico Border.*

71 David Barkin and Blanca Suarez, *El Fin de la Autosuficiencia Alimentaria* (Mexico City, 1982); Ruth Rama, "Some Effects of the Internationalization of Agriculture on the Mexican Agricultural Crisis," in Steven E. Sanderson, *The Americas in the New International Division of Labor* (New York, 1985).

72 Hart writes "Mexico in 1987 constitutes an economic and social disaster . . . 70 percent of the children suffer from malnutrition. . . . The World Health Organization estimates that 107,000 Mexican children died in 1983 from three diseases for which immunization is available." Hart, *Revolutionary Mexico,* 378.

73 Carlos Heredia and Mary E. Purcell, "The Polarization of Mexican Society," paper prepared for the NGO Working Group on the World Bank, Development Group for the Alternative Policies, Dec. 1994.

74 González, *Mexican Consuls and Labor Organizing,* 12, 14–15; James D. Cockcroft, *Mexico: Class Formation, Capital Accumulation, and the State* (New York, 1983), 91.

75 González, *Mexican Consuls and Labor Organizing,* chapter 6.

76 *International Report,* 12 (March, June 1994); 13, (Feb., July 1995). Raúl Fernández, "Perspectivas del Tratado de Libre Comercio de Norteamerica," *Deslinde* [Bogotá, Colombia], 13 (March–April 1993). James Cypher, "Developing Disarticulation Within the Mexican Economy," *Latin American Perspectives* (forth-coming 2002).

77 Victor S. Quintana, "La Catastrofe Maicera," *La Opinion,* April 17, 1999; Chris Kraul, "Growing Troubles in Mexico," *Los Angeles Times,* Jan. 17, 2000. Kraul writes that, due to corn imports from the United States, "one fifth of the 250,000 families who were working the land in Guanajuato in 1990 have since left their farms . . . a population shift that has been repeated across Mexico." The Free Trade Agreement "mandated the end of the costly subsidy program"; John Coatsworth, "Commentary" in Suarez-Orozco, ed., *Crossings,* 75–78; Philip Martin, "Do Mexican Agricultural Policies Stimulate Emigration?" in Bean, de la Garza, Roberts, and Weintraub, eds., *At the Crossroads.*

78 "A Call to Action is Needed at U.S. Border," *Los Angeles Times,* May 9, 1999; Mark Stevenson, "Border Factories Target of Fury over Mass Killings of Women," *Orange County (Calif.) Register,* April 4, 1999; Ham-Chande and Weeks, "A Demographic Perspective of the U.S. Mexico Border," in Weeks and Ham-Chande, eds., *Demographic Dynamics.*

79 Frank D. Bean and Marta Tienda, *The Hispanic Population in the United States* (New York, 1987), 110; Marcelo M. Suarez-Orozco, "Introduction: Crossings: Mexican Immigration in Interdisciplinary Perspectives," in Suarez-Orozco, ed., *Crossings,* 7, Gilda Laura Ochoa, "Mexican Americans' Attitudes and Interactions Towards Mexican Immigrants: A Qualitative Analysis of Conflict and Cooperation," *Social Science Quarterly,* 81 (March 2000), 84–105.

80 Gilbert G. González and Raúl Fernández, "Chicano History: Transcending Cultural Models," *Pacific Historical Review,* 63 (1994), 469.

Legacies of Discrimination

Angelo N. Ancheta

The year 1965 is a landmark in both the history of civil rights and the history of Asian Americans. In 1965, Congress passed the Voting Rights Act, a law designed to protect the most basic political right—the right to vote—and to eliminate racial discrimination in the electoral process. The act is responsible for eliminating state and local barriers to voting, and has encouraged the registration and participation of millions of voters. The passage of the Voting Rights Act came on the tails of Congress's passage of the Civil Rights Act of 1964, the most sweeping civil rights legislation enacted during the twentieth century. The 1964 act prohibits racial discrimination in public accommodations, in federally funded programs and activities, and, most broadly, in public and private employment.

The civil rights movement and the changes in racial attitudes that engendered the civil rights legislation of the 1960s also contributed to the passage of the Immigration Act of 1965. Prior to 1965, Asian immigration had been severely limited by discriminatory laws targeting migrants from Asian and Pacific Island countries. Laws dating back to the nineteenth century had excluded entire classes of Asian immigrants from entering the United States. After 1965, with the removal of a discriminatory system of quotas based on national origin, the immigration laws placed migration from Asia and the Pacific on an equal footing with migration from other parts of the world.

The Immigration Act of 1965 is a watershed in Asian American history. The 1965 act marked both the end of a decades-long era of overt governmental discrimination against Asian Americans and the beginning of an era of renewed immigration and population growth. The 1965 act was the culmination of several reversals in the law that rectified anti-Asian subordination by federal and state government. Laws that sanctioned discrimination against Asian Americans in immigration, naturalization, education, employment, property ownership, and family relations, including marriage, had all begun to fall during the 1940s and 1950s. By 1965, Congress could no longer countenance overt racial discrimination in the immigration laws.

Since the passage of the Immigration Act of 1965, Asian Americans have become the fastest growing racial group in the United States. Fueled primarily by immigration, the Asian American population doubled between 1970 and 1980, and doubled again between 1980 and 1990. Census Bureau figures for 1997 put the Asian and Pacific Islander population in the United States at close to ten million, and projections for the year 2000 put the population at over twelve million. A predominantly U.S.-born population in 1965, the Asian American population is today two-thirds immigrant. Among its members are native-born citizens whose family roots trace back as many as eight or nine generations in the United States; immigrants and the children of immigrants who came after 1965; and refugees from Vietnam and other South-east Asian countries who entered after the 1970s following the Vietnam War.

The subordination of Asian Americans did not simply end in 1965. The population growth of Asian immigrants has sharpened long-standing racial problems and ushered in new sets of problems. Subordination by government persists in the form of anti-immigrant laws having adverse effects on Asian Americans. Private subordination against Asian Americans—the subordination that arises in the everyday experiences of Asian Americans living and working in society—has changed over time, but many problems have remained constant. While attitudes regarding race have improved, racism and nativism continue to shape Asian American experiences, just as they did when the first waves of immigrant workers from Asia began settling in this country during the nineteenth century.

In this chapter, I examine the history of legal discrimination against Asian Americans. The history of laws that subordinated Asian Americans is often ignored in studies of civil rights. More importantly, though, many of the court decisions involving the rights of Asian Americans have contemporary value because they continue to be used as legal precedents. The focus of this history is governmental discrimination. Government has not been the only source of anti-Asian discrimination, but because the laws are expressions of societal values and ideologies, they embody many of the racial prejudices that continue to subordinate Asian Americans.

Immigration and Discrimination

The history of Asians in the United States is a long one, and can be traced as far back as the 1700s, when Filipino sailors traveling on trading ships settled in the bayous of Louisiana. Significant populations in Hawaii and the West came with the successive waves of laborers who entered the United States in the nineteenth and early twentieth centuries. In the 1840s Chinese immigrants began arriving in Hawaii to work on the plantations and on the West Coast to work in the gold mines and to help build the railroads. Japanese and Filipino workers entered in later years, as did smaller numbers of

Korean and Asian Indian immigrants. Economic demands for low-wage labor fueled migration, but economic recessions and overt racism led to intense discrimination against all of these populations in time.

Anti-Asian sentiment arose quickly with the arrival of Chinese laborers. In 1852, a California Assembly committee issued a report critical of Chinese labor, warning of "the concentration within our State limits, of vast numbers of the Asiatic races, and of the inhabitants of the Pacific Islands, and of many others dissimilar from ourselves in customs, language and education." John Bigler, the governor of California, soon called for legislative measures to "check [the] tide of Asiatic immigration" into California through targeted taxation. The nativist Know-Nothing Party, which had organized around anti-Catholic sentiment on the East Coast, organized around the growing anti-Chinese movement on the West Coast during the 1850s. Unions and political parties such as the Workingmen's Party adopted anti-Chinese platforms, and "anti-Coolie" clubs formed in California during the 1860s and 1870s.

When Chinese immigration was limited by federal law in the 1880s, Japanese, Korean, Asian Indian, and Filipino immigrants were recruited for low-wage work in Hawaii and the West Coast, but they too became targets of subordination. In 1905, delegates from over sixty labor organizations met in San Francisco to form the Japanese and Korean Exclusion League, which was later renamed the Asiatic Exclusion League. Organized around the threat of the "yellow peril" and the invasion of the "Asiatic horde," the league's constitution stated: "The preservation of the Caucasian race upon American soil . . . necessitates the adoption of all possible measures to prevent or minimize the immigration of Asiatics to America." The league even blamed anti-Asian violence on immigrants themselves: "In California the insolence and presumption of Japanese, and the immodest and filthy habits of the Hindoos are continually involving them in trouble, beatings. . . . In all these cases, we may say the Oriental is at fault."

Race riots instigated by white workers who resented competition from Asian workers were common on the West Coast. Anti-Chinese riots led to the deaths of dozens of Chinese laborers in California, Oregon, and other states during the late nineteenth century. Anti-Filipino riots took place in California and Washington during the 1920s and 1930s. In 1930, rioting in Watsonville, California, even arose in response to a local newspaper's coverage of the arrest of a Filipino man who had been seen walking with a white teenage girl, to whom he was engaged to be married. Fueled by angry rhetoric against Filipino workers, the four days of rioting included beatings, shootings, and an attack on a Filipino dance hall by four hundred white men.

Racial segregation was pervasive. Asian immigrants were often refused service in theaters, hotels, restaurants, or they were consigned to areas separate from a whites-only area. Housing segregation was also common. Asians were usually told by landlords and realtors, "No Orientals allowed" or "Only whites allowed in this neighborhood." Residential and commercial enclaves—Chinatowns, Little Tokyos, Little Manilas—developed in many cities because of segregation; they offered immigrants the services of boarding houses, hotels, restaurants, stores, churches, and recreation halls that were unavailable from whites-only institutions.

Restricted by both law and custom from entering the country in large numbers, Asian immigrant women faced severe forms of subordination in the United States. Societal discrimination and patriarchy within ethnic cultures placed Asian immigrant women in marginal economic roles as manual workers, seamstresses, cooks, cleaners, and washers. In the bachelor societies that dominated early immigrant communities, Asian women were often relegated to prostitution, exploiting themselves as cheap laborers and playing a role in the exploitation of migratory men who were unencumbered by families or the costs of raising children.

Anti-Asian sentiment engendered anti-Asian laws. The legal subordination of Asian Americans on the West Coast paralleled the treatment of African Americans in the South following Reconstruction: segregation was sanctioned and discriminatory laws abounded at all levels of government. Anti-Asian laws came in three forms: (1) federal naturalization laws that imposed a racial barrier on Asian immigrants seeking United States citizenship; (2) federal immigration laws limiting migration from Asian and Pacific Island countries; and (3) state and local laws discriminating against Asians, often based on their ineligibility for citizenship. One variation of this discrimination was the wartime treatment of Japanese Americans, who were relocated and interned in concentration camps during World War II. In the vast majority of cases, the courts upheld the constitutionality of anti-Asian legislation.

Racial Bar to Citizenship

In 1790, Congress passed a law to establish a uniform standard for naturalization. The Nationality Act of 1790 stated that "any alien, being a *free white person* who shall have resided within the limits and under the jurisdiction of the United States for a term of two years, may be admitted to become a citizen thereof." Asian Americans did not have a significant presence in the United States at the time, and the law was meant to exclude blacks and members of Native American tribes. In practice, however, the government denied citizenship to Asian immigrants for decades because they were not white.

In 1868, the enactment of the Fourteenth Amendment to the federal Constitution made clear that anyone born in and subject to the jurisdiction of the United States, including former slaves, would be an American citizen. Legislation passed by Congress in 1870 amended the naturalization law to conform with the intent of the Reconstruction amendments and allowed "aliens of African nativity and persons of African descent" to become naturalized citizens. However, Congress considered and rejected attempts to make Chinese immigrants eligible for citizenship under the 1870 law and retained the racial prohibition on naturalization for nonwhite immigrants. Eight years later, a federal court in *In re Ah Yup* upheld the racial bar against Chinese immigrants.

The racial restriction on naturalization even cast doubt on the eligibility of native-born Asian Americans for birthright citizenship under the Fourteenth Amendment. The issue was not resolved until 1898, with the United States Supreme Court's decision in *United States v. Wong Kim Ark.* Wong was born in San Francisco, California, to Chinese immigrants who were permanently residing in the United States. After returning from a trip to China in 1895, he was detained and prevented from entering the country on the grounds that he was not an American citizen. The Supreme Court ruled in his favor, holding that all persons born in the United States, even those born to parents ineligible for naturalization, are citizens of the United States. The Court stated: "The Fourteenth Amendment affirms the ancient and fundamental rule of citizenship by birth within the territory, in the allegiance and under the protection of the country, including all children born of resident aliens. . . ." But at the same time that it affirmed Wong's birthright citizenship, the Court acknowledged the power of Congress to deny citizenship to his parents: "Chinese persons not born in this country have never been recognized as citizens of the United States, nor authorized to become such under the naturalization laws."

The courts isolated Asians as the one racial group that would be ineligible for naturalized citizenship. In a series of cases during the 1920s, the United States Supreme Court ruled that, unless specifically exempted by Congress, Asians did not fall within the category of "free white persons." In *Ozawa v. United States,* the Supreme Court ruled on the question of a Japanese immigrant's eligibility for citizenship. Takao Ozawa, who had been raised and educated in the United States, did not challenge the constitutionality of the racial restriction. Instead, he argued that Japanese were included within the category "free white persons" because of skin color and other attributes. The Court rejected the argument, stating that skin color was not determinative and that "the words 'white person' were meant to indicate only a person of what is popularly known as the Caucasian race." Ozawa, according to the Court, was "clearly of a race which is not Caucasian."

In *United States v. Thind,* the Supreme Court ruled that Asian Indians were barred from naturalization, even though scientific evidence at the time indicated that Indians belonged to the Caucasian race. The popular conception of Caucasian, the Court noted, clearly excluded Indians: "It is a matter of familiar observation and knowledge that the physical group characteristics of the Hindus renders them readily distinguishable from the various persons in this country commonly recognized as white." The Court also indicated that the racial bar applied to other Asians as well: "There is much in the origin and historic development of the statute to suggest that no Asiatic whatever was included."

Congress even went so far as to strip United States citizenship from women who married Asian immigrants. The Cable Act, passed by Congress in 1922, stated that "any woman citizen who marries an alien ineligible to citizenship shall cease to be a citizen of the United States." Legal theories at the time mandated that citizenship between a husband and wife be unitary, with the laws favoring the husband's citizenship over the wife's. Under this reasoning, the government could take American citizenship away from any woman who married an immigrant subject to the racial bar.

Exceptions to the racial bar to naturalization did not come until the 1940s, largely in response to wartime alliances between the United States and particular Asian countries. Chinese immigrants were allowed to naturalize beginning in 1943; Indians and

Filipinos were allowed to naturalize beginning in 1946. It was not until 1952, 162 years after passing the Nationality Act of 1790, that Congress removed the racial limitation on naturalized citizenship.

Federal Laws of Exclusion

Racial barriers to naturalization prevented Asian immigrants from gaining full rights of citizenship; racial barriers to immigration prevented Asians from entering the country at all. Responding to claims of both unfair job competition from Asian immigrants and the purported racial inferiority of Asians, Congress passed a series of laws limiting Asian immigration into the United States during the late nineteenth and early twentieth centuries. Beginning with the exclusion of Chinese women under the Page Law of 1875, the laws first sought to curtail the immigration of Chinese, and in time extended the laws to include all Asians. The United States Supreme Court upheld the constitutionality of the immigration laws at every turn.

Anti-Chinese sentiment on the West Coast fueled the passage of restrictive immigration laws in the 1870s and 1880s. The Page Law of 1875 was directed at preventing the entry of prostitutes, but immigration officials effectively limited the entry of nearly all Chinese women by classifying them as prostitutes. In 1882, Congress passed the Chinese Exclusion Act, which excluded Chinese laborers for a period of ten years. The decline in Chinese immigration was precipitous: In 1882, over 39,000 Chinese entered the United States; in 1884, only 279 entered the country; and in 1888, only 10 were admitted. The Scott Act of 1888 expanded the 1882 act by prohibiting the entry of all Chinese laborers, including those who left the United States temporarily with return certificates. Conceding exceptional power over immigration to Congress and the federal government, the Supreme Court upheld the constitutionality of the Scott Act in *Chae Chan Ping v. United States (the Chinese Exclusion Case).* The Court stated in unambiguous terms that if "the government of the United States, through its legislative department, considers the presence of foreigners of a different race in this country, who will not assimilate with us, to be dangerous to its peace and security, their exclusion is not to be stayed."

Congress passed the Geary Act of 1892 to extend Chinese exclusion for ten more years and to respond to the racist claim that Chinese names and faces were all alike: the act's registration requirements were considered necessary to distinguish between Chinese who were legally in the country prior to exclusion and those who had been smuggled in afterward. Any Chinese immigrant who failed to register with the government within a year became subject to deportation. Among the requirements to obtain a certificate of residency was the testimony of at least one white person, who could act as a credible witness. In *Fong Yue Ting v. United States,* the Supreme Court relied on its earlier decision in the Chinese Exclusion Case and upheld the Geary Act's constitutionality. Congress renewed Chinese exclusion in 1902, and in 1904 Congress passed legislation that extended Chinese exclusion indefinitely. It was not until 1943, when China became an important ally of the United States during World War II, that the Chinese exclusion laws were repealed.

Japanese immigration to the United States began as the Chinese exclusion laws were taking effect. Closely regulated by the Japanese government, migration from Japan focused on sending laborers to Hawaii and California to work on plantations and farms. Although relations between the governments of the United States and Japan were cordial at the time, anti-Japanese sentiment became virulent on the West Coast and calls for restrictions on Japanese immigration resounded throughout the country. The placement of children of Japanese immigrants into San Francisco's "Oriental school," which had been established as a segregated school for the Chinese, raised the ire of the Japanese government and led to diplomatic discussions to address anti-Japanese sentiment in the United States. The result was an agreement negotiated in 1907 and 1908 between the two countries that voluntarily restricted Japanese immigration. Under the Gentlemen's Agreement, as it was commonly known, the Japanese government stopped issuing travel documents to workers destined for the United States. In exchange, the spouses and children of Japanese laborers could migrate to the United States.

Nativist sentiment against Korean and Indian immigrants also grew at the turn of the century, raising new demands for exclusion laws. Congress responded to the calls for Asian exclusion by passing the Immigration Act of 1917, which created a triangular "Asiatic barred zone" whose restrictions paralleled the exclusion of immigrants from China. The zone covered South Asia from Arabia to Indochina, and included India, Burma, Siam, the Malay states, the East Indian islands, Asiatic Russia, the Polynesian islands, and parts of Arabia and Afghanistan.

Seven years later, Congress passed the Immigration Act of 1924, a comprehensive immigration law that established national origin quotas based on the numbers of immigrants living in the United States as of 1890. Because of the demographic makeup of the United States in 1890, the quotas were biased heavily in favor of northern and western Europeans. The act also excluded any "alien ineligible to citizenship," which, because of the racial bar on naturalization, meant all Asians. The primary target of the exclusion was the Japanese, who were still subject to the Gentlemen's Agreement but had never been formally barred by the immigration laws.

Filipinos, who were United States nationals because of the Philippines' colonial status, were not affected by the 1924 act. Because of the need for low-wage labor, Filipino workers were recruited to Hawaii and the West during the 1920s. In time, anti-Filipino sentiment became as vitriolic as other forms of anti-Asian feeling, but exclusion could not be invoked against the inhabitants of an American colony. In time, the movement for Philippine independence combined with American nativism to promote Congress's passage of the Tydings-McDuffie Act in 1934. The act granted commonwealth status to the Philippines and led to independence in 1946. But the Tydings-McDuffie Act also divested Filipinos of their status as nationals, making those in the United States deportable unless they became immigrants. Between 1934 and 1946, Filipinos seeking to immigrate were subject to the immigration laws of 1917 and 1924, and an annual quota of only fifty visas was allocated for the Philippines. Like other Asians, Filipino immigrants were not "free white persons" and were therefore ineligible for naturalized citizenship.

By the 1920s and 1930s, Asian immigration had declined drastically and formed a minuscule percentage of the overall immigration into the United States. The Chinese and Filipino populations actually decreased over time, because of gender imbalances exacerbated by the immigration laws. The repeal of the Chinese exclusion acts in 1943 did little to change migration patterns because complete exclusion was replaced by an annual quota of only 105 visas. The 1952 McCarran-Walter Act revamped much of the immigration system, but retained the quota system of the 1924 act, which severely limited Asian immigration. The 1952 act also created an Asia-Pacific triangle, similar to the Asiatic barred zone in the 1917 act, from which a maximum of only two thousand immigrants could enter the United States each year. Individual quotas for each Asian country typically allowed only one hundred entrants per year. Racial bias within the McCarran-Walter Act was also manifested through restrictions on immigration to anyone who was of at least one-half Asian or Pacific ancestry, regardless of actual country of birth. It was not until reforms were enacted in the Immigration Act of 1965 that race-based exclusions were fully removed from the immigration laws.

State and Local Laws

State and local laws had the most profound effects on the lives of Asian immigrants and their families. Basic rights and liberties—to work, attend school, own property, operate a business, or even marry the person of one's choice—were limited by state and local laws. Some of the laws discriminated through explicit anti-Asian language, but most of the laws relied on the racial prohibition on naturalized citizenship to single out Asian immigrants. Legislative language to deny rights to "aliens ineligible to citizenship" had the clear intent and effect of subordinating Asians.

Chinese immigrants were targeted from the earliest days of their arrival into the United States. In 1852, the California legislature enacted a foreign miners' license tax, which imposed a three dollar monthly tax on every foreign miner who would not—and could not under federal law—become an American citizen. Until it was made void by the federal Civil Rights Act of 1870, the foreign miners' tax generated from one-fourth to one-half of California's total state revenue. In 1855, the California legislature passed a law entitled "An Act to Discourage the Immigration to this State of Persons Who Cannot Become Citizens Thereof," which imposed a landing tax of fifty dollars per person on shipowners transporting passengers ineligible for citizenship. The California legislature became even bolder over time, passing a law entitled "An Act to Prevent Further Immigration of Chinese or Mongolian to This State" one year later, and passing a law entitled "An Act to Protect Free White Labor against Competition with Chinese Coolie Labor" in 1862.

The courts were not immune from discrimination against the Chinese. In 1854, the California Supreme Court overturned the criminal conviction of George Hall, a white man who had been convicted of murdering a Chinese man based on the testimony of one white and three Chinese witnesses. The court ruled in *People v. Hall* that a Chinese witness could not testify against a white defendant in a criminal trial. Relying on a state law which stated that "[n]o Black or Mulatto person, or Indian, shall be allowed to give evidence in favor of, or against any white person," the court extended the discriminatory bar to include Chinese. The court offered three reasons for its decision: Indians and Chinese were of the same racial stock, the word "black" necessarily excluded all races other than Caucasian, and accepting Chinese testimony was just bad public policy. The ruling remained in effect for nearly twenty years.

Local ordinances imposed heavy burdens on immigrant workers and businesses. For example, San Francisco enacted a laundry ordinance in 1873 that imposed a tax schedule of $1.25 on laundries with one horse-drawn vehicle, $4 on laundries with two horse-drawn vehicles, $15 on laundries with over two horse-drawn vehicles, and $15 on laundries with no horse-drawn vehicles at all. The ordinance targeted Chinese laundries, since practically no Chinese laundry operated a horse-drawn vehicle. During the course of the next ten years, the city enacted over a dozen more laundry ordinances that were race-neutral on their face but were intended to discriminate against Chinese immigrants. San Francisco even enacted a "Cubic Air Ordinance," which required that living spaces have at least five hundred cubic feet of space per person; the ordinance was enforced only in Chinatown.

An exceptional court decision occurred in 1886, when the United States Supreme Court struck down one of San Francisco's ordinances in the land-mark case of *Yick Wo v. Hopkins*. Yick Wo, like most Chinese laundry owners in San Francisco in the 1880s, operated a laundry constructed of wood. The city's 1880 laundry ordinance governed the operation of laundries and prohibited wood construction. Yick Wo and two hundred other Chinese laundry owners were denied license renewals under the ordinance, even though they had been operating their laundries for over twenty years. Non-Chinese laundries (including ones with wooden buildings) were granted license renewals. The Supreme Court ruled in favor of the Chinese laundry owners, holding that the ordinance violated the equal protection clause of the Fourteenth Amendment. The Court stated: "No reason . . . exists except hostility to the race and nationality to which the petitioners belong, and which in the eyes of the law is not justified."

Yick Wo was an anomalous decision given the Court's rulings in other cases involving Chinese immigrants, and may have been due to the Court's strong adherence at the time to doctrines protecting business interests and the liberty of contracts. In any case, *Yick Wo* established two important principles that are still invoked in constitutional litigation: (1) noncitizens are protected by the equal protection clause of the Fourteenth Amendment, and (2) a neutrally written law can violate the Constitution if administered in a discriminatory manner.

Educational segregation was another common form of subordination. In 1860, California barred Asians, blacks, and Native Americans from attending the public schools.

Twenty-five years later, after the law had been declared unconstitutional, segregated schools were established in California. San Francisco set up "Oriental schools" for Chinese students and other Asian students. A federal court upheld the constitutionality of the segregated schools in 1903. Two decades later, the United States Supreme Court ruled in *Gong Lum v. Rice* that the placement of a Chinese student into a segregated school in Mississippi designed for the "colored races" did not violate the federal Constitution. *Gong Lum* was not overruled until the Supreme Court's decision in *Brown v. Board of Education* in 1954.

The right of Asian immigrants to own property was abridged through "alien land laws." California's Alien Land Law of 1913 targeted Japanese immigrant farmers by prohibiting persons ineligible for citizenship from purchasing land in the state and by limiting lease terms to three years or less. The law was expanded in 1920 to prevent U.S.-born children from gaining title to land and having their parents act as guardians. Both California's law and Washington State's Anti-Alien Land Act were challenged in the early 1920s. The United States Supreme Court ruled in favor of the states, holding that the equal protection clause was not violated in either case. The Court in *Terrace v. Thompson* made clear that Asian immigrants did not enjoy the same rights as citizens: "It is obvious that one who is not a citizen and cannot become one lacks an interest in, and the power to effectually work for the welfare of, the state, and, so lacking, the state may rightfully deny him the right to own and lease real estate within its boundaries." It was not until twenty-five years later that the Supreme Court struck down California's Alien Land Law as unconstitutional.

State laws even interfered with the basic family relationships of Asian Americans. In 1880, California enacted an anti-miscegenation law that prohibited marriages between whites and "Negroes, mulattoes, or Mongolians." The law was extended by the state legislature over fifty years later to include Filipinos, who had been ruled by a California appeals court to be members of the "Malay race." The effects of the anti-miscegenation laws included not only direct interference with personal relationships but the slow destruction of Asian American populations. Because male laborers formed most of the population within the Chinese and Filipino communities, anti-miscegenation laws combined with restrictive immigration laws to limit marriage and births. Anti-miscegenation laws against blacks and Asians were common in western states, and many laws remained on the books until the United States Supreme Court ruled them to be unconstitutional in 1967.

World War II Internment of Japanese Americans

Perhaps the most notorious form of discrimination against an Asian American community during the twentieth century was the relocation and internment of Japanese Americans during World War II. After the bombing of Pearl Harbor plunged the United States into war, antagonisms against Japan blurred with already heated animosity against Japanese Americans. Immediate calls for the removal of Japanese Americans from the West Coast resounded among labor, business, state and local politicians, and the military. Unlike the Japanese Americans in Hawaii, who constituted one-third of Hawaii's population, Japanese Americans on the West Coast formed less than 1 percent of the population and lacked any significant political power to oppose the calls for relocation.

Government intelligence reports of the time indicated that exclusion would be unnecessary, because the vast majority of Japanese Americans were loyal to the United States and did not pose a threat to national security. Nevertheless, on February 19, 1942, President Roosevelt issued Executive Order 9066, which authorized the secretary of war and his commanders to create military areas from which all persons could be excluded in the interest of national defense. Although also applicable to Germans and Italians, the order was targeted against Japanese Americans on the West Coast. A few weeks later, Lt. General John L. DeWitt, the western defense commander, instituted plans to evacuate all persons of Japanese descent from an area bordering the Pacific Ocean. Given only a few days to relocate, Japanese Americans quickly sold or abandoned their homes, and were allowed to carry only a few personal possessions with them. Although the original plan was to relocate communities to other parts of the country, the government interned Japanese Americans in guarded camps in the interior of the United States. Over 110,000 Japanese Americans, the majority of whom were United States citizens, were placed into thirteen isolated concentration camps for the remainder of the war. General DeWitt's oft-cited remark—"a Jap is a Jap"—encapsulated the popular sentiment blurring any distinctions between loyal Americans of Japanese ancestry and wartime adversaries of the Japanese empire.

The internment did not go unchallenged. Four Japanese Americans contested the government's military orders and appealed their cases to the United States Supreme Court: Minoru Yasui, Gordon Hirabayashi, and Fred Korematsu had each been arrested and jailed for violations of different military orders, and challenged their convictions as constitutional violations of due process and equal protection; Mitsuye Endo, who had been held in an assembly center and interned in both California and Utah, filed a writ of habeas corpus arguing that her detention by the federal government was illegal. In June 1943, in *Hirabayashi v. United States,* a unanimous Supreme Court upheld the constitutionality of a governmental curfew order. Relying on the government's argument that Japanese Americans had a "continued attachment" to Japan, the Court held that government possessed extraordinary powers during time of war and could issue an emergency order such as a curfew if necessary to protect the national interest. Noting that Hirabayashi's conviction involved a classification based on race, the Court nevertheless held that military necessity justified the classification. Deciding *Yasui v. United States* on the same day, the Supreme Court employed similar reasoning and reversed a lower court's finding that the curfew order was unconstitutional as applied to United States citizens.

In 1944, in *Korematsu v. United States,* the Supreme Court, in a six-to-three decision, upheld the constitutionality of the military's exclusion order. The Court wrote that "all legal restrictions which curtail the civil rights of a single racial group are immediately suspect" and that "courts must subject them to the most rigid scrutiny." However, the Court also stated: "That is not to say that all such restrictions are unconstitutional. . . . Pressing public necessity must sometimes justify the existence of such restrictions; racial antagonism never can." Despite the important language on the judiciary's strict scrutiny of racial classifications, the Court went on to hold that the exclusion of Japanese Americans from the West Coast was justified by military necessity. The Court yielded to the government's determination that the threat of espionage and sabotage by some was sufficient to justify the exclusion of all Japanese Americans. Discounting the centrality of race, the majority opinion concluded that Korematsu was not excluded because of racial hostility but because the United States was at war with Japan.

Decided on the same day as *Korematsu, Ex Parte Endo* was a victory for Mitsuye Endo but did little to change the legality of the exclusion orders. The Supreme Court skirted the issue of whether the internment was unconstitutional and limited its decision to the issue of whether Endo's detention was valid. The Court held that the government could not continue to detain concededly loyal American citizens. Finding no question of her loyalty to the United States, the Court ordered Endo's release. But, as Justice Frank Murphy noted in a concurring opinion, while Endo was allowed to leave the camps, she was still subject to military orders excluding her from the West Coast. With the war coming to a close, the exclusion orders were soon rescinded by the military, and Japanese Americans were allowed to return to the West Coast.

Four decades later, newly discovered documents showing that the federal government had altered a key government report and had suppressed evidence of Japanese American loyalty in the wartime trials and appeals were used to vacate the original convictions of Gordon Hirabayashi and Fred Korematsu. In both cases, the courts found that the government had committed prosecutorial misconduct. Min Yasui's conviction was also vacated by a federal district court, but without a finding of government misconduct; he passed away during the course of the appeal. Despite the decisions to vacate the original convictions, the United States Supreme Court opinions remain valid as legal precedents. It took the enactment of the Civil Liberties Act of 1988, which issued a formal apology for the internment and granted redress payments to internees, to close the chapter on one of the most ignoble episodes in American legal history.

Post-World War II Racial Reforms

Despite the federal government's discriminatory treatment of Japanese Americans, World War II helped bring in an era of gradual racial reform in the United States. The fight for democracy abroad had a powerful impact on attitudes toward race during the

1940s and 1950s. Although far from ideal, racial attitudes had begun progressing to a point where formal racial segregation, enforced by government, began losing its ideological power. The same era that saw the improved treatment of African Americans and new calls for desegregation also brought support for nondiscrimination against Asian Americans in the law.

The federal courts were among the first institutions to begin chipping away at state laws discriminating against Asian Americans. In 1948, in *Oyama v. California,* the United States Supreme Court held that California's Alien Land Act was unconstitutional. As a child, Fred Oyama had been granted title to land in California that his father Kajiro was unable to own because of the state's alien land law. During World War II, while the Oyama family had been interned, the state government attempted to seize the land because it had been sold in violation of the Alien Land Act. In a six-to-three decision, the United States Supreme Court struck down the act as unconstitutional because it violated the rights of Fred Oyama, an American citizen, under the equal protection clause. The Court stated that "the rights of a citizen may not be subordinated merely because of his father's country of origin." The Court avoided, though, the issue of whether Kajiro Oyama's rights had been violated as a noncitizen, which would have required the Court to overrule its earlier decisions upholding the alien land laws.

In 1948, in *Takahashi v. Fish and Game Commission,* the United States Supreme Court struck down a California statute that prohibited aliens ineligible for citizenship from fishing in the ocean waters off the California coast. In 1943, the state legislature had amended the California fish and game code to prohibit Japanese immigrants from obtaining commercial fishing licenses. In 1945, the legislature amended the law again to include all aliens ineligible for citizenship. Torao Takahashi had held a fishing license from 1915 to 1942, before he was interned, and had been denied a license under the amended law. The Supreme Court invalidated the law as an improper classification based on alienage. The Court held that the equal protection clause was violated because the state's interest in protecting its "proprietary interest in fish" was insufficient and that the state, unlike the federal government, had only limited power to make a classification based on alienage.

During the late 1940s and 1950s, legislatures and courts began a slow reversal of the earlier laws that discriminated against Asians. The Oregon Supreme Court declared the state's alien land law to be unconstitutional in 1949; the California Supreme Court followed in 1952; the Washington legislature repealed the state's alien land law in 1967. Laws discriminating against all racial minorities, including Asian Americans, were held to be unconstitutional violations of the equal protection clause. In 1948, in *Perez v. Sharp,* the California Supreme Court struck down the state's anti-miscegenation law as unconstitutional. The United States Supreme Court also held in 1948 that racially restrictive housing covenants, which had been commonly used to prevent Asian Americans from owning homes, were unconstitutional and could not be enforced by the courts. And the Supreme Court's landmark decision in *Brown v. Board of Education* in 1954 prohibited public school segregation and led to the dismantling of "separate but equal" schools for Asian Americans.

The federal government's reversal of discriminatory immigration and naturalization laws began in the 1940s and culminated with the passage of the Immigration Act of 1965. The Chinese exclusion laws were repealed in 1943, and Chinese immigrants were also allowed to become naturalized citizens. Asian Indian and Filipino immigrants gained the right to naturalize in 1946. Through the advocacy of organizations such as the Japanese American Citizens League, the 1952 McCarran-Walter Act removed the racial bar to naturalization. With the passage of the Immigration Act of 1965, formal barriers based on race and national origin were removed from the immigration laws.

The Immigration Act of 1965 abolished the Asia-Pacific triangle put into place by the 1952 McCarran-Walter Act and removed the discriminatory national origin quotas dating back to the immigration Act of 1924, which limited visas for most Asian countries to one hundred per year. The 1965 act set an allocation of twenty thousand visas for every country not in the Western Hemisphere, and established a preference system based on reuniting families and meeting the needs of the American economy through the entry of professional and skilled workers.

Anti-Immigrant Discrimination after 1965

Along with the civil rights legislation of the 1960s, the Immigration Act of 1965 marked a shift in the federal government's commitment to formal racial equality. Asian Americans have benefited directly from governmental prohibitions on discrimination in employment, education, housing, public accommodations, business, and immigration. In 1974, for example, the United States Supreme Court ruled in *Lau v. Nichols* that the San Francisco Unified School District violated Title VI of the Civil Rights of 1964 when the district discriminated against limited-English-speaking Chinese students by failing to provide equal educational opportunities through either bilingual or supplemental English instruction.

Governmental subordination of Asian Americans did not magically disappear with the passage of civil rights laws and nondiscriminatory immigration laws. Using 1965 as a watershed year, the history of legal discrimination against Asian Americans can be divided into two distinct eras: a pre-1965 era of explicit discrimination based on race, and a post-1965 era of implicit discrimination based on citizenship and immigration status.

Post-1965 Asian Immigration

The shift toward anti-immigrant laws is in part a reaction to the dramatic changes in the Asian American population that have arisen since 1965. In 1965, Asian Americans numbered approximately 1.4 million, constituting less than 1 percent of the nation's population. The majority of Asian Americans had been born in the United States.

When Congress passed the Immigration Act of 1965, few people at the time expected immigration from Asia and the Pacific to form a significant proportion of the new immigration flow to the United States. Testifying before Congress, Attorney General Robert Kennedy estimated that no more than five thousand immigrants from Asia and the Pacific would enter in the first year, and that there would be no significant increases in later years.

The estimates proved to be wrong, and immigration from Asia and the Pacific has grown from 7 percent of all legal immigrants in 1965 to about 40 percent during the 1980s and 1990s. Include with those immigrants who entered under the 1965 act the large number of Southeast Asian refugees who came to the United States following the Vietnam War, and the result is the extraordinary population growth in Asian American communities that we have witnessed over the past three decades.

The Immigration Act of 1965 created two vehicles for immigration to the United States, both of which spurred large numbers of Asian immigrants. Employment-based preference categories led to the entry of many immigrant professionals and technicians, particularly in the health care fields and the sciences. Family reunification led to the entry of large numbers of "immediate relatives"—parents, spouses, and unmarried minor children of United States citizens—who could enter in unlimited numbers. In addition, the family-based preference system authorized the limited entry of selected categories of relatives: spouses and unmarried children of lawful permanent residents; the adult children of citizens; and the brothers and sisters of citizens. The immediate family members of adult children and siblings could also enter as "derivative" beneficiaries. Once immigrant communities developed in the United States, they provided a base for the sponsorship of more immigrants; immigrants who became permanent residents and naturalized citizens could bring in additional family members through the preference system.

Although immigration from all of Asia and the Pacific has increased since 1965, the largest numbers of employment-based and family-based immigrants have come from the Philippines, China, South Korea, and India. Asian immigrants entering through the employment system are usually highly educated and often enter with significant financial resources. Family immigrants are more diverse, having a wider range of education and skill levels because their status is based solely on family relationships. English language ability also varies significantly, with immigrants from India and the Philippines usually possessing greater fluency because English is a language of instruction in those countries.

Since the mid-1970s, humanitarian admissions have been the major source of entry for Vietnamese, Cambodian, Laotian, and other refugees affected by the Vietnam War and the governments of Southeast Asia. The fall of Saigon in April 1975 led to a first wave of over 130,000 Southeast Asian refugees during eight months in 1975. Another wave of 380,000 Southeast Asian refugees arrived in the United States between 1979 and 1981. Additional Southeast Asian immigration has come through special legislation such as the 1987 Indochinese Refugee Resettlement and Protection Act, which allowed the entry of "Amerasian" children whose natural fathers were American servicemen during the Vietnam War.

Undocumented migration, which is difficult to measure because of its inherently secretive nature, also accounts for a significant number of Asian immigrants. Some undocumented Asians enter surreptitiously, through border crossings or port entries. The smuggling of Chinese immigrants, which gained national attention in 1993 with the sinking of the ship the *Golden Venture* near New York City, is one example. However, the vast majority of the Asian undocumented population fall out of legal status by overstaying on temporary visas or by violating the terms of a "nonimmigrant" visa, such as a student visa, by working without authorization. Precluded from lawful employment by the Immigration Reform and Control Act of 1986, undocumented immigrants form the work force for many underground economies that rely on exploitable labor, including agriculture, garment manufacturing, restaurant work, and domestic services.

Shifting Demographics

Taken together, these sources of immigration have led to most of the population growth of the Asian American population since 1965. The number of Asians who entered the United States through legal immigration was 1.6 million during the 1970s and 2.7 million during the 1980s. According to Census Bureau estimates, 86 percent of the Asian and Pacific Islander population growth during the 1990s is due to immigration, leading to projections that the Asian American population will number over 12 million by the year 2000. If immigration patterns continue, projections for the year 2050 put Asian Americans at close to 10 percent of the national population.

Once predominantly U.S.-born, the Asian American population is now largely immigrant. Nearly two out of every three Asian Americans are foreign-born, and approximately 40 percent of the population are not United States citizens. The growth of the Asian American population has also contributed, along with the growing population of Latinos, to significant shifts in urban demographics. The expansion of new immigrant populations and the long-standing migration of whites from urban cores to smaller cities and suburbs has transformed the racial character of the nation's cities. Most of America's largest cities—including New York, Los Angeles, and Chicago—are now "majority-minority," and many urban areas have concentrations of Asian Americans, Latinos, and African Americans living and working in the same neighborhoods.

Anti-Immigrant Legislation in the 1980s and 1990s

Anti-immigrant legislation enacted during the 1980s and 1990s has been in response to the large number of immigrants entering the United States from Asia and Latin America. The Immigration Act of 1965 removed explicit racial and national origin categories from the laws, but recent legislation has either created programs that have resulted in discrimination against Asian Americans or produced changes in the law that have adversely affected large numbers of Asian immigrants.

In 1986, Congress passed the Immigration Reform and Control Act (IRCA) to address undocumented migration to the United States. The law created an amnesty program to legalize undocumented immigrants who had lived in the United States since before 1982 or who had worked in agriculture for a minimal period. The law also established a system of employment verification and employer sanctions to limit the primary incentive for undocumented migration—jobs. All employers, both private and public, are required to verify the immigration status of newly hired employees, including United States citizens. Failure to verify an employee's status, or to knowingly hire an employee who lacks the authorization to work, subjects an employer to penalties.

Because of employer sanctions, discrimination against Asian Americans and Latinos increased significantly after IRCA went into effect. A report by the federal government's General Accounting Office issued in 1990 found a widespread pattern of discrimination against Asian Americans and Latinos—including American citizens. Nearly one of five employers surveyed by the GAO admitted that they discriminated on the basis of national origin or citizenship. Despite the GAO report and the recommendation of a federal task force, Congress chose not to repeal employer sanctions.

In the Immigration Act of 1990, Congress made significant changes to the immigration laws dealing with legal immigration. The 1990 act set an overall cap on legal immigration into the United States, retained the basic family reunification system set out in the 1965 act, and expanded the number of employment-based visa categories for highly educated and skilled immigrants. With Asian and Latin American immigration having dominated legal immigration since the 1970s, the law also established a visa lottery system for residents of countries that had not significantly used the family and employment preference systems. But the lottery system has racial and ethnic biases built into it: the beneficiaries of the lottery system are potential immigrants from Europe and Africa; excluded from the lottery are Asian countries such as China, India, South Korea, and the Philippines, and Central American countries such as Mexico and El Salvador.

In 1994, the voters of California passed Proposition 187, a ballot initiative designed to address immigration by denying basic rights and government services to undocumented immigrants. Under Proposition 187, undocumented immigrants are denied access to public school education, to nonemergency health care from state and local government providers, and to government social services. In addition, all individuals—both citizens and noncitizens—are required under the law to prove lawful immigration status in order to obtain a public school education, health care, or social services.

Although enjoined by the courts soon after passage, Proposition 187 had immediate effects on immigrants throughout the state; many immigrants removed their children from schools and avoided seeking health and social services. A number of immigrants died soon after the passage of Proposition 187 because they avoided medical services in fear of the law. Studies on hate violence in Los Angeles and other parts of California also showed a linkage between anti-Latino and anti-Asian violence and the passage of Proposition 187. Anti-immigrant sentiment expanded nationally after the passage of Proposition 187 in California. Similar ballot initiatives were unable to qualify for the ballots of other states, but efforts in Congress led to the passage of measures further limiting the rights of immigrants—both the undocumented and lawful permanent residents.

In 1996, Congress passed the Personal Responsibility and Work Opportunity Reconciliation Act, a comprehensive legislative package intended to overhaul the nation's welfare system. Designed to shift the burden of welfare financing and administration from the federal government to the states, the welfare reform legislation also contains provisions that discriminate against lawful permanent residents living in the United States by removing their eligibility for public entitlements, including Food Stamps and Supplemental Security Income for the elderly, blind, and disabled. The law also gives state governments the option of denying additional benefits, including Medicaid and Temporary Assistance for Needy Families. Although federal legislation enacted the following year would restore benefits to some permanent residents, the impact of the law on low-income Asian immigrants has been enormous, affecting the subsistence income of thousands of poor immigrants throughout the country. Reminiscent of the anti-Asian laws that subordinated "aliens ineligible to citizenship," the welfare reform legislation is race-neutral on its face, but its impact has fallen most heavily on the Asian American and Latino immigrant communities.

Congress's passage of the Illegal Immigration Reform and Immigrant Responsibility Act of 1996 soon after enactment of the welfare reform package marked another severe diminution of the rights of Asian immigrants. While the focus of the immigration reform law is on increasing border patrol resources to address undocumented migration, its scope extends to curtailing the rights of undocumented immigrants to receive federal grants, contracts, loans, or entitlements; limiting the due process rights of applicants for political asylum; and increasing enforcement of the immigration laws by local law enforcement. Although formal restrictions on legal immigration were removed from the final version of the legislation, the immigration reform law sets up economic barriers to family immigration by establishing minimum income requirements for sponsors of legal immigrants. Like the welfare reform legislation, the immigration reform legislation's most adverse effects fall primarily on Asian and Latino immigrants.

Lessons of Legal History

In closing this legal history of Asian Americans, I emphasize two points. First, while the history of Asian Americans is often ignored in general discussions of race, Asian Americans have in fact played an important role in the shaping of civil rights laws in the

United States. Despite the setbacks and adversity brought on by federal, state, and local laws, Asian Americans did not allow the laws to go uncontested. Many of these challenges succeeded in affecting legislation and the decisional law of the courts. For example, challenges to the discriminatory laws against Chinese immigrants during the mid-nineteenth century on the West Coast were integral to the passage of Reconstruction-era federal civil rights legislation.

Successful court decisions such as *Yick Wo v. Hopkins,* which established the rights of noncitizens to challenge laws under the equal protection clause, and *United States v. Wong Kim Ark,* which established birthright citizenship under the Fourteenth Amendment, are landmarks in U.S. legal history. Even the infamous case of *Korematsu v. United States,* which upheld the exclusion of Japanese Americans from the West Coast during World War II, established legal standards that were used to strike down laws mandating racial segregation. The passage of legislation such as the Civil Liberties Act of 1988, which granted redress payments to Japanese Americans, demonstrates that Asian Americans today are able to wield significant political influence in the area of civil rights.

Second, the patterns of discrimination that began in the nineteenth century with the first waves of immigrant laborers to the United States have been recurring themes in the statutes and court cases of the twentieth century. It is not a coincidence that the most virulent anti-Asian sentiment has occurred during economic recessions and depressions, when racial scapegoating typically peaks. But even during economic upturns, Asian Americans were consistently treated as foreigners, even, as in the case of the Japanese American internment, when they were United States citizens. Anti-Asian discrimination was explicit during the nineteenth century and for most of the twentieth century; race and nativism have been linked in the subordination of Asian Americans throughout the history of the United States.

Even after the 1960s, with the passage of expansive legislation prohibiting racial discrimination, anti-immigrant sentiment and anti-immigrant legislation have appeared, becoming even more prominent in the 1990s. During this decade, we have witnessed nativist scapegoating that rivals the explicitly racist rhetoric of the late nineteenth and early twentieth centuries. The fact that many of the anti-Asian court decisions from that earlier period—including *The Chinese Exclusion Case* and *Korematsu*—continue to be cited as valid legal precedents demonstrates that Asian Americans must be continually vigilant about abridgments of their rights.

At Exclusion's Southern Gate: Changing Categories of Race and Class among Chinese *Fronterizos*, 1882–1904

Grace Peña Delgado

Many images of the nineteenth-century overseas Chinese permeate the historical imagination: Cantonese men fleeing the war-torn province of Guangdong, sojourners searching for Gold Mountain, workers laying thousands of miles of track across the United States, and women working as prostitutes in California mining camps. The busy landscapes of American Chinatowns and the brimming detention barracks at the port of San Francisco also find their way into popular thought. Closer to their homeland, images of assiduous middle-men engaged in rubber and tin production in Malaysia and Thailand remind us that Chinese entrepreneurs met with frequent and open acceptance in these areas of the world. Multidirectional movements into Canada, Australia, and Cuba are also imprinted, although faintly, within collective historical memory.

These images exclude the complex social dynamics of Chinese living in the U.S.-Mexico borderlands.[1] While not as heavily populated with Chinese as other nations, Mexico was both host and home to several thousand Cantonese immigrants in the late nineteenth and early twentieth centuries. Chinese migration into Mexico coincided with an interest in populating and developing the Mexican North, but exclusion laws in the United States during the 1880s and 1890s also had a significant impact on the lives of Chinese immigrants in northern Mexico. Greeks, Syrians, Poles, Russians, Italians, Germans, and Hungarians settled in northern Mexico at the same time, but their movement between continents and countries did not raise the same types of questions about race and citizenship as that of the Chinese.

This essay brings together the stories of Chinese merchants and laborers at the U.S.-Mexico border in a time when racial ideologies profoundly determined their social marginalization and political exclusion in the United States. Racial ideologies did not, however, find uniform expression throughout the borderlands. As citizens or nationals of Mexico, the Chinese escaped ritualized practices barring their entry at the ports of San Francisco and New York when crossing at Mexico's national border. The privileges enjoyed by Chinese merchants and laborers in Mexico prompted border officials to recognize, rather than deny, the ability of Chinese to assert Mexican claims of citizenship and nationality. In the late nineteenth century, when a racialized discourse of exclusion entered the legal domains of the United States, Mexican civil society, especially in the North, was uniquely poised to absorb Chinese émigrés into its fold.

La frontera norte, long a place plagued by ethnic hostilities, teetered toward capitalist expansion during the late nineteenth century, although amid many uncertainties. To foster progress, Mexico's president, Porfirio Díaz, lured foreign investors with the promise of profits and immigrants with the favorable circumstances of opportunity. Although Díaz's open economic policies were in direct contrast to those adopted in China and the United States, what yielded results for the Chinese was that Mexican civil law accorded them rights equal to those of Mexicans. This ran counter to policies in China and the United States. Mexico's northern neighbor barred the entry of Chinese laborers with the passage of the Chinese Exclusion Act of 1882. Although merchants, diplomats, teachers, travelers, and students were permitted entry, the hardening of exclusion laws ten years later curbed the admission of many exempt Chinese. Furthermore, U.S. state and federal courts no longer gave citizenship to Chinese. By 1890, Chinese living in the United States had few formal privileges and protections compared to those who held U.S. citizenship. China also practiced policies of exclusion. Until 1893, Qing dynasty (1644–1911) strictures forbade the reentry of émigrés returning from abroad. Repatriation occurred only when imperial authorities realized the value of remittances from overseas Chinese to their nearly bankrupt regime.[2]

The reception of Chinese tells us about more than just their treatment in places they come from and settled; it tells us about the historical circumstances that scripted their sojourning experiences in Mexico and the United States. In fact, what is significant is not exclusion or inclusion, but rather than immigration restrictionism as understood at the U.S.-Mexico border did not always assume racialized forms. Officials soon discovered that political rights and economic motivations of the Chinese were more tenacious than the bite of U.S. exclusion. Despite the appearances of a closed U.S. border, the Chinese, occupying a range of positions between citizen/national/foreigner and merchant/laborer, carved out a social space for themselves s border crossers and *fronterizos* in northern Mexico.

Class determined the most fundamental level of participation for Chinese merchants and laborers in northern Mexico, due in large part to the nature of Chinese exclusion laws in the U.S. during the last two decades of the nineteenth century.

Merchants, enlisting the aid of Mexican and U.S. officials, petitioned for their entry north as Mexican citizens. This strategy suggests that the pliability of Mexican citizenship and nationality, at least for two decades, trumped the narrow confines of Chinese exclusion laws. Laborers, on the other hand, faced greater legal barriers to crossing the border, yet they also exercised more than nominal control over their deportation hearings. If they demonstrated Mexican citizenship or residency, they were deported to Mexico, not China. For both Chinese merchants and laborers, inclusion in the Mexican national community provided a means to contest exclusion laws and state-sponsored campaigns against them. How they used Mexican nationality and citizenship to defend their interests reveals much about the shifting notions of racial and national identity in the borderlands, while highlighting the legal and practical limits to exclusion and it enforcement in this continental crossroads.

Where East Meets West and South Meets North

As early as 1889, Chinese began traveling to Baja, California Norte and Sonora to cross into the United States, thereby evading the barriers posed by the 1882 Chinese Exclusion Act. When, for example, a Chinese ship arrived in San Francisco in 1893, eighty-four Cantonese émigrés transferred to the *New Berne*, a U.S. steamship that frequented Mexican ports.[3] This roundabout course had practical advantages. By crossing the Mexican border, Chinese could avoid prolonged detentions at the port of San Francisco. Disembarking at Mexican port cities of Mazatlán, Guaymas, La Paz, San José, Cabo San Lucas, Ensenada, or Magdalena Bay, they traveled overland through Baja California or Sonora.[4] Their growing presence in Mexico indicated that many were crossing illegally through one of the last frontiers of the United States. Given its proximity to several hundred miles of coastline, it was no surprise that the borderlands would become a major Chinese thoroughfare into the United States.

In stark contrast to U.S. policies, Mexico encouraged Chinese immigration in the late nineteenth century. The 1886 *Ley de extranjería y naturalización,* passed under President Porfirio Díaz, lured foreign settlers to Mexico with liberal ideals of citizenship and nationality. The Mexican government was particularly interested in attracting immigrants from abroad to the sparsely populated borderlands, since the *científicos* believed the Mexican peasant was inherently incapable of building and participating in a modern, industrial society. They saw European immigrants, especially those practicing Roman Catholicism, as ideal. Yet there were few incentives for would-be immigrants: Apache, Yaqui, and Seri Indians continued to dominate the border region, there were few waterways for irrigation development, and access to arable land was limited. With the exception of colonies of Russians and European Jews in Baja California, greater opportunities pulled immigrants of European descent to the United States or elsewhere.[5]

The Chinese, nonetheless, participated in the new immigrant experiment in northern Mexico. Between 1890 and 1895, Mexican government officials reported that over

4,350 Chinese landed at the Pacific ports of Salina Cruz and Mazatlán and Gulf ports of Tampico and Veracruz.[6] Commercial and agricultural opportunities drew many to the territory of Baja California Norte and the states of Coahuila, Chihuahua, Sinaloa, and Sonora. Sonoran census records of 1890 reported 229 Chinese living and laboring in the state as hotel workers, cooks, launderers, ranchers, merchants, and skilled tradesmen. Chinese later gained a foothold in local manufacturing and sale of apparel, shoes, and men's furnishings, quickly dominating what little small-scale manufacturing existed in the state. In 1895 the census recorded 126 men and eleven women living in the port city of Guaymas, 84 in the mining camp of Minas Prietas, 46 in the capital of Hermosillo, and 16 in the border town of Magdalena.[7] By 1900 Sonora was home to the largest Chinese population in Mexico, with over 850.

Substantially fewer Chinese lived just west in Baja California.[8] San Diego customs officials enumerated more than a hundred Chinese in Baja California Norte during the late 1880s, many ostensibly working in the mining and fishing enterprises of the Chinese Six Companies.[9] Although the demand for labor may have lured more Chinese into the peninsula, these projects eventually collapsed.[10] Over the next decade, the lack of employment and investment opportunities stunted the growth of the Chinese population. By 1900 only 188 Chinese resided in Baja California Norte.[11] Despite the demographic and economic differences between Baja California Norte and Sonora, the Chinese in both areas found themselves in relatively flexible circumstances. Exclusion laws in the United States, along with the push for immigration and development in northern Mexico, placed several choices in the hands of the Chinese: the possibility of settlement, the opportunity to naturalize, or the challenge of crossing the U.S. border. The lives of Chinese merchants narrate this interlacing history.

In 1879, Lee Sing, an ambitious young merchant, established a dry goods business with his brother in Tucson, Arizona. The small store, stocked with items such as beef jerky, beans, and whiskey, was quite enterprising in the context of the burgeoning Tucson economy. Financial connections with prominent Jewish businessman Louis Zeckendorf made his business prospects bright.[12] Sing's own success inspired expansion into the production and sale of shoes in Nogales, Arizona. Over the next few years, Sing's second business enterprise flourished with the economy of this booming border town, but by 1889 the operation of his businesses took a back seat to his personal priorities. After some years of engagement to a Mexican woman, Sing decided to liquidate his assets and properties in Nogales and Tucson in order to marry, relocate to Sonora, and become a Mexican citizen.

After his wedding in Mexico, Sing established stores in the Sonoran towns of Imuris, La Cienega, and Santa Ana. Like many Chinese proprietors in northern Mexico, Sing lived in a transnational world. He established financial and familial ties in both the United States and Mexico, holding investments with his brother in Tucson while creating a home and family in Sonora. Yet his growing wealth and economic status did not necessarily guarantee trouble-free entry into the United States. During a routine trip north in 1893, Sing was detained by Arizona border inspectors and questioned about his status as a merchant. The thirty-two-year-old Sing was fortunate; he was able to call on Mexican and American officials for assistance. D. A. Moreno, president of the border city of Santa Ana, verified Sing's *ciudadania* (citizenship), his eleven years of residency in Mexico, his marriage to a Mexican woman (and the fact that he was father of three Mexican children), his annual income of eight to ten thousand pesos, and his ownership of a local general store. Also persuasive were the confirmation by the prefect of Magdalena, Ignacio Bonillas, of the merchant's real estate holdings, and Sing's affidavit to the American consul at Nogales, Sonora, Josiah E. Stone.[13]

This overwhelming record of settlement held sway, and officials permitted Sing to pass freely across the border over the next four years. No single aspect, be it merchant status, Mexican citizenship, or familial roots in Sonora, determined entry. All were important, and all would have an impact on local enforcement of Chinese exclusion laws. It is useful to compare Sing's situation to that of most Mexicans, who were relatively free to cross the border during the 1890s; they were stopped at the border only when customs officials suspected them of evading paying appropriate tariffs, or smuggling contraband whiskey, cigars, and opium.[14] Unlike the Chinese, Mexicans' proof of citizenship or nationality was not required to pass into the United States. A Mexican national simply declared his name to U.S. customs officials and paid whatever duty or fine was due. Chinese residents of Mexico, by contrast, were always stopped at the border with the assumption that they were "aliens" in the region.

Claims of Mexican citizenship and nationality yielded positive results when immigrant officials stopped and detained Chinese border crossers. In fact, most Chinese merchants who asserted such privileges benefited from the rights bestowed on Mexicans at the U.S. southern line: they gained legal entry north. Moreover, conscious assertions of *mexicanidad* on the part of Chinese border crossers indicate that membership in the Mexican polity had not yet assumed narrow and ethnically confining requisites associated with the postrevolutionary identity of *mestizaje*. While Mexican nationality, and its subsequent power at the U.S. southern border, continued to perplex immigrant and customs officials attempting to make sense of rather extraneous exclusion laws, Chinese merchants continued to cross, although their movements were not always effortless.

The 1897 murder of Lee Sing's brother in Tucson, Arizona, threw the orderly world of the shoe merchant into confusion. Unbeknown to Sing, trouble began almost immediately with his arrival in Tucson to settle his dead brother's estate. After an eight-year absence, no one recognized Sing. Immigration officials and residents assumed he was a laborer illegally in the country. Unaware of these suspicions, Sing began to take care of his brother's affairs, selling his dry goods store to a local Chinese merchant for three thousand dollars. Somewhere along the way, sentimentality took over, and Sing contemplated relocating his wife and their three young children to Tucson.[15] He returned to Imuris and persuaded his wife of the town's virtues, including the quality of its schools. Sing then left for Tucson to arrange for the move, leaving with his wife the money and documents related to the sale of his brother's property.

Sing passed without incident across the international border. Once in Tucson, he took up short-term residency at the Star Laundry, a downtown shop in the Old Pueblo owned by an elderly friend of Sing, Sam Lee. It was here that a local passerby, who had witnessed Sing ironing what were later determined to be his own clothes, mistook the merchant for a laborer. Not surprisingly, this type of manual activity threw Sing's status as merchant into question. In a matter of a day, Tucson immigration officials arrested Sing, believing he was a laborer illegally in the United States. As the merchant's lengthy testimony revealed, the exchange of money in the form of a wage never occurred between Sam Lee and Lee Sing. The proprietor of the laundry washed his guest's clothes free of charge, and if any ironing was to be done, Sing would have to do it himself.

Sing's experience was a common one among Chinese merchants in the United States. According to historian Lucy Salyer, merchants could be stopped at "every hamlet, village and town . . . on the charge of being a laborer who has failed to register."[16] A similar predicament held true for Mexican merchants Ah Suey, Hi Chung, Wong Nam, Wong Fong, and Mary Fong of southern Arizona.[17] All gained admission into the United States, albeit after a period of detention, questioning, and litigation. Declarations of citizenship and merchant status aided their disputes. The territorial court even recognized the dual residencies of merchants Mary and Wong Fong as Tombstone, Arizona, and San Pedro, Sonora, Mexico. The couple, as a result, operated stores on both sides of the border while maintaining their home in Tombstone.[18] Likewise, legal maneuverings and the assertion of Mexican citizenship eventually freed Sing from the grip of the territorial courts.[19]

Citizenship, family, and merchant status would remain the cornerstones of Mexico's Chinese business community over the next five decades. Their place in Mexican society allowed Chinese merchants to exert control and influence in their national lives while maintaining fluid relationships and identities across borders. As more Chinese from Sonora and Baja California insisted on traveling into the United States, customs officials stopped and detained Chinese merchants with growing frequency.[20] Patterns of transnational travel, social ties, and economic activity, however, were not so easily broken. U.S. customs officials wrestled with this social reality, as well as the ambiguities of enforcing exclusion laws. Some consular officials began to feel that temporary Chinese travel into the United States should be allowed within the framework of exclusion laws. Within this ambiguous and negotiable intersection between formal law and social reality, requests by Chinese merchants to enter the United States were, more often than not, resolved in their favor.

Sifting Through and Enforcing the Law

By the mid-1890s, the difficulties of determining admission or exclusion of Chinese overwhelmed U.S. immigration officials.[21] Understaffed and ill-equipped, customs collectors and immigrant inspectors vastly underestimated the force of this new diaspora seeking entry—legally and illegally—into the United States. To assist in this complex and challenging task, the Bureau of Immigration in 1895 created the Chinese Bureau, which shared with customs agents the responsibility of enforcing exclusion laws. Yet this new body hardly seemed in a position to enforce exclusion laws along the Mexican border. At the port of San Francisco, the Chinese Bureau was part of a vast administrative organization under the control of the customs collector. By contrast, only five permanent-status customs officials ran the entire San Diego customs station in 1891. Equally undermanned were the customs offices in Tucson and Nogales, Arizona. To guard the 300-mile border with Sonora, both stations shared two collectors, two Chinese inspectors, and one mounted inspector.[22]

These officials were keenly aware that the lack of sufficient personnel brought even more pressure to bear on their daily responsibilities. The duties incumbent on customs officers—searching all incoming vessels, determining the appropriate duties for taxable items, tracking and fining smugglers of cigars, mescal, sheep, and opium—were made more demanding when deciding whether to admit Chinese originating from Mexico. Exclusion laws, customs officials soon discovered, were not only wholly inadequate and too general, they were often irrelevant. Their misgivings about the law engendered a frequent reliance on Mexican officials, who reluctantly assisted U.S. customs officials. Enforcing Chinese exclusion laws also dramatized the often circumspect political relationship between the United States and its southern neighbor.

Frustrated by the ability of Chinese laborers to slip through the unguarded border, customs agents soon realized that effective patrolling of the border meant monitoring the activities of the Chinese from within Mexico. In 1890, when eighty Chinese landed in Mazatlán, Sinaloa, and Guaymas, Sonora, the fear of a Chinese invasion loomed in the mind of San Diego customs collector John R. Berry. "It looks as if the experiment had been tried of entering Chinamen in this round-about way and in small numbers," he reported, "and having proved successful an attempt is being made to operate the plan on a larger scale."[23] To his satisfaction (but also to his annoyance), Mexican constables, not U.S. customs officers, caught thirteen out of eighty Chinese south of Tijuana. Because U.S. customs agents could not cross into Mexico, informal arrangements with Mexican constables were necessary to capture those Chinese attempting to cross the line. Happenstance placed the constables, on duty for no more than thirty minutes, in the path of the border crossers.[24]

Berry now sought to formalize enforcement of exclusion laws, seeking among other things to expand the power of his inspectors south into Mexico. He began to negotiate with Mexican customs officials and the governor of Baja California Norte immediately following the capture of the Chinese laborers. He asked M. G. Montaño, collector of customs at Tia Juana, Baja California, to allow his men to pursue Chinese into Mexican territory. "It is the desire of the Government of the United States to scrupulously respect the desire of the Government of Mexico, and I have no doubt it is equally the desire of the Mexican Government to extend to the Government of the United States such international courtesies as may be practical and that may be necessary," he wrote.

"If it is consistent with your wishes and within the scope of your official authority, I would respectfully request that you issue a permit for the Chinese inspectors . . . to cross."[25]

Governor Luís E. Torres responded by authorizing limited power to U.S. customs inspectors in Mexico to cross the border.[26] His hesitation to offer full border-crossing privileges was not so surprising considering that just two months earlier Baja California Norte had been subject to filibustering attempts by a marauding band of Americans.[27] Not wanting to disrupt economic relations with the United States, Torres sought a balance between maintaining friendly relations between the two republics and reasserting Mexican sovereignty.[28] Inspectors could enter as private citizens, he explained, but could "do nothing as a United States official" once in Mexico.[29] Left neither with the capacity to detain nor the power to arrest, mounted inspectors decided to monitor the movements of Chinese from the ports of Ensenada and La Paz.

The ability of inspectors to warn agents at the border about potential Chinese movements from the coast yielded modest results yet did not solve the problem of what to do with the Chinese once they reached Arizona.[30] Chinese laborers stopped at the Arizona-Sonora border were not always subject to the same exclusionary practices as those entering elsewhere. Arizona's Territorial Commissioners did not automatically deport Chinese from Mexico to China. Instead, they recognized Chinese residency in Mexico and, by extension, valued Chinese community life there. These actions also indicate that Arizona officials acted outside the predominant racial ideology of the day when interpreting exclusion laws. With virtually no legal precedents to guide decision making, or political pressure to sway their judgment, the actions of Arizona Territorial officials reveal that customs officials found themselves in the position to interpret exclusion law based on their own understanding of Chinese life at the border.

Territorial Commissioners Louis C. Hughes, Allen R. English, and D. J. Cumming made distinctions between border crossers and border residents—those Chinese laborers sojourning through Mexico and those from Mexico. Until roughly 1900, Chinese laborers of Mexican citizenship or nationality crossing the border were simply deported to Mexico, the most favorable outcome possible for Chinese laborers at the time. Chinese with no claims to Mexican residency or citizenship continued to risk crossing into the United States from Mexico, even if it meant deportation to China.

In the hot summer months of 1890; twenty-two Chinese with names like Ta Ho, Ah Cheong, Hom Jung, Gwan Gong, and Ning Saung Hoe were captured and imprisoned in Nogales and Tucson.[31] They were not residents of Mexico and had no other intention except to cross into the United States. Without any legal representation, each of the laborers signed an affidavit, translated into Chinese by interpreter C. Richards, about the nature of the circuitous journeys that landed them in Arizona. The testimony of Ning Ah Goon was typical: "My name is Ning Ah Goon. I am 42 years old, was born in China. I am a laborer. I arrived in San Francisco from China Jan. 20 to Feb. 17–1890 on S. S. *City of Peking*. I then went to Guaymas Mexico where I arrived Feb 27–1890, I do not know from which vessel."[32] By the time these laborers completed their declarations there was no longer any question as to their status—they were Chinese laborers and nationals illegally in the United States and had to return to China. A month after their arrest, they were officially deported.

However, the fact that many Chinese laborers crossed the border with no claims to Mexican residence or citizenship did not deter Territorial Commissioners English, Cumming, and Hughes from seeking to verify Mexican citizenship and residency when possible. That same summer, they held thirteen Chinese laborers for illegal entry into Arizona. Sam Hing, Chu Yun, Charley Quong, and Charley Ah Fong, without the assistance of attorneys, asked not to remain in the United States but to be deported to Mexico.[33] To return to China would mean returning to the homeland with a dream of a better life in Mexico unfulfilled—or at the least, a bit delayed. Each defendant, self-identified as a laborer, declared nationality or citizenship in Mexico. Support for Sam Hing was especially evident. Tombstone residents Wong Lung and James Reese posted a hundred-dollar bond on behalf of Sam Hing. They also testified to Hing's activities in Tombstone and provided important documentation, hoping that their friend would escape deportation to China. After the proceedings were completed, territorial marshal R. H. Paul escorted Sam Hing, Chu Yun, Charley Quong, and Charley Ah Fong to the border town of Nogales, Sonora.

The language of the territorial court suggested that deportation of laborers to Mexico was not as significant as the deportation of laborers to China. English, Cumming, and Hughes viewed sending laborers to Mexico as a mere discharge. The order of deportation by Commissioner English underscored this point: "I certify the order on the 26th day of June, AD 1890, by carrying the defendant, Chin Yan, to Nogales, State of Sonora, Republic of Mexico, and there discharging him."[34] That "deportation" meant returning to China and "discharge" meant a short escort to the border town further obscured the intent of the law to prohibit entry. In effect, Chinese attempting to enter the United States at its southern border prompted Territorial Commissioners to weigh the significance of Mexican citizenship or nationality against exclusion laws that targeted Chinese originating from China. The largely informal category of "discharge" emerged from Chinese residents and citizens of Mexico who fell outside the official purview of exclusion laws. This discursive practice also allowed officials to maintain a guise of enforcing the law.

Not all appreciated the consequences of these distinctions. Exclusionists had good reason to fear a "Chinese invasion" from the southern border, because, in fact, several hundred Chinese began to pour into the Mexican port cities of Guaymas and Mazatlán intent on crossing into the United States by way of San Diego and Nogales.[35] Customs officials in San Diego echoed these concerns and were impatient with the Arizona practice of discharging Chinese. This practice, they felt, made a mockery of their exclusion efforts. "To take them to the line and turn them loose below it, does no good whatsoever, as they simply take the first opportunity to cross again," remarked collector Berry. "The farce enacted [occurs] when officials backs are turned [and] the opportunity is created for their returning again."[36]

For a while, conflicting perceptions about Chinese laborers from Mexico widened the divide between San Diego and southern Arizona officials. However, after 1900, mounting political pressure forced the hand of American immigration officials at the border. The actions that had once ensured deportation of laborers to Mexico and the travel of merchants to the United States became relics of the past. Rather than maintain immigration procedures based on the preservation of the transnational lives of Chinese laborers and merchants, American officials mimicked the restrictionist practices of the ports of San Francisco and New York. This meant that laborers were routinely deported to China while merchants' petitions to travel into the United States were received with intense circumspection.[37] Curiously, neither law nor statute mandated these changes.

By the early 1900s, the importance of Mexican nationality and citizenship lessened significantly. In 1902, exclusionists, responding somewhat to the high numbers of Chinese entering the United States through its southern border, suspended the immigration of Chinese laborers for another ten years. These laws made it nearly impossible for any Chinese person originating from Mexico to enter the United States. Even extraordinary diplomatic efforts by Mexican and American officials who advocated admission for Chinese Mexicans were no match for the enforcement of exclusion laws. The bureaucratic machinery also increased at the border when, in 1903, the Bureau of Immigration was placed under the authority of the Department of Commerce and Labor to strengthen controls at the Mexican border. At the beginning of the twentieth century, race, in effect, cast a wide net over Chinese Mexican merchants and many hundreds of laborers caught at the U.S. southern border and crossing into the United States from Mexico assumed greater organization. No longer were Chinese traversing through the border without the assistance of vast smuggling operations. *Coyotes* (smugglers) were but one link in a transnational network of human trafficking responsible for substantially increasing illegal entries from Mexico. Their activities, a direct response to the grip of Chinese exclusion laws, would continue to plague the U.S.-Mexico border over the next few decades.

A Nest of Corruption: Smuggling Chinese through the Underground Railroad

At the turn of the twentieth century, the sparsely populated border region around the twin border cities of Nogales, Arizona, and Nogales, Sonora, became the principal thoroughfare by which smugglers channeled Chinese from Mexican port cities of Salina Cruz, Manzanillo, Mazatlán, and Guaymas. Once across the international boundary, smugglers moved "contraband" Chinese to Los Angeles and San Francisco via southern Arizona. For those seeking to profit from the geographic convenience and economic demand of smuggling Chinese into the United States from the Arizona-Sonora corridor, the clandestine activity proved lucrative and reasonably easy to facilitate. With the exception of an occasional Southern Pacific train route or patrol by customs line riders on horseback, the barren Sonoran desert seemed an open field for Chinese traversing north.

The systematic practice of trafficking Chinese into the United States from Mexico began in the early 1900s along the Arizona-Sonora corridor. When a plot to smuggle 20,000 Chinese "coolies" from Guaymas was discovered in 1903, Arizona immigration authorities were already in the midst of exposing the so-called underground railroad. The stealthy movements of smugglers and their clients brought in thousands of Chinese by way of covert transportation on stagecoaches, boxcars, and burros. This method allowed for both the evasion of exclusion and the avoidance of deportation. Jim Bennett, the mastermind of this elaborate smuggling scheme that began in 1901, had controlled operations so meticulously that it took immigration officials over three years to uncover the plot. The clandestine route, originating in the Sonoran port city of Guaymas, meandered through Hermosillo, Cananea, Magdalena, and Naco. In Arizona the underground route twisted through the Santa Cruz and Santa Rita mountain ranges where border crossers took a respite in the railroad town of Fairbank, Arizona. Making Fairbank the main terminal of activity, Bennett was able to maintain a constant flow of Chinese border crossers from Sonora into southern Arizona.

Bennett's operation proved remarkably resilient even in the face of vigilant Chinese inspectors who were well aware of the existence of smuggling rings in the area. Rather than err on the side of haste, the success of the operation depended on time-tested relationships forged between the ringleader and his assistants. Relying entirely on his own careful discernment of character and temperament, Bennett hired men to generate business in Sonora, monitor the routines of immigrant agents, and harbor Chinese border crossers. Bennett's approach proved quite successful. His shrewd manner of selecting smugglers engendered such a high degree of confidence among fellow guides that the Fairbank gang was reputed to have netted thousands of dollars a month from their efforts. Without fear of detection, Bennett and his crew escorted Chinese laborers into the United States for a fee that ranged from $50 to $200.[38] Usually the collection of the full fare for passage occurred in the city of final destination. In other instances, the smugglers required a good-faith payment at Fairbank. As a longstanding rule, Chinese border crossers needed to prove to the smugglers that they possessed the full fee for passage before proceeding to California.[39]

The illicit activity that facilitated the passage of hundreds of Chinese into the United States relied on clever techniques of forgery and deception. Bennett's ring seemed heavily dependent on the efforts of three men, Lee Quong, Louis Greenwaldt, and B. C. Springstein.[40] While Quong escorted Chinese through the underground route, Greenwaldt and Springstein forged certificates of residence to ensure the safe passage of border crossers once in the United States. Greenwaldt, a former San Quentin convict who served a term of six years for Chinese smuggling in 1892, joined Springstein in Cananea, Sonora, to complete the forgery ring.[41] Armed with a metal plate for imprinting documents, rubber stamps, and a seal maker that impressed

"O. M. Welburn Internal Revenue Collector, First District of California," the Fairbank gang produced replicas of certificates of residence.[42] The team of Springstein and Greenwaldt duplicated over 300 certificates, and for $100 filled in the appropriate information for passage.[43]

As soon as Chinese nationals secured a certificate, they sojourned north with Lee Quong and one of his assistants. Quong, nicknamed "The Jew" and "Sheeney John" because he allegedly resembled someone of the "He brew race," employed Wonk Tunk and Charley Lee to aid him in the efforts to escort and harbor Chinese.[44] Fluent in English, Quong was also a part-time truck farmer in the area who, at times, sold his produce in nearby Bisbee and Tombstone. However, Quong's principal occupation was that of Chinese smuggler. Taking advantage of the long-distance patrolling techniques of immigrant inspectors, Quong and Tunk loaded Chinese posing as Mexicans into boxcars destined for northern Sonora. To blur the line between Chinese and Mexican, Quong and Tuck had their Chinese patrons "cut off their queues and dressed as Mexicans" to escape detection.[45] Once they were safely inside boxcars, Quong quickly refastened the door seal as if it had not been broken. In northern Sonora, the Chinese would travel to the final destination of Fairbank on a road not recently patrolled by inspectors. By closely monitoring the routines of Chinese inspectors, Quong could fairly easily determine the routes he and his clients could take into Fairbank. Bennett's guides and their patrons traveled without fear of detection and were relatively successful in gaining passage without incident.

Chinese inspector Charles Connell cracked the smuggling ring after months of trailing the Fairbanks gang. Appointed as inspector only eighteen months before the bust, Connell was no stranger to politically controversial activity. Born in Mount Vernon, Iowa, and educated on the East Coast, Connell arrived in Arizona during its pioneering days. At the age of twenty-one, in 1880, he administered the first census of the Apache Indians at the San Carlos Reservation.[46] Considered a foremost authority on the tribe, Connell served as a "diplomatic agent" to the Apache on behalf of the federal government.[47] Only a few years later, when the Spanish-American War broke out, Captain Connell continued his government duties as a secret service agent along the U.S.-Mexican border. From this experience, Connell reportedly carried a mental map of the entire Mexican border between El Paso and San Diego and "knew every trail, road, pass, canyon, mountain and water hole."[48] His experience as an Apache agent and wartime officer proved quite appropriate in Connell's future duties for the federal government, especially in his duties as Chinese inspector that began early in 1903.[49]

On a visit to Naco, Sonora with special immigrant agent V. M. Clark, Inspector Connell encountered two Chinese men who had in their possession blank certificates of residence. The two border crossers stated that they had secured their documents from Springstein. Connell, in an attempt to confirm their account, queried federal immigration authorities who had supposedly issued the official certificates of residence. Numbers located at the upper left corner of the documents in question seemingly confirmed their authenticity. As it turned out, Connell's watchful eye caught an inconsistency not found in official certificates of residence: an additional letter "m."[50] Even though Connell and Clark were acting outside their jurisdiction, they pursued the case into Sonora, arrested Springstein, and confiscated mounds of evidence against the ringleader.[51] Springstein confessed to his illegal activity soon after agents interrogated the smuggler in their "sweat box."[52] Among those implicated were Quong, Greenwaldt, and Bennett. Moreover, written evidence recounting the particulars of smuggling cast doubt on Quong's innocence. Connell came upon a letter written by Quong to his friend, Ho Kwong:

> Yesterday I received a letter from you acknowledging the receipt of $25 sent for urgent use and speaking of your having five pieces of merchandise [*sic*] there are white men who would take a hand if there should be customers to be smuggled over right along. . . . A few days ago they got Wong Shai In, Wong Chun Yick, Yee Tuk Wai, and several others . . . you cannot smuggle anybody out by the fast trains. . . . There are boats now coming from China to Guaymas, which will no doubt bring over a great many customers. Just as soon as you receive any let me know immediately without fail.[53]

With the arrests of Quong and Springstein, inspectors concentrated their efforts on apprehending the elusive Greenwaldt and Bennett. Greenwaldt, who possessed the original metal plate used to manufacture fraudulent certificates, managed to evade Connell. Before his escape to Vancouver, British Columbia, Greenwaldt left Springstein holding six hundred unused certificates of residence. Once Greenwaldt arrived in Canada, he immediately established a regular line of ships of Chinese nationals headed for the port of Guaymas.[54] Bennett, the founder of the line, also escaped the grips of Connell and lived in "princely fashion as an American capitalist in Mexico." With the conviction and deportation of Quong in June 1904, Arizona and Sonora's underground railroad ceased operation.[55]

Before his deportation, Quong revealed several poignant aspects of the smuggling ring. He testified that he witnessed Chinese being routinely packed into boxcars and provided with food and water in their trek toward San Francisco, the principal destination of most crossers. In one unfortunate incident, Quong described the capture of five Chinese crossers traveling in a Southern Pacific boxcar on their way to San Francisco. One crosser died of thirst along the way, and others suffered severe dehydration. Despite his detailed description of incidents of Chinese smuggling, Quong denied all participation in the ring and tried to preserve his status in the United States by producing a seemingly authentic certificate of residence issued out of San Francisco.[56] After hearing the testimony of Arizona residents Frank Meyer, Gus Klein, and George McDonald, authorities deported Quong to China.[57]

Exclusion's Southern Gate

From the early 1880s to the late 1890s, the lives of Chinese merchants and laborers at the U.S.-Mexico border were not always sharply constrained by social class, nationality, or race. Family ties, the search for work, and the maintenance of transnational economic exchange between Chinese merchants in northern Mexico and those in the

United States softened exclusionists' calls for the closure of the American southern border. Merchant fronterizos continued to travel to Chinatowns in San Francisco, Tucson, San Diego, Los Angeles, and El Paso to supply their stores and cultivate economic and social relationships. At the same time, their dealings with border officials demonstrate that they could not completely escape the forces of U.S. immigration restrictionism. In a similar fashion, the power of exclusion did not completely overtake Chinese laborers as they engaged in extraordinary measures to avoid deportation to China when caught at the border. Nonetheless, after 1900, the re-entrenchment of exclusion laws marked the Chinese of Mexico racially. Mexican nationality or citizenship no longer facilitated Chinese admission into the United States or deportations to Mexico, while smuggling emerged concomitantly with the intensification of exclusion, especially after the U.S. Congress extended the laws indefinitely in 1904.[58] The resonance of Chinese border life has modern-day reverberations for Mexicans crossing north. Chinese fronterizos and Mexican immigrants traversed the same routes and aspired to maintain similar transnational ties while facing comparable challenges at the border. Then and now, racialized borders remain constant expressions of immigration restrictionism, and the most poignant and enduring reminders of the immigrant experience.

Notes

I am grateful for the assistance of my colleagues and friends in this endeavor. Luís Leobardo Arroyo, Xiaolan Bao, Maria E. Ramas, Jessica Wang, and K. Scott Wong provided incisive and meaningful comment. Without the urgings of these individuals, this project would certainly have fallen quite short of the mark. Special thanks are due Julie Rivera for her timely assistance. Paul Worsmer, Director of Archival Operations at the National Archives and Records Administration, Pacific Region (Laguna Niguel), proves once again that the work of historians would be much more arduous if not for the genius of archivists.

1 This essay is part of a larger research project on the history of Chinese along the U.S.-Mexico border. See Grace Delgado, "In the Age of Exclusion: Race, Region, and Chinese Identity in the Making of the Arizona-Sonora Borderlands, 1863–1943" (Ph.D. diss., University of California, Los Angeles, 2000). My goal here, if only partially, is to uncover a history that shows Chinese life as simultaneously local and transnational. I draw on the seminal work of Charles Cumberland, Leo Michael Dambourges Jacques, and Evelyn Hu-DeHart. Building on some central experiences scholars have established as common ground, my work here advances our understanding of the Chinese in Mexico that reaches across national borders. See Charles C. Cumberland, "The Sonoran Chinese and the Mexican Revolution," *Hispanic American Historical Review* 40:2 (1960): 191–211; and the following essays by Evelyn Hu-DeHart: "Immigrants to a De-

veloping Society: The Chinese in Northern Mexico, 1875–1932," *Journal of Arizona History* 21 (1980): 49–86; "Racism and Anti-Chinese Persecution in Sonora, Mexico, 1876–1932," *Amerasia* 9 (1982): 1–28; and "Coolies, Shopkeepers, Pioneers: The Chinese of Mexico and Peru," *Amerasia* 15 (1989): 91–116. The most comprehensive work on the Chinese in Sonora remains Leo Michael Dambourges Jacques, "The Anti-Chinese Campaigns in Sonora, 1900–1931" (Ph.D. diss., University of Arizona, 1974).

2 The Qing dynasty perceived overseas Chinese as deserters, traitors, rebels, and conspirators who rejected their filial duties. Despite the possibility of harsh punishment upon their return, over 125,000 Chinese emigrated to the Americas by 1880. See Lynn Pan, ed., *The Encyclopedia of the Chinese Overseas* (Cambridge: Harvard University Press 1999), 98.

3 John R. Berry to J. G. Carlisle, Secretary of the Treasury, 1 April 1893. Record Group 36, San Diego Collection District, Letters Sent to the Secretary of the Treasury, 1892–1908 (9L-39) National Archives and Record Administration/ Pacific Region at Laguna Niguel (hereafter referred to as NARA/LN). San Diego Collection referred to hereafter as SDCD-LSST.

4 By 1890, the frequency of illegal border crossings prompted U.S. congressional members to form a subcommittee to inspect immigration issues at the San Diego–Mexico border. See San Diego Customs District-Special Agents, Letters Sent (SDCD-SALS), John R. Berry to Anthony Godbe, 8 December 1890.

5 Robert H. Duncan, "The Chinese and the Economic Development of Northern Baja California," *Hispanic American Historical Review* 74:4 (1994): 616.

6 Mexico, Ministero de Fomento, *Boletín semestral de la dirección general de estadística de la República Mexicana, año de 1892.* Número X (México, D.F.: n.p., 1892), 418–19; and Mexico, *Anuario estadístico de la República Mexicana,* vol. 15 (México: n.p., 1893–1899).

7 Miguel Tinker Salas, *In the Shadow of the Eagles: Sonora and the Transformation of the Border during the Porfiriato* (Berkeley: University of California Press, 1997), 225.

8 I use the contemporary term, "Baja," rather than the anachronistic "Lower California" when referring to both Baja California Norte and Baja California Sur.

9 Thomas Arnold to the Secretary of the Treasury, 25 February 1890. Record Group 36, San Diego Collection District, Outgoing General Correspondence (9L-38) 1885–1909, NARA/LN. Hereafter referred to as SDCD-OGC.

10 Duncan, "Chinese and Economic Development," 618.

11 Evelyn Hu-DeHart, "The Chinese of Baja California Norte, 1910–1934," *Proceedings of the Pacific Coast Council on Latin American Studies* 12 (1985–86): 15.

12 *United States v. Lee Sing,* 1412 AZ-CCF [Records of the District Court of the United States for the Territory of Arizona, First Judicial District, Criminal Case Files, 1882–1912]. A database of these records is in the possession of the author.

13 *United States vs. Lee Sing [alias Gee Sing],* 823 AZ-CCF.

14 Letters received from the Treasury Department, 1880–1909, box 3. Record group 36, San Diego Collection District, (9L-44), NARA/LN. Hereafter referred to as SDCD-LRTD.

15 *United States v. Lee Sing,* 1412 AZ-CCF.

16 Lucy E. Salyer, *Laws Harsh as Tigers: Chinese Immigrants and the Shaping of Modern Immigration Law* (Chapel Hill: University of North Carolina Press, 1995), 46.

17 *United States v. Ah Chung,* 1099; *United States v. Hi Chung,* 1100; *United States v. Ah Suey,* 1101; *United States v. Mary Fong and Wong Fong,* 1291 AZ-CCF.

18 *United States v. Mary Fong and Wong Fong,* 1291 AZ-CCF.

19 *United States v. Lee Sing,* 1422.

20 William Wallace Bowers to the Commissioner General of Immigration, 20 May 1902; SDCD-OGC.

21 In 1891 the Secretary of the Treasury supervised immigration and a year later established twenty-four customs inspection stations including those border districts in San Diego and Nogales. The primary focus of these districts in terms of immigration was to enforce Chinese exclusion laws. The Collector of Customs also received applications for return certificates from Chinese individuals wishing to travel abroad.

22 This statistic derives from a database of over six hundred Chinese exclusion and criminal case files from the Arizona Territory and Southern District Court of California. Compiled by the author, the database highlights twenty-three fields of information such as place of arrest, Chinese interpreter, deportation destination, and commissioner. The database draws from the following files of record group 21: Records of the District Court of the United States for the Territory of Arizona, First Judicial District, Chinese Criminal Case Files, 1882–1912 [AZ-CCF]; Chinese Exclusion Cases, 1886–1906 [AZ-CEC]; Commissioners' Early Case Files [AZ-CECF]; Commissioners' Dockets [AZ-CD]; and Commissioners' Case Files, 1882–1912, [AZ-CMCF]; NARA/LN. The database from hereafter is referred to as CEDZZCA (the Chinese Exclusion Case File Database for Southern Arizona and Southern California).

23 John R. Berry to L. S. Irvin, 3 April 1890, SDCD-OGC; John R. Berry to William Windom, 7 April 1890, SDCD-OGC.

24 John R. Berry to William Windom, 7 April 1890, SDCD-OGC.

25 John R. Berry to M. G. Montaño, 17 June 1890, SDCD-SALR [Special Agents Letters Received].

26 General Luís E. Torres to John R. Berry, 19 June 1890, SDCD-SALS.

27 *San Diego Union,* 21 May 1890.

28 *San Diego Union,* 23, 25 and 27 May 1890.

29 John R. Berry to T. J. Monahau, 18 November 1890, SDCD-SALS.

30 A. E. Higgins to William Windom, 12 July 1890, SDCD-OGC.

31 CEDAZCA, 378, 388, 390–410.

32 *United States v. Ah Hoon [alias Ning Hoon and Ning Ah Goon],* 398 AZ-CCF.

33 *United States v. Chu Yun [alias Chin Yan]*, 387; *United States v. Sam Hing*, 413; *United States v. Charley Quong*, 416; *United States v. Charley Ah Fong*, 417 AZ-CCF.

34 *United States v. Chu Yun [alias Chin Yan]*, 387 AZ-CCF.

35 W. W. Bowers to the Commissioner General of Immigration, 5 April 1902, SDCD-OGC.

36 John R. Berry to William Windom, 3 April 1890, SDCD-OGC.

37 The four exceptional cases are: *United States v. Fong Soon*, 568; *United States v. Ah Loo*, 944; *United States v. Hop Sam*, 1585; and *United States v. Yee Kim*, 1588 CEDAZCA.

38 *The Border Vidette*, 21 August 1901.

39 *The Bulletin: Sunday Magazine*, 21 August 1904.

40 Lee Quong was also known as Lee Quan. See *Bisbee Daily Review*, 18 August 1903.

41 *San Francisco Examiner*, 13 June 1904.

42 The Charles Connell Collection, Manuscript 188, Scrapbook of Charles Connell, newspaper article entitled "Chinese Ring Broken Up: Agent of Smugglers' Chief, Who Is a San Franciscan, Arrested and Outfit for Making Bogus Certificates Seized," Arizona Historial Society. Hereafter referred to as CCC-AHS.

43 *San Francisco Examiner*, 13 June 1904. Greenwaldt and Springstein sold blank certificates of residence for $50. See edition of 18 June 1904.

44 CCC-AHS, Scrapbook of John Murphy, folder 3, newspaper article entitled "Important Arrest of Chinese Smuggler: Inspector Connell Captures Lee Quan [*sic*] on the San Pedro River," not dated.

45 *San Francisco Bulletin*, 21 August 1904.

46 *Los Angeles Times*, 27 January 1931. Also see the *Los Angeles Examiner*, 26 December 1928 and *The Gazette and Republican*, 15 March 1931.

47 *Arizona Republican*, 12 April 1934. See CCC-AHS, box 2, folder II, paper entitled "Excerpt from McClintock's History of Arizona."

48 *Los Angeles Examiner*, 26 December 1928.

49 *Los Angeles Times*, 27 January 1931.

50 *Los Angeles Examiner*, 13 June 1904.

51 *San Francisco Examiner*, 13 June 1904. Part of the evidence included a camera and several fountain pens. Inspector Clark made Springstein demonstrate how he filled out the certificates, placed the seal on the document, and took the photographs.

52 *Los Angeles Examiner*, 13 June 1904. See also Charles Connell Collection, Scrapbook, newspaper article entitled "Chinese Ring Broke Up: Agent of Smugglers' Chief, Who Is a San Franciscan, Arrested and Outfit for Making Bogus Certificates Seized." AHS. The *San Francisco Bulletin* reports quite a different story about the breakup of the ring. The newspaper attributed the breakup to the daring persistence of Charles Connell. One day Connell pulled a lone Chinaman off a boxcar at Naco, Sonora, and was en route to Fairbank.

In his possession was a paper, which bore the name of Lee Quong. Connell, pursing his suspicions, discovered that Quong had also been harboring Chinese nationals at Crance Ranch. See 21 August 1904. See newspaper articles entitled "Connell Meets a Wily Chink" and "An Elusive Chink Caught" for the type of chivalrous portrayal of the inspector's exploits. The use of "chink" was quite common when referring to Chinese border crossers in Arizona newspapers. For those Chinese established in Tucson as legal residents, Arizona newspapers did not use these racial epithets. See the Scrapbook of Charles Connell, and box 2, folder 2, CCC-AHS. The American newspapers, *Harper's Weekly,* and *Harper's Weekly Illustrated Magazine* also use similar racist language. Similarly, Sonora educator and politician José María Arana espoused vitriol when referring to the Chinese as dogs, pestilence, and as "having the venom of serpents."

53 Scrapbook of Charles Connell, newspaper article entitled "Lee Quong Deported: Three Americans Testify Positively to His Identity." The letter written by Quong to Kwong is dated 23 April 1903. CCC-AHS. The *Bisbee Review* reported that only three hundred certificates were confiscated during the raid. See edition of 10 June 1904.

54 *Los Angeles Examiner,* 25 June 1904.

55 *The Bulletin,* 21 August 1904.

56 Connell Scrapbook, newspaper article, "Lee Quong to be Deported: Three Americans Testify Positively to His Identity," undated. Yet, another account reveals that the Chinese were smuggled into the United States embarking in El Paso via Yuma to San Francisco—the final point of destination. Connell has reported several incidents where Chinese who were loaded into boxcars died of thirst very quickly. See Connell Scrapbook, "How Chinks Were Smuggled." CCC-AHS.

57 Connell Scrapbook, newspaper article, "One Less Chink: Lee Quong Ordered Deported by Commissioner Pirtle," undated. For an account about the smuggling of Chinese into the United States, see W. W. Husband to Henry L. Stimson, Secretary of State, 6 June 1929. CCC-AHS. The Chinese Six Companies remained complicit in the smuggling rings that were expanded into underground routes of passage into Lower California.

58 The U.S. Congress passed this act on 29 April 1904. This new bill regulated Chinese immigration on the expiration of the 1894 treaty between China and the United States. In effect, the bill separated domestic legislation on Chinese immigration from treaty obligations with China. As a result, exclusion laws grew even more stringent while the Chinese were restricted from U.S. shores indefinitely.

The Invisible Immigrants

Eric Lai and Dennis Arguelles, Eds.

Cambodian Americans

Cambodians, also known as the Khmer, started arriving in the United States two decades ago in the aftermath of the Vietnam War. Survivors of a terrible genocide, nearly all of the more than 200 thousand Cambodian Americans of single and mixed-descent counted by the 2000 Census were once refugees or are children of refugees.

The Refugee Act of 1980 codified and strengthened the U.S. policy of aiding individuals fleeing persecution. Of the approximately 1.64 million refugees who have arrived in the United States since 1983, 39 percent fled from either Cambodia, Laos or Vietnam. The Refugee Act also strengthened today's asylum adjudication process and created a federal Office of Refugee Resettlement (ORR). Cambodians Americans were among the earliest beneficiaries of the ORR's programs.

While those pro-immigrant and humanitarian policies helped the Cambodian American population grow quickly during the 1980s and early 1990s, recent immigration trends have had an unfortunate and detrimental impact upon the Cambodian American community. A prime example is the June 2001 ruling by the U.S. Supreme Court, which found that it was illegal or the Immigration and Naturalization Service (INS) to hold a Cambodian man indefinitely if it cannot deport him in a reasonable time. At the time, Cambodia was one of the few countries that did not accept deportees.

Until this decision, despite civil and human rights concerns, individuals who had already served their criminal sentences were re-incarcerated and, in some instances, held for years in INS detention facilities and contracted jails across the country. Rather than release such people, the U.S. Government instead increased its efforts to make Cambodia accept deportees. Such a repatriation agreement was signed in the spring of 2002. In June of that year, six Cambodians were deported, with more slated for forced removal.

Looking Back at a Troubled Past

Located in the heart of Southeast Asia, Cambodia is a small country about the physical size of the state of Oklahoma, bordered by Laos, Vietnam, and Thailand. The country, despite being officially neutral, inevitably found itself embroiled in the Vietnam War and its own Communist uprising in the form of the Khmer Rouge, led by Pol Pot. From 1969 to 1973, the U.S. secretly conducted air-bombing raids on North Vietnamese troops over the Cambodian border, despite Cambodia's neutrality.

The bombings caused Cambodian civilian casualties and damage to land and property that added to ever-increasing anti-American sentiment and a rise in the support for the communist Khmer Rouge. The carpet-bombing of Cambodia's countryside by American B-52s has been identified as one of the most important factors in the rise of Pol Pot and the Khmer Rouge. When U.S. forces withdrew from the region in 1975, the Khmer Rouge soon defeated the U.S.-dependant Cambodian government.

After taking power in April 1975, the Khmer Rouge began to implement a wholesale restructuring of Cambodian society with the intent of creating an agrarian socialist state. The mechanism for this change was forced labor camps and the systematic murder of all political opposition, those of minority ethnic groups, individuals from religious, professional and educated segments of society, and all others who questioned the new order. The Khmer Rouge dissolved institutions such as banks, hospitals, schools, stores, religion, and attempted to unravel the fabric of the family. Children were separated from their parents to work in mobile groups or as soldiers.

In proportion, the genocide in Cambodia rivals that of the Jewish holocaust. During the Khmer Rouge's reign from 1975 to 1979, about one-third of the Cambodian population died by starvation, torture or execution—2 million in total. In 1979, the Vietnamese government wrested control of the country, putting an end to Khmer Rouge rule. With the fall of the Khmer Rouge and Vietnamese occupation, 600,000 refugees fled to refugee camps along the Thai border. Although refugees began arriving in the United States after the fall of Cambodia in 1975, the overthrow of the Khmer Rouge in 1979 marked the true beginning of the Cambodian mass exodus and arrival in America.

Immigration Patterns

The 1980 Census was the first to count Cambodians in the United States. It found 16,044, of which nearly half that number (7,739) had been admitted as refugees. During the 1980s, liberal refugee admission policies helped the Cambodian American population increase nine times to 149,047 in the 1990 Census. According to INS statistics, 114,064 Cambodians were admitted as refugees during the 1980s.

Refugee admissions tapered off sharply in the 1990s. From 1991 to 1998, only 6,150 Cambodians were admitted as refugees, according to the INS. The Cambodian community continued to grow, according to the 2000 Census. There are 171,937 Cambodians of single descent, a 13 percent increase over 1990, and 206,052 Cambodians, including those of mixed-race and mixed-ethnicity.

It should be noted that measuring the demographics of the Cambodian American community has historically been challenging; it is widely suspected that the community is repeatedly undercounted by the Census Bureau. A 1992 report sponsored by the Center of Survey Methods Research of the Census Bureau identified language barriers, mistrust of strangers and the government, and unusual residence and household composition as significantly affecting Census counts. That report recommended that "Cambodian" should be added to the list of Asian ethnicities in the Census questionnaire form to make it easier for respondents to identify themselves. Although there is a growing recognition that overly-broad ethnic categories can obscure communities with special needs, the Census Bureau declined to add "Cambodian" to its 2000 Census questionnaire.

Policy and Societal Challenges

Despite their unique position as Asian holocaust survivors and refugees, Cambodian Americans are still largely overlooked by policy makers. Since the implementation of 1996 immigration and welfare reform laws, Cambodians have been caught up in a dragnet of immigration policies and social service policies that limit benefits to non-citizens and require the mandatory detention and deportation of those convicted of crimes.

Although a number of Cambodians have managed to find success in the United States, many continue to face challenges related to their refugee resettlement experience. The donut shop business in California has felt the hand of Cambodian American entrepreneurship. It is estimated that as much as 90 percent of California's 5,000 independent donut shops are Cambodian owned. However, the community as a whole, according to 1990 Census data available at the time of this writing, still deals with a high poverty rate (47 percent), poor English fluency (56 percent are rated as "linguistically isolated"), and low levels of educational achievement (only 6 percent of Cambodians over the age of 25 have a bachelor's degree from a university).

Learning English is a challenge for many Cambodians, who by and large arrived with a lack of formal education. The Khmer Rouge genocide decimated the educated and professional classes. As a result, Southeast Asian refugees (not including the Vietnamese), of whom Cambodians are a prominent percentage, have the lowest educational level, averaging just 3.1 years of schooling before arriving in the United States. Refugees from Latin America have 11.0 years of schooling; refugees from Africa have 7.5 years before coming to America, according to an ORR report.

This language barrier has made it difficult for many first-generation Southeast Asian Americans to become full-fledged citizens because they are unable to pass the English-language portion of the citizenship test. Due to the fact their parents have not become citizens, the 1.5 generation of Cambodian Americans (young people who arrived as infants or small children but have largely grown up in America) remain non-citizens. This has made them particularly vulnerable to changes in U.S. policies directed broadly at "aliens" or non-citizens.

The legacy of the Cambodian holocaust creates some of the most challenging barriers to Cambodian American political empowerment. Having survived near-starvation, violence, and torture, many Cambodians in this country still continue to struggle with day-to-day survival and consequently lack interest in civic participation. Because of their histories of being oppressed by the government, some Cambodians continue to harbor fear and distrust of the government and remain largely ignorant of their civic responsibilities.

Upcoming data from the 2000 Census is expected to show improved statistics in areas like education, poverty, and language fluency, due to more second and third generation Cambodian Americans. The implication of how current U.S. policies are negatively impacting the Cambodian American community exposes need for greater representation, advocacy and civic participation on their behalf. In looking at the past twenty years of Cambodian American history, it is clear that the community has come along way in a short period, but there is still much work to be done. Through greater civic and political participation, Cambodian Americans can guide their own course, empower themselves, and foster positive community development.

—Porthira Chhim

The Hmong in America

The Hmong people are an ethnic group whose origins go back about 3,000 years in China. Most Hmong—about eight million—still live in southwestern China. Another four million live in the Southeast Asian countries of Thailand, Burma, Laos and Vietnam, where they immigrated during the 19th century following centuries of persecution in China. There, they existed mostly as farmers living in rural areas.

Before 1975, there were just a handful of Hmong in America, most of them university students from Thailand or Laos. The first Hmong migration of notable size to the United States began with the fall of Saigon and Laos to Communist forces in 1975. Many Hmong had worked with pro-American anti-Communist forces during the conflicts in Vietnam and Laos. As a result, they were subject to violence and retribution in Laos. Many Hmong escaped Laos to Thailand where they were incarcerated in refugee camps.

First Wave Settlement

From the late 1970s to the mid-1990s, large numbers of Hmong refugees were resettled in the United States. The peak was 1980, when 27,000 Hmong refugees were admitted. From 1981 to 1986, the number of Hmong refugees slowed to a few thousand each year, but admissions picked up again between 1987 and 1994, when about 56,000 Hmong refugees were accepted. After 1994, Hmong refugee admissions slowed to a trickle as most of the Thai camps were by now empty, with the remaining Hmong repatriated to Laos, Also, Hmong immigration based on family reunification remains low, especially compared to other Southeast Asian ethnic groups.

Where did the Hmong settle? With the first wave that arrived in the late 1970s and early 1980s, voluntary resettlement agencies consciously tried to disperse the Hmong around the country in a number of locales. At that time, sizeable Hmong populations could be found in East Coast cities like Providence, Rhode Island and Philadelphia, Pennsylvania; in Mid-western cities like Chicago, Des Moines, Iowa, and Kansas City, Kansas; and the western cities of Denver, Colorado, Missoula, Montana, Tulsa, Oklahoma, and Salt Lake City, Utah.

This strategy, however, proved unsuccessful in many instances. Several thousand Hmong, for instance, were settled in a poor, predominantly African American neighborhood in west Philadelphia, where they encountered much hostility and violence. Most of the Hmong moved out within several years. Also, many Hmong wished to be reunited with family and clan members. These reasons led to a massive shift of the Hmong population in the mid-to-late 1980s to central California cities like Fresno, Stockton and Merced, and, to a lesser extent, to Minnesota and Wisconsin. By 1990, Fresno and Central Valley cities like Sacramento, Stockton and Merced were the center of Hmong American population and community life. Census figures show that by far the largest Hmong population at this time was found in California, followed by Minnesota, Wisconsin, Michigan and Colorado. The 1990 census counted 94,439 Hmong Americans across the United States.

Heading to the Midwest and South

During the 1990s, the Hmong moved again: away from the West and towards the Midwest and the South. This shift was epitomized by the emergence of Minneapolis and St. Paul as the unofficial capitals of Hmong America, taking over from Fresno. About half of Hmong today live in the Midwest, mostly in Minnesota, Wisconsin and Michigan, compared to 41 percent in 1990. Meanwhile, the proportion of Hmong in the Western states fell to 42 percent in 2000 from 55 percent in 1990. Nine out of ten in the West lived in California, with much smaller communities found in Colorado, Oregon, Washington and Alaska. Around 6 percent of the Hmong now live in the South, an impressive increase from just 1.3 percent in 1990. This movement was focused within a few states, such as North and South Carolina. In 2000, the Hmong population numbered in the Northeastern states remained very small, at just 2 percent.

By 2000, there were 169,428 Hmong numbered in America, representing a nearly 90 percent increase in the population from 1990. Many agree, however, that the figure is probably a significant undercount. The Twin Cities claimed 40,707 Hmong residents. Second was Fresno, California, with 22,456. After Fresno, the largest Hmong populations in the United States in 2000 were found in Sacramento-Yolo, Milwaukee-Racine, and Merced.

Why did Minneapolis St. Paul emerge as the new Hmong American capital? The opportunity to make a better life seems to be at the heart of things.

"The cost of living is cheaper here than in California," Lee Pao Xiong, president of the Urban Coalition in St. Paul, told the Associated Press. "The quality of education is better here, and jobs are available here."

Xiong said he's recruited 10 families from his own extended family to come here from California in recent years. "They came here and they found jobs within a month or two and are making ten, eleven, twelve dollars an hour," he said.

A 2002 community directory provides listings of 13 Hmong community organizations and 39 Hmong religious congregations in the Minneapolis-St. Paul area. Whereas many Hmong in California's Central Valley have taken up their old occupations of farming, those in Minneapolis have found jobs working in factories. But there is a substantial emerging class of Hmong small business owners—many of them congregated near St. Paul's University Avenue, also known for its Vietnamese businesses—and college-educated Hmong professionals going into fields like law, medicine, and non-profit management. Hmong are opening restaurants serving Lao or Thai cuisine, though traditional Hmong dishes are available upon request. And the United States' first Hmong politician, a 32-year-old female lawyer named Mee Moua, was elected to the Minnesota State Senate in 2002.

In the Twin Cities metro area, most Hmong live in St. Paul, which also hosts an annual New Year celebration and a summer sports tournament that attracts thousands of Hmong to visit from around the United States.

Steady Climb into the Middle Class

The Hmong came to America less-prepared for the modern capitalistic society of their new home than most other immigrant groups. Most had been farmers in their native country, and did not graduate from high school or the equivalent. As a result, many Hmong families when they first arrived were forced to go on public assistance. In 1990, the median Hmong household income was about $11,000, compared to $30,356 among all Americans. 67.1 percent of Hmong lived below the poverty line in 1990, compared to about 13 percent of all Americans.

In 1990, only 15 percent of Hmong owned their homes. While income data for Hmong had yet to be released at the time of this writing, housing data from the 2000

Census shows considerable upward socioeconomic movement, as many Hmong settled into stable or more lucrative jobs. 54 percent of Hmong owned their homes by 2000, reported the *Minneapolis Star-Tribune* newspaper. While home ownership was low in California at just 19.3 percent, it was around 55 to 60 percent in states like Minnesota, Wisconsin, Michigan, and North Carolina.

Culture

Traditionally, the Hmong favor large families with many children. Some of this can be explained by the Hmong's traditional farming roots. As a result, Hmong households average more than six persons per house or apartment in Minnesota and Wisconsin, compared to about 2.5 persons among the entire population. This helps explain the huge Hmong American population growth between 1990 and 2000, despite the decline in refugee admissions after 1994. These demographic trends suggest the Hmong population will continue to be among the fastest growing Asian group in the United States in the coming decades.

The large number of Hmong children also makes the population very youthful. Around half or more of the Hmong in California, Minnesota, Wisconsin, North Carolina, and Michigan were under 18 years old in 2000—compared to about a quarter within the general population.

The Hmong are a fairly tight-knit group; many community leaders are old clan leaders or politicians from Laos and are their descendents and relatives. For instance, the Hmong general Vang Pao, who commanded the Hmong forces fighting against the Communist North Vietnamese, remains a political leader for many Hmong in America. After escaping Laos, Vang Pao moved to Orange County, California, and helped found a leading Hmong organization, Lao Family Community. Lao Family Community has branches nationwide, many of them run by people close to Vang Pao or his actual relatives.

Still, there is a new generation of Hmong leaders emerging. They are young, well-educated, and not necessarily willing to be as beholden to old loyalties based on clan affiliation. Cleaved along this generational divide, the younger leaders support the reform of some aspects of Hmong culture that may clash with American customs. For instance, Hmong womens' groups have campaigned against polygamy, domestic violence, and teenage brides—not common but not unheard of among more traditional Hmong. Other leaders are trying to tackle the increasing number of Hmong youth being lured into gangs.

And others are trying to encourage Hmong entrepreneurship, a traditional route to the middle-class for immigrants but one less common with the Hmong. Vang Pao, for instance, has established a program with St. Thomas University in St. Paul to provide technical assistance to Hmong small businesspeople. While Hmong Americans certainly face a number of challenges, they are moving forward into a brighter future.

—Mark E. Pfeifer

Laotian Americans: You're From Where?

Laotian Americans are a very diverse group of people, like the geography of their home country, which is simultaneously tropical and mountainous. Laos is approximately the size of Great Britain, but unlike that island nation, Laos is sparsely populated and landlocked, wedged between Burma (Myanmar), Cambodia, China, Thailand, and Vietnam. While usage standards differ, one increasingly popular trend is to use the term "Laotian" to refer to all people from Laos, regardless of their ethnicity. Since another section of this chapter focuses exclusively on Hmong Americans, who are predominantly from Laos, this section focuses on all of the other Laotian American groups.

As this short piece makes clear, Laotian Americans continue to be diverse in practically every respect: they speak several different languages in the home, follow many different religions, are dispersed throughout the United States, and fill niches at every point along the socioeconomic scale.

History and Culture

According to the 2000 Census, 198,203 Laotian Americans (not including Hmong, but including mixed-race and mixed-ethnicity Laotians) live throughout the United States. Nearly all of them either arrived in this country as refugees or are the children of refugees. Laotian refugees began to arrive in 1975, when the Communist Pathet Lao defeated the U.S. supported government of Laos. Resettlement in the U.S. increased dramatically in the late 1970s and 1980s, after hundreds of thousands of Laotians fled across the Mekong River to Thailand seeking safety in refugee camps.

Resettled refugees from Laos are extremely diverse in terms of culture and language. The dominant group are the Lao Loum, or Lowland Lao, who make up seven-tenths of the population back in Laos. But there are many ethnic minority groups, including the Hmong, most of whom come from upland areas, thus earning them the broad label, Highland Lao.

One such ethnic minority is the Khmu, from the highlands of northern Laos, who are one of the smallest refugee groups in the United States. An estimated half million Khmu live in the mountainous regions of northern Thailand, northern-Laos, northwestern Vietnam, and southwestern China. The ancient homeland of the Khmu is thought to be the area around the city of Luang Prabang in northern Laos. Today, about 4,000 Khmu live in the United States. More than half live in California, in tight-knit communities around the San Francisco Bay area and in Stockton.

Forced to flee conflict many times, the Thaidam people are sometimes referred to as "professional refugees." Uprooted from northern Vietnam in 1954 when the French were defeated, the Thaidam fled to Laos where they lived for only twenty years before seeking asylum again in 1975. About 3,000 Thaidam live in the United States, primarily in Iowa. With a warm welcome from the people of Iowa, the first group of Thaidam came to Des Moines and others quickly followed. Des Moines soon became known as the "free capital of the Thaidam people." Ethnically and linguistically, the Thaidam are related to the Lao and other "Tai" groups.

Community Challenges As Refugees

Because of their refugee status, Laotian Americans face many issues and challenges. Having been exiled from their country to start their lives over again, many Laotians are still facing economic hardship, lack of higher learning opportunities, lack of resources, and lack of cultural traditions, values, and language from their homeland. These issues have led to many problems that the community still faces today, namely juvenile delinquency, unemployment, and intergenerational differences.

As for the Iu-Mein (or Yao) ethnic group, an estimated 20,000 arrived in the United States beginning in 1981. Originally from China, the subsistence-farming Iu-Mien lived in small, mountain communities in Laos. Like the Hmong, they became targets of the Pathet Lao because of their participation with Americans in the "secret war" in Laos. This group arrived without a written language, little exposure to wage labor, and very little experience with formal schooling.

Because of these pre-existing conditions, many Iu-Mien lack the type of skills that today's workforce requires. They have to settle for jobs that require minimal skills to no skills at all, and as a result, they must double their time, or work two jobs just trying to make ends meet. One major consequence is that the children are left at home with little or no supervision. These children consequently suffer academically, because help is unavailable to them in their home environments. Because formal schooling is still a new concept to many of these ex-refugees, the concept of education and educational resources is far out of reach and will remain so unless something is done to introduce the importance of formal education to them. Much more needs to be done in order for these parents, and the Laotian community as a whole, to realize that success in education is a family journey, not just one child or one student's path.

Another current problem in the community is the high rate of Laotian American youth going to prison, reportedly the highest rate among all Southeast Asian youth. Many reasons can be cited for this problem, but lack of parental involvement is a major factor.

Grassroots Network for Educational Success

A total of 105,477 refugees arrived in the United States from Laos between 1979 and 1981, so federally-funded mutual assistance centers throughout the country were formed for these "first wave" refugees; however, many of these centers eventually closed due to lack of funding. Then from 1986 to 1989, a total of 52,864 "second wave" Laotians arrived. Since many mutual assistance centers no longer exist, many older Laotian American immigrants have returned to the community to establish grassroots organizations to help more recent Laotian immigrants. Currently, many non-profit organizations, such as the Southeast Asian Resources Action Center (SEARAC), Laotian American National Alliance, and the Lao American Women Association are playing key roles in the continuous support and advocacy for Laotian Americans.

Regardless of the initial challenges of adapting to a new country, many Laotians are able to find a means of fulfilling their educational goals, managing to overcome obstacles to higher learning. The student network database from the *Lao Vision* magazine website documents and profiles many success stories. Take Soulinhakhath Steve Arounsack who has succeeded despite having very little parental involvement or financial contribution. Through scholarship and grants, Arounsack has earned his bachelor and master's degree and is currently a Ph.D. student at the University of California, Davis. While some students have the ability to succeed, unfortunately not all students have the resources available to them to achieve higher learning—lack of financial resources remain a major challenge. As a result, many are forced, like their parents, to join the workforce with little or no skills, where they must work overtime just to make ends meet. Higher education and gainful employment are still a rare commodity, in the Laotian American community, bringing the "model minority" fallacy to light.

Most young refugees or children of refugees attribute their success to a growing network of Laotian Student Associations at college campuses. These associations provide academic support as well as a strong network of students who share similar cultural experiences. Student and professional groups are also influential, servicing the Laotian community. Satjadham (SJD), a Lao literary group on the Internet, promotes culture, tradition, and language through classical and new literature of Laos to first-generation Laotian Americans. SJD boasts more than 100 members—many are refugees or children of refugees, holding advanced degrees. *Lao Vision* magazine, founded by Kag Khetsavanh (a refugee himself) acts as a forum for educational, intergenerational, cultural, and traditional discussion for younger or first-generation Laotian Americans in the United States.

Maintaining Cultural Identity

One concern that the community now faces is declining cultural practices—which include traditions, values, and language—among a newer generation of Laotian Americans dispersed throughout the country. The 2000 Census figures show just how scattered the Laotian American community is. Predictably, the largest states are California, with around 65,000 Laotians and Texas, with nearly 12,000. But there are many Laotians scattered in the Midwest (Minnesota, Illinois, Wisconsin, and Iowa), and southern states like Georgia and North Carolina. This dispersal challenges a traditionally concentrated and inclusive community. Such Laotian American enclaves now exist, though still rare, in those states with a greater number of Laotian Americans, such as New Iberia in Louisiana, San Diego and Fresno in California, and the Washington D.C. metropolitan area.

The traditional Laotian American family extends beyond a nuclear one, with grandparents and elders serving as respected household leaders. The term "immediate family" includes everyone whose bloodline can be traced within the family. The grandparents, and in some cases, great-grandparents, act as a channel of communication, teaching culture, tradition, and language to the next generation within the extended family structure. Elders continue to pass down many folktales and stories to first generation Laotian Americans through oral tradition, an important aspect of Laotian culture. The oral culture is a significant teaching tool for the elders because many can only speak, but not write, in their own language; so telling *nitaan* (folklores and fables) is their way of sharing their wisdom and learning with younger family members.

Because heritage, culture, and language serve as solid family foundations, the widening cultural gap between older and younger generations has had a significant effect on family structure. Parent-child communication is directly linked to success in society and how cultural traditions and values are passed down. But language barriers between Laotian-speaking parents and their English-speaking children are making them unable to share their unique Laotian and American experiences with each other.

Most Lowland Lao practiced Theravadha Buddhism in Laos. It's a practice they have carried on in the United States, one which has been very helpful for community-building purposes. The Laotian community in the Washington D.C. area for example, gathers at Watlao Buddhavong (Lao Buddhist Temple), in Catlett, Virginia, to celebrate Buddhist holidays and rites. Thousands of Laotians across the nation gather there annually to celebrate Pimai (Lao New Year) in April and the Laotian national independence holiday, which occurs on July 19th. These temples provide a place for interaction among different generations of Laotian Americans and offer weekend language school and other classes like classical dance and music. Because the Lowland Lao have a long-established written language and a history of formal education through Buddhist temples, these classes are merely a continuation of the tradition of learning via temple teaching.

While embracing a new life in the United States, many Laotian Americans continue strictly to practice Laotian traditions through their wedding ceremonies, New Year celebrations, and Buddhist festivals and rites in their daily lives.

Conclusion

From 1975 to 1999, a total of 241,892 Laotian refugees have arrived in the United States. Because Laotian American settlement remains relatively new, more resources and assistance are needed in order for the community to successfully adapt to mainstream society. More importantly, social scientists and other professionals must make the distinction between those who are refugees and those who are immigrants. Different data should be collected, and other factors must be considered before this group can be or should be put on the same page as other Asian Pacific Americans. Social issues, such as gainful employment, higher learning, and familial harmony begin with education, resources, and opportunities for Laotian American community. The "know-how" and "show-me-how" must be shared within the community and within the society.

Ethnic division among Laotian Americans signifies the rich culture and abundant diversity. While embracing the differences, Laotian Americans must realize that one unified voice is a key to social, educational, and political advancement in the United States. As a people of a shared native land in a new nation, they must question, challenge, and demand their rights and privileges through this unified voice. Let's start with the Census count of Laotian Americans, which many of us believe is an undercount. Then add a new ethnic category to the 2010 Census, where Laotian Americans will be allowed to check the same box and specify their ethnicity, i.e. "Laotian American, Low-land Lao ethnicity." This would lead to an accurate count and fair representation of the ethnic diversity of Laotian Americans.

Within the grassroots community, it's also important that all generations of Laotian Americans—past, present, and future—focus on the common issues that face the community. Laotian ethnic diversity aside, one voice will be stronger than the myriad of voices that exist in the community today.

—Toon Phapphayboun, with contribution from Max Niedzwiecki of the Southeast Asia Resource Action Center.

Unveiling the Face of Invisibility: Exploring the Thai American Experience

When you think of "Thailand," what comes to mind? The image of the "Land of Smiles?" The sex industry? Spicy food? It is important that dominant perceptions are challenged and redefined by exploring the ethnic-specific experiences and diversities within the Thai American community. The unique history of Thai immigrants and their struggle for legitimacy within the Asian Pacific American coalition and the mainstream culture will offer a deeper understanding of Thai Americans.

Unlike the more established Asian ethnic groups such as the Chinese and Japanese communities, who first began immigrating in the late nineteenth century, the majority of Thai Americans came to the United States after the passage of the 1965 Immigration Act eliminated the national origins quota system and enabled more Asians to enter the United States. About 27 percent of all Thai Americans came prior to 1975.

Early and Contemporary Immigration Patterns

Between 1965 and 1975, students and professionals made up the first wave of Thai immigrants. The majority of the students sought a Western education because university degrees would mean social advancement in Thailand. The first wave of Thai immigrants settled predominantly east of the city of Hollywood near Los Angeles and other areas of Los Angeles County.

While many Thai immigrants did return to Thailand, the myth of the "American Dream" continued to lure many other Thai immigrants to America. During the second wave, between 1970 and 1980, public protests against the military dictatorship led many Thais to immigrate to other countries such as the United States. Along with the rising political tension, Thailand experienced increasing U.S. presence during the Vietnam War. Consequently, many Thai women married American servicemen who were stationed on military bases in Thailand, which were not removed until 1976. In addition, thousands of Thai nurses responded to the U.S. demand for nurses during this decade and brought their children with them.

The third wave of Thai immigration spans from 1980 to the present, as more students as well as professionals come to America. Because of the decreasing economic opportunities in Thailand, many Thais, especially from rural areas, entered the United States as "undocumented" immigrants and became the new "cheap labor" source in such labor-intensive industries as garment sweatshops.

The Birth of Thai Town and Other Thai Communities

According to a study conducted by the Thai Community Development Center (CDC), there are about 50,000 Thais living and working in Southern California. The largest Thai American community is in Los Angeles, with about 22,000 Thais. In Southern California, Thai families can find a support network and seek social services from churches such as the Wat Thai Buddhist Temple in North Hollywood and community centers like the Thai CDC. To accommodate the growing numbers of Thai immigrants in Los Angeles, the Royal Thai Consulate was established in 1980 to help with immigration policies and legal services.

There are growing numbers of Thai people uncounted by the U.S. Census: undocumented Thais and those who are mixed races (Laotian-Thai, Chinese-Thai, Cambodian-Thai) who may be classified as "Other Asian." Thus, exact figures of Thais in the United States are unknown. According to the 2000 Census, there are 150,283 Thais, including those who reported being Thai mixed with another Asian ethnicity (i.e. Chinese-Thai) or another race such as white or black—or just about one percent of all APAs.

The Thai American community is growing more dispersed, with an emerging population of Thais on the East Coast, particularly in New Jersey. Many Thai immigrants are students and plan to get their education at Ivy League universities, whereas others have established Thai restaurants and markets. Like other Asian immigrants, many first-generation Thais start their own businesses, such as in the restaurant industry. As such, Thai immigrants choose an alternative path of socioeconomic mobility and develop a kind of "ethnic enclave economy," a concept formulated by scholars Alejandro Portes and Min Zhou.

Given the fact that Thais in the United States are a relatively new community, how do Thai Americans figure in the larger APA coalition? Thai Americans are making strides to claim a sense of legitimacy and visibility through creation of Thai Town and community organizations. Located between Normandie and Western Avenues in Los Angeles, Thai Town was officially established in October 1999 and offers both the Thai community and visitors restaurants, entertainment, local businesses, and shopping.

Annually, the Thai community comes together to enjoy Thai Culture Day, which takes place in Thai Town on the last Sunday in September and celebrate with a parade of native costumes, art exhibits, and demonstrations of *muay Thai* (or Thai kick-boxing). One of the most important aspects of "Thai Town" is the economic possibilities it has provided for the Thai people. Chancee Martorell, director of Thai CDC, says the organization is assisting twenty-five Thais from the working-poor class to start their own businesses in Thai Town.

Preserving Culture in America

Many older Thais have shared Thai culture with their children by involving them in such activities as Songkran (the water festival in April) and celebration of the King and Queen's birthdays (November and August, respectively) at the Wat Thai Buddhist Temple. In addition to being a place of worship for about 90 percent of Thais in Southern California, the Wat Thai Buddhist Temple serves as a space where the Thai second generation can explore their connection with their ancestral homeland. The temple provides workshops and classes on Thai language, dance, and the arts.

Other temples have emerged to serve the Thai families dispersed throughout Southern California. The Buddhist Temple of America located in Ontario, California, was founded by my late father, Dr. Zhalermwudh Thongthiraj, who believed in fostering Thai unity and spreading Buddhist teachings to fellow Thais as well as non-Thais interested in learning about Buddhism.

Besides churches, there is an emerging leadership network among Thais that is making significant steps to bringing more visibility to the Thai American community. Established in 1994, the Thai CDC has worked passionately to empower and improve the working conditions of low-income Thais, such as in the 1995 El Monte Sweatshop case, in which 72 undocumented Thai immigrants were forced to sew clothes in slave-like conditions for up to 84 hours a week, as well as to advocate humane labor and immigration policies. The Thai CDC has become a key factor to increasing the legitimacy of Thai Americans, particularly in Southern California, by providing social and legal services to the Thai people, and developing leadership among Thai Americans through community service.

What has also helped bring more legitimacy and visibility to Thai Americans is the development of the "Thai American Experience" class at UCLA, the first of its kind in the nation. A few of the challenges of this course are 1) to enable Thai Americans to re-connect to their "native" or "ancestral" heritage and redefine what it means to be a "Thai American," "Thai Chinese," or "Thai Filipino" and 2) to acknowledge the historical experiences of Thai Americans not just as victims of institutional discrimination (e.g., the 1917 Immigration Law barred the immigration of those living in the "Asiatic Barred Zone" which included Thailand, then known as "Siam"), but also as potential agents of social change.

The Future of the Thai Community

As the Thai American community continues to grow in numbers and visibility, there are still prospects and challenges for Thai Americans to mainstream into American society. The Thai CDC is working in overdrive to ensure greater access to social services and economic opportunities, even taking calls from Thai people in Alaska. Director Martorell hopes the Thai CDC will work with Los Angeles city officials to "beautify" Thai Town—adding cultural symbols and a fountain in front of the Thai shopping plaza—as well as to continue their community economic development projects. The Thai CDC plans to work together with the Asian Pacific Islander Small Business Program to help the most in need entrepreneurs through workshops and individualized business counseling. Thus, the future of the "Thai American" community lies in creating more leadership and educating others about ethnic-specific issues impacting the Thai people.

The Thai American community is part of the larger APA coalition and together, all Asian ethnic groups, in direct and subtle ways, challenge the stigma of being "perpetual foreigners," defined by mainstream representation of Asians as un-American and inassimilable.

—Rahpee Thongthiraj

Section 2

Culture

Breathing the Ancestors

Georgiana Valoyce-Sanchez

We have come to bury our dead. It is still dark. The dirt road leading down to Abalone Cove is rutted, and we bounce and sway in our seats as the van slowly winds its way down to the rocky shore. The people waiting below in the mist are like apparitions of the Ancestors we have come to return to the ocean. It is low tide, but the ghost-gray waves breaking along the dark shore leap high and wild, churning earth, rocks, and shells in their wake. Christ has arrived before me, shaking salt water from his hair, walking among the men in the darkness. He has walked these shores before, thousands of years before the first Christian missionaries ever arrived here. It is an old covenant, reflecting the light of Kakunupmawa, Mystery Behind the Sun.

The ashes of the Ancestors are close by. I cannot see them, but I know they are here. Several weeks before, I went with other Native Americans from different tribal cultures to the Arco Refinery in Carson, California, to discuss the reburial of the sixty or more Native people who had been found there. We walked in silence among the skeletal remains, the anthropologist hired by Arco making sure that we noted the evidence of violence on skulls and limbs. We are not sure who the people were, though some Chumash artifacts were also found with the bodies. The Chumash are my father's people, caretakers for thousands of years of a vast area of this land we now call Southern California. What we do know is that something terrible took place there.

We have been called to Abalone Cove by the Tongva/Gabrieleno people, the most likely descendants of the Ancestors. Because the remains of the Ancestors were found on acknowledged Tongva land, it is proper that the Tongva take responsibility for their reburial. The Tongva, particularly the Ti'at Society, have decided to cremate the remains and return the Ancestors to the ocean.

When the Catholic missionaries came to California, the Tongva people were given the name "Gabrieleno," for the Mission San Gabriel, just as my father's people were given the name "Barbareno," for the Mission Santa Barbara, our original names subjugated, lost. Diegeno, Luiseno, Gabrieleno, Ventureno, Barbareno, Purismeno, Obisbeno . . .

We are still veiled in darkness, but the ocean is silver-gray in Abalone Cove. Dawn is just beyond the cliffs. What is this sorrow I feel?

The night before my father died, I attended a women's sweat. The heat and steam inside the darkness of the sweat lodge seemed unbearable. I was in the womb of God, unable to be born. *Creator, mercy. Please help my father to have a good death.* I could not take the suffering one minute longer, until the woman next to me, in pain from sitting on the hard earth, asked me to rub her back. The next day, my father died with all his loved ones around him. A good death. Simple acts. And we are born.

I dance in a circle of new light. Dawn has come to Abalone Cove. We are holding hands, dancing in a circle, a Friendship Dance some tribal cultures call it. We pray and dance to the Sunrise Song, to the Water Song, to the Rock Song. Sun-splashed ocean, dark cliffs, shadows, rocky shore move past me as if I were standing still and they were dancing in the round. Circles, circles everywhere, from sun to galaxies, plants on the hillside, animals scurrying to their homes, ocean life, every living cell of our bodies, and seabirds flying overhead.

I cannot understand the words sung by the Western Shosone elder, but I understand their meaning—it is a great unknowing and it fills me with light. We offer Tongva and Chumash songs, Ancestor Songs and Healing Songs, songs with ancient words and meanings that we have remembered and reclaimed. I know these old songs—I have sung them before at other ceremonies—and I sing, respectful, serious. Inside, I am filled with joy, smiling.

The ashes of the Ancestors are carried to the beach in plastic bags by some of the Tongva people. Several small plastic bags from the crematorium, each containing the remains or partial remains of a person, are placed on the sand. I wonder if the mother, holding her baby, was cremated with her child.

My sister Susan and I are honored to be chosen to help prepare the Ancestors for their journey out to sea. We kneel on the beach and line two large boxes with cloth. My favorite sweat lodge towel is used to line one of the boxes. It is the same towel we draped over the steel bars of the rented hospital bed when my father was dying. A fine mist of ash rises as we empty the plastic bags. My sister and I glance at one another. "We are breathing the Ancestors," I say. "Yes," she says.

Chumash and Tongva men lift the *ti'at,* the traditional plank canoe of the Tongva so like our own *tomol,* carrying her to the ocean's edge on their shoulders. Her name is *Mo'omat 'Ahiko,* "Breath of the Ocean," and she is draped in a garland of sage. The boxes holding the Ancestors' ashes are covered in a beautiful purple cloth with black hibiscus blossoms printed on it. Susan has woven a wreath of sage for the Ancestors and it is placed on top.

The Tongva people carry the Ancestors' ashes to the *ti'at,* the rest of us walking in solemn procession behind them. Waves crash against the canoe, lifting her each time, tossing her against the rocks, and she reminds me of a wild mustang, straining to be free of the hands that try to hold her down. The captain enters the canoe and directs the people to place the boxes in the center of the *ti'at.* As always, the Ancestors are our ballast, the steadying point of our journey on Earth.

The paddlers and several other men begin to push the *ti'at* farther into the ocean, and she is bucking and heaving on the waves as the paddlers climb in and begin to paddle. Their long oars lift high into the air, circling down into the ocean and up again, like kayak paddlers, only with longer, larger paddles. They are beautiful to watch, and we pray earnestly for them to break beyond the pounding waves. Several of our men are still in the ocean, helping to push the *ti'at* into deeper water, and for a moment I am afraid she will not break free. *Creator, mercy.*

My brother John, who has followed the *ti'at* into the ocean, begins to sing the Dolphin Calling Song, praying for help for the paddlers. It is an old prayer, an old story: our people walking across a rainbow bridge, some falling into the depths of the ocean only to be saved, changed into dolphins by the compassion of Hutash, the Spirit of the Earth, and Kakunupmawa. "*'Alolk'oy! 'Alolk'oy!*" Dolphin! Dolphin! And the *ti'at* breaks free of the waves—*Mo'omat 'Ahiko* is out into the open sea, long oars rising and falling, and she is skimming over the water. We sing, we sing, and our tears mingle with our shouts of encouragement. Farewell, Ancestors! Good-bye! Welcome home.

. . .

The captain of the *ti'at* told us later that when the boxes containing the ashes of the Ancestors were lowered into the ocean they sank immediately, slowly descending into the depths. Bubbles, like a thousand little breaths, rose from below, whispering in some ancient language as they broke through the ocean's surface. I hear them sometimes.

I breathe the Ancestors and they breathe me. Because I breathe the Old Ones, because I love the Mystical Heart of Christianity, because I find goodness and truth in all the world's religions, I don't quite fit anywhere. I am an anomaly.

Sometimes, I am like the *Mo'omat 'Ahiko,* tossed between deep ocean and rocky shore. It is a difficult place to be, but I know this—God, Kakunupmawa, Mystery Behind the Sun, is good. Life with Hutash, the Spirit of the Earth, is good. I have been given teachers, ceremonies, stories, and songs; with the Ancestors, they are my ballast, my steadying point as I head out for the deep.

Reflections on the Positions and Problems of Black Women in America

Niara Sudarkasa

Introduction

I wish to express my thanks to the Sisters for inviting me to speak today. It is a challenge and an honor for me to share with you some of my reflections on the positions and problems of Black women in America.

Obviously this is a subject that is most difficult to cover in a short time. The very phrase "the position of Black women" is likely to call to mind several important topics, each of which could occupy all the time I have allotted to me. For example, one could discuss: (1) the position of Black women in the economic, political, and educational spheres relative to Black males, white females, and/or white males; or (2) the question of the historical position of Black women *vis-a-vis* Black males within the family; *or* (3) the position of Black women *vis-a-vis* various liberation movements with which women of different strata or circumstances see themselves allied.

When one mentions the "problems" of Black women, our minds naturally move to issues such as: (1) their right of access to education and employment; (2) the problem of obtaining equal pay for equal work; (3) the problems of the working mother—how can she adequately combine her roles within the home and those without?

Rather than try to discuss any of these issues in isolation, what I will try to do in this address is to suggest a *strategy for the analysis* of our positions and problems. It is my view—and it has been that of many of our heroines and heroes in the forefront of the

---

Black movement in different eras—that one of the responsibilities of the academic or the intellectual is to help clarify the positions from which we struggle. Today I shall try to place the problems and positions of Black women in a historical perspective. My overall thesis is that in order to deal most effectively with our problems as women we must make a holistic, systemic appraisal of our position as Black people. That done, we should be in a position to chart a course of action that is complementary to—and undertaken in collaboration with—Black men.

In America, the socioeconomic status of all Black people is defined primarily by reference to race. Historically, African males and females were brought here together in captivity, and the patterns of brutality, exploitation, denigration, and degradation which characterized slavery were extended to male and female alike.

Even though gender provided one basis for the division of labor among the enslaved Africans, it nevertheless does not seem to make sense historically to say that Black women were *either* more or less exploited than Black men. Both genders were brutalized to the degree, and in the manner, that it was possible in a given situation. The fact that Black women were raped is neither more nor less an outrage than the fact that Black men were beaten, castrated, or lynched.

The fact that Black men were denied the right to live out the role of husband to the women they chose as wives or the role of father to their children, is no less an abuse nor any less critical to an understanding of the future development of Black families than is the fact that many Black women, of necessity, had to assume the role of family head.

After Blacks were officially declared "emancipated" from slavery, it was race rather than gender that continued to be the dominant criterion by which their access to resources, opportunities, or occupations was determined. The fact that in some parts of the country, during certain specified periods, access to jobs or education might have been easier for either Black women or for Black men is really quite beside the point. *All* black people were severely circumscribed and discriminated against in their quest for equality in America.

It is absurd to claim (as some have done) that, historically, white males and Black women are the two groups who have always been free in America. I would challenge anyone who makes such a statement to document the area in which Black women have occupied positions of authority, exercised power, been accorded rights and privileges, had access to economic opportunities or otherwise exhibited the freedom which was and is characteristically afforded to white males.

It is equally misleading, in my view, to claim that Black women are *more* oppressed than Black men because of the (so-called) "double jeopardy of racism and sexism." Those who espouse this view appear to me to be substituting analogy for analysis. The mere fact that we are female and Black does not mean that our plight has been any worse than that of Black males. For every instance of denial of rights to Black women, a comparable instance of denial of rights to Black males can be cited. The fact that the income of Black women is less than that of Black men is certainly not proof that they are "more oppressed" than Black men. The systematic imprisonment and murder of Black males, particularly those in the age group of 18 to 30, is unsurpassed as a weapon of oppression and a means of undermining the survival of Blacks in America. In the past, it was Black men, not Black women, who were systematically hunted and eliminated, and this is as important to note as is the fact that a Black woman might be denied a job which would be given to a Black man. The systematic elimination of Black males, which has been documented by the sociologist Jacquelyne Jackson and others, is as important a fact of our history as is the legacy of sexual exploitation of Black women by white males.

The point is that we Blacks have been beguiled into debating the quality and quantity of the oppression meted out against us rather than recognizing the necessity to take a united stand against individuals and institutions that would perpetuate that oppression. I am reminded, whenever I hear these debates, of the fact that as a people we are all too ready to allow others to formulate the issues that will concern us; and determine the priorities in our lives as well as in our political movements.

In the 1950s and early 1960s, we were drawn into debates as to whether slavery in Latin America was more humane than slavery in the United States; in recent times we have spent a lot of time arguing as to whether, historically, Black families in America were mainly headed by single parents or by two parents. In both cases, I ask myself: So what? I doubt that the enslaved Africans in Latin America, grovelling under the whip of their Brazilian or Colombian masters, appreciated the fact that their enslavement was "more humane" than that in the United States. Whether Blacks had mainly two-parent-headed families or one-parent-headed families is far less important than the fact that it was *the flexibility of our family structure* that allowed us to survive and to thrive in America. As scholars, we should try to understand how we can maintain such adaptability in our institutions in the face of a hostile environment.

A similar point can be made with respect to arguments over whether Black women are more oppressed or less oppressed than Black men. The fact is that we are a people entering the twenty-first century in virtual bondage in some places and virtually without equality anywhere. The reversal of this situation requires conscious commitment, sustained struggle, and continuous collaboration and cooperation on the part of Black men and women, old and young.

What are some of the implications of a perspective such as the one I have presented here for the direction of Black women's activism?

The first and most obvious point is that I do not consider it possible to divorce Black *women's* liberation from Black *people's* liberation any more than Black male liberation can be divorced from Black female liberation.

Many Sisters make the mistake of attributing their lack of equality to Black males. This is as myopic a view as that which blames Black women for the attempted emasculation of Black men. It is incontrovertible that historically Black *people* were subjugated by white people. The fact that *some* Black men and some Black women were (and are) instruments in the systematic discrimination against our people must be incorporated into any analysis and into any plan for change. *However,* the fact of the existence of Black agents of discrimination cannot be construed to mean that they are the source of that discrimination.

Not only must Black people clearly recognize where we must place our emphases if we want to effect change, we must also appreciate the systemic nature of the inequities we face. One of the effects of our absorption into this system of inequities and inequalities is the inculcation in us of many of that system's values. Thus, certain segments of the Black population, male and female, emulate or espouse the patterns of interaction and the values of the very power groups that sustain these inequalities.

Some Black men, for example, have consciously or unconsciously adopted attitudes toward Black women that echo the attitudes that white men have historically exhibited toward their women. This is a complicated matter, but the fact that some of the most militant of Black males of the 1960s could advocate that Black women occupy a position distinctly behind or underneath Black males, indicates the extent to which the perspective of some white males on domestic and interpersonal relations had been adopted by some Black male leaders. Despite the fact that these Black males said they were looking to their African heritage as a guide to societal building for the future, the domestic and political philosophy they espoused reflected more of a Victorian English heritage than it did an indigenous African heritage. For in most of the African societies from which most Blacks in the Americas were taken, women have traditionally occupied roles that were conceptualized as complementary rather than subordinate to those of men. West African women were involved in the production and distribution of vital goods and services in their societies; they had political structures and occupied political offices which paralleled those of men; in their roles as mothers, wives, sisters, and daughters, they were intricately involved in decision making within both "domestic" and "public" groups within their societies.

This point leads me to the second major implication of my analysis of the situation of Blacks in America, and that is that Black women cannot, indeed will not, accept the notion that Black liberation depends upon Black women's subjugation. As Linda LaRue (1970), Maulana Ron Karenga (1975a; 1975b), and a number of others have argued, Black women must be encouraged to perform various strategic functions in our society rather than be confined to stereotypical roles which white men defined for white women and against which white women themselves are presently rebelling.

This is not to say that I advocate "doing your own thing" as a viable tactic in the strategy for Black liberation. Sisters and Brothers must realize that the "do your own thing" mentality is a hallmark of the individualism which undergirds the economic and political system that has oppressed us. The liberation of Black people, in my view, will unquestionably necessitate our building communities and societies around values that derive from our African past. As Professor Victor Uchendu recently pointed out in a lecture here at the University of Michigan, *the African world-view stresses a person's obligation and duty as well as his or her rights and privileges.* This means that in Africa, in the area of economic activities as in the area of domestic or political affairs, personal choices, and personal decisions were (and to a great extent still are) made against the background of consideration of duty to one's family, community, or society. In other words, in Africa, one did not (or does not) "do one's own thing" in the sense that one does in the U.S.A.

Thus, while I do not accept the notion that Black women must be forced into exclusively domestic roles or be limited to pursuing professions stereotypically earmarked for those of our gender, I do recognize that *the family is an institution that has a critical role to play in Black liberation.* As such, the family will demand the continued support of Black women as well as Black men. As women, we have historically been a pivotal force in the family and we should continue to be.

One of the most critical roles that Black women have to play within the family involves the socialization of Black children. It is imperative that we inform ourselves in order to enlighten our children; it is imperative that we understand our position as a people in America and in the world in order to educate our children to their position; it is imperative that we involve ourselves in the effort to change that position in order to inspire our children to follow our example.

A third major point that follows from my assessment of the position of Blacks in America is that any analysis which we make of a particular aspect of the life of Black women or of a particular problem that faces Black women, should be made in the context of our overall situation as Black people. For example, one of the issues which most incenses Black women and men is the issue of what is euphemistically termed "family planning." On the one side are the Brothers and Sisters who argue that white America is using birth suppression techniques as a genocidal weapon against Blacks. On the other side are Blacks who maintain that Black women must be allowed to "control their own bodies," which means among other things that they must be able to prevent or eliminate unwanted pregnancies.

It would seem to me that Black women who are concerned about our right to control our own bodies should also maintain that as a people we must have the right to decide to have children as well as the right to determine when we will stop having them. We should have the right to decide if, and under what circumstances we want to utilize contraceptives or to have abortions. At present too many Black women are *forced* to practice birth suppression in the name of "family planning." The situation is compounded by the fact that Black women (here and in Africa) often become virtual guinea pigs on whom pills, drugs, and other devices are forced even though the effects of these drugs and devices are by no means well researched.

The position which I take here does not deny an individual Black woman the right to choose, in consultation with others or by herself, to prevent or to abort pregnancies. At the same time, it recognizes the potentially injurious effects of linking social services needed by Black women to policies that virtually force them to submit to birth suppression programs if they are to get the wherewithal for their daily survival.

I might add, incidentally, that white women who are concerned with control over their bodies might stop to ask why it is that some of the same people who are against abortion and birth control for whites (including poor whites) are in favor of such programs among the Blacks in general, and poor Blacks (who "cannot afford large families") in particular. The fact is that if Blacks had equitable access to jobs, if historically they had been given fair compensation for their labor, if the opportunities in this country were equally available to all, then many of those who are poor could afford the families they desire to have. In the whole equation, more weight must be given to attaining economic parity and less attention given to "family planning" in isolation from other factors.

I would remind you of my reason for referring to the debate over "family planning" within the Black community. It was (and is) my contention that the analysis of any particular issue that relates to Black women should be approached from a holistic, systemic point of view. What I suggest is that this issue should be looked at in its historical context and from the point of view of the group as a whole as well as from the point of view of the individual.

In general, I have tried to make a case, in this relatively brief talk, for the fact that the treatment of women of African descent in America derives fundamentally from the fact of our blackness, not from the fact of our being women. In fact, as I often state, following Linda LaRue (1970:38), Blacks and some other non-whites in America have experienced what can be called oppression—i.e., systematic, cruel, and inhuman deprivation. White women in America have experienced what can be called suppression—they have been restrained and restricted, but as a group they have not experienced oppression.

Both racism and sexism represent facets of the same drive toward dominion that characterizes the predominantly male, Euro-American power structure. Historically, Black women's exploitation and abuse by white men and women was primarily an expression of racism, with sexism as an added dimension. (Black females were not even regarded as women in the same sense as their white "mistresses.") White women were the victims of sexism primarily perpetrated by men of their own group. Yet, there is no denying that the ideology of male dominance was (and is) pervasive throughout the society, and accepted, therefore, by the majority of Black males as well as white males. Sexism was (and is) displayed by Black men as well as by whites.

Nevertheless, the predominance of racism over sexism in America is evidenced by the fact that Black men were (and still are) required to show the utmost respect for white women, and usually paid with their lives for acts of abuse, alleged or real, against them. On the other hand, the disrespect and/or abuse of Black women by Black men, and even more so by white men, was (and is) often ignored. Sometimes, in some places, it even was (and is) encouraged.

The predominance of racism over sexism in America has made it difficult for Black women and white women to agree on what constitutes "women's liberation." To say this is not to say that Black women cannot find common cause with white women on certain issues. To the extent that white women are genuinely prepared to incorporate demands of equality for all women into their programs for change, then of course Black women can support such programs. However, in my experience, I have found that white women rarely work for equal justice for all women even though they usually verbalize such a sentiment. When affirmative action programs for "women" are established, these are usually headed and staffed primarily by white women, whereas non-white women are usually forced to turn to the minorities' advocates for assistance. This illustrates the fact that *race and not gender is still the primary demarcator of groups in this country* and in many other places throughout the world. One would hope that with the maturity of the women's movement, race will no longer be a source of privilege *or* persecution, at least not in our half of the world.

Let me conclude by amplifying a point which I made at the beginning. Black women, like Black men, in all walks of life can play a strategic role in our advancement and liberation. Those of us who are ensconced in academia should repay those Blacks over whose sweat and, in some instances, over whose blood we were put here, by utilizing our skills to help in the analysis of our situation, and by directing our skills toward the transformation of that situation.

I see the work of this Conference as falling entirely within that charge. I hope that we will take our tasks seriously and that we will approach our deliberations in the spirit of Sisterhood.

A Myth and a Movement

Helen Zia

In the 1960s, a new stereotype emerged on the American scene. As urban ghettoes from Newark, New Jersey, to Watts in Los Angeles erupted into riots and civil unrest, Asian Americans suddenly became the object of "flattering" media stories. After more than a century of invisibility alternating with virulent headlines and radio broadcasts that advocated eliminating or imprisoning America's Asians, a rash of stories began to extol our virtues.

"Success Story: Japanese American Style" was the title of an article that appeared in *The New York Times Magazine* on January 9, 1966. A few months later, *U.S. News & World Report* produced a similar piece entitled "Success Story of One Minority Group in the United States," praising Chinese Americans while making transparent comparisons to African Americans: "At a time when Americans are awash in worry over the plight of racial minorities, one such minority, the nation's 300,000 Chinese Americans, is winning wealth and respect by dint of its own hard work . . . Still being taught in Chinatown is the old idea that people should depend on their own efforts—not a welfare check—in order to reach America's 'Promised Land.' "

The radical attitude shift was a too familiar experience for Asian Americans who had seen many iterations of the "friend today, foe tomorrow" treatment. Nor was the link to urban uprisings an accident. Where Asians had previously been the economic wedge to distract labor unrest, in the 1960s they were refashioned as a political and social hammer against other disadvantaged groups. The "model minority" was born.

The new stereotype proved tenacious, surfacing like clockwork whenever the Westinghouse Science Talent Search winners or other scholastic prizes were announced, with tales of stunning accomplishment by Asian immigrant youngsters who had just learned to speak English. The "model minority" myth presented its own quandary: should Asian Americans accept, if not embrace, this "good" stereotype as an improvement over the "inscrutable alien enemy" image of the previous hundred years?

In the 1960s, a new generation of Asian Americans was preparing to reject all stereotypes, preferring instead to find its own self-definition. One of the unacknowledged consequences of the civil rights movement and the war in Vietnam was their impact on the consciousness of the postwar generation of Asian Americans—primarily the second- and third-generation Japanese, Chinese, and Filipino Americans. The call by African Americans for equality resonated among Asian American youth, appealing to their sense of justice as well as their own experiences as a racial minority.

The young Asian Americans, inspired by the movement for Black Power, declared "Yellow Power" and "Yellow is beautiful." They believed that the various Asian immigrant groups had common interests and experiences in America that transcended cultural differences and historical animosities from centuries of war and conflict in Asia. This was a radical departure from the views of the immigrant generations that identified more closely with "over there." It was a declaration that, for Asian Americans, our identities and futures held much in common with other Asians in the United States. The burgeoning Asian American student movement found a target in the Vietnam War. Asian Americans were outraged at the government's willingness to dehumanize and reduce Vietnamese people to mere body counts on the evening news.

Nineteen sixty-eight marked the coming out of this new movement, as Asian American students, along with other students of color, conducted militant student strikes at San Francisco State College (now University) and the University of California at Berkeley. In the course of the organizing, the words "Asian American" made their debut. At Berkeley, the pan-Asian cluster of students needed a name; they didn't want to use the word "Oriental," which was seen to represent the European colonialist view of Asia. Yuji Ichioka and Emma Gee, then graduate students, are credited with coining the moniker.

Among the demands the student strikers in San Francisco and Berkeley fought for—and won—were educational programs that taught their history in America. Out of these student movements, the first Asian American studies programs in the country were established as part of new ethnic studies departments at San Francisco State and Berkeley and, soon after, the Asian American Studies Center at UCLA. Other universities on the West Coast followed as Asian American scholars began to reclaim the rich history of Asians in America.

The Asian American esprit spread rapidly along the West Coast. Students at college campuses in the San Francisco Bay Area and Los Angeles founded groups under the same name, Asian American Political Alliance, to signal their unity. The following year, students on the East Coast established a network of Asian American Student Associations. The movement wasn't limited to students. In New York, two middle-aged Japanese American Nisei women, Kazu Iijima and Minn Matsuda, organized Asian Americans for Action in 1969 to protest U.S. imperialism in Vietnam.

As more young Asian Americans studied law and became public-interest lawyers, they began to fight discriminatory practices against Asian Americans in the courts. In 1972, the first class action suit brought for Asian Americans by Asian American attorneys was won by a San Francisco attorney named Dale Minami, against the Blue Shield insurance company for discriminatory employment practices. Minami and other Asian American lawyers founded the Asian Law Caucus, and went on to file other civil rights suits to stop the San Francisco police from making dragnet arrests of Chinatown youths; to end discriminatory hiring practices by the San Francisco Fire Department, which opened employment to minorities and women for the first time; and to restore jobs to Filipino American security guards who were fired because they spoke English with an accent.

The young activists created organizations that advanced a pan-Asian vision and have become community institutions: from the Asian Law Caucus in San Francisco to the Asian American Legal Defense and Education Fund and Asian Americans for Equality in New York, to the Asian American Resource Center in Boston and Leadership Education for Asian Pacifics in Los Angeles. Other ethnic-based organizations, such as Chinese for Affirmative Action, the Organization of Chinese Americans, and the Japanese American Citizens League, took on a more pan-Asian scope. Professional and business organizations followed suit, with the formation of national groups such as the National Asian Pacific American Bar Association and the Asian American Journalists Association. Even the federal government recognized the necessity for a statistical and programmatic category for Asian Americans.

Having their own pan-Asian organizations gave Asian American activists a base from which to launch campaigns against racism and discrimination. As new kids on the block, they coexisted uneasily—and at times conflicted—with the more established and conservative community groups. Old-time Chinatown organizations active since the exclusion years were staunchly anti-Communist and allied with the government of Taiwan; they opposed the younger groups that seemed, and often were, so radical and leftist. Among Filipino Americans, the older organizations supported the regime of Ferdinand Marcos, while many youths were seeking its overthrow.

Most of the efforts by the young Asian Americans were directed at grass-roots community issues: organizing sweatshop workers in Chinatowns, for example; or at bringing other issues into the Asian American community, such as opposition to apartheid in South Africa. Pan-Asian issues that linked the various Asian communities periodically caught fire. In San Francisco, efforts to evict fifty-five elderly Filipino American retired migrant workers from their home, the International Hotel, began in the late 1960s, as developers of the new financial district continued to dismantle the last pieces of what used to be a ten-block Manilatown. Asian American community activists fought the evictions with a broad multiracial coalition, mobilizing several thousands of protesters for tenants' rights and community control—a nine-year battle that finally ended in 1977 when police on horseback and in riot gear broke through the demonstrators' barricades.

A national Asian American campaign to win a new trial for death row inmate Chol Soo Lee, a Korean American immigrant, began in 1977 when Pulitzer Prize-nominated journalist K. W. Lee (not related) began to raise questions about the conviction. For the first time, a broad coalition was forged between Korean Americans and the multi-ethnic Asian American communities. They gathered more than 10,000 signatures on petitions and raised $175,000 in donations, resulting in a new trial and the release of Lee in 1983.

One of the most stunning civil rights victories was won in the early 1980s when the wartime convictions of three Japanese Americans were overturned. Gordon Hirabayashi, Fred Korematsu, and Minoru Yasui had resisted curfew orders for Japanese Americans and internment notices during World War II—and were sent to prison. Forty years later, researchers Aiko and Jack Herzig and Peter Irons discovered that federal officials had altered and destroyed evidence upholding the loyalty of Japanese Americans. With this new information, pro bono legal teams in three cities—San Francisco; Portland; Oregon; and Seattle—succeeded in getting the cases of the three men reopened on the grounds that fundamental injustices had occurred. The lead attorneys—Lori Bannai, Rod Kawakami, Dale Minami, and Peggy Nagae—were all third-generation Sansei whose work vindicated their Nisei parents and Issei grandparents. Together with the findings of a congressional commission in 1983 that the internment was not justified but driven by "race prejudice, was hysteria, and a failure of political leadership," these various efforts paved the way for a national apology and federal legislation providing redress to surviving internees. Members of Congress Norman Mineta and Robert Matsui, both of California, led the legislative movement that culminated in the Civil Liberties Act of 1988, after a national campaign won the support of whites, African Americans, Christians and Jews, women, gays and lesbians, and many others. The young Asian American movement was providing a legacy for all Americans.

Detroit Blues: "Because of You Motherfuckers"

Helen Zia

I arrived in Detroit in 1976 with little more than my beat-up Chevy Vega, a suitcase, a few boxes, and about a hundred dollars. My first order of business was to find a job, preferably at an auto factory. I was on a mission, a grand adventure, to learn what it meant to be an American in America's heartland. I was finally doing what we had talked about endlessly in college—going to the grass roots, the workplaces and neighborhoods where we could learn from the people who were the real makers of history. This was not the road my ancestors had planned for me.

Like many Asian American immigrant parents, mine had instilled in me the virtues of education and scholarship. But our family's tiny baby novelty business offered little exposure to possible careers. My parents had few ideas of where my studies might take me. I was so unsure of what to do in my life beyond college that I did what any good Asian American child would do: I applied to medical school. Though I majored in public and international affairs, and minored in East Asian Studies and student activism, I also took a few pre-med courses—just to be safe. I even got accepted, and within days of starting on my M.D. I began to realize I had made a terrible mistake. But my filial obligation to my parents—and my entire line of ancestors—was a core part of my Chinese heritage, so I stayed on.

After struggling for two years, I finally mustered the courage to ruin forever my parents' dream—and that of nearly every Asian immigrant parent—to have an offspring who is a doctor, who will care for them in their old age. I quit medical school, spurning my path to respectability, wealth, and filial nirvana. But I was clueless about what to pursue instead. I still wanted to be part of the big social changes I discovered during

---

the student protest years. My equally idealistic friends encouraged me to move to Detroit, which they viewed as the real America. My parents saw this as further evidence that I had lost my mind.

Almost immediately, I landed a job as a large-press operator at a Chrysler stamping plant, making car hoods, fenders, and other parts. I joined the United Auto Workers union. In a factory of several thousand workers, I was one of perhaps three Asian faces; I definitely stood out. I was a rarity on the streets of Detroit as well, with its 60 percent African American population and the rest mostly working-class whites, many from the South. At the time, Detroit had only 7,614 Asian Americans in a population of 1.2 million—not even one percent of the city.

I didn't go to Detroit to find a large Asian American population, but I had hoped to find some palatable Chinese food. I was unhappy with the restaurants in the diminutive and decaying Chinatown, whose residents seemed too old and fragile to move elsewhere. Desperate, I asked my co-workers at the stamping plant where to go.

"Stanley's is the happening place for Chinese food," the African American autoworkers unanimously told me. I wouldn't have been so trusting had I recalled that any dish more exotic than sweet and sour pork unnerved many of my black friends. At Stanley's, I wasn't surprised to find that the cocktails wore pink umbrellas. But I was stunned by the gigantic, flaky dinner rolls that accompanied my order. Rice was optional, and everything was smothered in heavy brown gravy. I didn't fault Stanley's—like Chinese everywhere in the diaspora, they had to survive and adapt to the environment. But if culinary influence was an indication of political status in Detroit, Asian Americans weren't even on the map.

Two years later, I was no longer a press operator. As easily as I found my job at the auto plant, I lost it, along with some 300,000 other autoworkers in the devastating collapse of the auto industry. I was learning more about "real Americans" than I ever imagined; my biggest lesson was that we were not so different. There was the occasional racial confrontation—like the drunken worker who pointed her finger in my face and said, "I don't care if you're from Jap-pan, the Philipp-eenes or Ha-wah-yeh, you're on my turf," but she was the rare exception. Standing together on the assembly line and the unemployment line, we shared our lives and recognized our common humanity.

In the midst of that social upheaval, I discovered journalism. I began writing for the *Detroit Metro Times* and other "alternative" news publications I wrote about the auto industry and the labor movement for *Monthly Detroit* magazine, then joined the staff of a new city magazine, *Metropolitan Detroit.* I spent my days reporting on the life and trends that made Detroit dynamic. Asian American issues were not among them.

The last thing I expected to find in Detroit was an Asian American mandate that would compel the scattered groups across the nation into a broad-based pan-Asian movement. I was in for a big surprise.

In the years leading up to the summer of 1982, Detroit was a city in crisis. Long lines of despair snaked around unemployment offices, union halls, welfare offices, soup kitchens. Men and women lost homes, cars, recreational vehicles, summer cottages, and possessions accumulated from a lifetime of hard work in a once-thriving industry. They were named the "new poor." For many, gloom turned to anger as they searched for the cause of their miseries.

At first, the companies blamed the workers for incompetence and malaise, for wanting too much in exchange for too little. The workers, in turn, pointed to decrepit factories and machines that hadn't been upgraded since World War II, profits that had been squandered and not reinvested in plants and people. The government was faulted for the usual reasons. Before long, however, they all found a common enemy to blame: the Japanese.

While Detroit had once scoffed at the threat of oil shortages, Japan's automakers were busily meeting the demand for inexpensive, fuel-efficient cars. In 1978, a new oil crisis and subsequent price hikes at the gas pumps killed the market for the heavy, eight-cylinder dinosaurs made in Detroit, precipitating the massive layoffs and a crisis throughout the industrial Midwest. The Japanese auto imports were everything the gas-guzzlers were not—cheap to buy, cheap to run, well made and dependable. They were easy to hate.

Anything Japanese, or presumed to be Japanese, became a potential target. Japanese cars were easy pickings. Local unions sponsored sledgehammer events giving frustrated workers a chance to smash Japanese cars for a dollar a swing. Japanese cars were vandalized and their owners were shot at on the freeways. On TV, radio, and the local street corner, anti-Japanese slurs were commonplace. Politicians and public figures made irresponsible and unambiguous racial barbs aimed at Japanese people. Lee Iacocca, chairman of the failing Chrysler Corporation and onetime presidential candidate, jokingly suggested dropping nuclear bombs on Japan, while U.S. Representative John Dingell of Michigan pointed his fury at "those little yellow men."

Bumper stickers threatened "Honda, Toyota—Pearl Harbor." It felt dangerous to have an Asian face. Asian American employees of auto companies were warned not to go onto the factory floor because angry workers might hurt them if they were thought to be Japanese. Even in distant California, Robert Handa, a third-generation Japanese American television reporter, was threatened by an autoworker who pulled a knife and yelled, "I don't likee Jap food . . . only like American food."

I had lost my job at Chrysler in the first round of layoffs, four years earlier, but every time I drove my car I was grateful that it was American-made. The tension was an ominous reminder of dangerous times past. It seemed only a matter of time before the anger turned to violence.

That summer, a twenty-seven-year-old man named Vincent Chin was destined to become a symbol for Asian Americans. Vincent was a regular Detroit guy who happened to be of Chinese descent. Cheerful and easygoing, Vincent was a recent graduate of Control Data Institute, a computer trade school, and worked as a draftsman during the day and a waiter on weekends. He liked nothing more than spending a lazy afternoon fishing with his buddies. He hadn't been touched by the Asian American movement and knew little of the violence endured by past generations of Asians in America. But he had felt the sting of racial prejudice and witnessed the hardships of his immigrant parents, who worked in the laundries and restaurants of Detroit.

On June 19, 1982, a week before his wedding, Vincent's pals took him out for the all-American ritual the bachelor party. They went to Fancy Pants, a raunchy striptease bar in Highland Park, a tattered enclave of Detroit, near the crumbling mansions once home to auto magnates and Motown stars and only blocks away from the abandoned buildings where Henry Ford manufactured the Model T. Vincent, who grew up in that neighborhood, had been to Fancy Pants several times before.

That night, his mother admonished him, "You're getting married, you shouldn't go there anymore."

"Ma, it's my last time," he replied.

"Don't say 'last time,' it's bad luck," she scolded, conjuring up old Chinese superstitions.

At the lounge, two white men sat across the striptease stage from Vincent and his three friends—two white men and one Chinese American. Ronald Ebens, a plant superintendent for Chrysler, and his stepson, Michael Nitz, a laid-off autoworker, soon made it clear that they found Vincent's presence distasteful. The friends of the groom-to-be were paying the dancers handsomely to shower their favors on Vincent. According to witnesses, Ebens seemed annoyed by the attention the Chinese American was receiving from the nude dancers. Vincent's friends overheard Ebens say "Chink," "Nip," and "fucker." One of the dancers heard him say, "It's because of motherfuckers like you that we're out of work." Vincent replied, "Don't call me a fucker," and a scuffle ensued. Nitz's forehead was out, possibly by a punch or chair thrown by Vincent. Both groups were ejected from the bar.

Ebens and Nitz hunted for Chin and the other Chinese man in his group. In the dark summer night, they drove through the area for a half hour with a neighborhood man whom they paid to help them "get the Chinese." Finally they spotted Vincent and his friend in front of a crowded McDonald's on Woodward Avenue, Detroit's main central thoroughfare. Creeping up behind the Chinese Americans, Nitz held Vincent Chin down while his stepfather swung his Louisville Slugger baseball bat into Vincent's skull four times, "as if he was going for a home run." Two off-duty cops who were moonlighting as security guards witnessed the attack. The impact of the blows broke a jade pendant that Vincent wore—to some Chinese, a sign of bad luck. Mortally wounded, Vincent died four days later. His four hundred wedding guests attended his funeral instead.

The *Detroit Free Press* featured the bridegroom's beating death on its front page, telling of Vincent's life and hopes for his marriage, but offering no details of his slaying—none of the circumstances were yet known. Detroit's Asian Americans, unaccustomed to any media coverage, took notice. But they remained silent even though many believed that race was a factor in the killing. The community was small and unorganized. Conventional wisdom of the "don't make waves" variety admonished that visibility could bring trouble. Even if they wished to protest, they had no advocacy or watchdog group to turn to. It seemed that the matter would end there. I read the story with sadness and alarm, too aware of the racial tensions swirling around the region. I wondered how this Chinese American came to be killed, when there were so few Asian Americans in Detroit. As an enterprising young journalist, I clipped the story out and filed it, certain that there was a bigger story behind Vincent's death.

Nine months later, on March 18, 1983, new headlines appeared on the front pages of Detroit's two dailies: "Two Men Charged in '82 Slaying Get Probation" and "Probation in Slaying Riles Chinese." It seemed to be the courtroom conclusion to Vincent Chin's death. The two killers pleaded guilty and no contest to savagely beating Chin to death; each received three years' probation and $3,780 in fines and court costs to be paid over three years. The judge, Charles Kaufman, explained his reasoning: "These aren't the kind of men you send to jail," he said. "You fit the punishment to the criminal, not the crime." The lightness of the sentence shocked Detroit. Two white killers were set free in a city with a population more than 60 percent black, where African Americans routinely received harsher sentences for lesser crimes. The sentence of probation drew cries of outrage. Local pundits harshly criticized Judge Kaufman. "You have raised the ugly ghost of racism, suggesting in your explanation that the lives of the killers are of great and continuing value to society, implying they are of greater value than the life of the slain victim . . . How gross and ostentatious of you; how callous and yes, unjust . . ." wrote *Detroit Free Press* columnist Nikki McWhirter.

The Detroit News reporter Cynthia Lee, herself a Chinese American from Hawaii, interviewed members of the Chinese American community, who voiced their disbelief. "You go to jail for killing a dog," said Henry Yee, a noted local restaurateur who was described as the "unofficial mayor of Chinatown." Vincent's life was worth less than a used car, cried a distraught family friend.

The reaction within the Detroit area's small, scattered Asian American population was immediate and visceral. Suddenly people who had endured a lifetime of degrading treatment were wondering if their capacity to suffer in silence might no longer be a virtue, when even in death, after such a brutal, uncontested killing, they could be so disrespected. Disconnected, informal networks of Asian Americans frantically worked the phones, trying to find some way to vent their frustrations and perhaps correct the injustice.

I, too, was stunned. Here was the incredible ending to the story I had clipped out for future reference. I felt distraught, betrayed—and furious. The probationary sentences seemed to echo the familiar taunt, "a Chinaman's chance," that grim reminder of the days when whites lynched Chinese with impunity. The lessons from my Asian American student movement days came rushing back to me. After I read the articles, I telephoned the person named in the *Detroit News* article. Introducing myself to Henry Yee, whose common Chinese American name was the same as my older brother's, I offered to help in any way I could. Henry invited me to meet him and some others that afternoon. At Carl's Steak House, I met Henry Yee and Kin Yee (not related), president of the Detroit Chinese Welfare Council. A woman named Liza Chan, a Hong Kong-born attorney of my own generation, joined us. We talked generally about possible actions. The first step would be to conduct a larger meeting that could include more members of the Chinese and Asian American community.

The Chinese Welfare Council was the public face of the local branches of the Chinese Consolidated Benevolent Association and the On Leong Merchants Association, a tong, a form of Chinatown organization often associated with the seamier side of Chinese American ghettoes. In Detroit it served a social function. Both organizations had long histories in Chinatowns. The business association, also known as the Six Companies, began in San Francisco in the 1860s to provide public services denied to Chinese by local governments. The association arbitrated disputes, representing Chinese concerns to the city, state, and federal governments. The tongs, on the other hand, were alleged to conduct organized crime activities in Chinatowns, using their networks to run gambling, prostitution, drug-trafficking, and protection rackets. Some tongs performed legitimate community and civic functions; in Detroit, the Chinese Welfare Council and On Leong Merchants Association were well established, and both Henry Yee and Kin Yee were members.

Merchants were the Chinese pioneers in Detroit. In 1872, the first Chinese Detroiter, Ah Chee, arrived and set up a laundry business; subsequent arrivals did the same. The first Chinese restaurant opened in 1905. The Chinese business community hit its peak in the 1920s, when the city counted 300 Chinese laundries and 32 restaurants. Since that time, the Chinatown population and business base dwindled, becoming a mere shadow of its peak days.

Over the years, the Asian American population in the Detroit area changed considerably. The Immigration Act of 1965 had ushered in a new generation of Chinese immigrants, as well as those from Korea, the Philippines, and South Asia. Because the new immigration regulations heavily favored educated professionals, the newer Asian immigrants included highly trained scientists, engineers, doctors, and nurses. Many of the top researchers for the Big Three automakers were Ph.D.'s from throughout Asia. The professionals lived in the suburbs, far from Detroit's urban core and Chinatown. By the 1980s, Chinatown's shrinking base reflected the diminished role of the merchants. The children of the laundry and restaurant owners had gone to college and moved to the suburbs or to other cities. The family businesses in Chinatown faded.

The 1980 census reported only 1,213 Chinese in the entire city; while that is surely an undercount, the population was unquestionably small. On Leong ran the Chinese Culture and Recreational Center, offering activities for youth and English-language instruction to new immigrants. It also assisted the aging bachelor Chinese, settled disputes among immigrants, and maintained a cemetery plot for Chinese. If it had more nefarious pursuits, they weren't obvious, though the notorious Hong Kong–based chief of the national On Leong, Eddie Chan, was well known to the FBI and Interpol.

The Detroit Chinese Welfare Council represented Chinatown interests to the city and at political functions. Both groups were run by the same aging elders who realized they needed to bolster their membership by attracting new, and younger, blood. The late Vincent Chin was one of their younger members.

Vincent's background was like that of many second-generation Chinatown Chinese. His father, David Bing Hing Chin, had worked in laundries all his life, from the time he arrived from China in 1922 at the age of seventeen until his death in 1981, the year before Vincent was slain. He had served in the Army during World War II, which earned him his citizenship and the right to find a wife in China. Lily came to the United States in 1948 to be married, like so many other Chinese women of her generation, including my mother. Lily knew her husband-to-be's family, and looked forward to joining him in America. Lily's father opposed the move because his grandfather had worked on the transcontinental railroad, but was driven out. He feared Lily might face similar bigotry. In Detroit, Lily worked in the laundries and restaurants alongside her new husband.

In 1961, Lily and David Bing Chin adopted a cheerful six-year-old boy from Guangdong Province in China. Vincent grew up into a friendly young man and a devoted only child who helped support his parents financially. He ran on his high school track team, but he also wrote poetry. Vincent was an energetic, take-charge guy who knew how to stand up for himself on the tough streets of Detroit. But friends and co-workers had never seen him angry and were shocked that he had been provoked into a fight.

For Chinese Americans, the identification with the Chin family was direct. The details of the Chins' family history mirrored those of so many other Chinese Americans, who, like Lily and David, came from Guangdong Province. So did the military service that made it possible for Chinese American men to get married, and their work in the restaurants and laundries. Vincent was part of an entire generation for whom the immigrant parents had suffered and sacrificed. Other Asian Americans also found a strong connection to the lives of Vincent, Lily, and David Chin. Theirs was the classic immigrant story of survival: work hard and sacrifice for the family, keep a low profile, don't complain, and, perhaps in the next generation, attain the American dream. For Asian Americans, along with the dream came the hope of one day gaining acceptance in America. The injustice surrounding Vincent's slaying shattered the dream.

But most of all, Vincent was everyone's son, brother, boyfriend, husband, father. Asian Americans felt deeply that what happened to Vincent Chin could have happened to anyone who "looked" Japanese. From childhood, nearly every Asian American has experienced being mistaken for other Asian ethnicities, even harassed and called names as though every Asian group were the same. The climate of hostility made many Asian Americans feel unsafe, not just in Detroit, but across the country, as the Japan-bashing began to emanate from the nation's capital and was amplified through the news media. If Vincent Chin could be harassed and brutally beaten to death, and his killers freed, many felt it could happen to them.

After the news of the sentences of probation for Vincent's killers, his mother, Lily, wrote a letter in Chinese to the Detroit Chinese Welfare Council: "This is injustice to the grossest extreme. I grieve in my heart and shed tears in blood. My son cannot be brought back to life, but he was a member of your council. Therefore, I plead to you. Please let the Chinese American community know, so they can help me hire legal counsel to appeal, so my son can rest his soul."

As phone calls and offers of help from Chinese Americans and others poured in from all over the Detroit area, Henry Yee and Kin Yee called for a meeting on March 20, 1983, under the auspices of the Detroit Chinese Welfare Council at the Golden Star Restaurant in Ferndale, a working-class suburb just north of Detroit. Vincent had worked at the Golden Star as a waiter. The restaurant was three miles from the McDonald's on Woodward Avenue where he was killed.

One week after the sentencing, about thirty people crammed into the back dining room of the Golden Star. I had never been to the restaurant, but its familiar decor of red, black, and gold-speckled mirrors reminded me of Chinese restaurants everywhere. The lawyers stood at the front, fielding questions from the group. Barely a half dozen of them, they constituted the majority of Asian American attorneys in the entire state. Most were under thirty. None specialized in criminal law, but they agreed on one thing: once a sentence was rendered, little could be done to change it; the law offered few options. The impasse forced an uneasy quiet over the gathering, broken only by the low sounds of Lily Chin weeping at the back of the room.

Aside from Kin Yee, Henry Yee, and Liza Chan, whom I had just met, I knew no one at the meeting. At that moment I had to decide between being a reporter on the sidelines and being an active participant in whatever happened. I hesitated, then raised my hand. "We must let the world know that we think this is wrong. We can't stop now without even trying." At first there was no response. Then the weeping stopped. Mrs. Chin stood up and spoke in a shaky but clear voice. "We must speak up. These men killed my son like an animal. But they go free. This is wrong. We must tell the people, this is wrong."

With Mrs. Chin's words as a moral turning point, the group decided to press forward. The lawyers recommended a meeting with the sentencing judge, Charles Kaufman. But who would accompany Mrs. Chin and Kin Yee to meet the judge? Some of the lawyers stepped back, explaining how such an act might jeopardize their jobs. In a community with so little political clout, to be "the nail that sticks out" was an invitation to disaster. After another pause, a woman spoke up. "I'll meet with Kaufman." It was Liza Chan, the only Asian American woman practicing law in Michigan. I took on the task of publicizing the news that Asian Americans were outraged and preparing to fight the judge's sentence. From the beginning, women would play a major role in the case.

In the next few days, Liza and Kin attempted to meet with the judge, who by now was flooded by angry phone calls, letters, and media inquiries, as Asian Americans and others challenged his sentence. He skipped their appointment. When I joined Liza and Kin for the next scheduled meeting, we were told that the judge had suddenly decided to go on vacation. On a pro bono basis, Liza began the work of finding and interviewing witnesses to reconstruct what happened to Vincent Chin that fateful night, so that Mrs. Chin and the community could assess their legal options. It soon became clear that there were failures at every step of the criminal justice process. The police and court record was slipshod and incomplete. The police had failed to interview numerous witnesses, including the dancers at the bar and a man the killers hired outside the bar to help them "get the Chinese"; when Liza and I visited the arresting officer, he had the murder weapon, the Louisville Slugger baseball bat, sitting behind his desk. The first presiding judge had set the initial charges against the killers at second-degree murder, which other legal experts determined to be too low. Almost as outrageous as the sentence itself was the fact that no prosecutor was present when Judge Kaufman rendered his sentence of probation.

After the community meeting at the Golden Star, I issued our first press release. We were flooded with numerous requests for information and offers to help. Without an existing advocacy group to manage the community response, we decided some kind of organization would have to be formed. The founding meeting was set for the following week, after we contacted the various community groups, which were mostly religious, cultural, and professional in nature. The meeting would be held at the Detroit Chinese Welfare Council building.

On the evening of March 31, more than a hundred solidly middle-aged and mainly middle-class Asian Americans from towns surrounding Detroit packed the dingy, low-ceilinged hall. The threat of a Michigan frost still lingered, but the topic under debate this night was hot and unprecedented among Asian Americans: whether to form a pan-Asian organization that might seek a federal civil rights investigation in the slaying of Vincent Chin. There had never before been a criminal civil rights case involving anyone of Asian descent in the United States.

Once again, the gathering was mostly Chinese American, with a few other Asian ethnicities offering a thin slice of diversity. The imagery was staunchly conservative: a faded portrait of Chiang Kai-shek at the front, flanked by the red-white-and-blue—not Old Glory but the flag of Taiwan, the Republic of China.

The main order of business was to create an organization that could file petitions and legal actions, raise money, and organize the outcry for a response. The idea was to form an umbrella organization to coordinate the efforts of the area's varied Asian American groups. Members of some twenty groups had come that night, mostly Chinese, from the Association of Chinese Americans and the Greater Detroit Taiwanese Association, to such professional associations as the Detroit Chinese Engineers Association; cultural groups like the Chinese American Educational and Cultural Center; church organizations from the Chinese Community Church to the Detroit Buddhist Church; and a women's group, the Organization of Chinese American Women.

Detroit had not seen such a broad gathering of Chinese since the China War Relief effort of the 1930s. Non-Chinese were also represented, including the Japanese American Citizens League, the Korean Society of Greater Detroit, and the Filipino American Community Council.

The pan-Asian intent of the group became clear as the group discussed what to name the new organization. "Citizens for Fair Sentencing in the Cause of Vincent Chin" and "Justice Committee of the Chinese Welfare Council" were rejected as too narrow. "Chinese Americans for Justice" limited the concern to Chinese. The vote overwhelmingly went to "American Citizens for Justice," which offered an inclusive base and a vision for justice beyond a single case. The founding of the American Citizens for Justice, or ACJ, marked the formation of the first explicitly Asian American grassroots community advocacy effort with a national scope. Third-generation Japanese American James Shimoura was the first, and at the time only, non-Chinese to serve on the executive board. Japanese, Filipino, and Korean American groups joined in support, assured that they would be welcome. As word of our efforts spread; both white and black individuals also volunteered, making the campaign for justice multiracial in character.

That night, the new pan-Asian American organization drafted its statement of principles:

ACJ believes that:

1. All citizens are guaranteed the right to equal treatment by our judicial and governmental system;
2. When the rights of one individual are violated, all of society suffers;
3. Asian Americans, along with many other groups of people, have historically been given less than equal treatment by the American judicial and governmental system. Only through cooperative efforts with all people will society progress and be a better place for all citizens.

ACJ's first mandate was unambiguous: to obtain justice for Vincent Chin, an Asian American man who was killed because he looked Japanese.

Hard questions came quickly as the newly formed ACJ sought to gain supporters outside the Asian American community. Our first efforts at mounting a national media campaign were crude and amateurish as we learned the process of getting our news out; in the days before fax machines, each press release was hand-delivered, often by a retired Chinese American couple, Ray and Mable Lim. ACJ held its first news conference at the Detroit Press Club on April 15, 1983. The entire spectrum of local media appeared—it was big news to see Asian Americans coming together to protest injustice. To the reporters and the people of Detroit, Asian Americans seemed to emerge from nowhere. Our task, and mine in particular, was to educate them quickly, in sound bites, about Asian Americans.

An appearance that Liza Chan and I made on a popular African American talk radio program drew numerous calls from black listeners. Some were pleased that Asian Americans would reach out to their community to talk about this injustice. Others asked if Asians were just trying to "ride the coattails" of African Americans, and still others accused Asian people of prejudice against blacks. We tried to answer questions frankly, acknowledging that anti-black prejudice exists among some, but not all, Asian Americans, and that ACJ was trying to address racial bias and injustice against any group, including attitudes held by Asians. The talk shows gave us an opportunity to point out the contributions of Asian Americans to the civil rights struggles. The listeners' comments also underscored the need for us to bring such discussions to the more recent Asian immigrants who had arrived after the 1965 Immigration Act with little awareness of the U.S. civil rights movement.

The growing prominence of the case gave Asian Americans our first direct entry on a national level into the white–black race dynamic with an Asian American issue. We tried to explain that we recognized and respected African Americans' central and dominant position in the civil rights struggle; we wanted to show that we weren't trying to benefit from their sacrifices without offering anything in return. On the other hand, many European Americans were hostile or resistant to "yet another minority group" stepping forward to make claims. Underlying both concerns was the suggestion, a nagging doubt, that Asian Americans had no legitimate place in discussions of racism because we hadn't *really* suffered any.

Still, many did welcome Asian Americans into the civil rights fold, as a new voice from a previously silent neighbor. As ACJ began to make its case, African American organizations such as the umbrella Detroit-Area Black Organizations quickly endorsed ACJ's efforts. Its president, Horace Sheffield, became a dependable supporter at ACJ events, and Asian Americans reciprocated. The Detroit chapter of the NAACP, the largest chapter in the country, issued a statement about the sentence. Several prominent African American churches gave their support, as did the Anti-Defamation League of B'nai B'rith and the Detroit Roundtable of Christians and Jews. ACJ sought and won the support of other communities as well, including Latinos, Arab Americans, and Italian Americans. A diversity of women's groups from the Detroit Women's Forum to Black Women for a Better Society endorsed ACJ, as did a number of local political leaders from the president of the Detroit City Council to U.S. Representative John Conyers.

Many Asian Americans wanted to express their outrage, but were unsure how race fit in the picture. Their tentativeness about the issue of race was evident in ACJ's carefully crafted public positions. ACJ focused on Judge Kaufman's unjust sentence, deliberately not commenting on possible racial bias by the judge or the potential for a racial motivation in the killing of Vincent Chin. A few of us in the core organizing effort—attorneys Roland Hwang and Jim Shimoura, educator Parker Woo, and I—had an understanding of civil rights from the Asian American student movement days and felt that racism permeated the case on many levels. But we also knew that other Asian Americans would need to hear more conclusive evidence if they were to take a strong position on race.

ACJ waited to see if Liza Chan's interviews with witnesses would produce evidence of a racially motivated killing. I worded our press releases carefully to convey the context of our history with racism, while avoiding an outright accusation; one of the first ACJ press statements said: "This case has aroused the anger of the Asian community by recalling the days of 'frontier justice,' when massacres of Chinese workers were commonplace." News reporters, on the other hand, wanted ACJ to call Kaufman a racist. Journalists discovered that Kaufman had been held in a Japanese prisoner-of-war camp during World War II. ACJ refused the bait.

Soon the smoking gun the community needed appeared. A private investigator hired by ACJ to uncover the facts leading to Vincent's death reported that Racine Colwell, a tough blond dancer at the Fancy Pants, overheard Ebens tell Chin, "It's because of you motherfuckers that we're out of work." At a time when bilious anti-Japanese remarks by politicians, public officials, and the next-door neighbors spewed forth regularly, Asian Americans knew exactly what Ebens meant. A nude dancer with nothing to gain from her testimony had produced the link to a racial motivation that the community was waiting for. ACJ attorneys and leaders realized it was enough to charge Ebens and Nitz with violating Vincent Chin's civil rights. It was time to talk about race.

The next meeting of the ACJ was held at Ford Motor Company World Headquarters, in Dearborn. David Hwang, who had worked at Ford as a research engineer for thirty-six years, secured the use of the company cafeteria on a Sunday evening. More than two hundred people packed the cavernous room to hear updates on the legal efforts and to coordinate the grass-roots, volunteer work. A quick roll call identified Asian American employee groups from the top corporations of the Detroit area, from Burroughs and Detroit Diesel to General Motors and Volkswagen. The meeting's featured speaker from the U.S. Department of Justice explained the difficult process of getting the federal government to conduct a civil rights investigation. The FBI would need to show that there was a conspiracy to deprive Vincent Chin of his civil rights, he advised. The strong public outcry would also be a factor in its decision to investigate.

After the Department of Justice official left the meeting, a gray-haired engineer from General Motors raised his hand. In the clipped English of a native Cantonese speaker, he voiced the uneasiness of the crowd. "If we try to pursue a civil rights case," he asked, "is it necessary for us to talk about race?"

The simple question captured the race conundrum bedeviling Asian Americans. Should Asian Americans downplay race to stay in the "safe" shadows of the white establishment? Or should they step out of the shadows and cast their lot with the more vulnerable position of minorities seeking civil rights? Was there a third, Asian American way that would take sides with neither?

"We may alienate our supporters," argued an earnest-looking businessman, who voiced his fears that a stand on racism might affect an already fragile existence between black and white. "Could we win the NAACP but lose the FBI?" asked another.

Behind the discomfort of "talking about race" was the question of where Asian Americans fit in America, and, more important, where we wanted to be. Asian Americans had never been included in broad discussions on race, nor had we interjected ourselves. The questions were many. If race was such a volatile subject for whites and blacks, why should Asian Americans step in, to face potential wrath from one or the other, or both? Organizing over race might make us seem like troublemakers, as African Americans were often perceived, but we lacked the numerical strength and political power of blacks; if we stepped out of the shadows to make waves, wouldn't we risk becoming targets again?

One by one, people discussed their uncertainties. Those of us who had been involved with Third World movements knew the political theories about race and racism, but making the argument to struggling restaurant workers or comfortable professionals was another matter. Even in 1983, fifteen years after the term "Asian American" first designated a pan-Asian identity, civil rights and their importance to Asian Americans were simply not familiar at the grass-roots level of the Asian ethnic communities. We tried to give direct, even practical answers: yes, a civil rights suit would involve race, and if we wanted to pursue a federal case, we would have to get comfortable educating people—including ourselves—about our experiences with race. But remaining silent would not protect us from the anti-Japanese racial hostility all around us and we could all become targets anyway, the way Vincent Chin had.

Suddenly people began talking about the anger and frustration that brought them to this meeting, why they were touched and outraged by what happened to Vincent Chin. "I've worked hard for my company for forty years," said a computer programmer, his voice shaking. "They always pass me over for promotion because I'm Chinese. I have trained many young white boys fresh out of college to be my boss. I never complain, but inside I'm burning. This time, with this killing, I must complain. What is the point of silence if our children can be killed and treated like this? I wish I'd stood up and complained a lot sooner in my life."

The outrage overcame the fear. "We want to win this case, and we want equal justice for all, including Asian Americans," David Hwang reminded the group. In the end, we reached a consensus: to fight for what we believed in, we would have to enter the arena of civil rights and racial politics. Welcome or not, Asian Americans would put ourselves into the white–black race paradigm.

ACJ began to publicize its findings of racial slurs and comments made by Vincent Chin's killers and to call for a civil rights investigation. The backlash that some had feared was immediate. Non-Asians, most particularly those in a position to make policy on civil rights and race matters, openly resisted claims by Asians of racial discrimination and prejudice. Angry white listeners called in to radio talk shows to complain: "What does race have to do with this?" and "Don't white people have civil rights?"

White liberals were the most skeptical. When Wayne State University constitutional law professor Robert A. Sedler met with Liza Chan and other ACJ attorneys about the legal issues in a civil rights case, he told them to forget it. In his opinion, civil rights laws were enacted to protect African Americans, not Asians. Asian Americans cannot seek redress using federal civil rights law; besides, he said, Asians are considered white.

Sedler wasn't alone in this view. The American Civil Liberties Union of Michigan initially dismissed the outcry from Asian Americans as a law-and-order, "mandatory sentencing" movement. Later, as the community outrage continued, Howard Simon, its executive director, issued a report absolving Judge Kaufman of bias and blaming the prosecutors for failing to prepare the facts of the case for sentencing. The Michigan ACLU wasn't interested in the civil rights aspects of Chin's slaying.

Nor did the Detroit chapter of the National Lawyers Guild, which defined itself as part of the political left, find any connection between Vincent Chin's killing and racism. But the Guild's West Coast chapters, more familiar with Asian Americans' history with racial violence, mustered the votes to give the national endorsement to ACJ's efforts. A near mutiny broke out in the Detroit chapter, but the national body prevailed.

To build a broad coalition of support, ACJ decided to approach the United Auto Workers union, and not just for its powerful presence in Detroit. We felt that if we could change some of its members' anti-Japanese rhetoric, we might be able to prevent future attacks on Asian Americans—and possibly save lives. The UAW department of fair practices was across from Solidarity House, the international headquarters, so it was impossible to avoid the racially inflammatory signs and bumper stickers adorning the parking lot entrance. "300,000 Laid-Off Autoworkers Say Park Your Import in Tokyo" proclaimed one large sign; Volvos, VWs, Saabs, and other European imports apparently presented no problem. I recognized Joe Davis, the fair practices director, from my days as a Chrysler press operator, when he was president of a militant UAW local. Davis told us that the UAW condemned the attack on Vincent Chin. "But if he had been Japanese," noted Davis, an African American, "the attack would be understandable, and we wouldn't give you our support." I had a similar encounter with Doug Fraser, the former president of the UAW, at a reception. I had just shown a city council member, Maryann Mahaffey, a supporter of ACJ, the photo of a poster at Auto World theme park in Flint, Michigan, that featured a buck-toothed, slant-eyed car dropping bombs on Detroit—an example of autoworkers' racial hostility. Mahaffey showed the photo to Fraser, who burst into gleeful laughter—until he saw me standing nearby. As a former UAW member, I was embarrassed and repulsed by the union's acquiescence in racism. I recalled the violent anti-Asian campaigns of Samuel Gompers and wondered when the chain would be broken.

In spite of the backlash, local, national, and international support for ACJ's efforts was growing daily. The legal twists and turns garnered steady local news coverage, and the mobilization of Detroit's Asian Americans was an interesting new phenomenon for reporters. The Vincent Chin case broke into national news by a strange twist of fate. I had rented a car while my American-made auto was in the shop; as I waited at the car rental agency, I stood in line behind a woman with a *New York Times* notebook and copies of the two Detroit daily newspapers, each open to a story about the Chin case. I happened to be carrying several ACJ press packets and asked her if she wanted more information. She turned out to be Judith Cummins, a *New York Times* reporter in town visiting relatives. She wrote a story about the killing and the controversy, even though the local bureau chief had shrugged us off. Perhaps Cummins recognized the story's importance because she was African American and the bureau chief missed it because he was white; in any case, the *New York Times* coverage brought other national media interest, including national network news, TV news magazine specials, and an appearance on the Phil Donahue show.

It was the first time that an Asian American–initiated issue was considered significant national news. Ethnic media from the Asian American community, as well as foreign-language news media from China, Hong Kong, Taiwan, and Japan, followed the case closely—sending to Asia images of Asian Americans raising political Cain over issues of race, racism, and racial unity. As the news of the case spread, groups from all over the country and the world contacted ACJ to extend their support. We developed an international following. Several Chinese Canadian groups offered assistance, as did the North American representative of Taiwan; ACJ politely declined Taiwan's help, deciding not to accept money from foreign governments. Families of other hate crimes victims reached out from afar; a representative for the family of Steven Harvey, an African American musician who was killed by whites in Kansas City, came to an ACJ meeting. Asian Americans and African Americans pledged mutual support.

ACJ was pursuing a three-pronged legal effort. It called on Judge Kaufman, who finally heard arguments by Liza, to set aside his own sentence, since it was based on incomplete information. ACJ filed briefs with the Michigan Court of Appeals to overturn Kaufman's sentence. The third approach was the civil rights case. Kin Yee and Lily Chin went to Washington, D.C., to meet with William Bradford Reynolds, President Ronald Reagan's civil rights chief, about a federal civil rights investigation. As the local and state actions turned sour, the FBI began to take an interest in the case. To capture the mounting frustration of the community, the ACJ decided to hold a citywide demonstration at Kennedy Square in downtown Detroit, the site of many historic protests. We had held a number of noisy picket lines in front of City Hall, but there had never before been a protest in Detroit organized by the broad Asian American community. This would possibly be the first in the country outside the larger Asian American centers of New York City and the West Coast.

The "demonstration committee" was headed by David Chock, Michael Lee, and Man Feng Chang, all senior scientists from the General Motors Tech Center. They enlisted the help of other engineers, and joked that this would be the most precisely planned demonstration in history. The outpouring of support was unprecedented. Waving American flags and placards that demanded equal justice, hundreds of professionals and housewives marched alongside waiters and cooks from Chinese restaurants across the region. The restaurant owners shut their doors during the busy weekday lunch rush to allow employees and their own families to participate in the demonstration. Children and seniors, hunched and wizened, walked or rode in wheelchairs. Chinese, Japanese, Koreans, and Filipinos marched in pan-Asian unity. Support statements were made by the city's major African American and religious organizations, local politicians, and even the UAW. At the rally's emotional end, Mrs. Chin appealed to the nation. Through her tears, she said haltingly, "I want justice for my son. Please help me so no other mother must do this." Finally, the demonstrators marched to the Federal Courthouse singing "We Shall Overcome," and hand-delivered to U.S. Attorney Leonard Gilman a petition with three thousand signatures seeking federal intervention.

ACJ used the demonstration to launch its call for a federal prosecution of the killers for violating Chin's civil right to be in a public place, even if that place was a sleazy nude bar. In his speech to the demonstrators, ACJ president Kin Yee read the group's carefully worded position on race: "Eye-witnesses have come forward to confirm something that we suspected all along: that Vincent Chin was brutally slain as a result of a racial incident. Ronald Ebens, a foreman at Chrysler, was so consumed with racial hatred toward Asian people that he started a fight, blaming Asians for the problems of the ailing auto industry. Even non-minority immigrant groups like the Irish and the Poles have faced violence from others who blamed them for their problems. This misguided view encourages attacks on Asian American people and it must be fought against by all who cherish justice and have respect for human dignity."

In direct yet subtle terms, ACJ showed the ways in which Asian Americans had been made scapegoats for the ills of the modern American economy, naming anti-Asian violence as a present-day phenomenon that should concern all people. This created a framework for Asian Americans to organize nationally, and was a first step toward placing Asian Americans in the center of domestic and international economic, political, and social policy contexts. Across the country, in Los Angeles, San Francisco, New York, and Chicago—cities with far greater Asian American populations than Detroit's—pan-Asian coalitions were being built to support the campaign and to address anti-Asian violence in the local community. Fund-raising efforts nationwide encompassed the entire spectrum of Chinese American society, from the National On Leong Association and local chapters, the Chinese Consolidated Benevolent Association and the Chinese Hand Laundry Alliance, to overtly left-leaning groups like the Chinese Progressive Association and the Chinese Association for Human Rights in Taiwan. In between were civil rights groups like the Organization of Chinese Americans, Asian American Law Students Association, Chinese restaurants and business enterprises, and church groups. Dozens of chapters of the Japanese American Citizens League sent money, as did the Korean American Association of Illinois and the American-Arab Anti-Discrimination Committee. The broad cross section showed that the Vincent Chin case was able to overcome the forces of tradition and fear of the unknown, particularly in the arena of race politics. Asian Americans were finally joining together to correct perceived injustices.

Such unity was difficult to maintain. It was rare for the highly educated suburbanites who spoke the Northern Chinese Mandarin dialect to be aligned so closely with Cantonese-speaking Chinatown merchants and workers whose roots were in Southern China. In addition to differences in language, class, and kinship bonds, there was the political gap. Many business owners were Chiang Kai-shek loyalists and fervent anti-Communists, while the more left-wing groups openly supported Mao Tse-tung and the People's Republic of China.

Partly to avoid fractious conflict over "homeland" politics, the charter of the Organization of Chinese Americans, for example, expressly prohibited taking stands on international issues—a policy that is still in effect. ACJ's policy was to admit all who supported its goals, as long as they also maintained an open and tolerant policy toward others. Vincent Chin's story had struck such a raw nerve that Asian American groups were competing to be affiliated with ACJ. In San Francisco, with its rich profusion of Asian American groups, near warfare broke out among various factions. The first cracks appeared when the Chinatown business groups, a powerful constituency in San Francisco, withdrew their support of the case because leftist, pro-People's Republic groups were involved. They used their influence over several Chinese-language newspapers to criticize the fund-raising efforts.

Meanwhile, the leftists were at odds with one another. The Reverend Jesse Jackson's presidential campaign manager for Northern California, Eddie Wong, arranged for Jackson to stop in San Francisco's Chinatown to meet Mrs. Chin, who was attending local support events in California. Jackson became the first national political leader of any race to speak out against racial violence toward Asians. During Jackson's speech in front of a swarm of national reporters and TV cameras at Chinatown's historic Cameron House, where assistance had been provided to Chinese immigrants since 1874, the leaders of two rival leftist groups pinched and shoved each other, trying to elbow the other off the stage just beyond Jackson's view.

Despite the rumblings among the Chinese, ACJ continued to actively reach out to other Asian ethnicities. The second non-Chinese board member was Minoru Togasaki, a second-generation Japanese American. The Chinese speakers on the board felt worried that they might insult Min by mispronouncing his polysyllabic name, difficult for Chinese speakers accustomed to single-syllable ones. A practice session was held, with a room full of Chinese Americans gingerly repeating the name "To-ga-sa-ki" until they got it right.

Detroit's growing Korean community was represented by two large groups: the Korean Society of Greater Detroit, and the Korean American Women's Association. The two groups had rarely worked together. The Korean women were the wives of non-Korean GIs and were often looked down upon by other Koreans—but their support for the Vincent Chin case brought them together. The Filipino and South Asian populations were larger than any of the others and had well-established connections with both Republican and Democratic parties. Their political savvy and access to politicians made it clear to other Asian American groups why they needed to get involved in politics, which many new immigrants tended to shun.

At ACJ's first fund-raiser dinner, a prominent local citizen appeared, the architect Minoru Yamasaki, designer of the World Trade Center towers in New York and other buildings of world renown. Yamasaki, then seventy-three years old, unexpectedly came to join the gathering as an ordinary citizen. Looking dignified but frail, he rose up slowly from his seat with the assistance of a companion. A hush fell over the banquet room as Yamasaki said in a strong, clear voice, "If Asian people in America don't learn to stand up for themselves, these injustices will never cease."

The civil rights investigations dragged on. In November 1983, a federal grand jury indicted Ronald Ebens and Michael Nitz for violating Vincent Chin's right to enjoy a place of public accommodation; the trial would take place the following June. During this period, other racial attacks drew the attention of the Asian American community. In Lansing, Michigan, a Vietnamese American man and his European American wife were harassed and repeatedly shot at by white men shouting racial slurs. In Davis, California, a seventeen-year-old Vietnamese youth was stabbed to death in his high school by white students, while in New York a pregnant Chinese woman was decapitated when she was pushed in front of an oncoming subway car by a European American teacher who claimed to have a fear of Asians.

In other cities, Asian Americans followed the Detroit Asian American community's example and organized to track such incidents. In Boston, a pan-Asian group called Asians for Justice was formed after an escalating number of anti-Asian attacks against Japanese Americans, Chinese Americans, and Cambodian Americans, as well as the stabbing death of a Vietnamese American man. As such new groups raised public awareness about the particular kind of racial hostility against Asians, they prompted more people to come forward to file hate crime reports. The growing list of cases underscored the existence of racism against Asian Americans.

ACJ expanded its civil rights work from anti-Asian hate crimes. It took on employment and discrimination referrals; successfully lobbied the governor to create a statewide Asian American advisory commission; campaigned against offensive media images, like the poster of the slant-eyed car displayed in Flint, Michigan, and a children's TV program whose host, Jim Harper, appeared in yellowface as a sinister Fu Manchu character with a phony Asian accent. To reach out to children and young people, ACJ members Pang Man and Marisa Chuang Ming sponsored a ten-kilometer Run for Justice, while Harold and Joyce Leon's three daughters, professional violinists and a cellist with the world's leading symphony orchestras, performed a special benefit concert for ACJ.

When the federal civil rights trial began on June 5, 1984, in the court-room of Judge Anna Diggs Taylor, a dignified jurist who was one of the first African American women to serve on the federal bench, ACJ knew that the courtroom battle would be uphill. Many people had a hard time believing that Asian Americans experienced any kind of racial prejudice, let alone hate violence. What Asian Americans found to be racially offensive fighting words drew only shrugs from people who would otherwise never use racial epithets—at least not in public.

The words Racine Colwell, the stripper, heard—"It's because of you motherfuckers that we're out of work"—didn't contain a single racial slur. Asian Americans recognized that they were being singled out in that comment, but to others it was simply a true statement. Don Ball, the veteran *Detroit News* reporter covering the trial, wrote that such statements and the fact that Ebens and Nitz hunted for Vincent and his one Chinese buddy, while ignoring his white friends, were "flimsy evidence that Chin's slaying was racially motivated."

On June 28, the federal jury in Detroit disagreed, and found Ebens guilty of violating Vincent Chin's civil rights; Nitz was acquitted. The jury foreperson explained to filmmakers Christine Choy and Renee Tajima in their documentary *Who Killed Vincent Chin?* that Racine Colwell's testimony was the clincher—in Detroit, it was clear that "you motherfuckers" meant the Japanese, or people who looked like them. Ebens was sentenced to twenty-five years by Judge Taylor.

But the case won a retrial on appeal in 1986 because of pretrial publicity and evidentiary errors associated with audiotapes made of witnesses when ACJ was first investigating the case. It was a cruel irony that the very interviews that convinced Detroit's Asian American community and the U.S. Department of Justice of the killers' racial motivation would be used to grant Ebens's appeal. The new trial would be held in Cincinnati, where there was less chance that prospective jurors knew of the case.

Located across the Ohio River from Kentucky, Cincinnati is known as a conservative city with Southern sensibilities. Absent was the heightened racial consciousness of Detroit, with its black majority and civil rights history. If Asians were hard to find in Detroit, they were near-invisible in Cincinnati—but not completely invisible; on July 4, 1986, a gang of patriotic whites shot up the homes of Southeast Asian refugees in the city. When the jury selection process for the new trial began on April 20, 1987, potential jurors were interrogated on their familiarity with Asians. "Do you have any contact with Asians? What is the nature of your contact?" they were asked, as though they had been exposed to a deadly virus.

Their answers were even more revealing. Out of about 180 Cincinnati citizens in the jury pool, only 19 had ever had a "casual contact" with an Asian American, whether at work or the local Chinese takeout joint. A white woman who said she had Asian American friends was dismissed as though the friendship tainted her; also dismissed was a woman whose daughter had Asian friends, and a black man who had served in Korea.

The jury that was eventually seated looked remarkably like the defendant, Ronald Ebens—mostly white, male, and blue-collar. This time the jury foreperson was a fifty-something machinist who was laid off after thirty years at his company. This time the defense attorneys tried to argue that ACJ and the Asian American community had paid attorney Liza Chan to trump up a civil rights case; that argument was objected to by the prosecutors and overruled by the judge.

It was a terrible disappointment, but not a surprise, when the jury of this second civil rights trial reached its not-guilty verdict on May 1, 1987, nearly five years after Vincent Chin was killed. This jury, composed of people with so little contact with Asian

Americans and knowledge of our concerns, couldn't see how "It's because of you motherfuckers" might contain a racial connotation.

Mrs. Chin was distraught. "Vincent's soul will never rest. My life is over," she said. She cried every day for Vincent, when she awoke in the morning and when she lay down at night. Soon after, she moved to New York, then San Francisco, to stay with relatives. Detroit had too many hard memories. Once the legal proceedings were over, Mrs. Chin, disheartened by the failure of the courts to bring her son's killers to justice, moved to her birthplace in Guangdong Province, China, after spending fifty of her seventy years in the United States.

In a civil suit against Ebens and Nitz for the loss of Vincent's life, a settlement judgment of $1.5 million was levied in September 1987 against Ebens, who later told documentary filmmaker Christine Choy that Mrs. Chin would never see the money. He stopped making payments toward the judgment in 1989. At no point did Ebens ever publicly express remorse for taking Chin's life; he never spent a full day in jail. He and his wife, Juanita, moved several times, leaving a trail in Missouri and Nevada en route to whereabouts unknown.

ACJ, however, vowed to continue in its mission of equal justice for all. After the Cincinnati trial, its president, Kim Bridges, a Korean American, announced that ACJ was founding a Midwest Asian American Center for Justice.

Losing the legal effort in its first national campaign of this magnitude after five years of intensive organizing did not devastate the Asian American community; instead, it had been transformed.

The legacy of the Vincent Chin case has lived on, in mainstream America as well as the Asian American community. The documentary *Who Killed Vincent Chin?* is a staple on college campuses, retelling the story to generations of students. Musicians from balladeer Charlie Chin to jazz artist Jon Jang have created songs and musical arrangements about the struggle for justice in the Vincent Chin case. The Contemporary American Theater Festival of Shepherdstown, West Virginia, near Washington, D.C., commissioned playwright Cherylene Lee to write the play *Carry the Tiger to the Mountain;* West Virginia Governor Cecil H. Underwood used the issues raised by the play to launch a statewide dialogue on race, modeled after President Clinton's Race Initiative. Consuelo Echeverria, a Latina sculptor at Carnegie Mellon University in Pittsburgh, welded a life-size installation from forged steel auto parts, portraying the baseball bat slaying, called *Because They Thought He Was. . . .*

Los Angeles attorney and activist Stewart Kwoh, a MacArthur Fellowship "genius" award winner, attributes to the Vincent Chin case his inspiration for establishing the Asian Pacific American Legal Center of Southern California and the National Asian Pacific American Legal Consortium, which conducts an annual audit of anti-Asian hate crimes. New generations of Asian American activists, such as Victor M. Hwang, a civil rights attorney with the Asian Law Caucus in San Francisco, cite the influence of the Vincent Chin case on their desire to make a difference as Asian Americans.

Numerous scholars have studied the Vincent Chin case and its impact on the Asian American community. As Yen Le Espiritu, professor of Ethnic Studies at the University of California at San Diego, wrote in her book *Asian American Panethnicity:*

> Considered the archetype of anti-Asian violence, the Chin killing has "taken on mythic proportions" in the Asian American community (W. Wong 1989a). As a result of the Chin case, Asian Americans today are much more willing to speak out on the issue of anti-Asianism; they are also much better organized than they were at the time of Chin's death. . . . Besides combating anti-Asian violence, these pan-Asian organizations provide a social setting for building pan-Asian unity.

After a century of seeking acceptance by distancing from one another, Asian Americans were coming together to assert their right to be American.

Section 3

Contemporary Issues

American Indian Activism and Transformation: Lessons from Alcatraz

Troy R. Johnson, Duane Champagne, and Joane Nagel

The occupation of Alcatraz Island in 1969–71 initiated a unique nine-year period of Red Power protest that culminated in the transformation of national consciousness about American Indians and engendered a more open and confident sense of identity among people of Indian descent. Between 20 November 1969 and the Longest Walk in 1978, there were more than seventy property takeovers by Indian activists.[1] This series of collective actions is referred to as the Alcatraz–Red Power Movement (ARPM) because it started with—and was modeled after—the Alcatraz takeover. Certainly, many individual Indian people were politically active before and after this period, but what made the movement so powerful were the large numbers of *organized* demonstrations and the property seizures aimed at airing national and local Indian grievances.

The ARPM was predominantly a struggle to secure redress for overwhelming conditions of political, cultural, and economic disadvantage that mirrored the long history of Indian poverty, not only on reservations, but more recently in urban environments. Current theories of social movements focus on situations of group repression or disadvantage while emphasizing elements of individual and group choice, such as active leaders, effectively organized groups, formation of common group and individual interests, and the development of group ideology.[2] Both repressive and voluntarist elements must be analyzed to understand the rise, development, and decline of social movements. Voluntarist elements within the ARPM include charismatic leaders, the legacy of historical Indian resistance and social movements, the tactic of property seizure, a pan-Indian identity, formation of a national activist organization—in this case, the American Indian Movement (AIM)—and a common national agenda of self-determination for Indian people and communities. Other structural and voluntarist elements are situational and have to be understood within the specific historical context. Some of these situational events are the civil rights movement, the Vietnam War protests, widespread student activism, the rise of radical ethnic groups, the reluctance of the federal government to overtly repress social movements during the late 1960s and early 1970s, and the mass media attention heaped on many Indian takeovers, including Alcatraz Island.

Despite its influence, the occupation of Alcatraz Island has largely been overlooked by those who write or speak today of American Indian activism. Much has been written about the battles fought by Indian people for their rights to hunting and fishing areas reserved by treaties in the states of Washington, Oregon, Wisconsin, and Minnesota, as well as about Six Nations efforts to secure guaranteed treaty rights in the northeastern United States and Indian actions protesting the demeaning use of Native American mascots by athletic teams. The 1972 takeover of the Bureau of Indian Affairs (BIA) headquarters in Washington, D.C., and the 1973 occupation of Wounded Knee are also well known, as is the killing of the young Coeur d'Alene Indian Joseph Stuntz and also the deaths of two FBI agents on the Pine Ridge Reservation in 1975, which resulted in the imprisonment of Leonard Peltier. Yet it was the occupation of Alcatraz Island that launched the greatest wave of modern-day American Indian activism. In the pages that follow, we will describe and analyze the rise, organization, fall, and legacy of the Alcatraz–Red Power Movement.

The Legacy of Native American Activism

The ARPM protests were not unusual in that they were part of a long line of rebellions and social movements among Native Americans as means to resist colonial and U.S. control over their livelihood, culture, government, and resources. To better understand the ARPM, we will compare it with some of the major types of Indian movements occurring throughout history, pointing out similarities, differences, and important continuities.

Religious revitalization movements, numerous in Native American history, have provided spiritual solutions to the conditions of economic marginalization, political repression, and major losses of territory, as well as the ability to carry on traditional life. The more notable movements of this type include the Delaware Prophet (1760–63), the Shawnee Prophet (1805–11), the Winnebago Prophet (1830), the Ghost Dance of 1870, and the Ghost Dance of 1890, but there are also many local and lesser-known movements. In each of these, a prophet relied on ritual knowledge and power to gather a pan-Indian following either to fight against European invaders or to pray for a cataclysmic event that would restore the Indian nations to the peace, plenty, and life they had known before American or European intrusions.[3] Most of these movements were either militarily repressed or the followers abandoned them when the predicted events did not come to pass. In some cases, small groups continued in the religion, but there were no pan-Indian churches or enduring community change. Similar to the ARPM, the religious revitalization movements formed a multitribal gathering of adherents, and both movements were reactions to severe conditions of economic, political, and cultural deprivation. But the ARPM was secular, relying on physical tactics rather than spiritual solutions; and while the ARPM depended on charismatic leaders, it did not focus on prophets or the formation of new religious beliefs.

Social revitalization movements, most of which led to reformed religions with present-day practicing adherents, also served to establish modified forms of community organization designed to better accommodate American-style agriculture, reservation land, and political restrictions. These movements include Handsome Lake Church (1799–present), the Delaware Big House Religion (1760–1910), the Kickapoo Prophet (1830–51), the Shaker Church (1881–present), and the Native American Church (1800s–present). Multiple tribal groups gathered for the Kickapoo Prophet, Shaker Church, and Native American Church, while the Delaware Big House Religion and Handsome Lake Church were exclusively tribal in nature.[4] Unlike these social revitalization movements, the ARPM was not concerned directly with reconstituting Indian communities as a solution to poverty or with political marginalization. Rather, ARPM protests were aimed at getting the attention of U.S. officials and agencies to gain access to material resources to alleviate poverty and redress cultural and political repression. Building Indian colleges, creating Indian studies programs, and preserving Indian cultures through federally funded cultural centers and museums were goals that could be achieved while working within U.S. institutions. The ARPM did not require major institutional change within Indian or reservation societies but rather sought fairer treatment, the honoring of treaty obligations, and financial assistance from the federal government.

While the eighteenth and nineteenth centuries were studded with the rise of Indian religious movements, secular Indian movements have characterized much of the twentieth century. Early national Indian reform movements, led by organizations such as the Society of American Indians (SAI), were composed of well-educated Indian professionals who favored assimilation of Indian people into mainstream American society as the solution to the poverty and misery of reservation life. They formed national organizations and were involved in the Indian policy issues of the 1920s and 1930s.[5] Like the ARPM, the SAI worked within the larger U.S. societal framework, but the SAI's assimilationist stance generated much internal debate. The ARPM sought not assimilation but the preservation of Indian identity and culture. The SAI, however, sowed the seed for a national Indian policy and a lobbying force in American politics, which came to fruition with the formation of the National Congress of American Indians (NCAI) in 1944.

In the 1950s, the Six Nations peoples[6] used passive resistance and militant protests to block various New York State projects. For example, Tuscaroras and Mohawks demonstrated in opposition to the building of the Kinzua Dam in upstate New York, which required the displacement of Indians and the flooding of Indian land. Activism began to build in the 1950s, as more than twenty major demonstrations or nonviolent protests were orchestrated by Indian people. These demonstrations were aimed at ending further reductions of the Indian land base, stopping the termination of Indian tribes, and halting brutality and insensitivity toward Indian people. This rise in Indian activism was largely tribal in nature, however; very little, if any, pan-Indian or supra-tribal activity occurred. The militancy was primarily a phenomenon of traditional people typified by the participation of elders, medicine people, and entire communities, not the forging of alliances outside tribal boundaries, such as would later occur during the Alcatraz occupation and which characterized the Alcatraz-Red Power Movement.

A major example of tribally-based activism was the dispute over state taxes in New York in the late 1950s. In 1957, Wallace "Mad Bear" Anderson, a Tuscarora Indian, helped the Mohawk fend off a New York State income tax on the grounds of Indian sovereignty on Indian reservations. Anderson led a protest group of several hundred Indians from the St. Regis Reservation to the Massena, New York, courthouse, where they tore up summonses for nonpayment of state taxes.[7] In April 1958, Anderson led a stand against the tide of land seizures, a move that ultimately brought armed troops onto Indian land. The New York Power Authority, directed by its chairman, Robert Moses, planned to expropriate 1,383 acres of Tuscarora land for the building of a reservoir and the back-flooding of Indian lands. Anderson and others practiced such harassment tactics as standing in the way of surveyors' transits and deflating vehicle tires. When Power Authority workers tapped the Indian leaders' telephones, Tuscaroras switched to speaking their tribal language. When the Tuscaroras refused to accept the state's offer to purchase the land, one hundred armed state troopers and police invaded Tuscarora lands. They were met by a nonviolent front of 150 men, women, and children, led by Anderson, who blocked the road by lying down or standing in front of government trucks. At the same time, Seneca and Mohawk Indian people set up camps on the disputed land, challenging the state to remove them. Anderson and other leaders were arrested, but the media attention forced the Power Authority to back down. The Federal Power Commission ruled that the Indians did not have to sell the land, and the tribe did not sell. The *Buffalo Courier Express* reported that Mad Bear Anderson, more than anyone else, was responsible for the tribe's decision.[8]

Following the Six Nations' success in New York State, the Miccosukee Indian Nation of Florida summoned Anderson to help fight the federal government's attempt to take land from them as part of the Everglades Reclamation Project. In 1959, several hundred Indian people marched on BIA headquarters in Washington, D.C., to protest the government policy of termination of Indian tribes, and they attempted a citizen's arrest of the Indian commissioner. In California, Nevada, and Utah, the Pit River Indians, led by Chief Ray Johnson, refused $29.1 million of claims case money awarded by the government and demanded return of their traditional lands. The Pit River Indian people carried on their battle until 1972, at which time they reached a negotiated settlement for partial restoration of land and a monetary payment.

During the 1950s and 1960s, Indian resistance to U.S. policies was galvanized by the common threat of termination of reservation and tribal status. Termination policy sought to detribalize and liquidate Indian land, directly abrogating federal treaties and agreements. The NCAI was joined by organizations such as the Indian Rights Association and the American Friends Services Committee in their fight against termination. Today, the NCAI, composed of tribal representatives—each with one vote—works within the political system as a national lobbying group for tribal-reservation (but not urban Indian) interests. It presents legislation to Congress, serves as a legislative guardian over Indian issues, and organizes Indian support or opposition to congressional actions. By contrast, the ARPM used social protest rather than established political procedures, and it represented the interests and concerns of urban Indians as well as disfranchised reservation Indians, who often were unfriendly to the established tribal governments and their leaders. These differences in approach created tensions between the more established NCAI and certain ARPM organizations, such as AIM, during the 1960s and 1970s.

The federal government's policy of termination led to interest among Indians in strengthening Indian policy, and numerous Indian rights and protest organizations emerged in the early 1960s, most notably the National Indian Youth Council (NIYC). The NIYC was organized by young college-educated Indians following the American Indian Charter Convention held in Chicago in 1961. They adopted some of the ideas of the civil rights movement and staged numerous fish-ins in the Pacific Northwest, where Washington State was attempting to use state laws to restrict Indian fishing rights guaranteed by federal treaties.[9] The NIYC encouraged greater tribal self-sufficiency and autonomy and was therefore critical of federal and BIA policy. Although the group was active throughout the 1960s, it never got the media attention that the ARPM did in the 1970s, nor did it engage in the same protest tactics.

The rhetoric of Indian self-determination can be traced to the early 1960s, when Melvin Thom, a Paiute Indian from Walker River, Nevada, and the cofounder and president of the NIYC, recognized the need to alleviate the poverty, unemployment, and degrading lifestyles experienced by urban and reservation Indians. Thom realized that it was essential that Indian people, Indian tribes, and Indian sovereign rights not be compromised in the search for solutions to various problems. He said, "Our recognition as Indian people and Indian tribes is very dear to us. We cannot work to destroy our lives as Indian people."[10] He understood that family, tribalism, and sovereignty had sustained Indian people through the many government programs designed to destroy them as a people and to nationalize their traditional lands. The official government policy, dating back to 1953, was termination of the relationship between the federal government and Indian communities, meaning that Indian tribes would eventually lose any special relationships they had under federal law—for example, the tax-exempt status of their lands and federal responsibility for Indian economic and social well-being. In other words, Indian tribes themselves would be effectively destroyed. Thom described the termination policy as a "cold war" that was being fought against Indian people:

> The opposition to Indians is a monstrosity which cannot be beaten by any single action, unless we as Indian people could literally rise up, in unison, and take what is ours by force. . . . We know the odds are against us, but we also realize that we are fighting for the lives of future Indian generations. . . . We are convinced, more than ever, that this is a real war. No people in this world ever has been exterminated without putting up a last resistance. The Indians are gathering.[11]

Indian people wanted self-determination rather than termination. This included the right to assume control of their own lives independent of federal control, the creation of conditions for a new era in which the Indian future would be determined by Indian acts and Indian decisions, and the assurance that Indian people would not be separated involuntarily from their tribal groups.

The 1960s witnessed a continuation of localized Indian protest actions such as the brief Indian occupation of Alcatraz Island in 1964. Preceding this event, however, were the fish-ins along the rivers of Washington State. The fish-in movement began when tribal members and their supporters fished in waters protected by federal treaty rights but were restricted by state and local law enforcement. When Isaac Stevens was appointed governor of the new Washington Territory in 1853, he concluded the Medicine Creek (1854) and Point Elliott (1855) treaties, which guaranteed Indian rights to fish both on and off the reservation and to take fish at usual and accustomed grounds and stations. In the mid-1950s, state authorities tried to control Indian fishing in off-reservation areas on the Puyallup River. The Indians protested, arguing that these were "usual and accustomed grounds and stations" within the meaning of the 1854 and 1855 treaties. In 1963, the U.S. Court of Appeals upheld the rights of Indian people to fish in accordance with these treaties. In 1964, in defiance of the Supreme Court decision in *United States v. Winons* (1905), the state courts in Washington closed the Nisqually River to Indian fishermen in areas off the Nisqually Reservation. In the same year, the Survival of American Indians Association (SAIA) was formed as a protest organization to assert and preserve off-reservation fishing rights. Fish-ins were organized by SAIA and held at Frank's Landing on the Nisqually River. A large number of state and local law enforcement officers raided Frank's Landing in 1965, smashing boats and fishing gear, slashing nets, and attacking Indian people, including women and children. Seven Indians were arrested. Dangerous though they might be, the fish-ins nonetheless provided the Indian youth of Washington with an opportunity to express their disillusionment and dissatisfaction with U.S. society and also to protest actively the social conditions endured by their people. Celebrities such as Marlon Brando lent their names to bring national media coverage of these protest actions. The Indian people who participated in the fish-ins would later provide assistance to the occupiers on Alcatraz Island.

In March 1966, President Lyndon Johnson attempted to quiet the fears of Indian people. In a speech before the Senate, he proposed a "new goal for our Indian programs; a goal that ends the old debate about termination of Indian programs and stresses self-determination; a goal that erases old attitudes of paternalism and promotes partnership and self-help."[12] In October 1966, Senator George McGovern from South Dakota introduced a resolution that highlighted the increased desire of Indian people to be allowed to participate in decisions concerning their development. The frustration resulting from years of BIA paternalism and the new Indian awareness of their powerlessness resulting from years of neglect, poverty, and discrimination had finally attracted the attention of the bureaucracy in Washington, D.C.

In the summer of 1968, United Native Americans (UNA) was founded in the San Francisco Bay Area. Many of the Indian occupiers of Alcatraz Island were, or had been, members of UNA; many more were strongly influenced by the organization. UNA had a pan-Indian focus. It sought to unify all persons of Indian blood throughout the Americas and to develop itself as a democratic, grass-roots organization. Its goal was to promote self-determination through Indian control of Indian affairs at every level. Lehman Brightman, a Sioux Indian, was the first president of UNA.

The year 1968 closed with a confrontation between Canada, the United States, and members of the Iroquois League. Canada had been restricting the free movement of Mohawk Indians (members of the Iroquois League) between the United States and Canada, demanding that the Mohawk pay tolls to use the bridge and pay customs on goods brought back from the United States. Members of the Iroquois League felt that this was an infringement of their treaty rights granted by Great Britain, and members of the Mohawk tribe confronted Canadian officials as a means of forcing the issues of tolls and customs collections on the Cornwall International Bridge (the St. Lawrence Seaway International Bridge) between the two countries. The protest was specifically over Canadian failure to honor the Jay Treaty of 1794 between Canada and the United States.[13]

A number of Mohawk Indians were arrested for blockading the Cornwall Bridge on 18 December 1968, but when they pressed for presentation of their case in the court system, the Canadian government dismissed the charges. This protest action was not without precedent. In 1928, the Indian Defense League, founded in 1926, had argued that unrestricted rights for Indians to trade and travel across the U.S.-Canadian border existed based on the Jay Treaty of 1794 and the Treaty of Ghent in 1814. It was not until the 1969 concession, however, that the Canadian government formally recognized these rights, under article 3 of the treaty, and allowed Indians to exchange goods across the border, duty-free, and permitted unrestricted travel between the countries.[14]

The 1968–69 Cornwall Bridge confrontation also brought about the creation of *Akwesasne Notes*, an Indian newspaper, which began as an effort to bring news to Indian people regarding the crisis by reprinting articles from diverse newspapers. Edited by

Jerry Gambill, a non-Indian employed by the Canadian Department of Indian Affairs, *Akwesasne Notes* developed into a national Indian newspaper with a circulation of nearly fifty thousand. As a result of coverage in *Akwesasne Notes,* Cornwall Bridge became a prominent discussion topic for Indians across the nation. Later, the Alcatraz occupation would find an Indian media voice in *Akwesasne Notes.*

In addition to his newspaper work, Jerry Gambill assisted Ernest Benedict, a Mohawk Indian, in establishing the North American Indian Traveling College and the White Roots of Peace. The White Roots of Peace harked back to an earlier Mohawk group, the Akwesasne Counselor Organization, founded by Ray Fadden, a Mohawk Indian, in the mid-1930s. The counselor organization had "traveled far and wide inculcating Indian pride among Mohawk youth . . . hoping to influence a group of young Mohawk . . . to take up leadership roles in the Mohawk Longhouse."[15] This was largely an attempt by Fadden and other Mohawk to preserve and revive Iroquois lifeways. Seeing the spiritual crisis caused by the death of key elders and noting that many young Indians were moving away from the faith, Benedict and Gambill founded the White Roots of Peace, which was committed to the preservation of tradition by bringing back the Great Binding Law through speaking engagements to Indian and non-Indian communities and school audiences.

As part of this increase in Indian activism in the 1960s, the Taos Pueblo Indians of New Mexico reasserted their claims to ancestral lands. In 1906, the U.S. government had appropriated the Taos Blue Lake area, a sacred site belonging to the Taos Pueblos, and incorporated it into part of the Carson National Forest.[16] In 1926, the tribe, in reply to a compensation offer made by the government, waived the award, seeking return of Blue Lake instead. As a result, they got neither the compensation nor Blue Lake. On 31 May 1933, the Senate Indian Affairs Committee recommended that the Taos Pueblo Indians be issued a permit to use Blue Lake for religious purposes. The permit was finally issued in 1940. On 13 August 1951, the tribe filed a suit before the Indian Claims Commission seeking judicial support for the validity of their title to the lake. On 8 September 1965, the Indian Claims Commission affirmed that the U.S. government had taken the area from its rightful owners. On 15 March 1966, legislation was introduced to return Blue Lake to the Taos Pueblo Indians; however, the bill died without action in the Senate Interior and Insular Affairs Subcommittee. On 10 May 1968, House Bill 3306 was introduced to restore the sacred area to the tribe. Although it was passed unanimously in the House of Representatives, it once again died in the Senate Interior and Insular Affairs Subcommittee.[17]

The return of Taos Blue Lake became the centerpiece of Indian policy for the administration of Richard Nixon, the incoming president. Two other significant events also had a strong effect on Nixon's developing policy of Indian self-determination. First was the receipt of a study of the BIA by Alvin M. Josephy, Jr., entitled *The American Indian and the Bureau of Indian Affairs, 1969.*[18] In his report, completed on 24 February 1969, Josephy chastised the federal government for its ineptitude in the handling of Indian affairs. Specifically, he condemned the failure of various presidents to effect any change in the multilayered, bureaucratically inept BIA, the failure of the government's Indian education policy, and the high rates of unemployment, disease, and death on Indian reservations as a result of neglect of Indian people by the federal government. Second was the publication in 1969 of Edgar S. Cahn's *Our Brother's Keeper: The Indian in White America,* a study of the ineptitude of the BIA and an indictment of the BIA for its failure to carry out its responsibilities to the American Indian people.[19] Cahn highlighted the numerous studies of Indian people, all except one conducted by non-Indians, and stated that "recommendations have come to have a special non-meaning for Indians. They are part of a tradition in which policy and programs are dictated by non-Indians, even when dialogue and consultation have been promised."[20]

Other movements, such as the Alaska Native Claims Movement of 1960–71, raged on. This particular movement consisted of regional coalitions of over two hundred Alaska Native villages joined in a statewide land claims protest. A large land claims settlement was finally negotiated in 1971 whereby the Alaska Natives retained 44 million acres of land and received $962.5 million and other benefits.[21] The Alaska Native Claims Settlement Act (ANCSA) of 1971 became a model for many struggling indigenous movements around the world.

Indian protests for assertion of treaty-based fishing rights continued throughout the 1960s and early 1970s and were often associated with arrests and violence. In a 1970 protest over treaty fishing rights at Frank's Landing in Washington State, sixty Indians were arrested. SAIA members, led by Janet McCloud, a Tulalip Indian, gathered in Seattle and marched in protest at the federal courthouse. In January 1971, Hank Adams, a former member of NIYC and now a member of SAIA who had participated in a decade of fish-ins, was shot in the stomach by two white sport fishermen as he slept in his pick-up truck. Adams had been tending a set of fish nets for a friend on the Puyallup River. He survived the shooting, but the police, who sympathized with the non-Indian sport fishermen, disputed his account of the incident and did not search for his attackers. In February 1974, a federal judge, George Boldt, ruled in *United States v. Washington* to uphold the treaty rights of Indian people to fish at their usual and accustomed grounds and stations off reservation and "in common with" other citizens.[22]

Self-determination formed the logic for much tribally based litigation, lobbying, and protest action. The outlines of the Indian self-determination policy were formed during the late 1960s, when Zuni Pueblo took advantage of a little-known law to contract BIA services. The Zuni wanted to minimize BIA interference in their community, preferring to manage their own affairs. The success of the Zuni contracting of BIA programs came to the attention of Nixon administration officials, and the new self-determination policy announced in 1970 was based on contracting of federal and BIA services directly to tribal governments. However, the contracting mechanisms for enabling tribal governments to take advantage of the self-determination policy were not worked out until passage of the Indian Self-Determination and Education Act of 1975. Nevertheless, the new policy of self-determination was designed to give Indian people greater control over their communities, tribal governments, and reservation institutions, all of which had been managed by BIA officials since late in the nineteenth century. Although ultimately the effects of the self-determination policy were limited, most Indian communities strongly favored the new policy.

By the late 1960s and early 1970s, Native Americans thus had a rich and long legacy of social movements. Most were tribally centered around treaty or land issues. Others were multitribal, led by groups such as the NCAI and composed of loose coalitions of tribal groups or members allied temporarily to struggle against a common external threat, such as termination. Most Indian social movements revolved around issues of injustice, deprivation, or suppression, something they shared with the Alcatraz-Red Power Movement. The fact that the ARPM relied on a history of past incidents to inform and organize its members and leadership also was not unusual. The ARPM drew selectively on many elements of Indian history, especially symbols of resistance. Geronimo, the Apache leader who fought against U.S. control over reservation communities in the 1880s, was one such symbol for the Alcatraz Island occupiers. Custer's defeat in 1876 was used to symbolize Indian victory and defiance, and the Wounded Knee Massacre in 1890 became a major symbol of Indian repression during the Wounded Knee seizure in 1973.

The ARPM was very different from earlier and contemporary Indian social movements. Its members sought change and inclusion in U.S. institutions while preferring to retain Indian cultural identity. This was a form of nonassimilative inclusion that was not well understood at the time but later helped form the contemporary vision of a multicultural society. The defining characteristics of the ARPM were its emphasis on a supratribal identity and the tactic of property seizure, which was used only sparingly by other Indian social movements. Since most Indian people were repressed and marginalized throughout the 1960s, there was much activism, but nothing of the scale or significance of the Alcatraz–Red Power Movement in terms of tactics, new identity formation, visibility in U.S. society, and bringing attention to Indian issues. So we must look to other issues beyond the legacy of Indian social movements for explaining the rise of the ARPM, its goals, pattern of organization, and tactics, as well as its legacy.

Change and Protest in American Society

The occupation of Alcatraz Island occurred at the height of considerable urban unrest in the United States. To understand both the causes of the occupation and its consequences for American Indian activism, individual ethnic consciousness, and Native American community survival, it is important to recall the atmosphere of the 1960s and the changes underway in U.S. social and political life at the time.

The United States was deeply involved in an unpopular war in Vietnam. The new feminism was stirring, and the civil rights movement, Black Power, LaRaza, the Latino movement, the New Left, and Third World strikes were sweeping the nation, particularly its college campuses. While U.S. armed forces were involved in the clandestine invasion and bombing of Cambodia, the 1969 announcement of the massacre of innocent civilians in a hamlet in My Lai, Vietnam, burned across the front pages of American newspapers.[23] Ubiquitous campus demonstrations raised the level of consciousness of college students. People of all ages were becoming sensitized to the unrest among emerging minority and gender groups who were staging demonstrations and proclaiming their points of view, many of which were incorporated by student activists. Sit-ins, sleep-ins, teach-ins, lock-outs, and boycotts became everyday occurrences.

The occupation of Alcatraz Island was part of the much larger movement for social change, which had its roots in the 1950s and 1960s and was now being promoted by people of many colors, genders, and ages. The 1960s witnessed a marked upsurge in political awareness and activity sparked by events in the national arena such as the civil rights movement. The Student Non-Violent Coordinating Committee (SNCC), founded in April 1960, was made up of black-led, nonviolent sit-in activists. It combined with Students for a Democratic Society (SDS), founded in 1962, to form what came to be called the "New Left." Young black Americans were hearing an angrier and more militant voice, a voice coming from former members of SNCC and participants in the civil rights movement. Between 1964 and 1967, more than a hundred major riots and scores of minor disruptions occurred in cities across the country. By the end of 1968, racial upheavals had resulted in more than two hundred deaths and property destruction valued at approximately $800 million. It was during this time that the Black Panther Party (BPP) was born.[24]

The activist movements of the 1960s were marked by a variety of racial, class, and gender groups: young college students were joined by Vietnam veterans, gay rights activists, women's liberation activists; urban American Indian people, Mexican American farm workers, and members of LaRaza, the newly emerging Chicano/Chicana empowerment movement. These disparate groups came together in an era marked by dynamic personal change, cultural awareness, and political confrontation. Meanwhile, many Indian activists observed the civil rights movements and contemplated how this activity could be brought to bear on Indian issues.[25]

The Vietnam War came to be defined in the minds of many Indian men and women as a war fought to defend a freedom that they themselves had never experienced. While Indian people may have been the forgotten Americans in the minds of many politicians and bureaucrats during peacetime, this was not the case in time of war or national emergency. American Indians were required to serve and did so honorably: 1,000 in World War I; 44,500 in World War II; and 29,700 during the Korean conflict. The Vietnam War proved no exception, with a total of 61,100 Indians serving during that era.[26] Beginning with the commitment of troops to Vietnam in 1963, Indians either volunteered or were drafted into military service for this undeclared war against a people some Indian servicemen considered to be as much of an oppressed minority as American Indians themselves were. Mad Bear Anderson, the Tuscarora activist, visited Vietnam seven times and stated, "When I walk down the streets of Saigon those people look like my brothers and sisters."[27] Robert Thomas, a Cherokee anthropologist, commented that Indian people understood the war in Vietnam better than his university colleagues did: "The conflict in Vietnam was tribal in origin, and the Vietnamese were tired of the war machine flattening their crops."[28]

American Indians coming back from Vietnam faced difficult choices. Those who returned, or attempted to return, to life on the reservation found high unemployment rates, poor health facilities, and substandard housing conditions—as did Indian veterans coming back from World War II service. Those who elected to relocate or settle in urban areas encountered what can best be described as "double discrimination." First, they were faced with the continuing discrimination against Indian people that resulted in high unemployment, police brutality, and, very often, alcoholism and death. Second, they experienced the discrimination felt by other Vietnam veterans viewed as participants in an unpopular war; rather than being hailed as heroes or shown some measure of respect for their sacrifices, they were considered third-rate citizens and treated as outcasts. In an attempt to retreat for a period of time, to adjust to a changing society, or perhaps simply to acquire skills for future employment, many of the returning Indian veterans utilized their GI bill educational benefits and enrolled in colleges in the San Francisco Bay Area. Indian students from these colleges, many of them Vietnam veterans, filled the ranks of the rising Indian activism movement now emerging as "Red Power."

Organization and Protest in the Urban Environment

In 1990, more than 50 percent of American Indians lived in cities. This trend toward urbanization began during World War II as a result of wartime industrial job opportunities, federal policies of relocation (in tandem with the termination of tribal rights and the forced assimilation of Indians into non-Indian society), and the urbanization of the U.S. population as a whole. Many Native Americans migrated to the Bay Area during this time to work in defense industries; thousands of others were relocated there by the federal government. In the Bay Area, which was one of the largest of more than a dozen relocation sites, the newly urban Indians formed their own organizations to provide the support that the government had promised but had failed to deliver. While some groups were known by tribal names such as the Sioux Club and the Navajo Club, there were also a variety of intertribal organizations, including sports clubs, dance clubs, and the very early urban powwow clubs. Eventually, some thirty Bay Area social clubs were formed to meet the needs of the urban Indians and their children—children who would, in the 1960s, want the opportunity to go to college and better themselves.[29]

Many of these organizationally connected urban Indians were dissatisfied with conditions in the cities and on reservation homelands—specifically, with the lack of self-determination in both communities and with federal policies concerning Indian affairs. They represented a population that was poised on the brink of activism: disillusioned Indian youth from reservations, urban centers, and universities who called for Red Power in their crusade to reform the conditions of their people. Native American scholar Vine Deloria, Jr., in *Behind the Trail of Broken Treaties,* states: "The power movements which had sprung up after 1966 now began to affect Indians, and the center of action was the urban areas on the West Coast, where there was a large Indian population."[30]

These Red Power groups strongly advocated a policy of Indian self-determination, with the NIYC in particular emphasizing the psychological impact of powerlessness on Indian youth. This powerlessness and lack of self-determination was explained by Clyde Warrior, a Ponca Indian and cofounder of NIYC, when he told government officials in Washington, D.C., in 1967: "We are not allowed to make those basic human choices and decisions about our personal life and about the destiny of our communities which is the mark of free mature people. We sit on our front porch or in our yards, and the world and our lives in it pass us by without our desires or aspirations having any effect."[31] An article in *Warpath,* the first militant, pan-Indian newspaper in the United States, established in 1968 by UNA, summed up the attitude of the Bay Area Indian community: "The 'Stoic, Silent Redman' of the past who turned the other cheek to white injustice is dead. (He died of frustration and heartbreak.) And in his place is an angry group of Indians who dare to speak up and voice their dissatisfaction at the world around them. Hate and despair have taken their toll and only action can quiet this smoldering anger that has fused this new Indian movement into being."[32]

On 11 April 1969, the National Council on Indian Opportunity (NCIO), established by President Lyndon Johnson by Executive Order 11399, conducted a public forum in San Francisco before the Committee on Urban Indians. The purpose of the forum was to gain as much information as possible on the condition of Indian people living in the area so as to help find solutions to their problems and ease the tensions that were rising among young urban Indians. The hearings began with a scathing rebuke by the Reverend Tony Calaman, founder of Freedom for Adoptive Children. Reverend Calaman attacked the San Francisco Police Department, the California Department of Social Welfare, and the Indian child placement system, stating that the non-Indian system emasculated Indian people. When asked to explain, he said: "it is a dirty, rotten, stinkin' term [emasculation], and the social workers are doing it and the police officers are doing it when they club you on the head. It is a racist institution, just pure racism—and you all know what racism is, and you all know what racists are. Look in the mirror, and you will see a racist."[33]

Earl Livermore, director of the San Francisco American Indian Center, appeared next and concentrated his testimony on problems Indian people face in adjusting to urban living, particularly Indian students faced with unfavorable conditions in the public school system. Those conditions ranged from lack of understanding by school officials to false or misleading statements in school textbooks. Livermore pointed out that many of the textbooks in use damaged the Indian child's sense of identity and personal worth. His testimony also addressed urban Indian health problems, which often were the result of Indian people not being properly oriented to urban living and the frustration and depression that often followed. Lack of education, according to Livermore, resulted in unemployment, which in turn led to depression, which led Indian people deeper into the depths of despair. Alcoholism, poor nutrition, and inadequate housing were also highlighted as major problems.[34]

A total of thirty-seven Indian people took advantage of the opportunity to appear at the public forum to highlight the problems and frustrations felt by urban American Indians. Twenty-five of them would be among the occupiers of Alcatraz Island seven months later. Dennis Turner, a Luiseño Indian, testified before the committee about his personal frustrations resulting from the relocation program and about the inadequacy of the educational system to meet Indian needs. He also highlighted problems of inadequate housing and lack of counselors for Indian people newly relocated to the urban areas. More directly, Turner addressed the problem of governmental agencies such as the NCIO conducting hearings and making promises, and the frustration of seeing no change as a result of hearings such as the one before which he was presently testifying. Addressing LaDonna Harris, a Comanche Indian and chairperson of the Committee on Urban Indians, Turner stated: "After it's [the hearing] over with, you're going to wonder what is going to happen? Is something going to come off or not? The Indian is still hoping. If he keeps on hoping, he's going to die of frustration."[35]

In response to a press query, "Are you going to have some militant Indians?" Harris replied, "Heavens, I hope we will."[36] Her statement was, in fact, a look into the future, to plans not yet formalized but soon to capture the attention of Americans throughout the nation and to be played out as a nineteen-month drama on Alcatraz Island. But her premonition was not without precedent. In a 1969 meeting at the San Francisco Indian Center, Richard McKenzie, a Sioux Indian who was one of the members of a short-lived 1964 Alcatraz occupation party, recognized the uniqueness of the Indian situation as opposed to the civil rights movement. He said, "Kneel-Ins, Sit-Ins, Sleep-Ins, Eat-Ins, Pray-Ins like the Negroes do, wouldn't help us. We would have to occupy the government buildings before things would change."[37]

The rise of Indian activism was also prophesied by Walter Wetzel, the leader of the Blackfeet of Montana and former president of the National Congress of American Indians: "We Indians have been struggling unsuccessfully with the problems of maintaining home and family and Indian ownership of the land. We must strike."[38] Mad Bear Anderson, who had turned back the bulldozers when a dam was planned on Iroquois land, declared: "Our people were murdered in this country. And they are still being murdered. . . . There is an Indian nationalist movement in the country. I am one of the founders. We are not going to pull any punches from here on in."[39]

President Nixon's self-determination policy would be tested in California, particularly the Bay Area, which had become the hotbed for the newly developing Indian activism. Jack Forbes, a Powhatan/Lenape Indian and professor of Native American studies and anthropology at the University of California, Davis, became an advisor and mentor to many of the new Indian students. In the spring of 1969, Forbes drafted a proposal for a College of Native American Studies on one of the California campuses. American Indian or Native American studies programs were already being formed—for example, at UC Berkeley, UCLA, and San Francisco State College. These programs grew out of the Third World strikes in progress on the various campuses and included Indian students who would soon be intimately involved in the Alcatraz occupation: Richard Oakes, Ross Harden, Joe Bill, Dennis Turner, LaNada Boyer, and Horace Spencer.[40]

On 30 June 1969, the California legislature endorsed Forbes's proposal for the creation of a separate Indian-controlled university. Forbes wrote to John G. Veneman, assistant secretary of Health, Education, and Welfare, and requested that Veneman look into the availability of a 650-acre site between Winter, California, and Davis.[41] Additionally, in 1969, the Native American Student Union (NASU) was formed in California, bringing together a new pan-Indian alliance between the emerging Native American studies programs on the various campuses. In San Francisco, members of NASU prepared to test President Nixon's commitment to his stated policy of self-determination before a national audience by occupying Alcatraz Island. For Indian people of the Bay Area, the social movements of the 1960s not only had come to full maturity but would now include Indian people. In November 1969, American Indians moved onto the national scene of ethnic unrest as active participants in a war of their own. Alcatraz Island was the battlefield.[41]

The Alcatraz Occupations

In actuality, there were three separate occupations of Alcatraz Island.[42] The first was a brief, four-hour occupation on 9 March 1964 by five Sioux Indians representing the urban Indians of the Bay Area. The event was planned by Belva Cottier, the wife of one of the occupiers. The federal penitentiary on the island had been closed in 1963, and the government was in the process of transferring the island to the city of San Francisco for development purposes. But Belva Cottier and her Sioux cousin had plans of their own. They recalled having heard of a provision in the 1868 Sioux treaty with the federal government that stated that ownership of all abandoned federal lands that once belonged to the Sioux reverted to the Sioux people.[43] Using this interpretation of the treaty, they encouraged five Sioux men to occupy Alcatraz Island and issued press releases claiming the island in accordance with the treaty and demanding better treatment for urban Indians. Richard McKenzie, the most outspoken of the group, pressed the claim for title to the island through the court system, only to have the courts rule against him. More important, however, the Indians of the Bay Area were becoming vocal and united in their efforts to improve their lives.

The 1964 occupation of Alcatraz Island foreshadowed the unrest that was fomenting, quietly but surely, among the urban Indian population. Prior to the occupation, Bay Area newspapers contained a large number of articles about the federal government's abandonment of the urban Indian and the refusal of state and local governments to meet Indian people's needs. The Indian social clubs that had been formed for support became meeting places at which to discuss discrimination in schools, housing, employment, and health care. Indian people also talked about the police, who, like law officers in other areas of the country, would wait outside Indian bars at closing time to harass, beat up, and arrest Indian patrons. Indian centers began to appear in all the urban relocation areas and became nesting grounds for new pan-Indian, and eventually activist, organizations.[44]

The second Alcatraz occupation had its beginning on Bay Area and other California college and university campuses when young, educated Indian students joined with other minority groups during the 1969 Third World Liberation Front Strike and began demanding courses relevant to Indian students. Indian history written and taught by non-Indian instructors was no longer acceptable to these students, awakened as they were to the possibility of social protest to bring attention to the shameful treatment of Indian people. Anthropologist Luis S. Kemnitzer has described the establishment of the country's first Native American Studies Program at San Francisco State College in 1969—the spring before the occupation. The students involved in that program went on to plan the Alcatraz occupation:

> . . . a non-Indian graduate student in social science at San Francisco State who was tutoring young Indian children in the Mission District came to know a group of young Indians who . . . all had some contact with college and had come to San Francisco either on vocational training, relocation, or on their own. . . . Conversation with the student tutor led them to become interested in the strike and in exploring the possibility of working toward a Native American studies department.
>
> . . . the university and the Third World Liberation Front had started negotiations, and there was limited room for movement. . . . [LaRaza] agreed to represent the Indians in negotiations, and there was close collaboration between representatives of LaRaza and the future Native American studies students. I was one of the faculty members on strike, and, although I was not involved in the negotiations with the university administration, I was informally recruited by other striking faculty to help plan and negotiate with LaRaza.[45]

Richard Oakes was one of the students in the program. He came from the St. Regis Reservation, had worked on high steel in New York, and had traveled across the United States, visiting various Indian reservations. He eventually wound up in California, where he married a Kashia Pomo woman, Anne Marufo, who had five children from a previous marriage. Oakes worked in an Indian bar in Oakland for a period of time and eventually was admitted to San Francisco State College. In September 1969, he and several other Indian students began discussing the possibility of occupying Alcatraz Island as a symbolic protest, a call for Indian self-determination. Preliminary plans were made for the summer of 1970, but other events led to an earlier takeover. During the fall term, Oakes and his fellow Indian students and friends caught the attention of a nation already engrossed in the escalating protest and conflict of the civil rights movement as they set out across the San Francisco Bay for Alcatraz Island.[46]

The catalyst for the occupation was the destruction of the San Francisco Indian Center by fire in late October 1969. The center had become the meeting place for the Bay Area Indian organizations and the newly formed United Bay Area Indian Council, which had brought the thirty private clubs together into one large council headed by Adam Nordwall (later to be known as Adam Fortunate Eagle). The destruction of the center united the council and the American Indian student organizations as never before. The council needed a new meeting place and the students needed a forum for their new activist voice. The date for the second occupation of Alcatraz Island was thus moved up to 9 November 1969. Oakes and the other students, along with a group of people from the San Francisco Indian Center, chartered a boat and headed for Alcatraz Island. Since many different tribes were represented, the occupiers called themselves "Indians of All Tribes."[47]

The initial plan was to circle the island and symbolically claim it for all Indian people. During the circling maneuver, however, Oakes and four others jumped from the boat and swam to the island. They claimed Alcatraz in the name of Indians of All Tribes and then left the island at the request of the caretaker. Later that evening, Oakes and fourteen others returned to the island with sleeping bags and food sufficient for two or three days but left the next morning, again without incident, when asked to do so.[48]

In meetings following the 9 November occupation, Oakes and his fellow students realized that a prolonged occupation was possible. It was clear that the federal government had only a token force on the island and that so far no physical harm had come to anyone involved. A new plan began to emerge. Oakes traveled to UCLA, where he met with Ray Spang and Edward Castillo and asked for their assistance in recruiting Indian students for what would become the longest Indian occupation of any federal facility. Spang, Castillo, and Oakes met in UCLA's Campbell Hall, now the home of the American Indian Studies Center and the editorial offices of the *American Indian Culture and Research Journal,* in private homes, and in Indian bars in Los Angeles. When the third takeover of Alcatraz Island began, seventy of the eighty-nine Indian occupiers were students from UCLA.[49]

In the early morning hours of 20 November 1969, eighty-nine American Indians landed on Alcatraz Island in San Francisco Bay. These Indians of All Tribes claimed the island by "right of discovery" and by the terms of the 1868 Treaty of Fort Laramie, which gave Indians the right to unused federal property that had previously been Indian land. Except for a small caretaker staff, the island had been abandoned by the federal government since 1963, when the federal penitentiary was closed. In a press statement, Indians of All Tribes set the tone of the occupation and the agenda for negotiations during the next nineteen months:

> We, the native Americans, re-claim the land known as Alcatraz Island in the name of all American Indians. . . . [W]e plan to develop on this island several Indian institutions: 1. A CENTER FOR NATIVE AMERICAN STUDIES . . . 2. AN AMERICAN INDIAN SPIRITUAL CENTER . . . 3. AN INDIAN CENTER OF ECOLOGY . . . 4. A GREAT INDIAN TRAINING SCHOOL . . . [and] an AMERICAN INDIAN MUSEUM. . . . In the name of all Indians, therefore, we reclaim this island for our Indian nations. . . . We feel this claim is just and proper, and that this land should rightfully be granted to us for as long as the rivers shall run and the sun shall shine. Signed, INDIANS OF ALL TRIBES.[50]

The occupiers quickly set about organizing themselves. An elected council was put into place, and everyone was assigned a job: security, sanitation, day-care, housing, cooking, laundry. All decisions were made by unanimous consent of the people. Sometimes meetings were held five, six, or seven times per day to discuss the rapidly developing events. It is important to remember that, while the urban Indian population supported the concept of an occupation and provided the logistical support, the Alcatraz occupation force itself was made up initially of young, urban Indian students from UCLA, UC Santa Cruz, San Francisco State College, and UC Berkeley.[51]

The most inspiring person, if not the recognized leader, was Richard Oakes, described as handsome, charismatic, a talented orator, and a natural leader. The casting of Oakes as the person in charge, a title he himself never claimed, quickly created a problem. Not all the students knew Oakes, and, in keeping with the concepts underlying the occupation, many wanted an egalitarian society on the island, with no one as their leader. Although this may have been a workable form of organization on the island, it was not comprehensible to the non-Indian media. Newspapers, magazines, and television and radio stations across the nation sent reporters to the island to interview the people in charge. They wanted to know who the leaders were. Oakes was the most knowledgeable about the landing and the most often sought out, and he was therefore identified as the leader, the "chief," the "mayor of Alcatraz." He was strongly influenced by the White Roots of Peace, which had been revitalized by Ray Fadden, and Mad Bear Anderson. Before the Alcatraz occupation, in the autumn of 1969, Jerry Gambill, a counselor for the White Roots of Peace, had visited the campus of San Francisco State and inspired many of the students, none more than Oakes.[52]

By the end of 1969, the Indian organization on the island began to change, and two Indian groups rose in opposition to Oakes. When many of the Native American students left the island to return to school, they were replaced by Indian people from urban areas and reservations who had not been involved in the initial planning. Where Oakes and the other students claimed title to the island by right of discovery, the new arrivals harked back to the rhetoric of the 1964 occupation and the Sioux treaty, a claim that had been pressed through the court system by Richard McKenzie and had been found invalid. Additionally, some non-Indians took up residence on the island, many of them from the San Francisco hippie and drug culture. Drugs and liquor had been banned from the island by the original occupiers, but they now became commonplace.[53]

The final blow to the nascent student occupation occurred on 5 January 1970 when Oakes's thirteen-year-old stepdaughter, Yvonne, who was apparently playing unsupervised with some other children, slipped and fell three floors to her death down an open stairwell. The Oakes family left the island, and the two groups began maneuvering for leadership roles. Despite these changes, the demands of the occupiers remained consistent: title to Alcatraz Island, the development of an Indian university, and the construction of a museum and cultural center that would display for and teach non-Indian society the valuable contributions of Indian people.[54]

In the months that followed, thousands of protesters and visitors spent time on Alcatraz Island. They came from a large number of Indian tribes, including the Sioux, Navajo, Cherokee, Mohawk, Puyallup; Yakima, Hoopa, and Omaha. The months of occupation were marked by proclamations, news conferences, powwows, celebrations, "assaults" with arrows on passing vessels, and negotiations with federal officials. In the beginning months, workers from the San Francisco Indian Center gathered food and supplies on the mainland and transported them to Alcatraz. However, as time went by, the occupying force, which fluctuated but generally numbered around one hundred, confronted increasing hardships as federal officials interfered with delivery boats and cut off the supply of water and electricity to the island. Tensions on the island grew.[55]

The federal government, for its part, insisted that the Indian people leave, and it placed an ineffective Coast Guard barricade around the island. Eventually, the government agreed to the Indian council's demands for formal negotiations. But, from the Indian people's side, the demands were nonnegotiable. They wanted the deed to the island; they wanted to establish an Indian university, a cultural center, and a museum; and they wanted the necessary federal funding to meet their goals. Negotiations collapsed for good when the government turned down these demands and insisted that the Indians of All Tribes leave the island. Alcatraz Island would never be developed in accordance with the goals of the Indian protesters.[56]

In time, the attention of the federal government shifted from negotiations with the island occupants to restoration of navigational aids that had been discontinued as the result of a fire that shut down the Alcatraz lighthouse. The government's inability to restore these navigational aids brought criticism from the Coast Guard, the Bay Area Pilot's Association, and local newspapers. The federal government became impatient, and on 11 June 1971, the message went out to end the occupation of Alcatraz Island. The dozen or so remaining protesters were removed by federal marshals, more than a year and a half after the island was first occupied.[57] Some members of Indians of All Tribes moved their protest to an abandoned Nike missile base in the Beverly Hills, overlooking San Francisco Bay. While that occupation lasted only three days, it set in motion a pattern of similar occupations over the next several years.

The events that took place on Alcatraz Island represented a watershed moment in Native American protest and caught the attention of the entire country, providing a forum for airing long-standing Indian grievances and for expressing Indian pride. Vine Deloria noted the importance of Alcatraz, referring to the occupation as a "master stroke of Indian activism." He also recognized the impact of Alcatraz and other occupations on Indian ethnic self-awareness and identity: "Indian[n]ess was judged on whether or not one was present at Alcatraz, Fort Lawson, Mt. Rushmore, Detroit, Sheep Mountain, Plymouth Rock, or Pitt River. . . . The activists controlled the language, the issues, and the attention."[58] In 1993, Deloria reflected on the longer-term impact of the Red Power movement: "This era will probably always be dominated by the images and slogans of the AIM people. The real accomplishments in land restoration, however, were made by quiet determined tribal leaders. . . . In reviewing the period we should understand the frenzy of the time and link it to the definite accomplishments made by tribal governments."[59]

The Alcatraz occupation and the activism that followed offer firm evidence to counter commonly held views of Indians as powerless in the face of history, as weakened remnants of disappearing cultures and communities. Countless events fueled American Indian ethnic pride and strengthened Indian people's sense of personal empowerment and community membership. Wilma Mankiller, now principal chief of the Cherokee Nation of Oklahoma, visited Alcatraz many times during the months of occupation. She described it as an awakening that "ultimately changed the course of my life."[60] This was a recurrent theme in our interviews with Native Americans who participated in or observed the protests of that period:

> GEORGE HORSE CAPTURE: In World War II, the marines were island-hopping; they'd do the groundwork, and then the army and the civilians would come in and build things. Without the first wave, nothing would happen. Alcatraz and the militants were like that. They put themselves at risk, could be arrested or killed. You have to give them their due. We were in the second wave. In the regular Indian world, we're very complacent; it takes leadership to get things moving. But scratch a real Indian since then, and you're going to find a militant. Alcatraz tapped into something. It was the lance that burst the boil.[61]

> JOHN ECHOHAWK: Alcatraz just seemed to be kind of another event—what a lot of people had been thinking, wanting to do. We were studying Indian law for the first time. We had a lot of frustration and anger. People were fed up with the status quo. That's just what we were thinking. Starting in 1967 at the University of New Mexico Law School, we read treaties, Indian legal history. It was just astounding how unfair it was, how wrong it was. It [Alcatraz] was the kind of thing we needed.[62]

> LEONARD PELTIER: I was in Seattle when Alcatraz happened. It was the first event that received such publicity. In Seattle, we were in solidarity with the demands of Alcatraz. We

were inspired and encouraged by Alcatraz. I realized their goals were mine. The Indian organizations I was working with shared the same needs: an Indian college to keep students from dropping out, a cultural center to keep Indian traditions. We were all really encouraged, not only those who were active, but those who were not active as well.[63]

FRANCES WISE: The Alcatraz takeover had an enormous impact. I was living in Waco, Texas, at the time. I would see little blurbs on TV. I thought, These Indians are really doing something at Alcatraz. . . . And when they called for the land back, I realized that, finally, what Indian people have gone through is finally being recognized. . . . It affected how I think of myself. If someone asks me who I am, I say, well, I have a name, but Waco/Caddo—that's who I am. I have a good feeling about who I am now. And you need this in the presence of all this negative stuff, for example, celebrating the Oklahoma Land Run.[64]

ROSALIE McKAY-WANT: In the final analysis, however, the occupation of this small territory could be considered a victory for the cause of Indian activism and one of the most noteworthy expressions of patriotism and self-determination by Indian people in the twentieth century.[65]

GRACE THORPE: Alcatraz was the catalyst and the most important event in the Indian movement to date. It made me put my furniture into storage and spend my life savings.[66]

These voices speak to the central importance of the Alcatraz occupation as the symbol of long-standing Indian grievances and increasing impatience with a political system slow to respond to native rights. They also express the feelings of empowerment that witnessing and participating in protest can foster. Loretta Flores, an Indian women, did not become an activist herself until several years after the events on Alcatraz, but she has eloquently described the sense of self and community that activism can produce: "The night before the protest, I was talking to a younger person who had never been in a march before. I told her, 'Tomorrow when we get through with this march, you're going to have a feeling like you've never had before. It's going to change your life.' Those kids from Haskell (Indian Nations University) will never forget this. The spirits of our ancestors were looking down on us smiling."[67]

The Alcatraz-Red Power Movement: A Nine-Year Odyssey

The success or failure of the Indian occupation of Alcatraz Island should not be judged by whether the demands for title to the island and the establishment of educational and cultural institutions were realized. If one were to make such a judgment, the only possible conclusion would be that the occupation was a failure. Such is not the case, however. The underlying goals of the Indians on Alcatraz were to awaken the American public to the reality of their situation and to assert the need for Indian self-determination. In this they succeeded. Additionally, the occupation of Alcatraz Island was a springboard for Indian activism, inspiring the large number of takeovers and demonstrations that began shortly after the 20 November 1969 landing and continued into the late 1970s. These included the Trail of Broken Treaties, the BIA headquarters takeover in 1972, and Wounded Knee II in 1973.

Many of the approximately seventy-four occupations that followed Alcatraz were either planned by or included people who had been involved in the Alcatraz occupation or who certainly had gained their strength from the new "Indianness" that grew out of that movement. For example, on 3 November 1970, in Davis, California, "scores of Indians scaled a barbed wire fence and seized an old Army communications center . . . unimpeded by four soldiers whose job it was to guard the facility. Raising a big white tepee on the surplus Government property, 75 Indians occupied it for use in development of an Indian cultural center. Several veterans of the successful Indian invasion of Alcatraz Island a year ago took part in [the] assault."[68] Most occupations were short-lived, lasting only a few days or weeks, such as those that occurred during 1970–71 at Fort Lawton and Fort Lewis in Washington, at Ellis Island in New York, at the Twin Cities Naval Air Station in Minneapolis, at former Nike missile sites on Lake Michigan near Chicago and at Argonne, Illinois, and at an abandoned Coast Guard lifeboat station in Milwaukee.

A number of protest camps were established during the early 1970s, including those at Mount Rushmore and the Badlands National Monument. During the same years, government buildings also became the sites of protests, including regional Bureau of Indian Affairs offices in Cleveland and Denver, as well as the main headquarters in Washington, D.C. Many of these occupations took on a festive air as celebrations of Indian culture and ethnic renewal, while others represented efforts to provide educational or social services to urban Indians. The September 1971 attempted "invasion" of BIA headquarters was described as follows:

> A band of militant young Indians sought to make a citizens' arrest of a Federal official today and wound up in a noisy clash with Government guards at the Bureau of Indian Affairs. . . . [T]hey sought a conference with bureau officials on their contention that Indians were being denied basic rights. Some of the Indians . . . barricaded themselves in two rooms of the public information office on the first floor and others occupied Mr. Crow's [Deputy Commissioner of Indian Affairs] office on the second floor. . . . The invasion of the bureau was directed by the American Indian Movement and the National Indian Youth Council.[69]

As Indian activism in the 1970s progressed, some events were characterized by a more serious, sometimes violent tone, revealing the depth of grievances and difficulty of solutions to the problems confronting Native Americans after nearly five centuries of Euro-American contact. An example was the November 1972 week-long occupation of BIA headquarters. This unplanned takeover occurred at the end of the Trail of Broken Treaties, a protest event involving caravans that traveled across the United States to convene in Washington, D.C., the purpose being to dramatize and present Indian concerns at a national level. The inability of an advance party to secure accommodations in private homes and churches for several hundred exhausted Indians led to the occupation of BIA offices. Angry participants, many of whom mistakenly thought the federal government had agreed to provide housing and then reneged, literally destroyed the inside of BIA headquarters. They barricaded the doors with furniture and office equipment, soaking each pile with gasoline so it could be quickly ignited in the event of forced removal. They smashed plumbing fixtures and windows, covered the walls with graffiti, and gathered up BIA files and Indian artifacts to take back to their reservations. The protest ended a week later after a series of negotiations with federal officials. Damage to the building was estimated at $2.2 million.

During this period, the ARPM protest strategy began to shift from Alcatraz-style takeovers to different forms and terrains of contention linked to the organizational underpinning of supratribal collective action and its urban population base. Researchers and journalists generally reported that participants in activist events in 1970 and 1971 were Indians of varied tribal backgrounds who mainly lived in urban areas and were associated with the NIYC or some other supratribal organization—or else with AIM, the primary organization of the Red Power movement.[70] Before Alcatraz, AIM was essentially an Indian rights organization concerned with monitoring law enforcement treatment of native people in American cities. However, the occupation of Alcatraz captured the imagination of AIM as well as the rest of the country, and as a result, AIM embarked on a historic journey into Indian protest activism.[71]

The American Indian Movement, founded in Minneapolis in 1968, quickly established chapters in several U.S. cities. AIM's membership was drawn mostly from urban Indian communities, and its leadership and membership both tended to come from the ranks of younger, more progressive, and better educated urban Indians.[72] Although not involved in the initial takeover of Alcatraz Island, AIM played an important role in the spread of supratribal protest action during the 1970s and in shaping the Red Power agenda, tactics, and strategies for drawing attention to Indian people's grievances. Ward Churchill and James Vander Wall have noted that "the 19-month occupation [of Alcatraz] . . . demonstrated beyond all doubt that strong actions by Indians could result not only in broad public exposure of the issues and substantial national/international support for Indian rights, but could potentially force significant concessions from the federal government as well. . . . The lessons of this were not lost on the AIM leadership."[73]

The American Indian Movement was enormously influential, but its role in orchestrating Red Power protest events must not be overstated. While many collective event participants claimed AIM membership, the more common thread was education, urban ties, and Indian ethnic identification. AIM and its visible leadership provided a symbolic as well as an actual organizational point of entry for these potential participants in Red Power. Networks of urban Indian centers, Indian churches, and Indian charitable organizations helped plan and support collective actions by AIM.[74] Protest activities and strategies moved through Indian communities via Indian social and kin networks and by way of the "powwow circuit," which passed information along to Indian families who traveled between the cities and the reservations.[75] However, the most important factor contributing to AIM's influence on Red Power protest was probably its ability to use the news media—newspapers, radio, magazines, and television—to dramatize Indian problems and protests.

After visiting the Indians on Alcatraz Island and realizing the possibilities available through demonstration and seizure of federal facilities, AIM embarked on a national activist role. Its leaders recognized the opportunities when they met with the Indian people on the island during the summer of 1970 and were caught up in the momentum of the occupation. AIM leaders had seen firsthand that the bureaucracy inherent in the federal government had resulted in immobility: No punitive action had been taken thus far on the island. This provided an additional impetus for AIM's kind of national Indian activism and was congruent with the rising tide of national unrest, particularly among young college students.

AIM's first attempt at a national protest action came on Thanksgiving Day 1970 when its members seized the Mayflower II in Plymouth, Massachusetts, to challenge a celebration of colonial expansion into what had mistakenly been considered a "new world." During this action, AIM leaders acknowledged the occupation of Alcatraz Island as the symbol of a newly awakened desire among Indians for unity and authority in a white world. In his 1995 autobiography, *Where White Men Fear to Tread,* former AIM leader Russell Means has stated:

> [A]bout every admirable quality that remains in today's Indian people is the result of the American Indian Movement's flint striking the white man's steel. In the 1970s and 1980s, we lit a fire across Indian country. We fought for changes in school curricula to eliminate racist lies, and we are winning. We fought for community control of police, and on a few reservations it's now a reality. We fought to instill pride in our songs and in our language, in our cultural wisdom, inspiring a small renaissance in the teaching of our languages. . . . Thanks to AIM, for the first time in this century, Indian people stand at the threshold of freedom and responsibility.[76]

It was on Alcatraz, however, that the flint first met the steel; it was on Alcatraz that young Indian college students stood toe to toe with the federal government and did not step back.

After 1972, the involvement of urban Indian individuals and groups, such as AIM, in ARPM protests revealed tensions inside the Indian communities themselves—between urban and reservation Indians, between AIM and tribal governments, and between different age cohorts—often arising out of political divisions on the reservations. The tone of protest became less celebratory, less other-directed, and more harsh, more inward, and sometimes more violent. No single event of the Alcatraz–Red Power Movement more clearly illustrates the combination of Indian grievances and community tensions than the events on the Pine Ridge Reservation in South Dakota in the spring of 1973, a ten-week siege that came to be known as "Wounded Knee II."[77]

The conflict at Wounded Knee, a small town on the reservation, involved a dispute within Pine Ridge's Oglala Lakota (Sioux) tribe over its controversial tribal chairman, Richard Wilson. Wilson was viewed as a corrupt puppet of the BIA by some segments of the tribe, including those associated with AIM. An effort to impeach him resulted in a division of the tribe into opposing camps. The two camps eventually armed themselves and began a two-and-a-half month siege that involved tribal police and government, AIM, reservation residents, federal law enforcement officials, the BIA, local citizens, nationally prominent entertainment figures, national philanthropic, religious, and legal organizations, and the national news media.[78]

The siege began with the arrival of a caravan of approximately 250 AIM supporters, led by Dennis Banks and Russell Means, on the evening of 27 February 1973. Although the armed conflict that followed AIM's arrival is generally characterized as a stand-off between AIM and its supporters and the Wilson government and its supporters, the siege at Wounded Knee was really only one incident in what had been a long history of political instability and factional conflict on the Pine Ridge Reservation.[79] The next weeks were filled with shootouts, roadblocks, negotiations, visiting delegations, and the movement of refugees out of various fire zones. There were also moments of high drama. For example, on 11 March "the occupiers, together with a delegation of Sioux traditionals who had entered Wounded Knee during a truce, proclaimed the new Independent Oglala Nation, . . . announced its intention to send a delegation to the United Nations . . . [and] on March 16, 349 people were sworn in as citizens."[80]

When the siege ended on 9 May, after protracted negotiations between Leonard Garment, representing President Nixon, and AIM leaders Dennis Banks and Carter Camp, two Indians and one FBI agent were dead and an unknown number on both sides had been wounded. Wilson remained in office (though he was challenged at the next election), and many of the AIM members involved in the siege spent the next few years in litigation, in exile, and in prison.[81]

Although the action at Wounded Knee was inconclusive in terms of upsetting the balance of power in the Oglala Lakota tribal council,[82] the siege became an important component of the ARPM repertoire of contention. In the next few years, there ensued a number of both long- and short-term occupations. Many, but not all, of these occupations were similar to Wounded Knee in that they occurred on reservations and involved tribal factions associated with AIM or urban tribal members. These events included the six-month occupation of a former girls' camp on state-owned land at Moss Lake, New York, in 1974; the five-week armed occupation of a vacant Alexian Brothers novitiate by the Menominee Warrior Society near the Menominee reservation in Wisconsin in 1975; the eight-day takeover of a tribally owned Fairchild electronics assembly plant on the Navajo reservation in New Mexico in 1975; a three-day, followed by a one-day (several weeks later), occupation of the Yankton Sioux Industries plant on the reservation near Wagner, South Dakota, in 1975; and the week-long occupation of a juvenile detention center by members of the Puyallup tribe in Washington State in 1976.[83]

Red Power protests in the mid- to late 1970s were increasingly enacted in an atmosphere of heightened confrontation. The following, which took place in 1976, illustrates the tension of later activism:

> With little pomp, unobtrusive but heavy security and an impromptu Indian victory dance, the Federal Government today commemorated the 100th anniversary of the battle of Little Bighom. . . . Today on a wind-buffeted hill covered with buffalo grass, yellow clover and sage, in southeastern Montana where George Armstrong Custer made his last stand, about 150 Indians from various tribes danced joyously around the monument to the Seventh Cavalry dead. Meanwhile at an official National Park Service ceremony about 100 yards away, an Army band played. . . . Just as the ceremony got underway a caravan of Sioux, Cheyenne and other Indians led by Russell Means, the American Indian Movement leader, strode to the platform to the pounding of a drum.[84]

The last major event of the Alcatraz-Red Power Movement occurred in July 1978 when several hundred Native Americans marched into Washington, D.C., at the end of the Longest Walk, a protest march that had begun five months earlier in San Francisco. The Longest Walk was intended to symbolize the forced removal of American Indians from their homelands and to draw attention to the continuing problems of Indian people and their communities. The event was also intended to expose and challenge the backlash movement against Indian treaty rights that was gaining strength around the country and in Congress. This backlash could be seen in the growing number of bills before Congress to abrogate Indian treaties and restrict Indian rights.[85] Unlike many of the protest events of the mid-1970s, the Longest Walk was a peaceful event that included tribal spiritual leaders and elders among its participants. It ended without violence. Thus, Red Power protest had come full circle, from the festive Alcatraz days, through a cycle of confrontations between Indian activists and the federal government, to the traditional quest for spiritual unity that marked the end of the Longest Walk.

The decline of the Alcatraz–Red Power Movement is generally attributed to FBI suppression. That is probably only part of the story. AIM leaders were jailed, brought to trial, and many AIM members were found dead.[86] Internal debates in AIM underscored a long-standing split in the movement between those who preferred to work for the benefit of the urban Indian community using conventional methods of federal funding and community service and those who favored the activist national/supratribal agenda. The activist leadership began to withdraw from AIM: some moved on to other issues; some were kept busy fighting legal battles or serving jail time; and others were excommunicated from AIM by those who preferred more conventional tactics. Some leaders, disillusioned with the possibilities of attaining recognition of native rights within the United States, sought recognition of treaty, national, and humanitarian rights within international forums such as UNESCO. After 1978, AIM leaders pursued many of the same goals as ARPM leaders, but the tactic of property seizures—the defining characteristic of the ARPM—fell out of favor, signaling the end of a formative period of Red Power activism.[87]

In some sense, the ARPM was no longer needed. It had laid the foundation of Indian activism and achieved many of its goals, mostly by conventional means. More Indian students were attending college, by the early 1980s there were over a hundred Indian studies programs in the United States, many tribal museums had opened, the National Museum of the American Indian was being planned, and an international indigenous rights movement has been recognized by the United Nations. However, throughout the 1980s and into the 1990s, AIM remained a force in American Indian activism and consciousness, organizing and participating in protests in the Black Hills (Camp Yellow Thunder);[88] continuing the battle over land and grazing rights in Navajo and Hopi territory; protesting athletic team Indian mascots, gestures, logos, and slogans; and working for the repatriation of Indian burial remains, funerary items, and sacred objects.

Social scientists have written extensively on the consequences of activism for the individuals and communities involved in protest movements, which can be life-transforming events.[89] Doug McAdam has found, for example, that the lives of participants in the 1964 Freedom Summer voter registration campaign in the South were altered such that these activists remained ever different from their uninvolved contemporaries, and, furthermore, the effects of these changes extended well into their adulthoods.[90] In his study of labor actions and strikes, Rick Fantasia has found that the participants in such activism redefine themselves and others in terms of their awareness of class distinctions and power relations. He has also pointed out that the community divisions arising out of sustained protest can be long lived and sometimes bitter.[91]

Sometimes, individual communities are strengthened by their members coming together in protest action. For example, Annette Kuhlmann, Richard White, and Carol Ward have all found that many Native American communities have benefited from the involvement of former activists, whether as museum curators, newspaper editors, community or legal service providers, or tribal leaders.[92] Joane Nagel has argued that the activist period of the 1970s contributed to the cultural renaissance currently underway in many Indian communities in the form of tribal museum development, tribal language instruction, cultural preservation and apprenticeship programs, tribal history projects, and the preservation and reinstitution of ceremonial and spiritual practices.[93]

Perhaps the most profound effect of the Alcatraz-Red Power Movement was to educate and change the consciousness of people in the United States and around the world. By the 1980s, more Americans were familiar with Indian issues as a result of the attention brought to bear by ARPM activism. While Americans have generally demanded assimilation from Indians, the ARPM made the point that Indians have cultures, traditions, history, and communities that they want to preserve—but that they also want equal justice, economic opportunity, access to education, and more accurate portrayal of Indians in the media and in history books. Along with other ethnic group movements, the ARPM contributed to debate over multiculturalism within the U.S. national community. In the end, the Alcatraz–Red Power Movement may have strengthened and diversified U.S. society and made it a more tolerant place for all.

Notes

1 Stephen Cornell, *The Return of the Native* (New York: Oxford University Press, 1988), 180.
2 See R. H. Turner, "Collective Behavior and Resource Mobilization as Approaches to Social Movements," *Research in Social Movements, Conflict and Change* 4 (1981): 1–24; Charles Tilly, *From Mobilization to Revolution* (Reading, Mass.: Addison-Wesley); Doug McAdam, *The Political Process and the Development of Black Insurgency, 1930–1970* (Chicago: University of Chicago Press, 1982).
3 Michael Hittman, *Wovoka and the Ghost Dance* (Carson City, Nev.: Grace Danberg Foundation, 1990), 63–64, 182–94.
4 For a discussion of spiritual and social revitalization movements, see Duane Champagne, "Transocietal Cultural Exchange within the World Economic and Political System," in *The Dynamics of Social Systems,* ed. Paul Colomy (Newbury Park, Calif.: Sage, 1992), 120–53.
5 H. W. Hertzberg, *The Search for an American Indian Identity* (Syracuse, N.Y.: Syracuse University Press, 1971), 6.
6 Six Nations peoples consist of the Mohawk, Oneida, Onondaga, Cayuga, Seneca, and Tuscarora Indian tribes of the northeastern United States.
7 Guy B. Senese, *Self-Determination and the Social Education of Native Americans* (New York: Praeger, 1991), 146.
8 Ibid., 147.
9 Fay G. Cohen, *Treaties on Trial: The Continuing Controversy over Northwest Indian Fishing Rights* (Seattle: University of Washington Press, 1986), 69.
10 Quoted in Senese, *Self-Determination,* 145.
11 Ibid., 148.
12 Ibid., 144.
13 Troy R. Johnson, "Part 3: Native North American History, 1960–94," in *Chronology of Native North American History,* ed. Duane Champagne (Detroit: Gale Research, 1994), 355.
14 Ibid., 361–62.
15 Quoted in Senese, *Self-Determination,* 224.
16 Robert Hecht, "Taos Pueblo and the Struggle for Blue Lake," *American Indian Culture and Research Journal* 13:1 (1989): 55.

17 R. C. Gordon-McCutchan, *The Taos Indians and the Battle for Blue Lake* (Santa Fe, N. Mex.: Red Crane Books, 1991), xvi–xvii. This book recounts the story of the government taking of Blue Lake and the Taos Indians' successful campaign to recover it.

18 Alvin Josephy, "The American Indian and the Bureau of Indian Affairs, 1969: A Study with Recommendations," 24 February 1969. Report commissioned by President Richard M. Nixon.

19 Edgar S. Cahn, "Postscript," in *Our Brother's Keeper: The Indian in White America,* ed. Edgar S. Cahn (New York: New Community Press, 1969), 187–90.

20 Ibid.

21 R. D. Arnold, *Alaska Native Land Claims* (Anchorage: Alaska Native Foundation, 1978).

22 Cohen, *Treaties on Trial,* 82–83.

23 The Nixon presidential archives make no mention of the invasion of Cambodia, since it was largely a secret operation (thought poorly kept) at the time. President Nixon and his staff make direct analogies among the Indian people on Alcatraz, the events at My Lai, and the shootings at Kent State. It was agreed that the American people would not stand by and see Indian people massacred and taken off Alcatraz in body bags.

24 Judith Clavir Albert and Stewart Edward Albert, *The Sixties Papers: Documents of a Rebellions Decade* (New York: Praeger, 1984), 18.

25 Wub-e-ke-niew, *We Have'n Right to Exist* (New York: Black Thistle Press, 1995), xxxix.

26 Veterans Administration Statistical Brief, "Native American Veterans," SB 70-85-3 (October 1985), Washington, D.C.

27 Quoted in Stan Steiner, *The New Indians* (New York: Harper & Row, 1968), 282.

28 Ibid.

29 Joan Ablon, "Relocated American Indians in the San Francisco Bay Area: Social Interaction and Indian Identity," *Human Organization* 23 (Winter 1964): 297.

30 Vine Deloria, Jr., *Behind the Trail of Broken Treaties: An Indian Declaration of Independence* (Austin: University of Texas Press, 1985), 34.

31 Quoted in Alvin M. Josephy, Jr., *The American Indian Fight for Freedom* (New Haven, Conn.: Yale University Press, 1978), 84. Clyde Warrior is often referred to as the founder of the Red Power movement.

32 Quoted in Jack D. Forbes, *Native Americans and Nixon: Presidential Politics and Minority Self-Determination, 1969–1972* (Los Angeles: Americans Indian Studies Center, University of California, 1981), 28. Brightman founded and began publication of *Warpath* in 1968, providing a voice for the rising urban Indian youth groups.

33 Quoted in National Council on Indian Opportunity, "Public Forum before the Committee of Urban Indians, San Francisco, Calif.," 11–12 April 1969, 3

(hereafter NCIO, "Public Forum"). In the possession of Adam Fortunate Eagle, Fallon Indian Reservation, Fallon, Nev.

34 Joan Ablon, "Relocated Indians in the San Francisco Bay Area: Social Interaction and Indian Identity," *Human Organization* 23 (1964): 296–304.

35 NCIO, "Public Forum," 39.

36 Ibid., 41.

37 Quoted in Steiner, *New Indians,* 45.

38 Ibid.

39 Ibid.

40 Johnson, "Part 3," 355–57.

41 During this period, the University of California, Davis, was attempting to acquire the same site for its own use. It was the occupation of the intended site by Indian youth, some of which had been involved in the Alcatraz occupation, that ultimately led to success for the Indian-controlled university. In April 1971, the federal government formally turned this land over to the trustees of Deganawida-Quetzalcoatl (D-Q) University, a joint American Indian and Chicano university. One of the demands of the Alcatraz occupiers, in 1964 and again in 1969, was the establishment of an Indian university on Alcatraz Island. While this never occurred, the establishment of D-Q University was seen by many as the fulfillment of that demand.

42 Troy Johnson, *The Occupation of Alcatraz Island: Indian Self-Determination and the Rise of Indian Activism* (Urbana: University of Illinois Press, 1996). The occupations took place on 9 March 1964, the night of 9–10 November 1969, and 20 November 1969.

43 Belva Cottier interview with John Garvey, San Francisco, Calif., 13 May 1989. Copy in the possession of Troy Johnson.

44 NCIO, "Public Forum."

45 Luis S. Kemnitzer, "Personal Memories of Alcatraz, 1969" (chapter 7 of this volume), 114–15.

46 Johnson, *Occupation of Alcatraz Island,* 119.

47 Earl Livermore (Blackfoot) interview with John D. Sylvester, 8 April 1970, Doris Duke Oral History Project, University of Utah, Salt Lake City.

48 Johnson, *Occupation of Alcatraz Island,* 48.

49 Ibid.

50 "Unsigned Proclamation" reproduced in *Alcatraz Is Not an Island,* ed. Peter Blue Cloud (Berkeley, Calif.: Wingbow Press, 1972), 40–42.

51 Johnson, *Occupation of Alcatraz Island,* 71–72.

52 Ibid., 40–41.

53 Ibid., 154–55.

54 Ibid., 206.

55 Ibid., 152, 169.

56 Ibid., 182–83.

57 Ibid., 226.

58 Vine Deloria, Jr., "The Rise of Indian Activism," in *The Social Reality of Ethnic America,* ed. R. Gomez, C. Collingham, R. Endo, and K. Jackson (Lexington, Mass.: D. C. Heath, 1974), 184–85.

59 Vine Deloria, Jr., correspondence with the authors, 1993.

60 Wilma Mankiller telephone interview with Joane Nagel, Tahlequah, Okla., 27 November 1991. Transcript in the authors' files.

61 George Horse Capture telephone interview with Joane Nagel, Fort Belknap, Mont., 24 May 1994. Transcript in the authors' files. See also George Horse Capture, "An American Indian Perspective," in *Seeds of Change: A Quincentennial Commemoration,* ed. Herman J. Viola and Carolyn Margolis (Washington, D.C.: Smithsonian Institution Press, 1991).

62 John Echohawk telephone interview with Joane Nagel, Boulder, Colo., 9 July 1993. Transcript in the authors' files.

63 Leonard Peltier telephone interview with Joane Nagel, Leavenworth, Kans., 1 June 1993. Transcript in the authors' files.

64 Frances Wise telephone interview with Joane Nagel, Oklahoma City, Okla., 24 August 1993. Transcript in the authors' files.

65 Quoted in Judith Antell, "American Indian Women Activists" (Ph.D. diss., University of California, Berkeley, 1989), 58.

66 Grace Thorpe interview with John Trudell on "Radio Free Alcatraz," 12 December 1969. Transcript available from Pacifica Radio Archive, 3729 Cahvenga Boulevard, North Hollywood, CA 91604.

67 Loretta Flores telephone interview with Joane Nagel, Lawrence, Kans., 12 May 1993. Transcript in the authors' files.

68 "Indians Seize Army Center for Use as Cultural Base," *New York Times,* 4 November 1970, 6. This land later became the site of Deganawida-Quetzalcoatl (D-Q) University. See *Akwesasne Notes* (January–February 1971): 17.

69 William M. Blair, "24 Indians Seized in Capital Clash," *New York Times,* 23 September 1971, 49.

70 Ward Churchill and James Vander Wall, *Agents of Repression: The FBI's Secret War against the Black Panther Party and the American Indian Movement* (Boston: South End Press, 1988), 121; Rex Weyler, *Blood of the Land* (New York: Everett House, 1984), 24, 42–43; Peter Matthiessen, *In the Spirit of Crazy Horse* (New York: Viking, 1991), 37–40, 49–52; Alvin M. Josephy, Jr., *Now That the Buffalo's Gone* (New York: Knopf, 1982), 228–31.

71 Johnson, *Occupation of Alcatraz Island,* 219–20; Wub-e-ke-niew, *We Have the Right to Exist,* xl–xlvii.

72 Churchill and Vander Wall, *Agents of Repression,* 121.

73 Ibid. Ironically, several researchers also cite the role of common prison experiences in the formation of the American Indian Movement organization. See Matthiessen, *In the Spirit of Crazy Horse,* 34; Weyler, *Blood of the Land,* 35; Rachel

A. Bonney, "Forms of Supratribal Indian Interaction in the United States" (Ph.D. diss., University of Arizona, 1975), 154–55.

74 Fay G. Cohen, "The Indian Patrol in Minneapolis: Social Control and Social Change in an Urban Context" (Ph.D. diss., University of Minnesota, 1973), 52.

75 Ibid., 49–50; Jeanne Guillemin, *Urban Renegades: The Cultural Strategy of American Indians* (New York: Columbia University Press, 1975); Roy Bongartz, "The New Indians," in *Native Americans Today,* ed. H. M. Bahr, B. A. Chadwick, and R. C. Day (New York: Harper & Row, 1968), 495.

76 Russell Means with Marvin J. Wolf, *Where White Men Fear to Tread: The Autobiography of Russell Means* (New York: St. Martin's Press, 1995), 540.

77 Today, most commentators, participants, and observers refer to the 1973 siege at Wounded Knee, South Dakota, as "Wounded Knee." At the time, the press and commentators often called the siege "Wounded Knee II," to distinguish it from the U.S. 7th Cavalry's massacre of Lakotas which took place there in December 1890. See Robert Utley, *The Last Days of the Sioux Nation* (New Haven, Conn.: Yale University Press, 1963), 110.

78 See Edward Lazarus, *Black Hills, White Justice: The Sioux Nation versus the United States, 1775 to the Present* (New York: HarperCollins, 1991), chap. 12; Matthiessen, *In the Spirit of Crazy Horse,* chap. 3; Churchill and Vander Wall, *Agents of Repression,* chap. 5; Stanley D. Lyman, *Wounded Knee 1973: A Personal Account* (Lincoln: University of Nebraska Press, 1991); Rolland Dewing, *Wounded Knee: The Meaning and Significance of the Second Incident* (New York: Irvington, 1985).

79 For instance, Lazarus reports that, up to that point, the "Pine Ridge Sioux had never reelected a president to a second term" (*Black Hills, White Justice,* 309).

80 Ibid., 307.

81 The most celebrated of the cases involves Leonard Peltier, who was tried and convicted for the deaths of two FBI agents who were shot on the Pine Ridge Reservation in 1975. See Matthiessen, *In the Spirit of Crazy Horse,* 162.

82 For instance, Wilson remained in office and was reelected after a challenge by AIM leader Russell Means in 1974. Wilson died in 1990. See Churchill and Vander Wall, *Agents of Repression,* 189; Martin Waldron, "President of Oglala Sioux Is Re-elected," *New York Times,* 9 February 1974, 23; Matthiessen, *In the Spirit of Crazy Horse,* 581.

83 While several of these post-Wounded Knee occupations were marked by intratribal conflict, the Puyallup occupation of the detention center appears to have been undertaken by a unified tribe.

84 Grace Lichtenstein, "Custer's Defeat Commemorated by Entreaties on Peace," *New York Times,* 25 June 1976, II–1.

85 For a general description of anti-Indian backlash groups and activities in the late 1970s, see the series of articles in "Nationwide Backlash against the Indian

Tribes," the 18 July 1977 supplement of the *Yakima Nation Review:* Richard La Course, "Anti-Indian Backlash Growing; Tribes, Groups Form Defense Tactics"; Carole Wright, "What People Have Formed Backlash Groups?"; June Adams, "Three Major 'Backlash Bills' in Congress"; June Adams and Richard La Course, "Backlash Barrage Erupts across U.S." See also Fay G. Cohen, "Implementing Indian Treaty Fishing Rights: Conflict and Cooperation," in *Critical Issues in Native North America,* vol. 2, ed. W. Churchill (Copenhagen: International Work Group for Indigenous Affairs, 1991), 155–73.

86 Ken Stern, *Loud Hawk: The U.S. versus the American Indian Movement* (Norman: University of Oklahoma Press, 1994), 93–98. The deaths were never investigated, but Indian people suspect the FBI was involved.

87 See, for example, Wub-e-ke-niew, *We Have the Right to Exist,* xlv, 232–33; Josephy, *Now That the Buffalo's Gone,* 254–55.

88 Camp Yellow Thunder was established in the early 1980s to protest federal violations of Sioux treaties and the refusal of the federal government to return the Black Hills. See Lazarus, *Black Hills, White Justice,* 411–12; and Donald Worster, *Under Western Skies: Nature and History in the American West* (New York: Oxford University Press, 1992), chap. 8.

89 See, for example, Leila Rupp and Verta Taylor, *Survival in the Doldrums: The American Women's Rights Movement, 1945 to the 1960s* (New York: Oxford University Press, 1987); Doug McAdam, *Freedom Summer* (New York: Oxford University Press, 1988); Rick Fantasia, *Cultures of Solidarity: Consciousness, Action, and Contemporary American Workers* (Berkeley: University of California Press, 1988); Verta Taylor and Nancy E. Whittier, "Collective Identity in Social Movement Communities: Lesbian Feminist Mobilization," in *Frontiers in Social Movement Theory,* ed. A. D. Morris and C. M. Mueller (New Haven, Conn.: Yale University Press, 1992), 104–20; Joane Nagel, "American Indian Ethnic Renewal: Politics and the Resurgence of Identity," *American Sociological Review* 60 (1995): 947–65.

90 McAdam, *Freedom Summer.*

91 Fantasia, *Cultures of Solidarity.*

92 Annette Kuhlmann, "Collaborative Research on Biculturalism among the Kickapoo Tribe of Oklahoma" (Ph.D. diss., University of Kansas, 1989); Richard H. White, *Tribal Assets: The Rebirth of Native America* (New York: Henry Holt, 1990), 124; Carol Ward, "The Intersection of Ethnic and Gender Identities: The Role of Northern Cheyenne Women in Cultural Recovery," paper presented at the annual meeting of the Society for the Scientific Study of Religion, Raleigh, N. C., October 1993, p. 86.

93 Joane Nagel, *American Indian Ethnic Renewal: Red Power and the Resurgence of Identity and Culture* (New York: Oxford University Press, 1996), 195–200.

Selected Bibliography: Alcatraz and the Activist Period

Cornell, Stephen. *The Return of the Native: American Indian Political Resurgence,* New York: Oxford University Press, 1988.

Churchill, Ward, and James Vander Wall. *Agents of Repression: The FBI's Secret Wars against the Black Panther Party and the American Indian Movement.* Boston: South End Press, 1988.

Crow Dog, Mary, and Richard Erdoes. *Lakota Woman.* New York: Grove Weidenfeld, 1990.

Fortunate Eagle, Adam. *Alcatraz! Alcatraz! The Indian Occupation of 1969–71.* San Francisco: Heyday Books, 1992.

Johnson, Troy. *The Indian Occupation of Alcatraz Island: Indian Self-Determination and the Rise of Indian Activism.* Urbana: University of Illinois Press, 1996.

Matthiessen, Peter. *In the Spirit of Crazy Horse.* New York: Viking, 1991.

Means, Russell, with Marvin J. Wolf. *Where White Men Fear to Tread: The Autobiography of Russell Means.* New York: St. Martin's Press, 1995.

Nagel, Joane. *American Indian Ethnic Renewal: Red Power and the Resurgence of Identity and Culture.* New York: Oxford University Press, 1995.

Smith, Paul Chaat, and Robert Allen Warrior. *Like a Hurricane: The Indian Movement from Alcatraz to Wounded Knee.* New York: The Free Press, 1996.

Stern, Kenneth S. *Loud Hawk: The U.S. versus the American Indian Movement.* Norman: University of Oklahoma Press, 1994.

The Rise of Direct Action

S. Dale McLemore, et al

Power concedes nothing without demand.

—*Frederick Douglass*

When you are forever fighting a degenerating sense of "nobodiness"—then you will understand why we find it difficult to wait.

—*Martin Luther King, Jr.*

. . . while individual empowerment is key, only collective action can effectively generate lasting social transformation of political and economic institutions.

—*Patricia Hill Collins*

The Rise of Direct Action

Soon after the *Brown* decisions, there was a sharp increase in unemployment among African Americans. This decline in the economic circumstances of African Americans, coming as it did on the heels of great judicial victories, was particularly galling and decreased their faith in the value of changing laws. A more specific event, however, precipitated a new phase in the effort to ensure the civil rights of African Americans. On December 1, 1955, in Montgomery, Alabama, Mrs. Rosa Parks refused to yield her bus seat to a White person and was arrested. As the news of Mrs. Parks arrest spread, Black people in the city, at the urging of NAACP leader E. D. Nixon, began a boycott of the local buses. In less than a week, nearly all of the more than

40,000 Black citizens of Montgomery had rallied around the dynamic young pastor of the Dexter Avenue Baptist Church, Martin Luther King, Jr., in a massive boycott of the buses. At first, the boycott was intended to last only one day, but various incidents of harassment and intimidation by Whites led to a decision to continue the boycott indefinitely. This decision was followed by further acts of intimidation. For instance, on January 30, 1956, Martin Luther King's home was bombed; two days later, the home of E. D. Nixon also was bombed. On February 22, 24 Black ministers and 55 others were arrested for nonviolent protesting.

The confrontation between Blacks and Whites over segregation in Montgomery ended in the desegregation of the buses more than a year later. During that time, the bus boycott became a symbol of nonviolent protest throughout the world. Martin Luther King, Jr., became the leading spokesman for the philosophy of nonviolence and the most prominent figure in what rapidly became a new phase of the relations between Whites and Blacks in America. The events in Montgomery contributed to a growing conviction among Black Americans that, in King's words, "privileged groups seldom give up their privileges voluntarily." To promote the philosophy and practices of nonviolent protest, King founded the Southern Christian Leadership Conference (SCLC) in January 1957.

Increasing Militancy

The decade following the Montgomery bus boycott was filled with dramatic developments in American racial relations. Although the legal approach continued to play an indispensable role, various forms of direct action became far more popular, especially among young people. A sit-in by college students at a Woolworth's store lunch counter in Greensboro, North Carolina, in 1960 set off a veritable chain reaction of student sit-ins throughout the South. These events led rapidly to the formation of yet another organization devoted to nonviolent direct action, the Student Nonviolent Coordinating Committee (SNCC). Although the members of the new organization accepted the philosophy of nonviolence espoused by CORE and SCLC and were clearly inspired by Martin Luther King, Jr., they believed their goals could not be pursued vigorously enough within any of the existing organizations. The many lines of cleavage within the Black community became prominent once again. The older organizations, such as the once "radical" NAACP, were now regarded by many as "too conservative." Simultaneously, however, the older organizations were being changed by the "radical" tactics of direct action.

Amid charges of excessive "conservatism" and "radicalism," nearly all of the main Black protest groups adopted some combination of legal and direct-action methods, though the new organizations were in the vanguard. In this process, the entire civil rights movement became more militant. The battle cry "Freedom Now!" gradually gained acceptance even among many Black "conservatives." The NAACP, for example, sponsored many demonstrations during this period; and CORE pioneered still another new protest tactic by conducting an interracial "Freedom Ride" on a bus headed for New Orleans. Here, for the first time, White people joined in the protest. This ride ended when the bus was fire-bombed in Alabama, but many others were to follow. The representatives of the different protest organizations found that whatever their legal rights were supposed to be, sit-ins, kneel-ins, lie-ins, boycotts, picket lines, and freedom rides might each be met by mob violence, tear gas, police dogs, arrests, jail terms, and, in some cases, by death.

The tempo of direct action increased during the spring of 1963. As the number of demonstrations in the South reached a new high, the nonviolent technique was frequently used in the North as well. Two protests in 1963 stand out. The first of these took place in Birmingham, Alabama, which was a symbol of southern White resistance to desegregation. A coalition of Black leaders under the direction of Martin Luther King, Jr., joined an ongoing nonviolent protest campaign in Birmingham. The protests began with well-organized demonstrators going to jail for conducting sit-ins at lunch counters. Within a month, thousands of demonstrators, including King, had been jailed and many others had been physically assaulted by police. Later, protesters were met by police with clubs, high-pressure water hoses, cattle prods, and dogs. This attack on unarmed, unresisting men, women, and children aroused enormous national and international support, leading to a truce with Birmingham's business leaders. It was agreed that lunch counters, rest rooms, and other public places would be desegregated. The Birmingham protests had demonstrated dramatically that "the theory of nonviolent direct action was a fact".

A second outstanding protest of 1963 was a huge (approximately 250,000 people) March on Washington. Reviving the technique he had pioneered during the early years of World War II, A. Philip Randolph called for a massive protest march on the nation's capital to dramatize the problem of unemployment. The march captured the attention of the entire country. For millions of people, Martin Luther King, Jr.'s famous "I Have a Dream" speech encapsulated the aspirations of the civil rights movement. The march showed that the movement was beginning to look beyond direct-action protest toward a new focus on political action, beyond civil rights to a heightened concern for economic opportunity, and beyond appeals to the conscience of White people to a demand for equality.

The effects of the direct-action protests between 1956 and 1964 were mixed. In most states of the South, the protests had achieved rapid changes in desegregating restaurants, theaters, buses, hotels, and so on. Black men and women increasingly could expect to be served courteously; however, the protests had been less than successful in some states and had done little to bring about changes in segregated schooling, poor housing, and discrimination in law enforcement. Moreover, throughout 1964, instances of White violence increased. For example, three voter-registration workers (James Chaney, Andrew Goodman, and Michael Schwerner) were killed in Mississippi. Members of the KKK were suspected; and in 1967, seven of the suspects were convicted on civil rights charges.

Civil Rights Legislation

The escalation of violence by Whites weakened the allegiance of many Blacks to the philosophy of nonviolent resistance. As the limitations of direct action became apparent, Black leaders began to turn to different directions. The political pressure mounted by the March on Washington was increased through voter registration and "get out the vote" drives. With the strong support of President Johnson, President Kennedy's civil rights program was passed as the Civil Rights Act of 1964. This legislation prohibited discrimination in voting, public accommodations and facilities, schools, courts, and employment; however, official violations of the voting rights section of the law (Title I) continued in the South after the law was passed. In response to these violations, Martin Luther King, Jr. led a nonviolent demonstration in Selma, Alabama; and, shortly thereafter, Congress passed the Voting Rights Act of 1965. This law suspended all literacy tests for voters and permitted the federal government to station poll watchers in all of the states of the South.

The legislation of 1964 and 1965 marked the end of official segregation in America. Yet something was clearly wrong. The laws had not, in fact, ended discrimination; and, like the direct-action demonstrations that preceded them, they had had little visible effect on conditions in the Black ghettos of the cities. After a decade of notable victories, there still was pervasive unemployment, underemployment, and poverty. Many Black neighborhoods were characterized by high "street" crime, poor health and sanitation, poor housing, inferior schools, poor city services, high divorce and separation rates, low access to "city hall," demeaning and inadequate welfare services, high prices for inferior goods and services, and poor relations with the police. What now was to be done? An answer from the past attained renewed popularity.

Black Power

We mentioned earlier that the *Brown* decisions encouraged most Black Americans to believe the end of school segregation and other forms of inequality was near. We saw, however, that these hopes were soon dampened by the strong evidence—as in Montgomery and Birmingham—that many Whites intended to resist the Court's rulings in every way possible, including the use of violence. The primary reaction among Blacks to the massive resistance of the Whites, as noted earlier, was nonviolent protest. This was not the only reaction, however. Not since the days of Marcus Garvey had so many Black Americans been ready to listen to those who doubted the possibility or desirability of "integration" and who urged, instead, some form of separation. The organization that was best able to capitalize on this renewed interest in a separatist solution was the Lost Nation of Islam (the Black Muslims).

The Black Muslims had been led since the mid-1930s by Elijah Muhammad. They had been hard at work during the intervening years but had not attracted many converts; however, during the late 1950s and early 1960s, they attracted many new converts and a great deal of attention from the mass media. A new and dynamic

Muslim leader, Malcolm X, was a particularly effective advocate of the Black nationalist philosophy.

Renewed Black Nationalism. Malcolm X, who substituted an "X" for the surname his grandparents had received from their slave master (Little), became the minister of the large Muslim temple in Harlem. Like his teacher, Elijah Muhammad, Malcolm X emphasized that Black people must organize to regain their self-respect and to assert their collective power. Consequently, he and his followers sought some form of separation from White America. If the U.S. government would not pay the costs of sending Blacks to Africa, then, Malcolm X argued, the United States should set aside some territory within its borders so African Americans could move away from the Whites. Malcolm believed that such a separate territory should be given as payment for the long period during which Black slaves worked without pay to help build America.

Malcolm X was very interested in Africa and believed strongly that Black people throughout the world shared a similar destiny. In time, Malcolm and Elijah Muhammad came into conflict over various matters; and in 1964, Malcolm left Elijah's organization to found a rival Muslim group, the Organization of Afro-American Unity. The organization's charter emphasized the right of African Americans to defend themselves against violence in any way necessary. In addition to this "defensive" use of violence, however, some African Americans began to think in terms of attack. The most militant members of the group began to use the word "revolution" as more than a metaphor.

Violent Protests. The clearest evidence of a shift among some Blacks away from the acceptance of only "defensive" violence and toward the acceptance of "offensive" violence began to appear in 1964. For example, in July an off-duty New York City police lieutenant intervened in a dispute between some Black youths and a White man. When one of the youths attacked with a knife, the officer shot and killed him. Two days later, a rally called by CORE to protest the lynchings of civil rights workers in Mississippi led to a clash with police in which one person was killed. In the following days, a crowd attacked the police with Molotov cocktails, bricks, and bottles in the Harlem and Bedford–Stuyvesant areas of New York; the police responded with gunfire. Then, on a hot evening in August 1965, a California motorcycle patrol officer stopped a young Black man for speeding near the Watts area of Los Angeles. After the driver failed a sobriety test, he was arrested. The officer radioed for assistance while a large crowd of people gathered. When the prisoner's brother and mother arrived and began to struggle with the police, they too were arrested. As the police departed, the angry crowd threw stones at the police car.

Rumors that the police had beaten the intoxicated driver, his family, and a pregnant woman spread throughout the area. Later, groups of Black people stoned and over-turned some passing automobiles, beat up some White motorists, and harassed the police. The next evening, three cars were set on fire, snipers opened fire on the firefighters, and people began burning and looting stores and buildings owned by Whites. The burning, looting, and sniping then spread into the Watts area; and two city blocks on 103rd Street were burned out while firemen were held off by sniper fire. Late in the day, the governor of California ordered nearly 14,000 national guardsmen into the area to restore peace. Burning and looting spread into other parts of southeast Los Angeles, and the fighting between rioters, police, and guardsmen continued for two more days.

The Watts area rioting was the worst in America since the 1943 outbreak in Detroit. Thirty-four people were killed, over 1,000 were injured, and more than 600 buildings were damaged or totally destroyed. The pattern of burning and looting strongly suggested that the Black rioters had intentionally focused their attacks on food, liquor, furniture, clothing, and department stores owned by White people.

The level of Black protest increased during 1966. According to the National Advisory Commission, 43 major and "minor disorders and riots" occurred during that year, including a new outburst in Watts. Two of the major disorders in Chicago and Cleveland involved extensive looting, rock throwing, fire bombing, and shooting at the police. In each case, the disorders and riots were preceded by a history of dissatisfaction among Blacks in regard to police practices, unemployment, inadequate housing, inadequate education, and many other things; and they were usually precipitated by some seemingly minor incident, frequently involving the police. For example, in Chicago, the rioting commenced after police arrested a Black youth who had illegally opened a fire hydrant in order to cool off with water.

The heightened militancy of many African Americans and their impatience with the rate of social change were dramatized in a speech delivered by Stokely Carmichael. Like many Black leaders before him, Carmichael, the chairman of SNCC, urged Black people to "get together" in their own behalf. He rejected the idea that Black Americans could "get ahead" through individual ambition and hard work. What was needed, he said, was "Black Power." The slogan "Black Power" was not completely new; neither were the ideas of race pride and self-help suggested by it; however, the use of this phrase at this particular time took on special significance. The phrase was vague enough to encompass a wide range of perspectives. It symbolized the frustration of many integrationists as well as Black nationalists. In the minds of many White people, though, the slogan was identified primarily with Black revolutionaries and separatist organizations.

The increasing willingness of African Americans, especially the young adults, to demand an immediate end to racial inequalities and to back their demands with violence, if necessary, ushered in still another phase in Black–White relations. Just as the legal approach had been made secondary by the advent of widespread nonviolent protests, the use of violent methods now moved to the fore. As in the earlier shift, organizations, leaders, and methods that had at first seemed "radical" now seemed "conservative" by comparison. The level of violence was escalated again during 1967, with most of the disorders occurring in July.

The violent protests declined after 1968. The most influential Black leaders had never accepted the principles of separation or violent protest. For example, shortly before his assassination on April 4, 1968, Martin Luther King, Jr., argued that "the time has come for a return to mass nonviolent protest." In his view, nonviolence was more relevant as an effective device than ever before: "Violence is not only morally repugnant, it is pragmatically barren". Apparently, most African Americans soon accepted this assessment. By 1973, legal and political approaches to the solution of the problem of racial inequality had once again become the primary weapons of African Americans.

Declining Momentum. Civil rights activities by African Americans during the 1970s and 1980s were, in Brisbane's words, "calmer, more sober, more conservative." Global economic and political problems during the 1970s thrust such issues as inflation and military spending to the forefront. These changes were joined in the 1980s by a shift to the political right during the administrations of Presidents Ronald Reagan and George Bush. These social and political trends were reflected in a decreased willingness by the dominant group to support the social spending that was needed to maintain the levels reached during the 1960s. Even though many other groups—including women, homosexuals, the elderly, and the physically handicapped—also organized to combat discrimination and gain equal rights, the 1970s and 1980s witnessed a "dramatic loss of momentum". The U.S. Commission on Civil Rights expressed concern that in such matters as school and job desegregation, police protection, voting rights, housing, and affirmative action, the federal government's civil rights enforcement effort was not adequately funded and coordinated. In some cases, according to the Commission, changes in the laws have "aided and abetted the obstructionists." Numerous court rulings during the 1980s served to restrict the scope of effective minority action against civil rights violations. Even though the Civil Rights Act of 1991 reversed the effects of some rulings of the U.S. Supreme Court concerning discrimination in employment, the fact that the rulings had been made still increased the concern of many African Americans that their civil rights were in jeopardy.

Renewed Visibility of Black-White Conflict

There were numerous other signs in the 1980s that the gains of the 1960s and 1970s were under attack. Various incidents, often involving conflict with police officers, exploded into major urban riots. For instance, in Miami, Florida, three large disturbances took place during the 1980s. In 1980, 18 people were killed and more than 400 were injured in the Liberty City section; in 1982, two people were killed and more than 25 were injured in the Overtown section; and in 1989, six people were injured and 30 buildings were burned, again in Overtown, after a policeman killed an African American motorcyclist. These and many other events were reminders that America's racial problems had not been solved.

The Beating of Rodney King

These problems returned to national prominence and a higher place on the political agenda in 1991, after an African American man named Rodney King was arrested for traffic violations by four White Los Angeles police officers (one of the four was Hispanic). The arrest was videotaped covertly by a nearby citizen. The videotape, run repeatedly on national television, showed Mr. King writhing on the ground while being kicked and beaten with batons by the officers. According to press and television accounts, most viewers, White as well as Black, thought that the arrest and beating of Mr. King constituted a clear case of police brutality; consequently, when the officers were tried more than a year later, the nation was "stunned" (as many newspapers reported) by the acquittal of all four officers on the charge of "assault with a deadly weapon" and of three officers on the charge of an "excessive use of force as a police officer."

Major urban disorders erupted in several American cities, with the largest and most severe rioting of the twentieth century occurring in Los Angeles itself. The violence started in the Florence-Normandie area of South Central Los Angeles and spread southeast into Watts and north into Koreatown. As in the case of the Watts riots in the 1960s, Blacks were prominent among the rioters and non-Blacks were the main targets; but in this case, Hispanics also were prominent among the rioters, and Asians, principally Koreans (but also some Cambodians), were among the targets. City, state, and federal officials called for the rioting to end. Mr. King, in a halting yet eloquent appeal for peace, asked the crucial question: "Can we all get along?" Again, as in the 1960s, thousands of troops were rushed to the scene; and by the end of the first week in May, the explosion was over. Estimates of the deaths and damage vary; but at least 51 people were murdered, hundreds more were injured, and burning and looting were responsible for millions of dollars in damage. Twenty-seven of the victims of the rioting were Black. Whites were almost as upset about the videotaped beating as Blacks. Almost 86 percent of White Americans disagreed with the jury's decision, were angered by the absence of Blacks from the jury, and did not believe the trial should have been held in the lily-white suburban venue of Simi Valley.

Whites were much less likely than Blacks, however, to see the arrest of King and the release of the officers as evidence of a larger pattern of racism in the United States. A TIME/CNN poll taken during this period made clear some of the differences between the views of Black and White Americans concerning the state of race relations in the United States. Consider the answers to the following questions: "Have prejudice and discrimination against Blacks become more prevalent in recent years?"—54 percent of the Blacks and 31 percent of the Whites answered "yes"; "Would the verdict [in the King trial] have been different if the police and the man they had beaten had all been White?"—82 percent of the Blacks and 44 percent of the Whites answered "yes"; "Which makes you angrier, the verdict or the violence that followed?"—twice as many Blacks as Whites said the verdict made them angrier, whereas almost three times as many Whites as Blacks said the violence made them angrier (Ellis 1992:28); and when asked to give "the reason for the jury's not-guilty verdict," 45 percent of the Blacks and

12 percent of the Whites said "racism". Blauner emphasized that White Americans tend to view racial incidents as aberrations in American life, whereas Blacks believe that racism is a central part of American society.

The O. J. Simpson Trial

Four years after the trial of Rodney King's assailants, another spectacular trial divided the nation largely along racial lines and once again focused attention on racial relations. A popular and wealthy African American former professional football player and movie star, O. J. Simpson, was accused of murdering his former wife, Nicole Brown Simpson, and her friend Ron Goldman. Both Ms. Simpson and Mr. Goldman were White. The trial lasted 9 months and was followed on television by millions of viewers throughout the United States and in other countries. Reactions to the trial seemed to be especially shaped by race, and sometimes by gender. Almost every opinion poll taken during the trial showed a gap of about 40 percentage points between the views of Blacks and Whites. Most Whites held fast to the belief that Mr. Simpson was guilty; most Blacks maintained that he was innocent. The polls suggested that Blacks held a deep suspicion of the police and the criminal justice system. A verdict of "not guilty" was decided by a jury panel of nine Blacks, two Whites, and one Hispanic. Ten jury members were women and two were men.

The testimony and racial attitudes of a witness for the state, police detective Mark Fuhrman, were key elements in the trial that fanned racial tensions. In the tapes, which were played in court as evidence, the former detective used the word "nigger" more than three dozen times and talked about police officers who routinely perjured themselves, destroyed evidence, arrested people without probable cause, and beat confessions out of those they arrested. Many Black police officers did not see the attitudes expressed on the tapes as surprising or exceptional. Many White officers were upset by the tapes and said they did not reflect the views of most people in Los Angeles or in the police department.

Reactions to the trial among residents of Los Angeles and elsewhere also split along racial lines. Whites claimed the press and Black leaders were blowing the significance of the tapes and the extent of racial prejudice out of proportion. Blacks claimed that the tapes demonstrated the racism that Black Americans experience almost daily and that there was a police conspiracy to frame Mr. Simpson. The idea of a police conspiracy seemed bizarre to many Whites; but, as explained by the president of the Los Angeles Urban League, it seemed bizarre only because the police treat the members of the White and Black communities quite differently. Many Blacks view the police as "an occupying force" characterized by brutality and deep-seated racism.

When the verdict "not guilty" was read on October 3, 1995, the *New York Times* reported that 400 African American students at the historically black Morehouse College roared and cheered; Whites who stopped work to watch the jury decision on television responded with disbelief and anger. Both Blacks and Whites felt that the case exacerbated the already simmering ethnic and racial tensions in America, and numerous editorials appeared in newspapers throughout the United States commenting on the racial implications of the trial. Cornel West, an African American professor at Harvard, stated that the Simpson verdict represented "the first time in history that a majority Black jury has wielded an apparatus of state power against the will of the nation's white citizenry."

The racial disagreement seen in these incidents (and dramatized in the riots) certainly shows that the long road of change traveled by Black and White Americans since 1619 has not yet produced the levels of merger called for by the various ideologies of assimilation. Many Black Americans are disappointed, angry, and bitter and do not believe that they yet have achieved equality as citizens. Even the new Black middle class has not overcome fully the barrier of racism. Hochschild attributed the continued elusive racial bias that African Americans face in the United States to "the permanence of racism." In her interviews with Blacks she found that despite the gains made in many areas, successful Blacks still contend with "inhospitable personnel officers, informal social ostracism, excessive penalties for mistakes, exclusion from communication networks, resistance from subordinates, assumptions about cultural and personal inferiority, lower ratings from bosses, and 'ghettoized' assignments."

Some Corporate Cases

In 1994, in the largest court case in the history of the public accommodations section of the 1964 Civil Rights Act, Denny's restaurant chain was ordered to pay millions of dollars to Black customers who were discriminated against in its restaurants. Employees testified that they were told to follow what were called "Blackout" policies to keep African American customers to a minimum, including actions taken against military officers, police officers, teachers, and government officials. Whites were seated ahead of Blacks; Blacks were seated in the rear of the restaurant and service to them was slow; Blacks were asked to pay before eating, were required to make minimum purchases, and were even sometimes "locked out" of the restaurants. These policies resulted in service so disrespectful to African Americans that it would be hard to deny racist intent.

Just a year earlier, a federal court approved one of the largest financial settlements in a class action race discrimination suit against another restaurant chain, Shoney's. Employees of Shoney's charged that the chain deliberately shunted Blacks into low-paying, low-visibility kitchen jobs, when it hired them at all, and clearly showed a preference for Whites. In 1994, the U.S. Department of Labor, the federal agency responsible for protecting workers' rights, also settled the largest race discrimination suit ever brought by government workers. African American employees claimed that they had been unfairly dismissed, demoted, or denied promotion in 1981, 1983, and 1984. The Justice Department also reached out-of-court settlements in 1995 with a number of banks accused of showing bias in lending to Blacks. The suit contended, among other things, that banks refused to allow African Americans to clear poor credit histories, an opportunity normally given to Whites. It also maintained that banks required Blacks to meet unnecessarily high standards to qualify for loans and denied Black applicants mortgages at a rate about five times the denial rate of White applicants.

Another major discrimination case focused nationwide attention on Texaco, Inc., the fourteenth largest corporation in the United States. In November 1996, a Texaco executive released secretly recorded tapes of a meeting in which senior Texaco executives planned the destruction of documents requested in a Federal discrimination lawsuit. The tape recordings also showed the executives berating minority employees with racially insulting language. Six Texaco employees had previously sued the company alleging that Texaco fostered a racially hostile environment and systematically discriminated against minority employees in promotions. Newspaper editorials and comments from other minority employees noted that the only thing unusual about the Texaco case was that racism was reported. Although Texaco had antidiscrimination policies, equal opportunity programs, and appropriate channels for filing discrimination complaints in place, the White managers and executives operated by their own, often discriminatory, rules with little corporate oversight. Texaco's chairman and chief executive expressed dismay at the blatant racism captured on the tapes. Faced with threats of a national boycott of Texaco products, the corporation settled the discrimination suit by agreeing to pay damages to employees who claimed discrimination, raise salaries for Black employees, provide diversity training programs, and create an independent task force to oversee the changes. Farley pointed out that these continuing successful law suits about employment discrimination are indications of persistently unequal opportunities for African Americans in the job market, which result in a growing gap in earnings between Blacks and Whites.

Our sketch has shown that African Americans moved slowly and painfully out of slavery to citizenship and out of rigid segregation and the denial of equal rights to a legal and official form of equality. But the many evidences that "old-fashioned racism" has been replaced to some extent by "modern racism," and the widespread belief among African Americans that the gains of the 1960s have been eroded, make the careful analysis of social and economic changes and trends all the more important. We turn, therefore, as we have previously in the cases of the Japanese and Mexican Americans, to the question of the extent to which assimilation has occurred between Black and White Americans.

African American Assimilation

Cultural Assimilation

Each ethnic group we have considered so far has faced the question, "As we adopt American culture, what shall become of our own culture?" We saw that, although there are important group differences in this respect, each group has made an effort to retain, transmit, and elaborate its heritage. The tendency of an ethnic group to attempt to adopt these strategies has been shown to be intimately related, among other things, to whether a group has entered the country voluntarily. As a rule, groups that have come into the United States voluntarily have been more willing to undertake cultural assimilation than have Mexican Americans and American Indians. From this perspective, we should expect that African Americans would have been very resistant to cultural assimilation. Even though they were separated from their homelands, the separation did not arise in any way from a dissatisfaction with life in the old country or the desire to start anew in another land; thus, like Mexican Americans and American Indians, Africans initially did not wish to undertake cultural assimilation. Apparently, however, they had little choice. Those who survived the horrors of being captured, bought, and transported to America were in an extremely poor position to retain, transmit, or elaborate their heritage. The entire system of American slavery was constructed to strip the slaves of their cultures, to destroy the link between Africans and their past, and to replace their cultures with ways of thinking and acting that were deemed appropriate for slaves.

It has become increasingly accepted that Black Americans succeeded, nevertheless, in constructing a distinctive culture based on their African roots. To illustrate, Levine found that a number of the characteristics of African cultures, such as the high praise given to verbal improvisation, have remained central features of Black American culture. Levine argued that it is a mistake to assume, however, that cultural elements must be unchanged in order to be derived from African traditions. In his view, "Culture is not a fixed condition but a process. . . . The question is not one of survivals but of transformations". Gutman also believed that some important continuities existed between the lives of the plantation slaves of the early nineteenth century and those of rural Mississippi Blacks in the third decade of the twentieth century.

The Moynihan Report. An incendiary implication of the view that the African heritage was effectively destroyed by slavery is that the present culture of African Americans may be a "distorted" or "pathological" version of White American culture. Proponents of this belief argue that the transmission of such a culture from one generation to the next gives rise to many of the problems facing Black Americans today (e.g., poverty and unemployment, high street crime rates, and many single-parent families and teenage pregnancies).

An important application of this argument holds that the "deficiencies" of Black culture may be seen in the "breakdown" of the Black family. Although this view has been common, its direct political impact is generally traced to an explosive document prepared by Daniel P. Moynihan to help shape the federal government's War on Poverty. This document, commonly called the Moynihan Report, was based on the assumption that "at the heart of the deterioration of the fabric of Negro society is the deterioration of the Negro family". This "deterioration" was judged, in turn, to be the lasting result of the indescribable oppression experienced during slavery. Moynihan referred to a "tangle of pathology" in the Black family that resulted in lowered levels of education and school attendance, lowered income, lowered IQs, and high rates of arrest, delinquency, unemployment, and narcotics use. The Moynihan Report called for government action to enhance "the stability and resources of the Negro American family".

Notice that this "legacy of slavery" analysis is consistent with Elkins' view that the modern problems facing Black Americans are a lingering consequence of the extraordinary harshness of the slavery period. This perspective, many critics have noted, emphasizes the effects of past racism but ignores or minimizes the effects of present racism. In this way, the modern social problems of Black Americans appear to result from *their* inability to take advantage of opportunities rather than from the majority's failure to expand opportunities. Many people think this view "blames the victim."

An Ethnic Resource Model. As the results of Moynihan's analysis became generally known, many scholars reacted angrily. Although his description of the severity of the effects of the slavery period was generally accepted, his conclusions concerning their modern effects were not. Critics attacked the idea that the problems of Black Americans stemmed from the presumed weaknesses and failures of the Black family. They emphasized, instead, the many strengths, resources, and achievements of the Black family. The work of these scholars supported an ethnic-resource model that suggested that cultural strengths have protected the Black family through the devastating effects of slavery and through more recent patterns of Black male unemployment. Cultural resources also have fostered adaptive marriage and family patterns that help families keep functioning through extreme hardships. Hill, for instance, argued that Black families emphasize strong kinship bonds, hard work and ambition, and an equalitarian (rather than a "matriarchal") authority pattern. These elements buffer the deleterious effects of male unemployment and White discrimination. Moreover, accumulating evidence supports the idea that the extended family, rather than the nuclear family, is the proper unit of analysis for studies of the strengths and weaknesses of the Black family.

Gutman provided additional support for the ethnic-resource model. His analysis of slave marriages and families showed that despite the undeniable hardships and restrictions of slavery, Black slaves placed a high value on family stability and responsibility. A subsequent study comparing Black and White family structure in Philadelphia in 1850 and 1880 found that roughly three-quarters of the families in both groups consisted of two parents and their dependent children. The study found also that the households of former slaves were more likely than other Black households to be headed by couples.

Slavery surely narrowed the choices available to the slaves; but, according to ethnic resource theorists, these downtrodden people were able, nevertheless, to create both an effective culture and a distinctive social identity that were rooted in, and transmitted by, families. From this perspective, contemporary family problems are not a continuing legacy of slavery but, rather, are the result of contemporary structural problems rooted in continuing racism.

We see once again in these opposing interpretations of Black family problems—the legacy of slavery versus the ethnic resource model—a clash of cultural and structural explanations of social events.

Contemporary Families. This clash of explanations entered the political arena during the 1990s in heated debates about "family values" and appropriate family forms. These issues have been illuminated by social research concerning changes occurring in American families. Tucker and Mitchell-Kernan, for example, looked at trends in African American family formation and found very rapid changes among Black families in marriage rates, divorce rates, household structure, participation in the labor force by women, and households with children in poverty; but they also found that these trends are pervasive in families throughout American society. Today there are more births out of wedlock, more divorces, and more nonfamily living arrangements among *all* ethnic groups.

The proportion of families headed by husbands and wives has declined in recent decades among both Blacks and Whites, although the decline among Blacks has received more notice. Families headed by husbands and wives comprised about 82 percent of White families and 46 percent of Black families in 1998. As the number of families headed by husbands and wives has declined, the number of children living in one-parent homes has risen. In 1990, 19 percent of all White children, 30 percent of all Hispanic children, and 55 percent of all Black children lived in one-parent homes. Blacks as a group were less likely to marry than either Whites or Hispanics, but this was not the case 50 years ago.

The causes of these changes in family organization are still the subject of intense debate among scholars of family life. The prevailing view appears to be that Black Americans have responded in adaptive ways to economic and social changes beyond their control and, in so doing, have constructed a resilient new culture. From this perspective, the higher frequency of family problems such as father-absent households and unwed teenage mothers is created by contemporary discrimination (in all its forms) against African Americans and cannot be explained in terms of cultural shortcomings having their origins in the period of slavery.

This view has been met by proponents of the cultural perspective who charge that the myth of the completely disorganized and passive slave community has been replaced with the opposite myth of the utopian slave community. Patterson, for instance, argued that the slave system's "ethnocidal assault on gender roles, especially those of father and husband" devastated the Black community and still must be counted as a major (though not exclusive) factor in an understanding of the contemporary problems of Black families. Among the continuing consequences of slavery's "centuries-long holocaust," Patterson stated, are "deep scars in the relations between Afro-American men and women."

These competing positions make clear that much remains to be done before we will have an adequate understanding of the lengthy and complicated processes involved in the cultural assimilation of African Americans. It seems clear that the African Americans have "helped to create themselves out of what they found around them"; but it also may be the case that we still do not recognize fully the protracted and destructive effects of the American system of slavery on the African American family.

The "Million Man March." Two weeks after the O. J. Simpson verdict, African Americans used a public march with the theme of unity and the responsibility of Black men to their community to call attention to the needs of the Black family and to focus attention on Black pride and Black culture. The march was organized by Minister Louis Farrakhan, the controversial leader of the Nation of Islam. Some epithets used in media commentaries about the march denounced Farrakhan as a "Booker T. Washington conservative," "a Marcus Garvey black nationalist," an "anti-Semite," a "race-baiter," a "sexist," and a "homophobe." Some prominent Black leaders and organizations were unwilling to endorse or participate in the demonstration because of Mr. Farrakhan's role.

Others claimed that the media were trying to shift the focus from problems in the Black community to White anxiety and emphasized that the demonstration was about concerns much bigger than Mr. Farrakhan. The National Urban League president described the peaceful protest as the "largest family-values rally in the history of America." The march was seen by many as a way to counter the overwhelmingly negative images of Blacks, particularly Black males, that dominate the media. Attracting between 400,000 and 1 million Black males to Washington, D.C., and exceeding the turnout at the March on Washington in 1963, the Million Man March was said to celebrate the majority of Black men who work hard, support their families, and contribute to their communities. Glenn Loury, a conservative Black economist, claimed that the majority of Blacks are part of the middle and working classes, but that the 10 percent who are poor and have multiple problems have come to represent the entire Black community.

Minister Farrakhan, one of the last speakers at the all-day rally, delivered a lengthy speech concerning inspiration, White supremacy, a conspiracy against Blacks in White America, and the need for Black nationalism. He criticized the dominant group for giving too little attention to the problems of Black teenagers in trouble, double-digit unemployment rates among Black workers, and Black families that are falling apart because they do not have adequate incomes. Additionally, he called for Blacks to practice "boot-strap capitalism." The appeal by Blacks to Blacks, with no clear role for White people, called for the regeneration of the Black family, Black pride, and strong African American role models.

The march was an acknowledgment of the reality of Black culture and the view that its development is a positive thing. The participants also clearly wished, however, to be an integral part of mainstream America—to have good jobs, better incomes, and strong families. As is true for many African Americans, the marchers were committed to both Black culture and mainstream culture—an option we have referred to as cultural assimilation by addition. Indeed, many scholars have suggested that Blacks and Whites of the same social class levels are more alike than different in their values, behavior, and family organization. We conclude, therefore, that although African Americans are not identical to middle-class Anglo Americans in culture, their level of cultural assimilation is high.

Secondary Structural Assimilation

There can be no doubt that since emancipation African Americans have moved in many important ways toward the goal of full secondary assimilation; however, it is equally clear that a number of gaps still exist between the levels of Whites and Blacks in significant matters such as jobs, income, education, and housing. Moreover, as we shall see, if contemporary trends continue, the differences in these areas will not disappear soon.

Occupations. Whites, of course, always have been more heavily concentrated than Blacks in the higher-prestige, better-paying jobs, and they still are. For example, although the proportion of Black males in professional and managerial jobs increased almost sixfold between 1940 and 1980, their proportion in those top jobs was still lower than among White males in 1994. The pattern among Black and White females was similar. Despite a more than threefold increase in professional jobs and a more than fivefold increase in jobs as proprietors, managers, and officials, Black women in 1980 had not reached the levels of White women in 1940, and they were less likely to be employed as professionals than White women or White men. By 1994, the percentage of Black women in professional and managerial jobs had risen further but was still below that of White women in similar jobs (20.1 versus 31.1 percent). Two other points are of particular interest here. One is a dramatic change in the proportion of Black women working in domestic service. In 1940, 60 percent of the employed Black women were household workers. By 1984, only 5.9 percent of the employed Black women held such jobs. In the 1980s, the percentages of primary professional occupations held by Blacks of both sexes were teacher (9.7) and nurse (7.5).

The overall occupational distribution of Blacks has become more similar to that of Whites. Between 1940 and 1980, the index of occupational dissimilarity for Black and White males fell from 43 to 24, showing a large movement in the direction of occupational assimilation. This movement was not uniform within the various regions of the country, however. Studies based on a different measure of occupational assimilation showed that occupational inequality *increased* in the South during the 1940s and 1950s, but that, as Blacks moved out of the South, there were real improvements in employment opportunities during the 1970s. Cohn and Fossett suggested that variations in racial employment inequality can be attributed to factors such as regional differences in economic growth, size of the major firms doing the hiring, differing employer practices, and labor union strength.

Although the occupational "upgrading" revealed by these statistics is encouraging for those who favor secondary assimilation as a goal, five additional considerations are in order. First, since Blacks are more likely than Whites to occupy the lower positions of pay and prestige within each occupational category, occupational assimilation probably would still be incomplete even if the index of occupational dissimilarity were zero. Second, on the basis of detailed analyses of occupational data, Farley and Allen found that the rate at which Blacks were moving into high-prestige jobs during the 1970s slowed during the 1980s. Third, rapid technological and economic changes, such as increasing automation and the transfer of unskilled jobs to other countries, are permanently displacing Black workers who are concentrated in the secondary labor market. Fourth, the basic reading and math skills of young Black male workers in the 1990s were not, on average, as well matched to changing patterns in the demand for labor as were the basic skills of young Whites who had the same years of schooling and lived in the same regions. Finally, the apparent reductions in occupational inequality cited before are based on figures for Blacks who are a part of the employed labor force; but large numbers of Blacks are unemployed, underemployed, or are employed at substandard wages.

For most of the years between 1955 and 1975, the unemployment rate for Black males was roughly twice as high as for Whites; and after 1975, the gap widened. In 1994, approximately 13 percent of the Black population 16 years and older was unemployed compared to 5.7 percent of the White population of the same age. Although the economic recovery of the 1990s benefited both Black and White workers, gaps remained, with Black unemployment, at 9.6 percent in 1998, still over twice that of White unemployment. Throughout this time, unemployment among Black teenagers was exceptionally high. Research suggests that since 1940 the economic status of older Black workers stabilized relative to Whites but that of younger workers deteriorated in the late 1980s and the 1990s. Thus, although Black males are now more likely to get jobs that previously were "reserved" for Whites, they still are much less likely to get a job at all.

Incomes. There has been a definite increase in Black incomes since the 1950s, both in dollars and in purchasing power, but there still are large gaps between the incomes of Blacks and Whites. Overall, the median incomes of Black families increased more rapidly during the 1980s than the median income of White families, but the overall gap between the two groups changed little during the decade. In 1989, Black families received an average of 62 cents for each dollar White families received. In 1994, African American men working full-time, year-round earned a median income about 72 percent as high as non-Hispanic White men, and African American women earned a median income about 85 percent as high as non-Hispanic White women.

These comparisons, taken together, suggest real increases in the incomes of African Americans but only a modest movement toward equality with Whites. Perhaps even more revealing is a comparison of the total average wealth (as opposed to annual incomes) of Black and White Americans. U.S. Bureau of the Census figures released in

1990 showed that the estimated median net worth of Black American households was about one-tenth that of White households ($4,169 versus $43,279). Oliver and Shapiro argued that systemic economic barriers—such as historically low wages, discrimination in institutions, limited access to capital, the rise of suburbs, and the growth of inner-city ghettos—have impaired the ability of Blacks to accumulate wealth over the generations and have contributed significantly to Black and White inequality.

As shown in our comparisons of Mexican American and Anglo incomes, the general figures we have presented conceal many specific differences of importance. For instance, women typically have lower incomes than men, and since a higher percentage of Black families are headed by women, a higher percentage of Black families are poor. To illustrate, the median family income of Black two-parent households in 1989 was about 3.3 times as high as the median for Black female-headed households ($31,757 versus $9,590;). Also, as in the case of the Mexican American–Anglo comparison, some of the differences in per capita incomes between Blacks and Whites is due to the higher educational levels of Whites. Once again, we see that to estimate the income "costs" of discrimination against a minority group, it is necessary to "match" the groups being compared in many important respects.

Through an approach of this type, Farley and Allen showed that in 1985, even when the employed workers of the groups were matched in several pertinent ways, there still was a substantial difference in earnings between Black and White males (over $3,000) that may have been the result of discrimination. This difference, moreover, represented the reversal of a trend toward greater similarity between the earnings of Black and White males that had been underway for four decades; therefore, for Black men at least, it would appear that the effect of discrimination on earnings increased during the early 1980s. The results of the analysis for women, however, contained a surprise. To begin with, employed Black women earned an average of about $650 *more* in 1980 and about $800 more in 1985 than did White women; and had the Black women been identical to White women in the respects considered in this study, then the gaps *in favor* of Black women would have increased to around $1,100 in 1985; but as Hacker observed in a similar type of study, "The comparative status of women warrants only a muted cheer" because women of both races are underpaid. For Blacks of both sexes, however, educational gains (especially at the college level) appear to make a substantial difference in the incomes they receive. Because of the close relationship of education and income, estimates of Black progress in the area of income usually focus on changes in the level of education and on changes in patterns of schooling (e.g., desegregation). The following section looks at educational attainments of African Americans.

Education. In *An American Dilemma,* Myrdal saw education as a solution to America's race problem. Education represented a vehicle for combating racist beliefs as well as a means of improving the material conditions of Blacks. Prior to emancipation, the vast majority of Blacks were given no formal schooling; consequently, changes in the level of education among African Americans since the Reconstruction period have been enormous. In 1870, 80 percent of African Americans were illiterate; in the same year, illiteracy among Whites stood at 12 percent. By 1970, these levels had fallen to approximately 4 percent of all Blacks over 14 years old and to less than 1 percent for Whites of the same age group. Race differences in illiteracy rates in the 1980s and 1990s were negligible, even though the definition of literacy involved more complex functional literacy skills compared to the earlier measures, which were usually determined by the ability to sign one's name.

The absolute gains in years of school completed since the 1940s have been much greater for Blacks than for Whites. By the 1960s, racial differences in school enrollment were basically nonexistent; and, by 1990, 88 percent of Blacks between 5 and 20 years of age were enrolled in school, compared to 89 percent of Whites in this age group. In 1992, there was no substantial difference between Blacks and Whites in the median number of years of school completed.

Students who drop out of high school face a more difficult road to success than their peers who finish high school or college. The school dropout rate is highest among students living in low-income families; and, as a consequence of poverty, a larger, but statistically insignificant, proportion of Blacks than Whites leave school before the completion of high school. Overall, however, within low-, middle-, and high-income groups, there were few differences between the high school dropout rates of Whites and Blacks during the 1980s and early 1990s.

This review of educational progress demonstrates that in terms of illiteracy, school enrollment, and dropping out of school, Blacks have achieved near parity with Whites. The findings show that the educational patterns of African and White Americans are moving in the direction of complete educational assimilation. These findings do not show, however, that the overall educational gap between Blacks and Whites has closed or will soon close. For instance, even though in 1994 the percentage of those who had completed only high school was slightly higher among Blacks than Whites (36.2 versus 34.5), and students from the two groups went on to college in equal proportions (17.5 percent), a substantially higher percentage of the White students graduated from college (15.1 versus 9.5); and, proportionally, more than twice as many Whites as Blacks obtained an advanced degree (7.9 versus 3.4). Overall, the gap between the two groups in the percentage of those completing college doubled from 5 percent in 1960 to 10 percent in 1994.

As in the case of income gains, Black progress in education, though real, is a part of a general increase within American society. Such an increase within a given group may or may not keep pace with that of the total population. As we have seen, even when a group's level is rising, the absolute differences between groups may actually widen. Also, the educational increases for African Americans do not necessarily pay off in comparable salaries. According to a 1993 Census Bureau report, higher education translated into greater earning power for both Blacks and Whites; but Whites gained more.

Educational levels, of course, reveal little concerning educational quality. If, as the *Brown* decisions state, segregated schooling is damaging to those who are set apart, then the continuation of segregated schools reduces the quality of education for Blacks. From this standpoint, educational assimilation is incomplete as long as the schools are segregated or classrooms within desegregated schools remain segregated. Although a substantial amount of school desegregation occurred between 1968 and 1973, primarily because of court-ordered busing, many urban schools remained segregated despite court-mandated desegregation plans or voluntary actions. Although many minority students and White students benefited from desegregation remedies, the gains often came with high economic, educational, and personal costs—especially for Black and Hispanic children from low-income families who attended inner-city public schools.

Residential Segregation. The national trend is toward less segregation in many cities, but the historical development of metropolitan areas and local conditions within them affect the patterns. In some areas of the South, for example, housing patterns still reflect the effects of slavery and the plantation economy. In the antebellum South, the slaves and their families commonly lived in the backyards of the White masters. Although Whites typically enjoyed superior dwellings, Blacks and Whites were found side by side in various parts of the cities; consequently, the level of residential segregation at that time was typically less than it is in most parts of the United States today. Even when the Jim Crow system of deliberate, legal segregation came into being between 1890 and 1920, the southern pattern of interracial housing was not much affected. In the "Southern Plan" of segregation, it was unnecessary to force Blacks into racially separate geographical areas. Both tradition and the Jim Crow system created such a vast social distance between the races that residential closeness did not threaten the respective social "places" of the two races. As African Americans began to stream out of the South during World War I, however, they entered northern states in which they were, in most respects, legally equal to Whites. Certain facts of northern life, nevertheless, prevented Blacks from dispersing throughout all parts of the cities.

There was, first of all, an economic barrier. Like the European immigrants before them, most Blacks could afford to live only in the least expensive areas of the cities. But also of great importance, was that Black people faced an enormous amount of legal and extralegal housing discrimination. Even when African Americans had the money to afford housing outside of the ghettos, they usually were unable to purchase it.

Comprehensive, detailed studies of trends in housing segregation in the United States prior to 1940 are unavailable. Some studies of selected cities, however, suggest that residential segregation increased gradually from emancipation to World War I and then accelerated sharply until 1930. Using housing information published by the U.S. Bureau of the Census, Taeuber and Taeuber calculated residential segregation indexes (indexes of dissimilarity) for 109 American cities during 1947–1960 and for 207 cities in 1960. Their analysis established two important points. First, the average level of residential segregation of Blacks and Whites in American cities by 1940 was very high in every region of the country. Second, although there was a slight decline in residential segregation between 1940 and 1960 in most of the 109 cities that were studied, the declines were usually small, and the patterns within the cities varied. For instance, some cities had an increase in residential segregation during one or both of the two decades studied.

What has happened to residential segregation in U.S. cities since 1960? Blacks have continued to move into the central cities, whereas Whites have continued to form suburban rings around them. This pattern has raised some questions about whether analyses of residential segregation should focus on metropolitan areas rather than on central cities and also has led to conflicting conclusions about the direction of residential segregation. Although some studies have found that during some periods the level of African American residential segregation has declined little or has remained about the same, a number of other studies have shown that the efforts to reduce segregation in some American cities and metropolitan areas with large Black populations have been effective. Farley and Allen, for instance, have shown that among the 25 central cities with the largest Black populations, all but two (Philadelphia and Cleveland) experienced some decline in Black–White residential segregation between 1970 and 1980. Overall, declines occurred during the decade in 20 of the 25 cities. In a similar study of all metropolitan areas in the United States using 1990 data, Harrison and Weinberg found decreases in the residential segregation of Blacks in most of the metropolitan areas. The declines were substantial in 18 large areas, most of which were in Florida and Texas. During the entire period from 1960 to 1990, the average level of residential segregation of Blacks in American cities declined from a segregation index of about 86 to an index between 64 and 69, depending on the study.

Farley and Frey found that, although segregation varied widely among cities, the segregation of Blacks remained much greater than that of Hispanics and Asians. The average segregation score in 1990 for Blacks was 20 points above the average score for Hispanics or Asians. Farley and Frey also identified four practices that exacerbated segregation: (1) mortgage lending policies were discriminatory, (2) Blacks who sought housing in White areas faced intimidation and violence, (3) suburbs developed strategies for keeping Blacks out, such as zoning laws, real estate agents who dealt only with Whites, and intimidation by the local police, and (4) federally sponsored public housing encouraged segregation.

The persistence of residential segregation has led to legal battles similar to those that have occurred in the effort to desegregate schools, jobs, voting, public accommodations, and other social arenas. For example, agreements among homeowners to sell their homes only to members of certain groups have been declared illegal, rules requiring segregation in federally funded housing have been removed, and open-housing laws have been passed. And, in 1968, Congress passed the Fair Housing Act barring "racial discrimination on the part of any parties involved in the sale, rental, or financing of most housing units".

It is clear that in the 1980s and 1990s, income and educational gains made by African Americans since World War II have not been translated commensurately into residential assimilation. High-status Blacks are much more likely than high-status Whites to live in "poorer, more dilapidated areas" that are "characterized by higher rates of poverty, dependency, crime, and mortality". Many affluent Black families also choose to live in expensive all-Black suburbs. Massey and Hajnal proposed that segregation patterns in the United States have consistently evolved to minimize White–Black contacts, with only the level of segregation changing over time. They concluded that racial segregation in the United States resembles the apartheid system that previously existed in the Union of South Africa. In the United States, Blacks have been forced into segregated suburbs and channeled into segregated cities through institutionalized discrimination in the real estate and banking industries, racially biased public policies, and persistent White prejudice. Farley and Frey noted that while racial attitudes have changed, with most Whites endorsing the *principle* of equal opportunities for Blacks in the housing market, Whites, nevertheless, were uncomfortable when numerous Blacks moved into their neighborhoods; and they were reluctant to move into predominantly Black neighborhoods.

In a study of Los Angeles, California, Bobo and Zubrinsky found, in a survey of the attitudes of Whites, Asians, Blacks, and Hispanics, that stereotypes of Blacks and Hispanics as being unintelligent, preferring welfare, and being hard to get along with were most consistently important among White respondents. For Whites, sharing residential areas with any subordinate group, but especially with Blacks, brought the threat of a loss of advantages in relative status. The researchers concluded that Black–White separation was likely to continue, even in a diverse city such as Los Angeles, because Whites viewed desegregation as undermining their superior status.

Our consideration of changes in occupations, incomes, educational levels, and housing patterns suggests that, on average, African Americans have been moving slowly during recent decades toward the patterns found among Whites, though there are significant differences in the experiences of males and females in these respects, and the movement toward assimilation was halted or slowed during the 1970s and 1980s. When compared to an ideal of complete secondary assimilation, all of the changes we have discussed are small. For this reason, most observers appear to agree with Farley that although gains among Blacks "are widespread," Blacks "will not soon attain parity with whites."

Primary Structural Assimilation

The gains previously discussed show that Black–White relations in the United States are changing as the social and historical contexts of racial relations change, individuals' attitudes change, and younger people replace the older generation who experienced legal segregation. Many interactions between Blacks and Whites that were once infrequent, and often illegal, now occur with little notice (e.g., swimming, dancing, eating together, dating, mixed schools, churches, public transportation, and sports teams). Between 1964 and 1974, researchers at the University of Michigan's Institute for Social Research found an increase in contacts between Blacks and Whites in neighborhoods and on the job as well as in schools. The Michigan studies reported that the proportion of Whites who had no Black friends declined from about 80 percent in 1964 to about 60 percent 10 years later. According to research compiled by the Committee on the Status of African Americans, Blacks and Whites share a substantial consensus, in the abstract, on the broad goal of a desegregated and equalitarian society. Nearly 100 percent of Blacks surveyed in studies of racial attitudes endorsed the principles of school desegregation and free residential choice; they also reported that race would not be a deciding factor in their voting patterns. However, for Whites, these principles of equality are endorsed less when social contact is close, of long duration, frequent, and involves significant numbers of African Americans. The committee concluded that race still matters greatly in attitudes and behaviors in the United States. There remains a reluctance on the part of Whites to live in racially mixed neighborhoods as Blacks and Whites are treated differently in many situations. There continues to be an awkwardness in interracial, interpersonal relationships. In the midst of closer ties in terms of culture, employment, and incomes, resistance to high levels of primary structural assimilation continues to be high.

For example, Schofield reported that evidence from a wide variety of situations, ranging from conflicts between youth gangs of different ethnic and racial backgrounds to racial incidents on college campuses, showed that serious problems still exist in intergroup relations. Because of pervasive residential segregation, children often have their first close and extended contacts with those from different racial and ethnic groups in school. Many of those relationships are no longer just between Blacks and Whites. With minority group members becoming an increasingly large proportion of the U.S. population, children in the schools are likely to encounter multifaceted, multiethnic situations. Schofield also emphasized the difference between mere desegregation, which results in a racially mixed environment, and true integration, which refers to positive relations among members of different groups. Schofield noted that because of anxiety and uncertainty about dealing with out-group members, resegregation or clustering in racially homogeneous groups results. As noted in an earlier study by Hallinan and Williams of over a million high school friendship pairs, only a few hundred cross-race friendships developed. In colleges and universities as well, it is common for Black students to form their own sororities, fraternities, and political organizations. The reasons usually given by Black students for the latter phenomenon is that "such activities make predominantly White campuses more hospitable".

In a report on diversity at the University of California at Berkeley, group interviews with students were used to explore primary structural relationships. Black students reported that the environment they encountered on the campus was one in which racial and ethnic segregation was "everywhere" and they perceived subtle and pervasive racism. They felt that students were "categorized," "labeled," and "stereotyped" according to their perceived group identity. Black students coming from predominantly White high schools discovered that they were no longer the "token Black person," burdened with constantly explaining what it was like to be Black. They joined clubs and organizations that celebrated and affirmed their African American identity and culture. However, Black students also experienced new pressure from African Americans to make decisions about friends, social networks, and even who they would sit with at lunch, on the basis of race. Some felt ill at ease in the White community and not really accepted by their own group.

Black students from desegregated urban high schools or from predominantly Black schools had an easier adjustment to racially mixed social groupings. Many Black students were sensitive to their high visibility in mostly White classes at Berkeley and felt that they were the subjects of subtle discrimination by professors, teaching assistants, and other students. Many felt that ethnic and racial politics on the campus forced them to choose "what kind of Black" they were going to be—one who was committed to Anglo conformity, pluralism, or separatism. Many Black students said they associated mostly with other Black students where they were less likely to be rejected or stereotyped.

Presumably the changes in legal and social segregation that have occurred since the 1950s should have helped turn many of the increased personal contacts into friendships. In fact, this has happened; but, as shown by the studies cited above, as important as these reported changes are, they are modest in relation to the Anglo conformity ideal of complete primary assimilation.

Marital Assimilation

Interracial marriage—especially of Blacks with Whites—has long been a subject of interest. An understanding of this process, though, has been complicated by laws in many states prohibiting Black–White intermarriage, by differences in recordkeeping procedures, and by a trend toward removing racial identifications from marriage records. In 1967, when the Supreme Court ruled that laws prohibiting interracial marriages were unconstitutional, 16 states still had them. At that time, too, only three states (Hawaii, Michigan, and Nebraska) published official records on interracial marriages. By 1976, the effort to remove racial identifications from marriage records had been successful in seven states and the District of Columbia. Also, the social practice of designating those with any Black ancestry as Black has meant that the children of interracial marriages are identified only as African American. When those children marry, efforts to determine the number of racial intermarriages are complicated further.

Despite the technical problems created by these conditions, some excellent studies have been conducted. Some of the main findings of these studies are that (1) out-marriages among Blacks have been much less common than out-marriages among other racial and ethnic groups; (2) the rate of Black–White intermarriage went up rapidly during the 1960s and nearly doubled in the 1980s and 1990s; and (3) the declining pool of Black males who are eligible as marriage partners has resulted in more Black families that are headed by women who have never married and has encouraged those who do marry to marry outside their racial group.

In a study of interracial marriages in Los Angeles during the years 1948–1959, Burma found that Black males were much less likely to marry out than were Japanese, Chinese, Filipino, or Native American males and that Black females were even less likely to marry out than were Black males. Even after all the turmoil and change of the 1960s, Blacks were still found to be the least likely of 35 different American racial and ethnic groups to marry out. Lieberson and Waters, showed that although Black women seemed less likely to marry within their group than in the past, the probability of in-group marriages is still *very much* higher than among any of the 21 other groups included in their analysis. To be more specific, almost 99 percent of Black women in their first marriages had married Black men.

Even though the level of Black out-marriage is still extremely low when compared to other racial and ethnic groups, the rate of change has jumped noticeably since 1960. Monahan conducted a nationwide survey of Black–White intermarriage and found that the total proportion of mixed marriages rose from 1.4 per one thousand marriages in 1963 to 2.6 in 1970. By 1990, the rate was nearly 4 per one thousand marriages. Throughout this period, the proportion of Black–White intermarriages was three to four times higher in the North than in the South, though the rate of increase was much faster in the South than in the North, and highest in the West. Altogether, the rates of intermarriage of African Americans and Whites nearly doubled over the years 1980–1996, but such behavior was still relatively rare. Only about 1 percent of African American women and 3 percent of African American men were interracially married.

In their analysis of data from the 1980 census, Lieberson and Waters found that although the first marriages of Black women under the age of 25 were still very likely to have been with Black men, the younger women were much more likely to have interracial marriages than older Black women. According to 1980 census data on interracial married couples, of Black–White interracial couples about 3 percent were marriages of White husbands and Black wives, 10 percent were Black husbands and White wives, and 5 percent were Black spouses with spouses of backgrounds other than Black or White, such as American Indian, Japanese, or Chinese. Older Blacks were more likely than younger Blacks to wish to maintain their group boundaries and culture and, therefore, to oppose interracial dating. Better-educated Blacks and those with higher family incomes were less likely than other Blacks to oppose interracial dating and interracial marriages.

In 1954, the National Opinion Research Center began asking those who participated in the General Social Survey how they felt about intermarriage. At first only 4 percent of the White population approved of such a possibility. Since that time, responses to the intermarriage question have shown a steady movement up, but there has been less approval for intermarriage than for equity in jobs and for school desegregation. For example, in 1972 two in five Whites interviewed believed that intermarriages between Blacks and Whites should be illegal; this proportion fell to one White in five nearly two decades later. In 1991, some 66 percent of the Whites polled in the General Social Survey still disapproved of racial intermarriage. A Gallup Poll in 1983 also found that 22 percent of Blacks expressed disapproval of interracial marriages. These considerations all suggest that the color line will be slow to shift.

Other Forms of Assimilation

Black Americans appear to be simultaneously adapting to many aspects of Anglo-American culture while preserving and elaborating a distinctive African American culture, and their level of secondary assimilation is generally rising. But although Blacks and Whites seem to be coming together in cultural and secondary structural ways, they appear to be remaining largely apart in their private relations and identificational commitments. W. E. B. DuBois emphasized an African American duality or "double consciousness" when he wrote that "One ever feels his twoness,—an American, a Negro; two souls, two thoughts, two unreconciled strivings. . . . He simply wishes to make it possible for a man to be both a Negro and an American, without being cursed and spit upon."

Despite all of the legislation designed to prevent discrimination, even middle-class African Americans still face discrimination in jobs, incomes, education, housing, and public places and "speak again and again of 'living in two worlds' ". Such circumstances show that identificational, attitudinal, and behavioral assimilation are far from complete; and our findings concerning the differences in the opinions of Blacks and Whites following the riots in Los Angeles in 1992 and the trial of O. J. Simpson show that value and power conflicts between the groups are very much alive.

The contemporary pattern of Black–White relations suggests that African Americans may be moving toward the goal of ideal pluralism; but for those who advocate pluralism, there is no assurance that Black culture will survive either the centripetal pressures of Anglo conformity, on the one hand, or the centrifugal pressures of separation, on the other.

African American "Success"

We indicated earlier that in very broad terms a split long has existed between those who favor hereditarian explanations of group differences in worldly (or material) "success" and those who favor environmental answers. In our analysis, though, hereditarian answers have been shown to rest on invalid assumptions concerning races and racial membership; therefore, we have emphasized the split that exists between environmentalists who stress either cultural or structural explanations of differences among ethnic groups (i.e., those who attribute group differences primarily to the different norms, values, and motives of their members as compared to those who attribute group differences to such "material factors" as income differences and the many social forces that help create those differences). We have examined this pair of theoretical preferences in our discussions of the worldly success of the Japanese and Mexican Americans and also in our discussion of the controversy concerning the possible role of the Black family in the analysis of the modern social problems that are most prevalent among African Americans.

We turn now to a broader comparison of various ideas concerning the worldly "success" of African Americans.

Growing African American Affluence

A report by O'Hare, Pollard, Mann, and Kent showed that the number of affluent Blacks—those with yearly incomes of $50,000 or more—has grown substantially since the 1960s. In 1989, nearly one in seven Black families was affluent, compared with one out of every seventeen in 1967. The researchers explained this change as a product of the civil rights legislation that opened up opportunities in education and employment for Blacks and also of the economic expansion that followed the 1981–1983 recession. These middle-class adults are the first generation of African American children to benefit from desegregated schools, expanded higher-education opportunities, and equal employment laws. The children of the 1960s reached middle age in the 1980s and 1990s, the age when increased educational attainment begins to pay off financially. The report showed that the affluent Blacks are well educated (32 percent college graduates), own their own homes (77 percent), are in their prime earning ages (66 percent are age 35–55), are married (79 percent), and live in the suburbs. Like affluent White families, most Black families reach the $50,000-a-year income level by combining earnings from two or more family members. Less than 2 percent of Black single adults have personal incomes that could be considered affluent. Although these figures suggest that economic assimilation is occurring among this group of Black families, we have seen also that, overall, Blacks have lower participation in the labor force, higher unemployment rates, and greater percentages of single-parent households than Whites.

One interesting finding about successful Black women and men concerns tension between them. Black women professionals report that they feel pressure to be less successful because their accomplishments exacerbate White society's emasculation of Black men; at the same time Black men complain that there is little in textbooks or the media about Black fathers who are present in their families. There are gender differences, too, in the job market. For example, among Black college faculty, accountants, executives, and middle-class magazine readers, more men report racial discrimination in hiring but more women report racial discrimination in advancement; also while as many Black women as men have professional jobs, well-educated Black men have always earned more than well-educated Black women. Wilkinson pointed out, however, that although gender does contribute significantly to social inequality, sex and gender are less potent forces in the lives of African Americans than class or race.

The "Culture of Poverty" Explanation

During the 1960s, the "culture of poverty thesis," attributed initially to anthropologist, Oscar Lewis, became a popular explanation for the persistence of poverty among families in general. The basic idea of the culture of poverty thesis is that poor people develop particular patterns of values and ways of coping with their difficulties and pass these patterns down essentially intact from one generation to the next. Such values and behavior, according to this thesis, prevent poor people from taking school seriously or from working hard when they get a job; the poverty of one generation breeds and ensures the poverty of the next. Unless the poverty cycle is broken, this thesis states, children of such families are destined to learn the same "defective" pattern of behavior exhibited by their elders.

Most of the research conducted to determine whether poor people do, as the culture-of-poverty thesis claims, possess a distinctive culture has not supported this idea. For example, the belief that poor Black males do not take seriously the matter of getting and keeping jobs has been vigorously challenged by Liebow, who maintained that what looks like a "present orientation" to the middle-class observer is, in fact, a "future orientation." The poor Black worker is no less aware of the future than is his or her middle-class critic; but, Liebow said, these two people are looking at very different futures. The Black worker is facing a future "in which everything is uncertain except the ultimate destruction of his hopes and the eventual realization of his fears". Thus, Liebow argued, when a poor Black man squanders a week's pay it is not because he is unconcerned with his future. He does so precisely because he is aware of the future and its dim prospects.

Many critics of the culture of poverty thesis have seen it (along with the Moynihan thesis) as an elaborate way to shift the responsibility for social change away from the White majority and onto the shoulders of the minority, saying something must be wrong with *them.* The implication of this is clear: Black people must relinquish their own culture and become more like White Americans.

An "Underclass"? Many observers have expressed the fear that the most disadvantaged of the inner-city dwellers, the "hard-core" poor, are becoming so separated from the rest of the society that there is a danger they will become a permanent "underclass." Hochschild presents strong evidence that, for perhaps the first time in American history, a group of poor Blacks have become so alienated that they threaten the existence of stable communities. She contended that most poor Blacks have continued to pursue the American dream of "success" through legitimate hard work and have rejected succeeding financially through drug sales, gaining concessions through protest and violence, or withdrawing from all effort. But, she warned, there is no reason to expect society's "luck" in these respects to last if the discrepancy between their hopes for success and the realities they face each day continues to grow.

A Selective Mobility Explanation

In 1978, sociologist William J. Wilson wrote a controversial book, *The Declining Significance of Race,* based on the thesis that race as a factor affecting socioeconomic status was diminishing. Stated briefly, the reasoning behind this thesis is as follows: Throughout the long years between the beginnings of African American slavery and the end of World War II, practically all Blacks, professionals as well as the poor, were members of an oppressed lower caste. Under these conditions, Black people's racial affiliation rather than their economic circumstances determined their chances for occupational advancement; therefore, the inequalities between Blacks and Whites were, strictly speaking, *racial* in nature. Since World War II, however, the United States has seen the creation of a significant Black middle class, as discussed earlier, among whom occupational advancement depends more on *class* location than on racial membership. The result is a growing cleavage *within* the Black community in which socioeconomic classes have become more visible. In short, well-educated Blacks increasingly have opportunities for occupational advancement that are similar to those of Whites, whereas the uneducated members of all groups, including Whites, increasingly descend into a growing population of multiracial poor.

Wilson's conclusion that the life chances of Blacks had more to do with their economic class position than with their day-to-day encounters with Whites angered many scholars and stirred a debate that has not yet been settled. At the time of the publication of *The Declining Significance of Race,* the Association of Black Sociologists (ABS) published a denunciation of the book and accused Wilson of omitting significant facts "regarding the continuing discrimination against Blacks at all class levels," of misinterpreting some of the facts presented, and of drawing unwarranted conclusions. The ABS members were "outraged over the misinterpretation of the Black experience" and "extremely disturbed over the policy implications" of the book. Wilson, of course, was aware that in matters such as public school education, residential segregation, and full political participation, racial antagonism was still very much alive. He also recognized that older Black workers, due to the historic effects of discrimination, did not earn the same incomes as Whites. His argument, however, was that as younger talented and educated Blacks entered the labor market in competition with Whites, the racial barriers to advancement would be largely eliminated.

Wilson expanded his analysis of the ghetto poor in another controversial book, *The Truly Disadvantaged.* He acknowledged that despite the Great Society programs of the 1960s, the proportion of Black births occurring outside of marriage and the proportion of Black families headed by women had both risen. He also acknowledged that welfare dependency, violent crime, and increased joblessness among Blacks had reached "catastrophic proportions". In Wilson's view, problems such as poverty, unemployment, street crime, and teenage pregnancy cannot be explained fully as simple consequences of either culture or discrimination. He stated that explanations must include "societal, demographic, and neighborhood variables," and argued that "the sharp rise of Black female-headed families is directly related to increasing Black male joblessness". In a third important book, *When Work Disappears,* Wilson proposed that many of the problems in the inner-city neighborhoods are fundamentally a consequence of the disappearance of work. Wilson acknowledged that cultural factors do play a role, but he argued that the loss of blue-collar jobs, the relocation of other jobs to the suburbs, the lack of locally available training and education, and the dissolution of government and private organizations that once supplied job information and employment opportunities have had devastating effects on the Black urban poor and their families.

We have seen in this brief summary that many questions concerning the "success" of African Americans are still unanswered. How one interprets these persistent differences in levels of achievement—as a consequence of lesser abilities, biases, an oppositional culture, differences in family income or education, barriers of social class, regional economic changes, or differences in cultural capital—has implications for policies that facilitate assimilation. Some of the evidence reviewed so far shows that in the important areas of occupations, income, and education, racial differences have declined substantially. These findings show that as a group African Americans *are* succeeding in some ways and that the gains *are* significant. But we also saw that in some ways the gaps between the achievements of Blacks and the rest of the population are growing. It is possible, as Wilson contended, that better-educated Blacks have taken advantage of the opportunities created by the civil rights movement and have moved out of the inner cities, leaving behind an increasingly visible group of poor Blacks.

The Entrepreneurial Option

Many minority groups, both within the United States and throughout the world, have reacted to dominant-group hostility by becoming middleman minorities or by developing a secure economic base within an ethnic enclave. We may now wonder: To what extent have Black Americans relied on self-employment as a response to hostility? O'Hare reported that while the number of Black-owned firms was less than 15 per 1,000 population, the comparable figures for some other minorities were as follows: Korean Americans more than 102; Asian Indian Americans about 76; Japanese Americans 66; and Cuban Americans about 63. The figures also showed, however, that the number of Black-owned businesses grew in the years 1972–1987 from over 187,000 to over 424,000. Nevertheless, this mode of adaptation to out-group threat was still comparatively low among African Americans. Why was this true?

Lieberson listed several important factors to be considered in comparing the economic success of Asian Americans and African Americans, including a greater opportunity for "Asian groups to occupy special niches," an even higher level of hostility by Whites toward Blacks than Asians, and the higher level of economic competition presented to Whites by Blacks. Portes and Bach described various explanations of group differences in business success and concluded, as stated previously, that one way "up" is the development of an ethnic-enclave economy whose component firms function in ways that resemble those at the "center" of the economy rather than those at the "periphery." They agreed with Frazier that to develop an enclave economy a group must possess " 'a tradition of enterprise' based primarily on experience in 'buying and selling' ". In a comparison of Cuban-owned and Black-owned businesses in Miami, Wilson and Martin found that "the black business community appears to be merely an extension of the periphery economy" while the Cuban community had created an enclave economy.

The question of the business success of African Americans has been analyzed further by Butler. A major objective of Butler's analysis was to challenge the belief that African Americans do not have a strong tradition of business and self-help. He argued (1) that beginning during the colonial period, a noticeable segment of the African American population followed an entrepreneurial path similar to that of the middleman minorities; (2) that a substantial Black middleman economy was constructed before 1900; but that (3) with the development of the Jim Crow system, segregation forced Black business development to detour from the usual path of middleman groups and to develop, instead, as a truncated middleman minority. As the Black entrepreneurs were separated from White consumers, they became dependent on "Protected markets in personal services catering to other Blacks". Butler found that African American individuals became entrepreneurs and professionals within the Black community because they were cut off, or truncated, from the main business districts of America as a result of segregation. Racism forced them to do business exclusively within their own group. He argued that the modern-day descendants of Black Americans who engaged in business have inherited a philosophy of life and a way of adapting to extreme hostility resembling that of the descendants of other middleman minorities, and with similar socioeconomic consequences. Yet despite the racism that prevented them from continuing as middlemen, Butler found that there was "really no difference between the offspring of African Americans today whose parents, grandparents, and great-grandparents adjusted to America by self-help and the offspring of other self-help ethnic groups."

An important consequence of this historical pattern, Butler argued, is that African Americans have followed two routes to worldly success in American society, the immigrant model of assimilating into the mainstream and the entrepreneurial route as a truncated middleman minority. The first route to success, described in our discussion of the secondary assimilation of the new Black middle class, resembles what one would expect on the basis of the immigrant model. Despite the extremely high levels of discrimination against them, the new arrivals in the northern and southern cities, like many immigrants before them, worked hard to establish themselves in the society's mainstream and to make a place in the world for their children. Many third- and fourth-generation descendants of this group are now "making it in America." The second route to success, in Butler's view, stems from a strong, misunderstood, and underestimated tradition of business enterprise among African Americans. He stated that, with appropriate adjustments for new conditions, the example of the truncated middleman minority may afford a blueprint for adjustment for many of those African Americans who do not wish to follow, or are unable to follow, the immigrant model.

All of the arguments presented concerning the worldly success of African Americans are hotly contested and are of great public importance. As emphasized previously, positions taken in the public debate over what should be done to promote the assimilation of minority groups are closely connected to competing social policy views. Liberals, generally, stress the role of past and present discrimination and other structural factors in creating and maintaining group differences. Conservatives, on the other hand, focus strongly on the role of cultural differences as important causes of group differences in success. Wilson argued that his approach transcends the "simplistic either/or notions of culture versus social structure" by showing some of the links between these notions. Butler, too, argued that his approach "is neither conservative nor liberal" but rather one that encourages African Americans to consider "a path which has been followed for centuries by oppressed and outcast groups."

Regardless of the extent to which increases in the worldly success of African Americans depend on changes in Black culture, on a greater similarity of opportunities, or on "the dynamic interplay between ghetto-specific cultural characteristics and social and economic opportunities", it is probable that this issue will continue to animate political debates for some time to come. The disagreement over the question of the causes of African American success remind us that social-scientific theories and evidence frequently suggest certain practical steps that may be taken to solve social problems. It reminds us, too, that the various ideologies of group adjustment lie just beneath the surface of public debate over what should be done regarding the assimilation of minority groups.

The Need for Strangers

Proposition 187 and the Immigration Malaise

Marcelo M. Suarez-Orozco

On November 8, 1994, California voters overwhelmingly approved Proposition 187, known as the "Save our State" initiative. The Proposition read as follows:

> [The People of California] have suffered and are suffering economic hardship caused by the presence of illegal aliens in this state.
>
> That they have suffered and are suffering personal injury and damage caused by the criminal conduct of illegal aliens in this state.
>
> That they have a right to the protection of their government from any person or persons entering this country unlawfully.
>
> Therefore, the people of California declare their intention to provide for cooperation between their agencies of state and local government with the federal government, and to establish a system of required notification by and between such agencies to prevent illegal aliens in the United States from receiving benefits or public services in the State of California (Proposition 187: Text of Proposed Law).

Proposition 187 will, *inter alia,* exclude an estimated 400,000 undocumented immigrant children from public elementary and secondary educational institutions. The Proposition's incendiary language, and the unsettling debate around it (for example; see Noble, 1994; Ayres, 1994), is revealing of the anxieties produced by immigration today.

Sigmund Freud claimed that hysteria was the malaise of his civilization. As we approach the end of our century, hysteria over immigration has become one of the great discontents of our civilization. And as was the case in Freud's time, before we can cure this hysteria, we must carefully consider the relative importance of fact and fantasy in

---

its making. Slogans that new immigrants are driven into the wealthy post-industrial democracies by the magnet of the welfare state or to commit crimes may be catchy in political campaigns but are empirically dubious and intellectually dishonest.

Transnational Malaise and the Immigration Upheaval

What *are* some of the relevant facts? First, immigration is not a California problem, a Southwest problem, or even an American problem. With well over 100 million immigrants worldwide, immigration today is a global problem. In November 1994, voters in Flanders, Belgium, elected a member of the neo-Nazi Vlaams Blok party Mayor of the elegant city of Antwerp. The Vlaams Blok's narrow political platform is well captured in their slogan, "Our people first, seal our borders, send the immigrants home." Just a few months earlier in neighboring France, the outspoken Minister of Interior, Charles Pasqua, announced that his office would begin plans to send "boatloads and trainloads" of new immigrants and asylum seekers back home to North Africa. Paraphrasing Tolstoy's famous diagnosis, when it comes to immigration, all the families of the post-industrial democratic world are unhappy in the same way.

A second fact is that a big part of today's immigration crisis is of our own making. Policies to recruit foreign workers to feed the industrial nations' voracious appetite for inexpensive labor has ignited—via transnational labor-recruiting networks, wage differentials, and family reunification—much of the recent undocumented population movement. When he was a U.S. Senator, California's Governor Pete Wilson promoted policies to bring in temporary farm workers in response to the needs of California's big agro-businesses.

A third fact is that even in the context of severe anti-immigrant sentiment, the need for cheap foreign workers remains constant. In post-Proposition 187 California, agricultural enterprises fear labor shortages. Conservative analyst Martin Anderson—a former domestic policy advisor to President Reagan and now a Fellow at the Hoover Institute—has recently advocated new "guest-worker programs, under which foreign nationals who wish to work in the United States could do so lawfully, with dignity, with no threat of being hunted down and deported" (del Olmo, 1995: 2). In the past, many such "guest workers" have overstayed their permits. Furthermore, labor-recruiting networks—in certain sectors of the economy employers often prefer to hire the relatives and friends of immigrant workers they trust (see Waldinger, 1994)—generate new cycles of undocumented migration.

A fourth fact is that recent immigration has been a by-product of global economic and political transformations. Liberalization of Third World economies—in much of Latin America engineered largely by Harvard-trained economists—has stimulated migratory patterns. In Mexico and Central America a fierce pattern of competitive allocation of land between land-poor peasants and powerful transnational interests will continue to be a major factor in immigration. Over the next two decades NAFTA-related economic transformations will "push" perhaps two to three million Mexican farmers off the land.

Other transnational economic developments go hand-in-hand with immigration—be it legal or undocumented. The United States Treasury estimated that the January 1995 currency devaluation in Mexico would likely increase undocumented immigration to the United States by as much as 30 percent.

In Europe very similar dynamics exist. Even in the face of strong and growing anti-immigrant attitudes foreign workers will be vital to the economies of Belgium, France, and Germany. In the European case, political upheaval—including the end of Cold War and the spread of ethnonationalistic conflicts such as those in the former Yugoslavia—has accelerated population movements.

Proposition 187: Politics as Catharsis

Catharsis is defined as a discharge of emotions but not necessarily a cure of an underlying pathology. Proposition 187 may have served the voters of California as a discharge for emotions—anger and frustration with a severe economic recession which hit California particularly hard over the last four years; anger and anxieties about declining expectations, crowded schools, and stunning demographic changes (political minorities are fast becoming California's demographic majority); dislocations and apprehension brought about by seemingly unending cycles of deadly and costly disasters including earthquakes, urban wildfires, and most recently floods; and finally, rage and terror in the wake of the Rodney King beating, trials, and urban upheaval they generated. In short, Californians have had plenty of frustration, injury, and endangerment. Psychologists of varied theoretical orientations have identified frustration, endangerment, and injury as often leading to aggression. Whereas the underlying frustrations are varied and complex, lashing out at immigrants concentrates much anger and frustration into a single focus. Yet it is very unlikely that this discharge of anger will "cure" California's malaise.

Proposition 187 is both a beginning and an end. It is the beginning of a new kind of marginality in California. It is also the beginning of a long and costly legal battle over whether it is constitutional to keep undocumented immigrant children out of schools and ineligible to receive publicly funded health care. Hours after it was voted into law, Proposition 187 was challenged in the courts. Most of Proposition 187 will not be enforced, pending the outcome of the current litigation.

Proposition 187 can be seen as the end or climax of a series of developments. In the months leading to the November 1994 election, several polls suggested that many Americans felt "that immigration was now harmful" (Mills, 1994: 18).

Broadly speaking, the California referendum reflects six distinct but related areas of concern in the debate over the new immigrants. First, many Americans feel there are now too many immigrants coming into the United States. With over 700,000 new documented immigrants and an estimated 300,000 new unauthorized immigrants arriving each year, a historic high, many feel that immigration must be stopped.

A second fear relates to the fact that immigration controls—including employer sanctions—have largely failed to contain waves of new undocumented immigrants. As Demetrios Papademetriou, head of the Carnegie Endowment's Immigration Policy Program, put it, there is a feeling in the public that "immigration is out of control; our borders have fallen" (Weiner, 1993: 1).

The third concern relates to fears about the fact that the great majority of today's immigrants are culturally and ethnically different from the great bulk of the European-born immigrants of previous decades and centuries. Today 81 percent of all new arrivals are from Latin America, the Caribbean, and Asia. In contrast, in 1940 70 percent of all immigrants came from Europe.

Fourth, there is a related fear that the new immigrants and their children are not "assimilating" to the institutions of mainstream society in the way previous waves of European migrants assimilated. There is concern that new arrivals, particularly those from Latin America, do not seek citizenship as did previous waves of immigrants. Some have referred to Immigration and Naturalization Service figures suggesting that applications for naturalization (citizenship) from immigrants have dropped from 67 percent of all eligible immigrants in 1943 to only 37 percent in 1992 (Sontag, 1993: 1). In a related charge, some observers have asserted that the new arrivals share certain cultural values and attitudes that are simply not compatible with the norms of the dominant culture (see, for example, Brimelow, 1992).

Fifth, there is the explosive charge that the new arrivals are disproportionately contributing to the problem of crime in America. This is an empirically unfounded charge and an issue which cannot be addressed in detail in this article. Nonetheless, it contains powerful psychological overtones that I will explore.

The sixth concern relates to the fear of many that new immigrants have become a drain on the economy (see Huddle, 1993). That concern, one of the most often cited, deserves a more thorough analysis.

It is not by accident that Proposition 187 is a California product. California has the highest number of new immigrants: since the early 1990s, California has been receiving annually some 200,000 documented and an estimated 100,000 undocumented new immigrants. Furthermore, the new arrivals tend to be highly concentrated in certain areas. Los Angeles is today one of the largest cities of Spanish speakers in the world. Indeed, of the "estimated five million immigrants who moved to California since 1970, two-thirds moved to the vast sprawl of the Los Angeles basin" (Dunn, 1994: 3).

In the last few years California has been facing serious socioeconomic upheavals, including huge loses in its military-industrial base and other key industries. To make matters worse, California suffered a number of devastating—and costly—natural disasters including urban wild fires and earthquakes. The economic crisis led to severe budget cuts at the same time as many Californians were forced to rebuild their homes and their lives after the disasters. Surveys suggest that voters are particularly anxious about their socioeconomic losses and lack of security. This unhappy combination has ignited a furious debate about the "costs" and "benefits" said to be associated with the newest immigrants.

It is extremely difficult to calculate in a meaningful way the "costs" and "benefits" associated with a phenomenon as complex and multifaceted as immigration. There are, for example, short-term versus long-term "costs" and "benefits" that must be considered. There are also direct versus indirect "costs" as well as "benefits" associated with immigration. It is even more difficult to estimate the "costs" and "benefits" associated with the problem of undocumented immigrants—the data are simply not good enough.

An admittedly crass—but currently popular—index of economic "costs" is how much the new immigrants use in social services—welfare benefits (for which undocumented immigrants are not eligible), health care, costs associated with the criminal justice system, and costs associated with educating immigrant children in public schools. These "costs," some economists argue, can be evaluated against what immigrants "pay" in terms of taxes—local, state, and federal.

Yet even in making such rough estimates, economists have failed to arrive at a satisfactory consensus. Broadly speaking there are two schools of thought: those who see the new immigration as an economic burden and those who see the new immigration as an economic benefit. Those who see immigration as a burden maintain that the new immigrants simply cannot resist the seductive entitlements of the welfare state (Borjas, 1994: 76–80). According to this school of thought, the new immigrants end up "costing" more in terms of the services they use than they contribute through tax payments. In a highly publicized report, Rice University economist Donald Huddle concluded that immigrants—both legal and undocumented—"present in the United States in 1992 cost all levels of government that year more than $45 billion above and beyond the taxes they paid" (Huddle, 1993: 1).

Those who see the new immigration as an economic plus disagree. Indeed, they seem to speak another language altogether. Some experts have argued that the new arrivals—documented and undocumented—contribute far more to the economy than they use in services (Passel, 1994; Fierman, 1994: 67–75; Francese, 1994: 85–89). Passel re-examined Huddle's figures and concluded that far from "costing" more than $45 billion, immigrants—legal and undocumented—contributed a net surplus of $28.7 billion nationwide and a net surplus to the California economy of $12 billion (Passel, 1994: 1).

Other experts emphasize that beyond paying their fair share of the tax bill, immigrants generate a wealth of positive economic activity (Meissner, 1992). Some argue that recent arrivals have been critical in keeping within the United States low paying industries that would have likely migrated overseas without an immigrant labor force (see Rothstein, 1994: 48–63; Miles, 1994: 132). Other observers have noted that although there are regional differences, new arrivals do not on aggregate depress the wages of native workers (Fierman, 1994: 70).

Other researchers have noted that new immigrants played a critical role reinvigorating abandoned urban zones, opening ethnic businesses, and via the "multiplier effect," creating job opportunities for the native born. Fierman writes, "Compelling evidence even shows that immigrants boost overall employment on balance. . . . [F]or every one-hundred-person increase in the population of adult immigrants, the number of new jobs rose by forty-six. By contrast, for every one hundred new native-born Americans, the number of jobs rose by just twenty-five" (Fierman, 1994: 70). Yet others argue that immigrant workers will be increasingly critical when large numbers of baby-boomers begin to retire in large numbers and become consumers of social security and Medicare (Rothstein, 1994: 55–57; Francese, 1994: 89).

In short, there is ample evidence to reject the assertion that immigrants—both documented and undocumented—are the cause of economic hardship as the proponents of Proposition 187 have claimed. Even George Borjas, a controversial voice in the immigrant debate, concludes his somewhat sensationalist essay entitled "Tired, Poor, on Welfare" with a thoroughly uncontrovertial assessment, "At the national level, therefore, it would not be farfetched to conclude that immigration is near a washout" (Borjas, 1994: 78). Not farfetched at all! Likewise, Linda Chavez, hardly an advocate of open borders, writes. "Studies in the 1980s estimated that both legal and illegal immigrants were net contributors to the California economy paying more in taxes than they received in services and creating jobs rather than displacing American workers" (Chavez, 1994: 33).

There is enough evidence, therefore, to suggest that the current hysteria over immigration has little to do with objective measures of economic costs and benefits. Indeed, we concur with Nathan Glazer's observation that "economics in general can give no large answer as to what the immigration policy of the nation should be" (Glazer, 1994: 42).

Proposition 187 is based on another empirically dubious assertion: that Californians "have suffered and are suffering personal injury and damage caused by the criminal conduct of illegal aliens in this state" (Proposition 187). These psychologically charged indictments—drawn from powerful paranoid images of the "Other" as persecutorial criminal—are simply not based on any serious empirical evidence. The idea that undocumented immigrants, professional border bandits aside, are a major cause of serious crime in California today is empirically unfounded. If anything, the only serious empirical study of undocumented immigrants and crime suggests that they are far more likely to be the targets of violent crime than its perpetrators (Wolf, 1988).

In addition to its dubious assumptions about migrants and the economy and migrants and crime, Proposition 187 is based on the equally problematic assertion that "California's bounty of social services is the magnet drawing illegal immigrants across the border" (Noble, 1994: 11). Systematic studies suggest that it is simply not true that immigrants—documented or undocumented—are drawn by the "magnet" of the welfare state. Indeed, studies suggest that most new arrivals come to reunite with family members already in the United States, or in search of better employment opportunities (Cornelius, 1993: 31). Undocumented immigrants, furthermore, are already banned from receiving most social services. Some of the anxiety generated by the new immigration has to do with the fact that the federal government keeps the great bulk of the taxes generated by immigrants, whereas the local governments are responsible for providing most services—including health and education.

Texas, will follow the California example and enact similar laws in the near future.

What are the likely consequences of Proposition 187?

Proposition 187 will not add any resources to control the United States' international borders. Control of the U.S. borders is a responsibility of the Federal Government. Therefore, the State of California cannot have its own border control agenda independent of federal policy. Proposition 187 will not add any new equipment or border patrol agents along the Southern Border.

Although Proposition 187 bills itself as the "Save our State" initiative, there is some evidence to suggest that it may end up drowning the state. According to data provided by the independent office of California's Legislative Analyst, Proposition 187 may have devastating fiscal effects. The Legislative Analyst states,

> The most significant fiscal effects of this initiative fall into the following three categories,
>
> - Program Savings. The state and local governments (primarily countries) would realize savings from denying certain benefits and services to persons who can not document their citizenship or legal immigration status. These savings could be in the range of $200 million annually, based on the current estimated use of these benefits and services by illegal immigrants.
> - Verification Costs. The state, local governments, and schools would incur significant costs to verify citizenship or immigration status of students, parents, persons seeking health care or social services, and persons who are arrested. Ongoing annual costs could be in the tens of millions of dollars, with first-year costs considerably higher (potentially in excess of $100 million).
> - Potential Losses of Federal Funds. The measure places at risk up to $15 billion annually in federal funding for education, health and welfare programs due to conflicts with federal requirements. (Proposition 187; Analysis by the Legislative Analyst: 52).

In the words of Pat Dingsdale, President of the California State PTA, Proposition 187 "took a bad situation and made it much worse—$10 billion worse! Mean-while, Proposition 187 does absolutely nothing to beef up enforcement at the border or crack down on employers who hire undocumented workers" (Proposition 187; Rebuttal to Argument in Favor of Proposition 187). It is possible that the economic effects of Proposition 187 may be highly counterproductive—surely erasing any short term savings. There will also be costs associated with prosecuting those who refuse to report undocumented immigrants.

Given that there are no studies to support the assertion that immigrants come to California to plug into the welfare system, it is doubtful that, as its proponents predict, most new undocumented immigrants settled in the United States will return home as a result of Proposition 187. Furthermore, since many families are "mixed" in having both legal and undocumented members—a U.S. born child is a "legal" while there may be a Mexican-born undocumented child—it is very unlikely that a significant number of such "mixed" families will pick up and return to Mexico. Furthermore, the recent devaluation of the Mexican peso by 40 percent and the economic crisis in that country make it very unlikely that families will return *en masse.*

Proposition 187 requires school districts to verify the legal status of students in California. By January 1, 1996, the legal status of parents or guardians must also be verified by the schools. It is estimated that over 400,000 students could be expelled from California's public schools under the new law. Undocumented migrants will be also barred from attending community colleges, the California State University System, and the University of California System.

Under Proposition 187, undocumented immigrants are ineligible for all public health services, except for emergency medical care. (Undocumented immigrants are already ineligible for welfare programs.) State officers responsible for providing health, welfare, and public education services are required under the new law to report "suspected" undocumented immigrants to the United States Immigration and Naturalization Service. The costs associated with implementing these programs could be very high.

There may be additional costs associated with medical problems. There are preliminary reports that undocumented immigrants are now even more hesitant to obtain medical aid for fear of being reported to the INS. Some fatalities that could have been prevented have already been reported. As people fail to receive proper medical attention, serious—and, incidentally, much more costly—medical problems are likely to develop. Germs, unlike laws, do not discriminate: unvaccinated undocumented children will be equally contagious to citizens and immigrants alike.

Other costs which cannot be easily measured in dollars and cents will surely be paid. Given its vagueness, it is likely that the law would turn every immigrant (legal and undocumented), every person with an accent, every "foreign looking" person into a "suspect." This is likely to engender suspicion and mistrust, especially in a state with a large foreign-born population.

There is also the troubling issue of turning teachers, school personnel, health practitioners, and administrators into agents of the INS. If fully implemented, it is not clear whether these professionals—bound by their own professional code of ethics—will comply with their new responsibilities to report suspected undocumented immigrants to the INS. If non-compliance becomes a serious issue, there could be substantial costs associated with prosecuting and punishing professionals who refuse to obey the law. Furthermore, non-compliance would undermine the argument that undocumented immigration is undesirable—regardless of whether undocumented immigrants are a plus to the economy and to society at large—if for no other reason than by the fact that their very presence in the United States engenders contempt for the law.

There are reports that Proposition 187 has worsened the terror of "being caught" among undocumented immigrants. Proposition 187, if fully implemented, will surely engender a much wider circle of fear, from the ever-feared INS or *migra,* to teachers, school personnel, doctors, and nurses. It will reactivate and accentuate issues of marginality and shame, particularly among vulnerable undocumented immigrant children.

Immigration in the Western world today has all the features of a full blown hysteria: fact and fantasy have become hopelessly intertwined, generating a great deal of anxiety and rage. As in all hysterias, the current concern is out of proportion to the actual threat. The terror that ever growing "waves" of undocumented migrants and refugees are rushing to "flood" the shores of the more developed world is out of proportion to what is happening in reality. The United States today attracts only a small portion of the worldwide population of immigrants and refugees. Doris Meissner, the current INS Commissioner, wrote in 1992, "Whether motivated by economic or political reasons, or a mixture of both, the vast majority of migrants remain within their own countries. The next largest share move across national boundaries within the less-developed world, and a relatively small share cross borders to industrially advanced states" (Meissner, 1992: 66).

Melanie Klein elaborated the theory that we need others to contain our anxieties and focus our destructiveness (the "bad object"). Likewise, throughout much of history the Western world has had its need for "Others." At various times the Muslim world has been Europe's "outer Other," and the Jews have been its "inner Other." More recently, following the great atrocities of the Holocaust, the Western world saw the Soviet Union assume the place of the "Evil Empire." The Soviets, of course, played the role of the "bad guys" quite well. Indeed, during the Cold War the Soviet Union became a container of our anxieties and hatred. With the collapse of the Soviet system, the most recent container that kept our anxieties and sense of purpose in focus was broken. We are now looking for another container. We are, once again, in need of strangers: immigrants, mothers-on-welfare, gays be aware. . .

References

Ayres, B. Drummond. (1994a) "Curb on Aliens Dims Dreams in Hollywood." *The New York Times.* Nov. 11.

Ayres, B. Drummond. (1994b) "Court Blocks California on Alien Rules." *The New York Times.* Nov. 17.

Borjas, George. (1994) "Tired, Poor, on Welfare." In N. Mills, ed., *Arguing Immigration.*

Brimlow, Peter. (1992) "Time To Rethink Immigration?" *National Review.* June 22.

Brinkley, Joel. (1994) "California's Woes on Aliens Appear Largely Self-Inflicted." *The New York Times.* Oct. 15.

Brownstein, Ronald. (1994) "Wilson Proposes U.S. Version of Prop. 187." *Los Angeles Times.* Nov. 19.

Chavez, Linda. (1994) "Immigration Politics." In N. Mills, ed., *Arguing Immigration.*

Chavez, Lydia. (1994) "More Mexicans, More Profits." *The New York Times.* Dec. 9.

Cleeland, Nancy. (1994) "Judge Puts Hold on Most of Prop. 187." *San Diego Union-Tribune.* Nov. 17.

Clinton, Bill. (1995) "State of the Union Address." *Boston Globe.* Jan. 25.

Cornelius, Wayne. (1993) "Neo-Nativists Feed on Myopic Fears." *Los Angeles Times.* July 12.

Cowley, Geoffrey and Andrew Murr. (1994) "Good Politics, Bad Medicine." *Newsweek.* Dec. 5.

del Olmo, Frank. (1995) "Perspective on Immigration." *Los Angeles Times.* Jan. 31.

Dollard, J., L. W. Doob, N. E. Miller, O. H. Mower, and R. R. Sears. (1939) *Frustration and Aggression.* New Haven, Conn.: Yale Univ. Press.

Dunn, Ashley. (1994) "In California, the Numbers Add Up to Anxiety." *The New York Times.* Oct. 30.

Feldman, Paul and Rick McDonnell. (1994) "Prop. 187 Sponsors Swept Up in National Whirlwind." *Los Angeles Times.* Nov. 14.

Feldman, Paul and James Rainey. (1994) "Parts of Prop. 187 Blocked by Judge." *Los Angeles Times.* Nov. 17.

Fierman, Jaclyn. (1994) "Is Immigration Hurting the U.S.?" In N. Mills, ed., *Arguing Immigration.*

Francese, Peter. (1994) "Aging America Needs Foreign Blood." In N. Mills, ed., *Arguing Immigration.*

Freud, Sigmund. (1930) *Civilization and its Discontents.* Trans. and ed. by James Strachey. New York: W. W. Norton.

Fromm, Erich. (1973) *The Anatomy of Human Destructiveness.* New York: Henry Holt.

Glazer, Nathan. (1994) "The Closing Door." In N. Mills, ed., *Arguing Immigration.*

Huddle, Donald. (1993) "The Costs of Immigration." *Carrying Capacity Network.* July.

Kohut, Heinz. (1972) "Thoughts on Narcissism and Narcissistic Rage." *Psychoanalytic Study of the Child* 27: 360–400.

Klein, Melanie and Joan Riviere. (1964) *Love, Hate, and Reparation.* New York: W. W. Norton.

Kristeva, Julia. (1991) *Strangers to Ourselves.* New York: Columbia Univ. Press.

McCarthy, Cormac. (1994) *The Crossing.* New York: Knopf.

McDonnell, Patrick. (1994a) "Complex Family Ties Tangle Simple Premise of Prop. 187." *Los Angeles Times.* Nov. 20.

McDonnell, Patrick. (1994b) "Health Clinics Report Declines After Prop. 187." *Los Angeles Times.* Nov. 26.

MALDEF [Mexican American Legal Defense and Educational Fund]. (1994) "Temporary Restraining Order Granted Against Proposition 187." *News Release.* Nov. 16.

Meissner, Doris. (1992) "Managing Migrations." *Foreign Policy* 86(4): 66–83.

Miles, Jack. (1994) "Blacks vs. Browns." In N. Mills, ed., *Arguing Immigration.*

Mills, Nicolaus. (1994) *Arguing Immigration.* New York: Simon & Schuster.

Mitchell, Stephen A. (1993) "Aggression and the Endangered Self." *Psychoanalytic Quarterly* 62: 351–382.

Noble, Kenneth. (1994) "California Immigration Measure Faces Rocky Legal Path." *The New York Times.* Nov. 11.

Passel, Jeffrey. (1994) *Immigrants and Taxes: A Reappraisal of Huddle's "The Cost of Immigrants."* Washington, D.C.: The Urban Institute.

Pear, Robert. (1994) "Deciding Who Gets What in America." *The New York Times.* Nov. 27.

Plyler v. Doe: Appeal from the U.S. Court of Appeals for the Fifth Circuit. (1981) October Term of the United States Supreme Court.

Proposition 187 (1994) *Illegal Aliens. Ineligibility for Public Services. Verification and Reporting. Initiative Statute.* Sacramento, Calif.: State of California.

Rodriguez, Lori. (1994) "View of Reaction to Proposition 187." *Houston Chronicle.* Dec. 3.

Rothstein, Richard. (1994) "Immigration Dilemmas." In N. Mills, ed., *Arguing Immigration.*

Sanger, David. (1995) "Mexico Crisis Seen Spurring Flow of Aliens." *The New York Times.* Jan. 18.

Sherwood, Ben. (1994) "California Leads the Way, Alas." *The New York Times.* Nov. 27.

Sontag, Deborah. (1993) "Immigrants Forgoing Citizenship While Pursuing American Dream." *The New York Times.* July 25.

Suárez-Orozco, Carola and Suárez-Orozco, Marcelo. (1994) "The Cultural Psychology of Hispanic Immigrants." In T. Weaver, *The Handbook of Hispanic Cultures in the United States: Anthropology.* Houston: Arte Público Press, pp. 130–167.

Waldinger, Roger. (1994) "Black/Immigrant Competition Reassessed: New Evidence from Los Angeles." Unpublished manuscript. Department of Sociology. University of California, Los Angeles.

Weiner, Tim. (1993) "On These Shores Immigrants Find a New Wave of Hostility." *The New York Times.* June 13.

"Western Europe's Nationalists: The Rise of the Outside Right." (1994) *The Economist.* Oct. 15.

Wolf, Daniel H. (1988) *Undocumented Aliens and Crime: The Case of San Diego County.* La Jolla, Calif.: Center for U.S.-Mexican Studies, University of California, San Diego.

Wolf, Daniel H. (1994) "The Rae and Parker Study of Undocumented Alien Fiscal Impact: How Accurate?" Testimony to the Immigrant Hearing and Public Forum of Bill Morrow, Assemblyman, Seventy-Third District. Oceanside City Hall, Oceanside, Calif., December 9.

Wood, Daniel. (1994) "California's Prop. 187 Puts Illegal Immigrants on Edge." *The Christian Science Monitor.* Nov. 22.

Immigration Reform and Nativism

The Nationalist Response to the Transnationalist Challenge

Leo R. Chavez

On November 8, 1994, the voters of California overwhelmingly passed Proposition 187, which was, in the words of its supporters, to "Save Our State" by preventing "illegal aliens in the United States from receiving benefits or public services in the State of California."[1] As with many trends that begin in California, the anti-immigrant sentiment expressed in Proposition 187 rolled across the nation, as other states, some congressional representatives, and presidential candidates expressed the need to deny health care, education, and other publicly funded benefits to immigrants.

This chapter focuses on the "rhetoric of exclusion" embedded in the contemporary discourse on immigration reform.[2] The focus on anti-immigrant discourse reflects the notion that "the occasions, spaces, and modes of representation are themselves forms of power rather than mere reflections of power residing in the real, material 'facts of life,' and the 'big structures' through which the power of class, capital, or the state are expressed."[3] At the same time, the discourse of immigration reform is situated in a space that crosses over the borders of micropolitics and macropolitics. Local immigration reform discourse can become the national discourse, but in becoming national the local can become transformed.

As California's anti-immigrant discourse flowed across the nation, the anti- "illegal alien" focus of Proposition 187 broadened considerably. Discourse about immigration reform became a way of expressing anger about demographic changes brought on by immigration, targeting anyone who might be suspected of being "immigrant," "foreign looking," "un-American," or different. By eliminating or reducing these stigmatized groups, immigration reform would, in theory, "do something" about the source of the "problems" facing U.S. citizens, problems in the economy, education system, health care, and even the relations of local governments with the federal government. To the proponents of immigration reform, illegal immigrants are not the only problem; immigration in general is a threat to the "nation" that is conceived of as a singular, predominantly Euro-American, English-speaking culture. The "new" immigrants are *trans*nationalists, or people who maintain social linkages back in the home country; they are not bound by national borders and their multiple identities are situated in communities in different nations and in communities that cross nations.[4] Transnational migrants threaten a singular vision of the "nation" because they allegedly bring "multiculturalism" and not assimilation.[5] This was clearly part of U.S. Representative Newt Gingrich's intended message when, shortly after passage of Proposition 187, he promised that as Speaker of the House he would preside over a freewheeling congressional debate about the "cultural meanings of being American."[6]

Proponents of immigration reform, therefore, often cast their net on issues much wider than just illegal immigration. For example, flush with victory after passage of Proposition 187, the proposition's backers announced that their agenda was actually much broader and included affirmative action, bilingual education, and the promotion of English as the official language.[7] Their concerns led U.S. Representative Toby Roth (a Republican from Wisconsin) to introduce a bill that would effectively halt funding for bilingual education, abolish bilingual electoral ballots, and allow individuals to bring civil suits against institutions that violate English-only federal statutes.[8] The reason such a law is necessary, according to the bill itself, is because "It has been the long-standing national belief that full citizenship in the United States requires fluency in English."[9]

The question of who is an "American" and anti-immigrant discourse become entangled in revealing ways. For instance, on October 18, 1994, California State Senator Craven, a Republican from Oceanside, was quoted as saying "that the [California] state legislature should explore requiring all people of Hispanic descent to carry an identification card that would be used to verify legal residence."[10] By targeting "all Hispanics," citizens, legal residents, and undocumented immigrants, California Senator-Craven defines all Hispanics as belonging to a suspect class. Why Senator Craven focuses only on Hispanics is not clear. After all, California's ethnic diversity includes many other ethnic groups, including undocumented Canadians and Europeans who overstay their visas. Perhaps the answer has to do with the assumptions about social evolution and progress implicit in immigration discourse.

Discredited nineteenth-century scientific notions about social evolution continue to underlie present-day discourse on national encounters. This discourse positions Euro-Americans and Europeans at the top of a hierarchical ordering of civilized ("developed" and "technologically advanced" being common metaphors for this hierarchy) societies in contrast to less civilized ("less developed" and "technologically backward") societies. Senator Craven expressed these assumptions when addressing a senate hearing on migrant workers held in San Diego in February 1993; he said that "migrant workers were on a lower scale of humanity."[11]

Gifts to charitable organizations provide another example of how anti-immigrant sentiments extend beyond a concern with "illegal aliens." In Orange County, California, donors to charities are increasingly stipulating that those who receive their gifts not be illegal aliens. In some cases, the donors specifically state that the recipients should be English speaking, or even non-Latinos to ensure their citizenship status. As one director of a charitable agency said, "I had to find someone white and English-speaking" to receive the donations.[12]

Perhaps one of the clearest statements about the threat of immigration to the "complexion" of American society comes from Pat Buchanan, a presidential candidate during the 1992 and 1996 elections. Buchanan said: "A non-white majority is envisioned if today's immigration continues." Given this prognosis, he argues that America needs a "time out" from immigration.[13] Buchanan would like a moratorium on all immigration to the United States, not merely closing the borders to undocumented immigrants.

The extent to which the anti-immigrant debate is racially polarized is suggested by voting patterns in California. Proposition 187 passed with 59 percent of the votes cast. But white Californians, in particular, appeared to be expressing sentiments of unease over immigration. Two out of three voting whites in California (about 67 percent) voted for the proposition, a significantly larger proportion than the vote among African Americans and Asian Americans (about half of each group voted for it) and Latinos (only 23 percent voted for it).[14] The voting block provided by white voters ensured passage of Proposition 187. Importantly, even though whites account for about 57 percent of California's population, they account for about 80 percent of the voters, thus their views take on tremendous power. In contrast, while Latinos account for 25 percent of the state's population, they accounted for only 8 percent of those voting.[15] White voters in California appear to be sending a symbolic statement about their concern over immigration and the "new" immigrants.

Since passage of Proposition 187 by the voters of California, a number of U.S. Representatives and Senators have submitted bills dealing with the "immigration problem." Following the assumption put forward by proponents of Proposition 187, that social services, not jobs, are the magnet drawing undocumented immigrants to the United States, national immigration reform proposals target aid to immigrants.[16] For example, Representative Ron Packard (Republican from Oceanside) proposed denying illegal immigrants federal benefits offered to victims of flooding in California.[17] In June 1995, a House task force chaired by Representative Elton Gallegly (Republican from Simi Valley) submitted its report urging an approach similar to Proposition 187 at the national level. The task force commended denying all public services, except emergency health care, to undocumented immigrants. In order for hospitals to receive reimbursement for treating undocumented immigrants, however, they would have to notify the Immigration and Naturalization Service of the patients before they are discharged.[18] The task force also recommended allowing states to cut off public education to undocumented students. One of the task force's most contentious recommendations is to amend the U.S. Constitution to end automatic citizenship for U.S.-born children whose parents are undocumented immigrants.[19]

Representative Gallegly was an early proponent of this policy. In October 1991, he introduced legislation into Congress to amend the U.S. Constitution to deny citizenship to a child born in the United States if neither of the parents are citizens and if the child's mother is not at least a legal resident.[20] His argument is that even though this is a nation of immigrants, we must reduce immigration—both legal and undocumented:

> We must recognize, however, that the United States is also a nation of finite resources and opportunities which must be available to and shared by all its citizens. Today, in many parts of this country our cities and towns are being overrun with immigrants, both legal and undocumented, who pose major economic and law enforcement problems for local governments and place an added burden on their already strained budgets.[21]

Although Gallegly's legislation focuses on the children of undocumented immigrants, his statement clearly makes little differentiation between legal and illegal immigrants. He views immigrants generally as a "problem," as outsiders, regardless of immigration status. Thus, his attempts to stop conferring citizenship on the children of undocumented immigrants appears as but one part of a broader agenda to rid the country of all "outsiders," that is, immigrants and their U.S.-born children.

Perhaps the shift in focus from undocumented immigrants to legal immigrants became complete in June of 1995 when the U.S. Commission on Immigration Reform, headed by Barbara Jordan of Texas, recommended that legal immigration into the United States be sharply reduced.[22] President Clinton has also suggested that "You can make a good case for modest reduction of the quota on legal immigration."[23]

These emerging views on legal immigration set the context for national immigration reform proposals that target all immigrants, including those legally in the country. For example, Representative E. Clay Shaw, Jr. (a Republican from Florida), proposed that only citizens be provided benefits such as Aid to Families with Dependent Children, food stamps, and Medicaid. Denying these benefits to legal residents, would, according to Representative Shaw, take away the attraction of people to come to this country, that is, welfare and the social safety net.[24] In all, the Republican legislative program for immigration reform that was brought to the U.S. House of Representatives in Proposition 187's wake would deny sixty kinds of federal assistance to millions of legal immigrants, including health programs, Social Security, Supplementary Security Income, disability payments, housing assistance, childhood immunizations, subsidized school lunches, job training, and aid to the homeless.[25] On March 24,

1995, the House of Representatives passed the Personal Responsibility Act, which included many of these proposals to limit social services to legal immigrants.[26]

The U.S. Senate followed the House's example when it passed its own bill on welfare policy on September 19, 1995. The Senate's bill cuts fewer benefits for legal immigrants than the House's but also restricts benefits for naturalized citizens who immigrate after the bill's enactment.[27] If enacted, this would be the first time in U.S. history that government benefits were denied naturalized citizens because they were not born in the United States, thus establishing a two-tiered or segmented structure for citizenship. But even if these parts of the bill are ultimately dropped, they indicate the willingness of policy-makers to treat naturalized citizens differently from U.S.-born citizens. This is a sign of a major reconceptualization of the relationship of immigrants to the nation.

Finally, the U.S. Congress is considering legislation that would reduce the number of legal immigrants from 800,000 to about 535,000 per year. This reduction would be accomplished by eliminating several preference categories for family reunification, including the preferences for foreign adult children and parents of U.S. citizens and legal residents, and for adult brothers and sisters of U.S. citizens. The aim of eliminating these preferences is to stop the network migration of extended family members, while allowing nuclear families to continue to reunite in the United States. Eliminating these preferences would shut the door on an estimated 2.4 million foreigners—mostly Mexicans and Filipinos—waiting in queues to enter the United States on the basis of family ties.[28]

In sum, the nativist revolt against undocumented immigrants that began in California quickly reached national proportions, targeting all immigrants. The policy recommendations emanating from state and federal legislators and the discourse spewing forth from presidential candidates are of the sort not heard with such force since the nativist movements of the late 1800s and the early twentieth century. Should some of these proposals come to pass—especially such dramatic changes as a constitutional amendment to deny citizenship to children born in the United States, and distinctions between citizens by birth and those naturalized—then this round of nativism will have ushered in some of the most profound changes in how America—the United States—perceives itself as a community, as a people, and as a nation. Traditional definitions of who deserves to be an American and receive the benefits of the social contract are being challenged and redefined in unprecedented ways.

As the nation rushes along the anti-immigrant current, it is important to contemplate how we arrived at this juncture in our history and to analyze the underlying nature the attack on immigrants is taking and its implications for the future. Why this level of nativism now? Why do immigration reform proposals target mainly women and children? Or, to put it another way, why target reproduction of the immigrant labor force? And, what does this tell us about the production of immigrant labor that specific sectors of our economy have grown to depend upon?

The New Nativism in Historical Perspective

Why is anti-immigrant rhetoric so prominent in the contemporary discourse on the state of the nation? To answer this question, we must remember that Americans have always had a love-hate relationship with immigration, despite a congratulatory self-image as a "nation of immigrants." [For further treatment of the history of American nativism, see chapters 1 and 9–11 of this volume—*Ed.*] Because of America's history, "immigration" has become what anthropologists call a key symbol in American culture.[29] Immigration is such a central and powerful concept that it is endowed with a multiplicity of referents and meanings; it raises highly charged emotions, which can often be contradictory.[30] In short, nativism and xenophobia have been constant themes in American history, although they become prominent during specific historical moments. Contemporary anti-immigrant posturing can be traced to changes in immigration law, continued undocumented immigration, an economy undergoing repeated cycles of recession, and the end of the Cold War.[31]

In many ways, the "new" nativism sounds strikingly similar to the "old" nativism. In their book *The Immigration Time Bomb,* Richard Lamm, the ex-Governor of Colorado, and Gary Imhoff, an ex-official of the Immigration and Naturalization Service, warn about the perils of immigration in a way that is reminiscent of older laments:

> At today's massive levels, immigration has major negative consequences—economic, social, and demographic—that overwhelm its advantages. . . . To solve the immigration crisis, we Americans have to face our limitations. We have to face the necessity of passing laws to restrict immigration and the necessity of enforcing those laws. If we fail to do so, we shall leave a legacy of strife, violence, and joblessness to our children.[32]

More recently, Peter Brimelow, himself an immigrant from the Great Britain, has vociferously echoed Lamm and Imhoff's dark scenario for a future of continued immigration.[33] America's problems, according to Brimelow, are due to immigrants who lack the cultural background of earlier European, especially British, immigrants. He argues that America needs to "rethink" immigration and calls for a "time out" from immigration.[34] Failure to restrict immigration, Brimelow warns, will lead America on the road to becoming an "alien nation."

Discourse surrounding Proposition 187 and subsequent immigration reform resonate with Lamm and Imhoff's and Brimelow's views, with their heavy emphasis on the conflict and threat to the nation posed by transnational migrants who do not respect traditional borders and the sovereignty of nation states. In arguing for the urgency of their cause, the proponents of immigration reform often characterize the immigrant as the "enemy" in metaphors of war. Immigrants become the new threat to national security and identity, filling the void left by the loss of the old enemies after the collapse of the Soviet Union and the end of the Cold War. In this respect, the anti-immigrant discourse of the 1990s corresponds to the new vision of "America First" put forward by Pat Buchanan and increasingly touted by Republican presidential candidates. The anti-internationalist stance of "America First" enthusiasts carries with it "a kind of nativistic foreigner-bashing," according to Jeremy Rosner of the Carnegie Endowment for International Peace.[35]

Immigrants as foreigners who threatened the American way of life was a central part of the Proposition 187 campaign in California. Proponents of Proposition 187 banked on the widely held perception that an "invasion" of undocumented immigrants was the cause of California's economic problems and eroding the lifestyles of U.S. citizens to the point of reducing the nation to a "Third World" country.[36] The reference to "Third World" is a strategic marker that metaphorically alludes to social evolution and the threat of immigration leading to a de-evolution of "American civilization."

U.S. Representative Dana Rohrabacher (a Republican from Huntington Beach, California), in arguing for passage of Proposition 187 shortly before the election, carried the war metaphor even further when he said, "Unlawful immigrants represent the liberal/left foot soldiers in the next decade."[37] Another proponent of Proposition 187, Ruth Coffey, the director of Stop Immigration Now, frequently raised the specter of "multiculturalism," commenting that "I have no intention of being the object of 'conquest,' peaceful or otherwise, by Latinos, Asians, blacks, Arabs or any other groups of individuals who have claimed my country."[38] Of course, the irony of Ms. Coffey's statement appears to go unnoticed; as a result of the Mexican American War in the mid 1800s, the United States "conquered" California. An appeal to historical memory, however, can be subtle yet telling. Ronald Prince, one of the cofounders of the Save Our State (SOS) initiative, speaking to a gathering in Orange County, explaining how Proposition 187 would stop undocumented immigration, used a metaphor that harkened back to images of frontier justice, when Mexicans were routinely hanged by vigilante mobs: "You are the posse and SOS is the rope."[39]

Glenn Spencer, founder of the Voice of Citizens Together, a San Fernando Valley-based group that was a principal grassroots backer of Proposition 187, also put his views into a war metaphor framework. Before the November elections in California, he argued for passage of Proposition 187 because illegal immigration is "part of a reconquest of the American Southwest by foreign Hispanics. Someone is going to be leaving the state. It will either be them or us."[40] After the passage of Proposition 187, at a rally to deny public education to illegal immigrants and to denounce the Clinton Administration's proposed $40-billion aid package to Mexico, Spencer said, "It boils down to this: Do we want to retain control of the Southwest more than the Mexicans want to take it from us?" He went on to compare "the conflict" to the Vietnam war: "It's a struggle between two groups of people for territory."[41] Even when confronted with academic research that suggests immigrants generally assimilate and improve their economic well-being, Spencer's comment was that "What we have in Southern California is not assimilation—It's annexation by Mexico."[42]

Immigrants as a threat to national security, sovereignty, and control of territory is central to the war metaphors as used in debates about immigration. As Bette Hammond, the head of S.T.O.P.I.T. (Stop the Out-of-Control Problems of Immigration

Today), a Marin County-based group that was an early and key organizer on behalf of Proposition 187, put it: "We've got to take back our country."[43] Newt Gingrich, speaking about immigration reform, also raised the sovereignty issue: "If they're illegal, why aren't they gone? Whatever law we have to pass to be able to protect American sovereignty and to be able to say we're not going to have illegal people in the United States, we should pass."[44]

According to Linda B. Hayes, the Proposition 187 media director for southern California, the loss of U.S. territory can occur as a result of the rapid demographic shifts caused by Mexican immigration. As she wrote in a letter to the *New York Times,*

> By flooding the state with 2 million illegal aliens to date, and increasing that figure each of the following 10 years, Mexicans in California would number 15 million to 20 million by 2004. During those 10 years about 5 million to 8 million Californians would have emigrated to other states. If these trends continued, a Mexico-controlled California could vote to establish Spanish as the sole language of California, 10 million more English-speaking Californians could flee, and there could be a statewide vote to leave the Union and annex California to Mexico.[45]

Why people who left a country in search of economic opportunity and a better life would vote to return the state to that country is not explained. Nor is it clear why, in the year 2004, the children and grandchildren of immigrants—all U.S. citizens who did not grow up in Mexico and who will not have the same nostalgia for Mexico as their parents or grandparents—would vote to annex California to Mexico. Of course, such questions may be beside the point since nativist arguments rely more on emotional resonance than the marshaling of empirical evidence and support found in academic treatises.[46]

Proposition 187 and the proposals for immigration reform that followed, then, can be traced to xenophobia related to the changing complexion of immigrants, frustration with the ineffectiveness of the 1986 immigration law to control undocumented immigration, economic recessions, and a new nationalism. As anti-immigrant as the discourse appears, immigration reform targets predominantly women and children, that is, the reproduction of the immigrant labor force. Why is this and what does it mean?

Targeting Reproduction While Ignoring Production

Anthropologist Claude Meillassoux long ago reminded us of the importance of focusing on both production and reproduction when examining immigration.[47] Proposition 187 and most of the immigration reform proposals that followed it target social services, especially health care and education, as the principal attraction to immigrants, both legal and undocumented. The logic is that denial of social services to immigrants reduces the incentives for immigration and thus fewer immigrants will decide to come to the United States. This logic, however, targets reproduction—women and children—and does very little to stop the production-work of immigrant labor.

This is not to suggest that some proposals do not advocate increased funding for the Border Patrol and that the Justice Department does not occasionally "get tough" on employers, because both of these are true.[48] Rather, the point here is that most of the proposals for immigration reform focus on social services, targeting reproduction of the immigrant family and thereby reducing the costs associated with immigrant labor while maintaining, or even increasing, the profits of that labor. It is certainly true that immigrant families have reproductive costs, some of which are subsidized by society, such as education. Immigrant workers, on the other hand, have many benefits for production, since they cost society little to produce (the costs of raising and educating them were borne by their families and home societies), are often willing to perform low-wage work, are typically young and relatively healthy, and are often afraid to pursue, or are unaware of, their rights as workers. By targeting reproduction, immigration reform does very little to undermine the lucrative and highly profitable relationship between employers and workers.

Proposition 187 and most of the immigration reform proposals discussed above do not target production. They leave immigrant workers and their employers curiously out of the picture. For example, Proposition 187 did not advocate more funds for ensuring fair labor standards and practices, thus reducing the incentive for hiring immigrant, especially undocumented, labor. As Labor Secretary Robert B. Reich noted: "One reason that employers in the United States are willing to risk employer sanctions right now and hire illegal immigrants is because they can get those illegal immigrants at less than the minimum wage, put them in squalid working conditions, and they know that those illegal immigrants are unlikely to complain."[49] Nor did the proposition propose increased enforcement of employer sanctions. The implicit message is that we are going after the reproduction of the undocumented labor force not the laborer nor the employer.

The debate surrounding Proposition 187 provides further insight into this point. The proposition's proponents targeted those who are "breaking the law" and don't deserve social service benefits. Governor Wilson argued that "Californians are justifiably fed up with those who break the law and ignore the rules that govern a civilized society. Californians want people held accountable for their actions again—whether it's a career criminal, a deadbeat dad, or someone who violates immigration laws."[50] Proposition 187, however, targeted only undocumented immigrants' use of social services, not employers who might be breaking the law by hiring undocumented workers. Indeed, in correspondence between Pete Wilson and immigration authorities, Wilson often encouraged the immigration commissioner to stop raids on California companies, arguing that sweeping up undocumented workers caused unnecessary disruptions to business.[51] Such actions stand in marked contrast to anti-immigrant discourse, suggesting that production must be safeguarded but reproduction of the worker's family must be stopped.

Getting rid (the euphemism is "voluntary return migration") of spouses and children would reduce the costs associated with immigrant labor by removing those most likely to use social services. Parenthetically, a more cynical argument is that the objective in denying education and health care to undocumented immigrants is not to pressure them to return to their country of origin but to create a permanent underclass of low-educated, available low-wage workers. While I believe this is the practical outcome of the immigration reform proposals, I am assuming here that the goal of immigration reform is as stated: to remove the alleged incentives (social services) attracting undocumented immigrants to the United States. Research has shown, however, that undocumented immigrants come to the United States to work and rarely come to get an education.[52] It is the children of undocumented immigrants that are in the public school system. Research has also shown that immigrant women and children are more likely than immigrant men, especially among the undocumented, to use health services.[53] But even though they are more likely than adult males to use health services, immigrant women, particularly the undocumented, continue to face major health risks because they significantly underuse critical preventive medicine.[54] Despite the medical and financial implications, the first action Governor Wilson took after passage of Proposition 187 was to move to cut off prenatal care to undocumented women.[55] However, there is absolutely no evidence that if you deny health care for women and children, or deny education or school lunches for children for that matter, that it will do anything to reduce the economic magnet—jobs—that draws immigrant labor to the United States. This is true for both undocumented and legal immigration.

This relationship between production (positive) and reproduction (negative) is revealed most clearly in the proposals for a guest-worker program. At the same time that proponents of immigration reform appear to be clamoring for an end or reduction in immigration, there are serious proposals to bring foreign workers to the United States on a temporary basis to work in agriculture and highly competitive high-technology companies. Shortly after the November 1994 elections were over in California, Governor Wilson was in Washington promoting just such a new *bracero* or guest-worker program.[56] An advocate of providing California agribusiness low-cost seasonal labor (guest-workers) when he was a U.S. senator, Wilson again made his plea for a guest-worker program in an address to the Heritage Foundation. Wilson justified a guest-worker program as a way "to alleviate the pressure for illegal immigration created by Mexico's inability to produce enough jobs for its people." Wilson clearly stated his vision of a return to a use of primarily Mexican male labor that would exclude the workers' families: "It makes sense—it has in the past, it may well continue to do so in the future—to have some sort of guest-worker program. But not the kind of thing we have been seeing where there has been massive illegal immigration, where whole families have come and where they are . . . requiring services that are paid for by state taxpayers."[57] Harold Ezzell, a coauthor of Proposition 187 and a past official of the INS, has also suggested a guest-worker program as a means of meeting labor shortages that cannot be filled by U.S. workers.[58] Even Representative Gallegly, who is so adamant about denying citizenship to children born in the United States if their parents are not legal residents, acknowledged that there may be a need for immigrants to work in temporary jobs in the United States.[59]

This is the logical next step since a guest-worker program institutionalizes the perfect cost-benefit ratio for immigrant labor: bringing foreign workers produced with no costs and who are not allowed to bring their families, thus not incurring reproductive costs (health care, education) here. In essence, production without reproduction, workers without families, sojourners not settlers.

To a certain extent we have come full circle in the debate over immigration, especially immigration from Mexico. In 1911, the Dillingham Commission, which was established to study the immigration issue, argued that Mexican migration should be promoted as the best solution to the Southwest's labor problem.[60] Unlike Japanese, Chinese, and Southern and Eastern European immigrants, the Commission argued that Mexicans were "homing pigeons" who would work for a short time in the United States and then return to their families in Mexico. It even went so far as to exempt Mexicans from the head tax for immigrants that was established under the immigration laws of 1903 and 1907. The Commission's advocacy of single male workers allowed to work on a temporary basis—without their families accompanying them—was institutionalized in contract labor programs during the 1910s and later during the Bracero Program, which lasted from 1942 to 1964. Ultimately, however, even some temporary workers manage to bring their families to join them and become settlers. As Doris Meissner, Commissioner of the INS has observed, "History shows that every contract-worker program falls victim to the inexorable goal of workers who wish to reunite with their families or to become members of the community in which they work."[61]

Even undocumented workers, our unofficial guest-workers, and their families have a remarkable capacity to develop a sense of community in the United States.[62] Although they may have come originally as temporary migrants, over time they marry or bring their spouse and children to join them in the United States, have children born here who therefore become citizens (what I have termed "binational families"), have other relatives and friends living nearby, and have important networks in the labor market.[63] These social and familial developments increase the likelihood of settlement in the United States.[64]

Final Thoughts

What is new in the "new" nativism, perhaps, is the extent to which immigrants, even those who are legal residents and citizens, are being reimagined as less deserving members of the community.[65] What began as a prairie fire against undocumented immigrants quickly ignited into a major round of immigration reform, with immigrants facing denial of many social services. The benefits immigrants have historically brought to this "nation of immigrants" have become overshadowed by the cost of immigration. To be "immigrant" today is tantamount to being a "cost" to society, a cost that must be reduced if the nation is to get its house in order and balance its budget.

In the discourse of contemporary social sciences, immigrants have become the less moral, undeserving, and threatening Other in society.

In the current discourse on immigration, race matters but in a less than obvious way. As Balibar has noted, the category of immigration has replaced the notion of race. In other words, rather than speaking in terms of biological differentiation, genetic inferiority, or social evolution, proponents of immigration reform cloak a "neo-racism" in a language that talks about "scales of humanity," "us and them," "conquest and sovereignty" and "a nonwhite majority."[66] Such phrasing alerts us to the fact that the "new" immigration from Latin America, particularly Mexico, and Asia is qualitatively different from the "old" immigration from Europe.

The new immigrants pose a transnationalist challenge to a narrow nationalist construction of the nation. In this sense, the current wave of immigration reform proposals reflect a nationalist response to this transnational challenge. Immigrants, it is said, are harbingers of a "nonwhite majority," multiculturalism, and an end of English dominance. As a consequence, they are depicted as posing a threat to the fiction of the "national culture" and the nationalist order of society. They undermine the notion of a singular American identity. Immigrants, as the transnational movements of people across borders—both political and cultural—underscore the disorder inherent in the order implied by the fiction of a singular cultural heritage.[67]

Thus enters the recurrent contradiction in America's immigration history. On the one hand, there are those who have desired immigrant labor because it provides a valuable asset to the economy. On the other hand are those Americans who believe immigrants threaten that which is "American." The specific nature of that threat may find different emphasis during any particular historical moment. In the current epoch, the threat is both cultural and fiscal. The families of immigrant workers have costs to society. Reducing society's obligations and responsibilities to immigrant families is way of balancing the budget but not necessarily a way to produce healthy and educated members of society. Nor are such policies sure to reduce the flow of immigrants, legal or otherwise. What do we get, then, from this new round of nativism? Rather than giving us an accurate portrayal of immigrant motives and behavior, the discourse of immigration reform tells us more about the fears and character of a nation under stress. In this sense, the new nativism is a lot like the old nativism.

Notes

1 California Ballot Pamphlet 1994. On November 20, 1995, a federal district judge in Los Angeles ruled that the state of California is preempted from barring illegal immigrants from elementary and secondary education, and from federally funded health care and social welfare services. These issues are far from resolved, however, since the advocates for Proposition 187 intend to take their case to the U.S. Supreme Court. See Paul Feldman, "Parts of 187 Thrown Out," *Los Angeles Times* 21 November 1995: A1.

2 For an excellent analysis of the immigration debate in Europe, see Verena Stolcke, "Talking Culture: New Boundaries, New Rhetorics of Exclusion in Europe," *Current Anthropology* 36: 1–24, 1995.

3 Michael Peter Smith, "Postmodernism, Urban Ethnography, and the New Social Space of Ethnic Identity," *Theory and Society* 21: 493–531, 1992.

4 This view of transnational migrants converges with contemporary social theory. For example, see Linda Basch, Nina Glick Schiller, and Cristina Szanton Blanc, *Nations Unbound: Transnational Projects, Postcolonial Predicaments, and Deterritorialized Nation-States* (Amsterdam: Gordon and Breach, 1994). Also, postmodern definitions of identity critique the notion that a person must belong to only one community, geographically defined; rather, people have multiple and often contradictory identities, inhabiting a diversity of communities. See Michael Peter Smith, "Post-modernism, Urban Ethnography, and the New Social Space of Ethnic Identity," *Theory and Society* 21: 493–531, 1992. For a discussion of undocumented immigrants positioned in multiple communities, see Leo R. Chavez, "The Power of the Imagined Community: The Settlement of Undocumented Mexicans and Central Americans in the United States," *American Anthropologist* 96: 52–73, 1994; Roger Rouse, "Mexican Migration and the Social Space of Postmodernism," *Diaspora* 1: 8–23, 1991; and Michael Kearney, "Borders and Boundaries of State and Self at the End of Empire," *Journal of Historical Sociology* 4(1): 52–74, 1991.

5 Gebe Martinez and Patrick J. McDonnell, "Prop. 187 Forces Rely on Message—Not Strategy," *Los Angeles Times* 30 October 1991: A1.

6 Melissa Healy, "Gingrich Lays out Rigid GOP Agenda," *Los Angeles Times* 12 November 1994: A1.

7 Patrick J. McDonnell, "Prop. 187 Win Spotlights Voting Disparity," *Los Angeles Times* 10 November 1994: A3. See also Patrick J. McDonnell, "Is Prop. 187 Just the Beginning?" *Los Angeles Times* 28 January 1995: A1.

8 Charles King, "Too Narrow a View of Who's American," *Los Angeles Times* 21 September 1995: B11 (Orange County edition).

9 Charles King, "Too Narrow a View of Who's American," *Los Angeles Times* 21 September 1995: B11 (Orange County edition).

10 Maria C. Hunt, "Craven Says All Hispanics Should Carry I.D. Cards," *San Diego Union-Tribune* 18 October 1994: A1.

11 Maria C. Hunt, "Craven Says All Hispanics Should Carry I.D. Cards." *San Diego Union-Tribune* 18 October 1994: A1.

12 Leslie Berkman, "Some Attach Strings to the Spirit of Giving," *Los Angeles Times* 24 November 1994: B1 (Orange County edition).

13 Patrick J. Buchanan, "What Will America Be in 2050?" *Los Angeles Times* 28 October 1994: B11. See also John L. Graham, "Xenophobic Fears about a 'Nonwhite Majority' Are Nonsense," *Los Angeles Times* 27 November 1994: B17 (Orange County edition).

14 Patrick J. McDonnell, "Prop. 187 Win Spotlights Voting Disparity," *Los Angeles Times* 10 November 1994: A3. See also Philip Martin, "Proposition 187 in California," *International Migration Review* 24: 255–63, 1995.

15 Patrick J. McDonnell, "Prop. 187 Win Spotlights Voting Disparity," *Los Angeles Times* 10 November 1994: A3.

16 Kevin R. Johnson, "Public Benefits and Immigration: The Intersection of Immigration Status, Ethnicity, Gender, and Class," *UCLA Law Review* 42(6): 1509–75, 1995.

17 Lisa Richwine, "Packard Vows to Bar Illegal Immigrants from Flood Aid," *Los Angeles Times* 14 January 1995: B1 (Orange County edition).

18 Marc Lacey, "New Task Force Targets Illegal Immigration." *Los Angeles Times* 16 March 1995: A3.

19 Marc Lacey, "Immigration Report Gains Key Support," *Los Angeles Times* 30 June 1995: A34.

20 Elton Gallegly, "Gallegly Seeks to End Automatic Citizenship for Illegal Alien Children," press release of October 22, 1991, from the Office of Congressman Elton Gallegly, Washington, D.C., 1991.

21 Elton Gallegly, "Time to Amend Our Birthright Citizenship Laws," speech presented by Rep. Gallegly in the House of Representatives, October 22, 1991. Copy in author's files.

22 Janet Hook, "Immigration Cutback Urged by U.S. Panel," *Los Angeles Times* 8 June 1995: A1.

23 Alison Mitchell, "President Rebuts Some GOP Themes on Economic Woes," *New York Times* 5 September 1995: A1.

24 Elizabeth Shogren, "Plans to Cut Safety Net Leave Legal Immigrants Dangling," *Los Angeles Times* 21 November 1994: A1.

25 Aaron Epstein, "GOP Targets Legal Noncitizens," *Orange County Register* 27 December 1994: A1.

26 Elizabeth Shogren, "House OK's Welfare Overhaul that Cuts off Aid Guarantees," *Los Angeles Times* 25 March 1995: A1.

27 Elizabeth Shogren, "Senate Approves Shifting Control of Welfare to States," *Los Angeles Times* 20 September 1995: A1.

28 "Congress Moves on Immigration Reform," *Migration News* 2(10) October 1995: 1. Philip Martin, editor, *Migration News,* 1004 Eagle Place, Davis, CA 95616.

29 Clifford Geertz, *The Interpretation of Cultures* (New York: Basic Books, 1973).

30 See, generally, Stephen Steinberg, *The Ethnic Myth: Race, Ethnicity, and Class in America* (Boston: Beacon Press, 1981); John Higham, *Strangers in the Land: Patterns of American Nativism* 1860–1925 (New York: Atheneum, 1985 [1955]); Stephen Jay Gould, *The Mismeasure of Man* (New York: W. W. Norton, 1981); Rita J. Simon, *Public Opinion and the Immigrant* (Lexington, MA: Lexington Books, 1985).

31 On these issues, see David M. Reimers, *Still the Golden Door: The Third World Comes to America* (New York: Columbia University Press, 1985); Frank D. Bean, Barry Edmonston, and Jeffrey S. Passel, *Undocumented Migration to the United States* (Washington, DC: Urban Institute Press, 1990); Rita J. Simon, *Public Opinion and the Immigrant* (Lexington, MA: Lexington Books, 1985); and Wayne A. Cornelius, "America in the Era of Limits," *Working Paper No. 3* (La Jolla, CA: Center for U.S.-Mexican Studies, University of California, San Diego, 1980).

32 Richard D. Lamm and Gary Imhoff, *The Immigration Time Bomb* (New York: Truman Talley Books, 1985).

33 Peter Brimelow, *Alien Nation: Common Sense About America's Immigration Disaster* (New York: Random House, 1995).

34 Peter Brimelow, "Time to Rethink Immigration?" *National Review* 22 June: 30–46, 1992.

35 Jim Mann, "GOP Candidates Warm to Anti-Foreign Policy," *Los Angeles Times* 24 September 1995: A3.

36 Gebe Martinez and Patrick J. McDonnell, "Prop. 187 Forces Rely on Message—Not Strategy," *Los Angeles Times* 30 October 1994: A1.

37 Gebe Martinez and Patrick J. McDonnell, "Prop. 187 Forces Rely on Message—Not Strategy," *Los Angeles Times* 30 October 1994: A1.

38 Gebe Martinez and Patrick J. McDonnell, "Prop. 187 Forces Rely on Message—Not Strategy," *Los Angeles Times* 30 October 1994: A1.

39 Patrick J. McDonnell, "Prop. 187 Heats up Debate over Immigration," *Los Angeles Times* 10 August 1994: A1.

40 Gebe Martinez and Patrick J. McDonnell, "Prop. 187 Forces Rely on Message—Not Strategy," *Los Angeles Times* 30 October 1994: A1.

41 Patrick J. McDonnell, "Is Prop. 187 Just the Beginning?" *Los Angeles Times* 28 January 1995: A1.

42 Spencer was quoted in Patrick J. McDonnell, "Study Disputes Immigrant Stereotypes, Cites Gains," *Los Angeles Times* 3 November 1995: A1. He was responding to the study "The Changing Immigrants of Southern California" by Dowell Myers, the first report from the research project California Immigration and the American Dream: Integration and Advancement of the New Arrivals (Los Angeles: School of Urban and Regional Planning, University of Southern California, November 1995).

43 Patrick J. McDonnell, "Prop. 187 Heats up Debate over Immigration," *Los Angeles Times* 10 August 1994: A1.

44 Melissa Healy, "House GOP Charts California Agenda," *Los Angeles Times* 13 November 1994: A1.

45 Linda B. Hayes, "Letter to the Editor: California's Prop. 187," *New York Times* 15 October 1994: 18.

46 For a discussion of the issues related to return migration among undocumented immigrants from Mexico and Central America, see Leo R. Chavez,

Shadowed Lives: Undocumented Immigrants in American Society (Ft. Worth: Harcourt, Brace and Jovanovich College Publishers, 1992).

47 Claude Meillassoux, *Maidens, Meal and Money: Capitalism and the Domestic Community* (Cambridge: Cambridge University Press, 1975).

48 James Bornemeier, "Clinton Moves to Curb Illegal Immigration," *Los Angeles Times* 8 February 1995: A3. See also Janet Hook, "Clinton Moves to Speed Deportations," *Los Angeles Times* 7 May 1995: A1.

49 James Bornemeier, "Clinton Moves to Curb Illegal Immigration," *Los Angeles Times* 8 February 1995: A3.

50 Pete Wilson, "Sowing the Ground for a Better California," *Los Angeles Times* 24 October 1994: B11 (Orange County edition).

51 Paul Jacobs, "Wilson Often Battled INS, Letters Show," *Los Angeles Times* 25 September 1995: A3.

52 Leo R. Chavez, "Settlers and Sojourners: The Case of Mexicans in the United States," *Human Organization* 47: 95–108, 1988.

53 Leo R. Chavez, Wayne A. Cornelius, and O. W. Jones, "Mexican Immigrants and the Utilization of Health Services," *Social Science and Medicine* 21: 93–102, 1985; and Leo R. Chavez, Estevan T. Flores, and Marta Lopez-Garza, "Undocumented Latin American Immigrants and U.S. Health Services: An Approach to a Political Economy of Utilization," *Medical Anthropology Quarterly* 6: 6–26, 1992. Ruben Rumbaut, Leo R. Chavez, Robert Moser, Sheila Pickwell, and Sam Wishik, "The Politics of Migrant Health Care: A Comparative Study of Mexican Immigrants and Indochinese Refugees in San Diego," *Research in the Sociology of Medicine* 7 (Greenwich, CT: JAI Press, 1988), pp. 143–202.

54 Leo R. Chavez, Wayne A. Cornelius, and O. W. Jones, "Utilization of Health Services by Mexican Women in San Diego," *Women and Health* 11: 3–20, 1986.

55 Paul Feldman and Rich Connell, "Wilson Acts to Enforce Parts of Prop. 187; 8 Lawsuits Filed," *Los Angeles Times* 10 November 1994: A1.

56 Ronald Brownstein, "Wilson Proposes U.S. Version of Prop. 187," *Los Angeles Times* 19 November 1994: A1.

57 Ronald Brownstein, "Wilson Proposes U.S. Version of Prop. 187," *Los Angeles Times* 19 November 1994: A1.

58 Frank del Olmo, "Open the Door to Mexican Workers," *Los Angeles Times* 31 January 1995: B9 (Orange County edition).

59 Marc Lacey, "New Task Force Targets Illegal Immigration," *Los Angeles Times* 16 March 1995: A3.

60 Alejandro Portes and Robert L. Bach, *Latin Journey: Cuban and Mexican Immigrants in the United States* (Berkeley: University of California Press, 1985).

61 Doris Meissner, "Contract Workers: Human Exploitation," *Los Angeles Times* 30 January 1995: B9 (Orange County edition).

62 Leo R. Chavez, "The Power of the Imagined Community: The Settlement of Undocumented Mexicans and Central Americans in the United States," *American Anthropologist* 96: 52–73, 1994.

63 Leo R. Chavez, "Settlers and Sojourners: The Case of Mexicans in the United States," *Human Organization* 47: 95–108, 1988.

64 Leo R. Chavez, Estevan T. Flores, and Marta Lopez-Garza, "Here Today, Gone Tomorrow? Undocumented Settlers and Immigration Reform," *Human Organization* 49: 193–205, 1990.

65 Benedict Anderson, *Imagined Communities* (London: Verso, 1983).

66 Etienne Balibar, "Is There a 'Neo-Racism'?" In *Race, Nation, Class: Ambiguous Identities,* Etienne Balibar and Immanuel Wallerstein, eds. (New York: Verso, 1991), 17–28.

67 I credit Javier Inda with the notion of (dis)order, as he discussed it in "The Anthropology of Transnationalism," 1994 mimeo.

Executive Order No. 9066

February 19, 1942
Authorizing the Secretary of War to Prescribe Military Areas

Whereas, The successful prosecution of the war requires every possible protection against espionage and against sabotage to national defense material, national defense premises and national defense utilities as defined in Section 4, Act of April 20, 1918, 40 Stat. 533 as amended by the Act of November 30, 1940, 54 Stat. 1220. and the Act of August 21, 1941. 55 Stat. 655 (U.S.C., Title 50, Sec. 104):

Now, therefore, by virtue of the authority vested in me as President of the United States, and Commander in Chief of the Army and Navy, 1 hereby authorized and direct the Secretary of War, and the Military Commanders whom he may from time to time designate, whenever he or any designated Commander deem such action necessary or desirable to prescribe military areas in such places and of such extent as he or the appropriate Military Commander may determine, from which any or all persons may be excluded, and with respect to which, the right of any person to enter, remain in, or leave shall be subject to whatever restriction the Secretary of War or the appropriate Military Commander may impose in his discretion. The Secretary of War is hereby authorized to provide for residents of any such area who are excluded therefrom. Such transportation, food, shelter, and other accommodations as may be necessary, in the judgment of the Secretary of War or the said Military Commander and until other arrangements are made, to accomplish the purpose of this order. The designation of military areas in any region or locality shall supersede designation of prohibited and restricted areas by the Attorney General under the Proclamation of December 7 and 8, 1941, and shall supersede the responsibility and authority of the Attorney General under the said Proclamation in respect of such prohibited and restricted areas.

Source: Franklin D. Roosevelt, The White House, February 19, 1942.

I hereby further authorize and direct the Secretary of War and the said Military Commanders to take such other steps as he or the appropriate Military Commander may deem advisable to enforce compliance with the restrictions applicable to each Military area herein above authorized to be designated including the use of Federal troops and other Federal Agencies, with authority to accept assistance of state and local agencies.

I hereby further authorize and direct all Executive Department, independent establishments and other Federal Agencies, to assist the Secretary of War or the said Military Commanders in carrying out this Executive Order, including the furnishing of medical aid, hospitalization, food, clothing, transportation, use of land, shelter, and other supplies, equipment, utilities, facilities and service.

This order shall not be construed as modifying or limiting in any way the authority granted under Executive Order 8972. dated December 12. 1941, nor shall it be construed as limiting or modifying the duty and responsibility of the Federal Bureau of Investigation, with response to the investigation of alleged acts of sabotage or duty and responsibility of the Attorney General and the Department of Justice under the Proclamation of December 7 and 8, 1941, prescribing regulations for the conduct and control of alien enemies, except as such duty and responsibility is superseded by the designation of military areas thereunder.

Korematsu v. United States

Decided December 18, 1944

Mr. *Justice Black* delivered the opinion of the Court.
Mr. *Justice Frankfurter,* concurring.
Mr. *Justice Roberts,* Mr. *Justice Murphy,* and Mr. *Justice Jackson,* dissenting.

Certiorari to the circuit court of appeals for the ninth circuit.

Certiorari, 321 U.S. 760, to review the affirmance of a judgment of conviction.

1. Civilian Exclusion Order No. 34 which, during a state of war with Japan and as a protection against espionage and sabotage, was promulgated by the Commanding General of the Western Defense Command under authority of Executive Order No. 9066 and the Act of March 21, 1942, and which directed the exclusion after May 9, 1942 from a described West Coast military area of all persons of Japanese ancestry, held constitutional as of the time it was made and when the petitioner—an American citizen of Japanese descent whose home was in the described area—violated it. P. 219.
2. The provisions of other orders requiring persons of Japanese ancestry to report to assembly centers and providing for the detention of such persons in assembly and relocation centers were separate, and their validity is not in issue in this proceeding. P. 222.
3. Even though evacuation and detention in the assembly center were inseparable, the order under which the petitioner was convicted was nevertheless valid. P. 223.

Solicitor General Fahy, with whom Assistant Attorney General Wechsler and Messrs. Edward J. Ennis, Ralph F. Fuchs, and John L. Burling were on the brief, for the United States.

Messrs. Saburo Kido and A. L. Wirin filed a brief on behalf of the Japanese American Citizens League; and Messrs. Edwin Borchard, Charles A. Horsky, George Rublee, Arthur DeHon Hill, Winthrop Wadleigh, Osmond K. Fraenkel, Harold Evans, William Draper Lewis, and Thomas Raeburn White on behalf of the American Civil Liberties Union, as amici curiae, in support of petitioner.

Messrs. Robert W. Kenney, Attorney General of California, George Neuner, Attorney General of Oregon, Smith Troy, Attorney General of Washington, and Fred E. Lewis, Acting Attorney General of Washington, filed a brief on behalf of the States of California, Oregon and Washington, as amici curiae, in support of the United States.

Mr. *Justice Black* delivered the opinion of the Court.

The petitioner, an American citizen of Japanese descent, was convicted in a federal district court for remaining in San Leandro, California, a "Military Area," contrary to Civilian Exclusion Order No. 34 of the Commanding General of the Western Command, U.S. Army, which directed that after May 9, 1942, all persons of Japanese ancestry should be excluded from that area. No question was raised as to petitioner's loyalty to the United States. The Circuit Court of Appeals affirmed,[1] and the importance of the constitutional question involved caused us to grant certiorari.

It should be noted, to begin with, that all legal restrictions which curtail the civil rights of a single racial group are immediately suspect. That is not to say that all such restrictions are unconstitutional. It is to say that courts must subject them to the most rigid scrutiny. Pressing public necessity may sometimes justify the existence of such restrictions; racial antagonism never can.

In the instant case prosecution of the petitioner was begun by information charging violation of an Act of Congress, of March 21, 1942, 56 Stat. 173, which provides that

". . . whoever shall enter, remain in, leave, or commit any act in any military area or military zone prescribed, under the authority of an Executive order of the President, by the Secretary of War, or by any military commander designated by the Secretary of War, contrary to the restrictions applicable to any such area or zone or contrary to the order of the Secretary of War or any such military commander, shall, if it appears that he knew or should have known of the existence and extent of the restrictions or order and that his act was in violation thereof, be guilty of a misdemeanor and upon conviction shall be liable to a fine of not to exceed $ 5,000 or to imprisonment for not more than one year, or both, for each offense."

Exclusion Order No. 34, which the petitioner knowingly and admittedly violated, was one of a number of military orders and proclamations, all of which were substantially based upon Executive Order No. 9066, 7 Fed. Reg. 1407. That order, issued after we were at war with Japan, declared that "the successful prosecution of the war requires every possible protection against espionage and against sabotage to national-defense material, national-defense premises, and national-defense utilities. . . ."

One of the series of orders and proclamations, a curfew order, which like the exclusion order here was promulgated pursuant to Executive Order 9066, subjected all persons of Japanese ancestry in prescribed West Coast military areas to remain in their residences from 8 P.M. to 6 A.M. As is the case with the exclusion order here, that prior curfew order was designed as a "protection against espionage and against sabotage." In Hirabayashi v. United States, 320 U.S. 81, we sustained a conviction obtained for violation of the curfew order. The Hirabayashi conviction and this one thus rest on the same 1942 Congressional Act and the same basic executive and military orders, all of which orders were aimed at the twin dangers of espionage and sabotage.

The 1942 Act was attacked in the Hirabayashi case as an unconstitutional delegation of power; it was contended that the curfew order and other orders on which it rested were beyond the war powers of the Congress, the military authorities and of the President, as Commander in Chief of the Army; and finally that to apply the curfew order against none but citizens of Japanese ancestry amounted to a constitutionally prohibited discrimination solely on account of race. To these questions, we gave the serious consideration which their importance justified. We upheld the curfew order as an exercise of the power of the government to take steps necessary to prevent espionage and sabotage in an area threatened by Japanese attack.

In the light of the principles we announced in the Hirabayashi case, we are unable to conclude that it was beyond the war power of Congress and the Executive to exclude those of Japanese ancestry from the West Coast war area at the time they did. True, exclusion from the area in which one's home is located is a far greater deprivation than constant confinement to the home from 8 P.M. to 6 A.M. Nothing short of apprehension by the proper military authorities of the gravest imminent danger to the public safety can constitutionally justify either. But exclusion from a threatened area, no less than curfew, has a definite and close relationship to the prevention of espionage and sabotage. The military authorities, charged with the primary responsibility of defending our shores, concluded that curfew provided inadequate protection and ordered exclusion. They did so, as pointed out in our Hirabayashi opinion, in accordance with Congressional authority to the military to say who should, and who should not, remain in the threatened areas.

In this case the petitioner challenges the assumptions upon which we rested our conclusions in the Hirabayashi case. He also urges that by May 1942, when Order No. 34 was promulgated, all danger of Japanese invasion of the West Coast had disappeared. After careful consideration of these contentions we are compelled to reject them.

Here, as in the Hirabayashi case, supra, at p. 99, ". . . we cannot reject as unfounded the judgment of the military authorities and of Congress that there were disloyal members of that population, whose number and strength could not be precisely and quickly ascertained. We cannot say that the war-making branches of the Government did not have ground for believing that in a critical hour such persons could not readily be isolated and separately dealt with, and constituted a menace to the national defense and safety, which demanded that prompt and adequate measures be taken to guard against it."

Like curfew, exclusion of those of Japanese origin was deemed necessary because of the presence of an unascertained number of disloyal members of the group, most of whom we have no doubt were loyal to this country. It was because we could not reject the finding of the military authorities that it was impossible to bring about an immediate segregation of the disloyal from the loyal that we sustained the validity of the curfew order as applying to the whole group. In the instant case, temporary exclusion of the entire group was rested by the military on the same ground. The judgment that exclusion of the whole group was for the same reason a military imperative answers the contention that the exclusion was in the nature of group punishment based on antagonism to those of Japanese origin. That there were members of the group who retained loyalties to Japan has been confirmed by investigations made subsequent to the exclusion. Approximately five thousand American citizens of Japanese ancestry refused to swear unqualified allegiance to the United States and to renounce allegiance to the Japanese Emperor, and several thousand evacuees requested repatriation to Japan.[2]

We uphold the exclusion order as of the time it was made and when the petitioner violated it. Cf. Chastleton Corporation v. Sinclair, 264 U.S. 543, 547; Block v. Hirsh, 256 U.S. 135, 154–5. In doing so, we are not unmindful of the hardships imposed by it upon a large group of American citizens. Cf. Ex parte Kawato, 317 U.S. 69, 73. But hardships are part of war, and war is an aggregation of hardships. All citizens alike, both in and out of uniform, feel the impact of war in greater or lesser measure. Citizenship has its responsibilities as well as its privileges, and in time of war the burden is always heavier. Compulsory exclusion of large groups of citizens from their homes, except under circumstances of direst emergency and peril, is inconsistent with our basic governmental institutions. But when under conditions of modern warfare our shores are threatened by hostile forces, the power to protect must be commensurate with the threatened danger.

It is argued that on May 30, 1942, the date the petitioner was charged with remaining in the prohibited area, there were conflicting orders outstanding, forbidding him both to leave the area and to remain there. Of course, a person cannot be convicted for doing the very thing which it is a crime to fail to do. But the outstanding orders here contained no such contradictory commands.

There was an order issued March 27, 1942, which prohibited petitioner and others of Japanese ancestry from leaving the area, but its effect was specifically limited in time "until and to the extent that a future proclamation or order should so permit or direct." 7 Fed. Reg. 2601. That "future order," the one for violation of which petitioner was convicted, was issued May 3, 1942, and it did "direct" exclusion from the area of all persons of Japanese ancestry, before 12 o'clock noon, May 9; furthermore it contained a warning that all such persons found in the prohibited area would be liable to punishment under the March 21, 1942 Act of Congress. Consequently, the only order in effect touching the petitioner's being in the area on May 30, 1942, the date specified in the information against him, was the May 3 order which prohibited his remaining there, and it was that same order, which he stipulated in his trial that he had violated, knowing of its existence. There is therefore no basis for the argument that on May 30, 1942, he was subject to punishment, under the March 27 and May 3 orders, whether he remained in or left the area.

It does appear, however, that on May 9, the effective date of the exclusion order, the military authorities had already determined that the evacuation should be effected by assembling together and placing under guard all those of Japanese ancestry, at central points, designated as "assembly centers," in order "to insure the orderly evacuation and resettlement of Japanese voluntarily migrating from Military Area No. 1, to restrict and regulate such migration." Public Proclamation No. 4, 7 Fed. Reg. 2601. And on May 19, 1942, eleven days before the time petitioner was charged with unlawfully remaining in the area, Civilian Restrictive Order No. 1, 8 Fed. Reg. 982, provided for detention of those of Japanese ancestry in assembly or relocation centers. It is now argued that the validity of the exclusion order cannot be considered apart from the orders requiring him, after departure from the area, to report and to remain in an assembly or relocation center. The contention is that we must treat these separate orders as one and inseparable; that, for this reason, if detention in the assembly or relocation center would have illegally deprived the petitioner of his liberty, the exclusion order and his conviction under it cannot stand.

We are thus being asked to pass at this time upon the whole subsequent detention program in both assembly and relocation centers, although the only issues framed at the trial related to petitioner's remaining in the prohibited area in violation of the exclusion order. Had petitioner here left the prohibited area and gone to an assembly center we cannot say either as a matter of fact or law that his presence in that center would have resulted in his detention in a relocation center. Some who did report to the assembly center were not sent to relocation centers, but were released upon condition that they remain outside the prohibited zone until the military orders were modified or lifted. This illustrates that they pose different problems and may be governed by different principles. The lawfulness of one does not necessarily determine the lawfulness of the others. This is made clear when we analyze the requirements of the separate provisions of the separate orders. These separate requirements were that those of Japanese ancestry (1) depart from the area; (2) report to and temporarily remain in an assembly center; (3) go under military control to a relocation center there to remain for an indeterminate period until released conditionally or unconditionally by the military authorities. Each of these requirements, it will be noted, imposed distinct duties in connection with the separate steps in a complete evacuation program. Had Congress directly incorporated into one Act the language of these separate orders, and provided sanctions for their violations, disobedience of any one would have constituted a separate offense. Cf.

Blockburger v. United States, 284 U.S. 299, 304. There is no reason why violations of these orders, insofar as they were promulgated pursuant to Congressional enactment, should not be treated as separate offenses.

The Endo case, post, p. 283, graphically illustrates the difference between the validity of an order to exclude and the validity of a detention order after exclusion has been effected.

Since the petitioner has not been convicted of failing to report or to remain in an assembly or relocation center, we cannot in this case determine the validity of those separate provisions of the order. It is sufficient here for us to pass upon the order which petitioner violated. To do more would be to go beyond the issues raised, and to decide momentous questions not contained within the framework of the pleadings or the evidence in this case. It will be time enough to decide the serious constitutional issues which petitioner seeks to raise when an assembly or relocation order is applied or is certain to be applied to him, and we have its terms before us.

Some of the members of the Court are of the view that evacuation and detention in an Assembly Center were inseparable. After May 3, 1942, the date of Exclusion Order No. 34, Korematsu was under compulsion to leave the area not as he would choose but via an Assembly Center. The Assembly Center was conceived as a part of the machinery for group evacuation. The power to exclude includes the power to do it by force if necessary. And any forcible measure must necessarily entail some degree of detention or restraint whatever method of removal is selected. But whichever view is taken, it results in holding that the order under which petitioner was convicted was valid.

It is said that we are dealing here with the case of imprisonment of a citizen in a concentration camp solely because of his ancestry, without evidence or inquiry concerning his loyalty and good disposition towards the United States. Our task would be simple, our duty clear, were this a case involving the imprisonment of a loyal citizen in a concentration camp because of racial prejudice. Regardless of the true nature of the assembly and relocation centers—and we deem it unjustifiable to call them concentration camps with all the ugly connotations that term implies—we are dealing specifically with nothing but an exclusion order. To cast this case into outlines of racial prejudice, without reference to the real military dangers which were presented, merely confuses the issue. Korematsu was not excluded from the Military Area because of hostility to him or his race. He was excluded because we are at war with the Japanese Empire, because the properly constituted military authorities feared an invasion of our West Coast and felt constrained to take proper security measures, because they decided that the military urgency of the situation demanded that all citizens of Japanese ancestry be segregated from the West Coast temporarily, and finally, because Congress, reposing its confidence in this time of war in our military leaders—as inevitably it must—determined that they should have the power to do just this. There was evidence of disloyalty on the part of some, the military authorities considered that the need for action was great, and time was short. We cannot—by availing ourselves of the calm perspective of hindsight—now say that at that time these actions were unjustified.

Affirmed.

Notes

1 140 F.2d 289

2 Hearings before the Subcommittee on the National War Agencies Appropriation Bill for 1945, Part II, 608–726; Final Report, Japanese Evacuation from the West Coast, 1942, 309–327; Hearings before the Committee on Immigration and Naturalization, House of Representatives, 78th Cong., 2d Sess., on H. R. 2701 and other bills to expatriate certain nationals of the United States, pp. 37–42, 49–58.

Minidoka Internment National Monument

Minidoka Internment National Monument was established in 2001 as the 385th unit of the National Park System to commemorate the hardships and sacrifices of Japanese Americans interned there during World War II. Also known as the 'Hunt Camp', the Minidoka Relocation Center was a 33,000-acre site with over 600 buildings and a total population of about 13,000 internees held from Washington, Oregon, and Alaska. It was in operation from August 1942 until October 1945.

The Monument is located between the towns of Twin Falls and Jerome, Idaho in south central Idaho. There are no facilities or services at the site and the boundaries are not well marked. Many buildings and features that were part of the center are located on private property surrounding the Monument. Please do not enter any private property. We are working to establish relationships within the community to preserve the significant remaining components of the Relocation Center and to provide visitor services.

Executive Order 9066

In the 1800's, many emigrants from Japan crossed the Pacific Ocean to seek economic opportunity in America. While some originally intended to return to their birthplace, many eventually established families, farms, businesses, and communities. America became their new home, yet the pioneers (Issei) and their American-born children (Nisei) encountered various forms of racial prejudice in the United States. Congress passed laws prohibiting resident aliens from owning land or obtaining citizenship. Quotas were set restricting the flow of new arrivals. With the rise of militarism in Japan in the early 1900's, newspapers often fanned the flames of prejudice.

Japan's attack on Pearl Harbor on December 7, 1941 intensified hostility towards Japanese Americans. Some newspaper columnists and politicians treated all people of Japanese ancestry as potential spies and saboteurs. As wartime hysteria mounted, President Franklin D. Roosevelt signed Executive Order 9066 on February 19 1942. This authorized the U.S. military to remove "any or all persons" from the West Coast, but was targeted specifically to Japanese Americans and Japanese resident aliens.

Japanese American Internment During World War II

Following the signing of Executive Order 9066, over 120,000 persons of Japanese ancestry (Nikkei) living on the West Coast were forced to leave their homes, jobs, and businesses behind and report to designated military holding areas. This constituted the single largest forced relocation in U.S. history. Temporary assembly centers were located at fairgrounds, racetracks, and other make-shift facilities. Some 7,100 future Minidoka residents were first incarcerated at the Puyallup assembly center known as 'Camp Harmony.' Despite its innocuous name, it was no summer camp. Barbed wire fences surrounded the camp, armed guards patrolled the grounds, and movement between different areas of the camp was strictly controlled. It would be four to five months before the ten relocation centers established by the Wartime Relocation Authority were activated.

Living Conditions at Minidoka

The first internees at Minidoka arrived to find a camp still under construction. There was no hot running water and the sewage system had not been constructed. The initial reaction to the stark landscape by many was one of discouragement. Upon arriving, one internee wrote:

> "When we first arrived here we almost cried, and thought that this is the land God had forgotten. The vast expanse of nothing but sagebrush and dust, a landscape so alien to our eyes, and a desolate, woebegone feeling of being so far removed from home and fireside bogged us down mentally, as well as physically."

The camp consisted of administration and warehouse buildings, 36 residential blocks, schools, fire stations, an assortment of shops and stores, and a cemetery. Internees built baseball diamonds and small parks with picnic areas. Their baseball team was virtually unbeatable. Taiko drumming and other musical groups were formed, and a newspaper was published, the *Minidoka Irrigator.*

Each residential block included twelve barracks-style buildings, each divided into six small one-room apartments, a communal dining hall, a laundry facility with communal showers and toilets, and a recreation hall. Provisions within the barracks consisted of Army issue cots and a pot-bellied stove. Light was provided by a single hanging bulb. Scraps of lumber were utilized to make furniture. Coal for the stoves and water had to be hand carried. When coal supplies ran low, sagebrush was gathered and burned.

The hastily built barracks buildings were little more than wooden frames covered with tarpaper. They had no insulation. During the winter of 1942 temperatures plunged to −21 degrees Fahrenheit. Over 100 tons of coal a day was needed for heating the buildings in the camp. Spring, with its ankle deep mud and blinding dust storms, was followed by scorching heat and temperatures soaring to 104 degrees Fahrenheit. An accidental drowning in the North Side Canal prompted internees to build a swimming hole to cope with the oppressive heat.

Many living in the rural communities outside the camp thought that the internees were being "coddled," a perception that still persists today. For those inside the camp confined within barbed wire fence, with watchtowers and armed guards, the perception was considerably different.

Despite the harsh conditions at Minidoka, internees were resourceful. To create beauty in an otherwise dismal landscape, paths were lined with decorative stones and both traditional Japanese and vegetable and flower gardens were planted. Some of these impressions are still visible today, yet most traces of daily life at Minidoka are now gone.

Wartime Efforts

The relocation centers were subject to the same wartime rationing as the rest of the country. Materials considered to be vital to the war effort were recycled. The camp at Minidoka was almost a self-sustaining community complete with vegetable gardens and hog and chicken farms. Japanese Americans interned at Minidoka were also an indispensable source of labor for southern Idaho's agricultural-based economy.

> "The Hunt residents were credited with possibly saving hundreds of thousands of dollars in crop losses in the local sugar beet and potato crops as well as in canneries, lumber mills, etc. in the region during the three years the center existed."
>
> *North Side News 8/5/82*

Internees cleared and cultivated 950 acres of inhospitable land and constructed the ditches and canals needed to irrigate them. After the camp closed in October 1945, these lands were divided into smaller farms and auctioned to the highest bidders or given to WWII veterans along with two buildings. Their names were drawn by lottery. Nisei were excluded from both the lottery and sale of the farms. Many of the buildings from the camp were also disbursed to government agencies and nonprofit organizations. Today, most of the former Relocation Center remains privately owned farmland.

A Question of Loyalty

Segregation in the camps was achieved by employing what came to be known as the "loyalty questionnaire." The questionnaires were originally designed for determining suitability for military service. Two controversial questions were included. Those who answered "no" to both questions were labeled the "No-No's" and shipped to Tule Lake, California, the camp for 'dissenters.' Many at Tule Lake who answered "yes" to both questions were shipped to Minidoka, a camp for 'loyal' internees.

Could This Happen Again?

It has been described as one of the worst violations of constitutional rights in American history and yet few Americans raised their voices in protest of the removal order. More than two-thirds of the internees were American citizens by birth. The system of checks and balances that was supposed to protect their rights and freedoms failed.

In 1988, the Civil Liberties Act acknowledged the fundamental injustice of the evacuation, relocation, and internment of citizens and permanent resident aliens of Japanese ancestry during World War II. A formal apology by the U.S. Government was made, as well as restitution to those individuals who were interned. And most importantly, the Act provides for a public education fund to finance efforts to inform the public about the internment so as to prevent the recurrence of any similar event.

The 442nd Regimental Combat Unit

"You fought not only the enemy but you fought prejudice—and you have won."

President Truman addressing members of the 442nd at the White House in 1946

Despite their internment, most Japanese Americans remained intensely loyal to the United States, and many demonstrated their loyalty by volunteering for military service. They were segregated into all Japanese American combat and intelligence units commanded by non-Japanese Americans. Of the ten relocation centers, Minidoka had the highest number of volunteers, about 1,000 internees—nearly ten percent of the camp's total population during its peak. The 442nd combat fought in France and Italy alongside the Battalion from Hawaii (also composed of Japanese Americans) and was the most decorated unit of its size in American military history. During WWII, 73 soldiers from Minidoka died while fighting for their country and two received the Congressional Medal of Honor.

U.S. Civil Liberties Act of 1988

August 10, 1988

"The Congress recognizes that, as described in the Commission on Wartime Relocation and Internment of Civilians, a grave injustice was done to both citizens and permanent residents of Japanese ancestry by the evacuation, relocation, and internment of civilians during World War II.

As the Commission documents, these actions were carried out without adequate security reasons and without any acts of espionage or sabotage documented by the Commission, and were motivated largely by racial prejudice, wartime hysteria, and a failure of political leadership.

The excluded individuals of Japanese ancestry suffered enormous damages, both material and intangible, and there were incalculable losses in education and job training, all of which resulted in significant human suffering for which appropriate compensation has not been made.

For these fundamental violations of the basic civil liberties and constitutional rights of these individuals of Japanese ancestry, the Congress apologizes on behalf of the Nation."

Based on the findings of the Commission on Wartime Relocation and Internment of Civilians (CWRIC), the purposes of the Civil Liberties Act of 1988 with respect to persons of Japanese ancestry included the following:

1. To acknowledge the fundamental injustice of the evacuation, relocation and internment of citizens and permanent resident aliens of Japanese ancestry during World War II;
2. To apologize on behalf of the people of the United States for the evacuation, internment, and relocations of such citizens and permanent residing aliens;

3. To provide for a public education fund to finance efforts to inform the public about the internment so as to prevent the recurrence of any similar event;
4. To make restitution to those individuals of Japanese ancestry who were interned;
5. To make more credible and sincere any declaration of concern by the United States over violations of human rights committed by other nations.

Enacted by the United States Congress, August 10, 1988

"The Congress recognizes that, as described in the Commission on Wartime Relocation and Internment of Civilians, a grave injustice was done to both citizens and permanent residents of Japanese ancestry by the evacuation, relocation, and internment of civilians during World War II.

As the Commission documents, these actions were carried out without adequate security reasons and without any acts of espionage or sabotage documented by the Commission, and were motivated largely by racial prejudice, wartime hysteria, and a failure of political leadership.

The excluded individuals of Japanese ancestry suffered enormous damages, both material and intangible, and there were incalculable losses in education and job training, all of which resulted in significant human suffering for which appropriate compensation has not been made.

For these fundamental violations of the basic civil liberties and constitutional rights of these individuals of Japanese ancestry, the Congress apologizes on behalf of the Nation."

Based on the findings of the Commission on Wartime Relocation and Internment of Civilians (CWRIC), the purposes of the Civil Liberties Act of 1988 with respect to persons of Japanese ancestry included the following:

1. To acknowledge the fundamental injustice of the evacuation, relocation and internment of citizens and permanent resident aliens of Japanese ancestry during World War II;
2. To apologize on behalf of the people of the United States for the evacuation, internment, and relocations of such citizens and permanent residing aliens;
3. To provide for a public education fund to finance efforts to inform the public about the internment so as to prevent the recurrence of any similar event;
4. To make restitution to those individuals of Japanese ancestry who were interned;
5. To make more credible and sincere any declaration of concern by the United States over violations of human rights committed by other nations.

Legal and Civil Rights Issues in 2020: Civil Rights Policy

William R. Tamayo

An examination or projection as to the legal and civil rights issues that will likely exist as a result of the increase in the Asian Pacific American population requires, at the outset, a premise for the assertion that the social category will be relevant in the year 2020.

Furthermore, this analysis rests on an assumption that our collective goal as defenders of civil rights is to ensure that the experiment of democracy known as the United States can live up to the ideals it professes to uphold: equality, full opportunity, inclusion, democratic rights, and respect for civil rights.

This analysis as presented rests on the following premises and assumptions about life in 2020:

1. Racism against nonwhites will still be an integral component of the United States economy and cultural life both institutionally and socially;
2. While legal forms of blatant racism will likely remain unlawful, a national consensus for a coherent or uniform remedy for the social impact of centuries of systemic racism will still be lacking;
3. "Asian Pacific American," as a category created by and asserted in response to racism, will still be relevant both as a political vehicle and as a category to measure the impact of inequality; and
4. Immigration from Asia will likely be from the "developing" Asian countries, e.g., Philippines, India, China, Korea, many of which still are undergoing massive upheavals around issues of civil liberties, democracy, labor rights, and freedom of movement.

Initial demographic projections assert that the Asian Pacific American population in the year 2020 will be 18–20 million, representing a near tripling of the 1990 population. Immigration from Asia will be a major source of this growth. Thus, the majority of the community will likely be foreign born, and a significant portion non-citizens. This "foreign-born" characteristic combined with a relatively small voting bloc will still leave Asian Pacific Americans in a weak political position to make civil rights gains or to implement civil rights agendas on a national scale, but may be able to impact or sway local elections and activities.

The State of the World in 2020

Without a doubt, a projection of legal and civil rights issues must consider the state of the world in 2020—its economic health, its environmental health, whether peace or wars dominate the political landscape, and whether massive migration of labor (especially from Asia) to countries of real and perceived opportunities will continue.[1] Should political and economic instability and upheavals continue in the sending countries and other Asian nations, it can be expected that immigration—legally and illegally—from Asia will continue. As of January 1992, over 1.5 million persons from Asian countries (representing 53.2 percent of the worldwide list) were on visa waiting lists, with the Philippines (472,714) leading all countries worldwide.[2] (The top seven sending countries are all Asian nations except for Mexico, which ranks second in the numbers of its citizens registered for visas.)[3] This number does not even begin to include the numbers of relatives who will migrate as "immediate relatives"[4] of United States residents, a number which could, at least for some countries, represent twice as much as those on the preference waiting list.[5]

Some countries worth close observation for students of demography and migration include Burma, Thailand, Pakistan and Indonesia. As more and more movements for democracy demand changes but are met with resistance (in the form of violence and repression) from existing governments, and as economies in Asia fail to meet the basic needs of the vast majority of the population, there will be steady streams of migration from these countries.

At the same time, attempts to develop East Asia into a major "economic union," similar to the European Economic Community, could and are alleged to lead to greater prosperity throughout the region. Consequently, this could conceivably reduce the need for workers to migrate from Asia to the United States, and affect immigration projections.[6]

On the other hand, the state of the U.S. economy and its ability to "absorb" newer immigrants will pose issues. That is, other "Western" or capitalist countries could be the recipient of the new migrations of Asian labor. As evidenced by migrations in the late 1980s and early 1990s, Asian workers are also migrating to England, Western Europe, Middle East, Australia, and Canada.

Not surprisingly, however, this massive migration of Asians and others has precipitated a resurgence and growth of anti-immigrant and racist movements represented in spontaneous outbursts and uprisings of white youths to organized and well-financed electoral movements, e.g., "Le Pen" in France and anti-immigrant movements in Germany in 1992. Reminiscent of anti-immigrant movements that dotted the history of the United States[7]–and that were forerunners to fascist and neo-fascist movements in Wes tern Europe in the 20th century, these movements have, unfortunately, gained wider acceptance among white Americans and Europeans. Institutional support through government and private parties has similarly created a more fearful climate and pressed civil rights advocates.

Nevertheless, it is likely that given the projections for the Asian Pacific American population in 2020, any analysis on the civil and legal rights issue of that year will be impacted by perceptions both in fact and fiction, that there will be even more persons of Asian descent migrating to the United States. The fear of more "yellow and brown hordes" being absorbed into an unstable and declining economy will have great social implications.

The State of the U.S. Economy and Social Relations

The national state of social relations, particularly around such a fundamental issue as racism, will greatly determine the civil rights agenda of Asian Pacific Americans. The social issues, however, are inextricably intertwined with the health of the U.S. economy and with the willingness of leaders to put forth and to finance a progressive social rights agenda. Unfortunately, the experiences of 1992 and the 12 previous years when national leadership "planned" social policy based on "racial polarization" rather than "racial inclusiveness and unity" do not give ground for optimism. This catering to a "white, native-born consensus" based on some notion of preserving a perceived birthright has been at the cornerstone of social policies negatively affecting civil rights, immigration policy, and labor policy. The disturbing rise of explicitly racist and proviolence organizations, the rise of similarly inclined politicians (and the frightening followers), and the failure of national leadership to quell this growth lays fundamental problems for all racial minorities including Asian Pacific Americans. Aside from catering to traditions of racism, these proponents have also taken on the bashing of immigrants (read: nonwhite immigrants) as part of their crusade. Proposed measures from militarizing the U.S.-Mexico border, to increased immigration raids in Asian and Latino communities, to outright denials of labor protections to immigrants have been part of these proponents' arsenal.

If the United States economy is relatively healthy in 2020, then racial relations should be improved.[8] However, increased economic instability combined with racist and nativist appeals by national figures will lead to continued divisiveness and set the stage for increasing legal and civil rights issues for Asian Pacific Americans and other nonwhite communities.

Simultaneously, the relationships of our community to its allies in the broader civil rights community will determine the agenda. Given the near tripling of our population by 2020, the concerns of the community will have to be part of a broader national civil rights agenda. *That agenda will have to take on an internationalist perspective based on full civil and democratic rights for all regardless of race, national origin, and immigration status if it is to adequately address the civil rights concerns of largely immigrant, nonwhite communities.* In addition, it will be incumbent on civil rights leadership to build viable and operational multiracial and multicultural coalitions with matching agendas.

Inherent to forging the relations of the civil rights coalition is a grappling with a lingering issue of whether Asian Pacific Americans will "be used" by Whites against other minority groups, and whether other minority groups, i.e., Blacks and Latinos, will view Asian Pacific Americans (or some ethnic groups) as indistinguishable from a political and economic view from Whites (who will presumably still direct most major corporations and be the majority of elected officials in 2020). Professor Mari Matsuda warned that Asian Pacific Americans had better understand the fundamental characteristics that tie people of color within the social dynamics of U.S. society lest they be used as buffers between Whites and other communities of color.[9] Inherent in that relation, however, is an incumbent duty for Asian Pacific Americans to stand with their brothers and sisters of color in addressing all issues of racism together in both time and place.

Legal Issues for Asian Pacific Americans

Asian Pacific Americans as workers, women, gays and lesbians, consumers, immigrants, non-citizens, and general members of U.S. society will be loaded with a myriad of legal problems. Following, however, are particular legal issues which will likely emanate from the discrimination based on race, national origin, class, sex, and immigration status—categories of discrimination that are impacted by the existence of an Asian Pacific American category.

Labor Rights

Overwhelmingly, Asian Pacific Americans are working class, non-professional people (despite perceptions by the public and representations by the media). Recent immigrants and even those with residency over ten years overwhelmingly dominate the light manufacturing and service sectors and lower-paying positions in the medical and clerical industries.[10] The vast majority, similar to most Americans, are not represented by unions, and are not aware of their rights as workers. Thus, abuse of these workers from harassment, non-payment of overtime salaries, undercutting wages, and harsh working conditions in violation of labor laws, will likely continue. The attempts of certain industries to curb labor-law protections in the 1980s (often with Administration backing) serve as a harbinger of the types of labor battles that Asian workers will face in 2020. As international and domestic competition among industries heightens, it can be expected that various "cost-saving" measures will be utilized. The prospects for organized labor to rebound from its losses in the 1980s and 1990s and to be more inclusive of Asian Pacific American workers and their needs will also impact the landscape within which labor rights will be asserted.

Special attention will need to be given to the fact that the majority of Asian immigrants will be *women*. Aside from issues arising in other arenas, e.g., domestic violence, the fact that many of the immigrant workers will be women will also give rise to increasing attention to issues of sexual harassment, sex discrimination in employment, and employment of women in traditionally low-paid jobs, e.g., garment and service. The necessary components to setting the agenda for combatting this discrimination will, in part, have to be the empowerment of women of color within national women's organizations and unions and the effort of those organizations to be as aggressively inclusive as the times demand.

Furthermore, with its poverty rate being twice that of Whites, and with 50 percent of Southeast Asians living in poverty,[11] the community will have to grapple with the consequences of having a generation or two of our community virtually locked out of mainstream life. Poor educational performances, limited employment opportunities, and an increasing trend for youth to turn toward anti-social behavior as an economic necessity, will likely mark the life of refugees and their children.

The Glass Ceiling and Approaches to Affirmative Action

While the issue of the "glass ceiling," i.e., lack of promotion of racial minorities to management positions, and related issues of affirmative action have been on the agenda for the last few years, there is a strong likelihood that they will remain as issues three decades from now. The nearly three decades since the passage of Title VII of the Civil Rights Act of 1964 have clearly shown a glaring disparity between Congress' professed intent to eradicate discrimination and the harsh and stark reality created by decades of inequality. For while some minorities have been promoted to positions in management, management in corporations does not even begin to mirror the demographic profile of the working community. Hopefully, the Civil Rights Act of 1991 will have created a more favorable legal climate within which programs for aggressive affirmative action will find their way to general acceptance. However, if there is a continued polarization, and in view of the fact that the existing Supreme Court has conservative members who will likely be serving on the court for two or three more decades, the prospects for favorable anti-discrimination legal precedents appears dim. Thus, the Asian Pacific American legal and civil rights community will need to develop more creative approaches—both legally and legislatively.

On another front, Asian Pacific Americans will have to articulate a clearer approach to affirmative action and will have to answer some hard questions regarding the collective applicability of affirmative action to a community which has distinct ethnic communities with varied histories in the United States. Some of the questions include: Will recent immigrants be able to claim that they inherit the impact of decades of discrimination against other Asian groups and thus are entitled to affirmative action remedies? When there is underrepresentation of some Asian Pacific Americans, e.g., Filipino Americans, in certain jobs or college admission slots, but not of other groups, e.g., Japanese Americans, is this a cause for complaint? Will the relatively more affluent position of Asian Americans relative to other minority groups, i.e., Blacks and Latinos, render the claims for affirmative action less meaningful, particularly since the bulk of Asians migrated in more recent years when laws against discrimination have already been passed?

Immigrant Rights

Given the overwhelming immigrant character of our community and the expected increase past the year 2020, expanding and protecting the rights of immigrants—documented and undocumented—to be free from discriminatory treatment will fill the civil rights agenda. The onslaught upon the rights of immigrants will likely come in these forms, as our history shows:

- attempts to curb Asian and other immigration through legislation aimed at decreasing family unity;[12]
- further restrictions on the due process rights of immigrants in court and administrative proceedings so as to expedite deportation;
- legal and quasi-legal restrictions on the rights of immigrants (both documented and undocumented) to public benefits and social services (assuming both will still exist in 2020);
- increased use of force in restricting immigration and enforcing immigration laws;
- the building of more immigration detention centers in order to incarcerate immigrants and deprive them of access to legal representation and social services;
- the growth of xenophobic movements expressed through violence, legislation, media, etc.;
- curbs on the numbers of refugees admitted from war-torn, politically unstable, or economically devastated countries.

Defenders of immigrants rights in our community will be forced to strengthen with even greater fervor the internationalist, humanitarian, and pro-civil rights moorings upon which to analyze and critique the above expressions of anti-immigrant sentiments.[13] Furthermore, the issues will require an astute and thorough understanding of the political economy of the sending nations that prompts this massive migration. The political instability of the sending nations will have to be addressed as we attempt to seek refugee protections or "safe haven" status for those fleeing persecution from those countries.

Inherent to this responsibility will be the task of working more closely with other immigrant communities that will similarly be impacted by U.S. foreign policy considerations, political upheaval in sending countries, and the response of the U.S. government. The commonalities for seeking a more unified agenda to address these civil rights concerns will be more vivid.

One major issue that appears likely for addressing will be the increasing demands of certain U.S. industries for already-trained skilled workers from abroad rather than investing in the existing workforce through job training and better education. While some in our community will view this avenue for migration as a positive opening to increase immigration, it raises substantial public policy questions, and asks the Asian Pacific American community where it stands on the issue of protecting and improving the domestic workforce through corporate and governmental investment. Asian Pacific American leaders will have to demand, as will other communities, especially those communities of color hardest hit by the callous indifference to improving the education and job skills of U.S. workers, that government and business look first to retraining the domestic labor force before seeking skilled labor from abroad. Simultaneously, however, knowing well that much of that skilled immigrant labor will enter into the social dynamics of U.S. racism and xenophobia, and employment discrimination or abuse, we will have to defend their rights as immigrants and workers.

Language Rights

Short of English becoming the universal language of the world (God forbid!), our community will be filled with "language minorities," i.e., non- or limited-English-speaking communities. The issue becomes more complex since our community shares no common language, but instead is a polyglot of languages and dialects, each with a distinct historical development. Nevertheless, lack of access to services, lack of access to the ballot, and discrimination in employment because of being a language minority will likely be issues in 2020. The successful effort to have the bilingual voting materials provisions of the Voting Rights Act reauthorized in 1992 (to be valid until 2007) will hopefully create more favorable conditions for their maintenance and expansion in 2020.

"English-Only" rules in the workplace,[14] or terminations from or denials of employment based on accent discrimination will likely continue in view of the increasing and constant immigration from Asian countries. It could be expected that there will be legislative, referendum, or initiative measures that will be introduced to make English the "official language" of the United States or of various states in order to present some alleged "uniformity" in communication which will supposedly improve relations. Asian Pacific American civil rights advocates will have to respond to these thinly guised racist and exclusionary attempts to further disempower and disenfranchise language minority communities. Again, it will be incumbent for Asian Pacific Americans to be active players in insuring that the broader civil rights community places the defense of language minorities on its agenda of action.

Hate Violence

Disturbingly and unfortunately, hate violence will likely be an issue in 2020 unless there is a major turnaround in the approach to social problems. The increasing polarization of the country around race, compounded by the fierce international competition in business and by decreasing economic and employment opportunities, have laid the seeds for increasing hate crimes and violence. Asian Pacific American advocates will continue to press states to enact laws allowing the prosecution of acts of violence as "hate crimes" (which enhance the sentences), and to press local prosecutors and state attorneys general to bring cases against the perpetrators.

On a national scale, these advocates will have to pierce and thoroughly discredit the "racialized patriotism" which serves as the cornerstone or rationale for a perceived duty to bash persons of Asian descent whether they be foreign-born or eighth-generation Americans. This daunting task will also require demands for quick and responsive action from federal officials and from United States and Asian corporate officials to denounce acts of anti-Asian violence.

Voting Rights

Asian Pacific Americans on a national scale actively participated in the redistricting process for the first time in 1991–92. While not all proposed plans were adopted, Asian Pacific Americans served notice on legislatures and city councils that we were stepping forward to defend our rights under the Voting Rights Act, and placed into the public record the historical discrimination suffered by Asian Pacific Americans in voting. While Asians in 1992 were 10 percent of the California population, there had been no Asians in the state legislature for 11 years. Asians were 3 percent of the national population, but less than 1 percent of the House of Representatives. In 2020, with an expected Asian Pacific American national population of 5–6 percent, and a California population of 15–20 percent, ensuring adequate representation at all electoral levels will be a major civil rights concern. Challenges to at-large election schemes which have historically served to exclude minorities from city councils, boards of supervisors, and school boards, will be needed.

Is There Power in Numbers?

Although Asians will number 20 million in 2020, we will likely still represent only 5–6 percent of the national population. In some states, e.g., California, we could likely be 15–20 percent of the population. Adding to this factor are projections that there will be no racial group that constitutes a majority. Perhaps Washington, D.C., will finally give some favorable attention to this population. However, articulating a civil rights agenda for Asian Pacific Americans will necessitate a conscious summation of the collective experiences garnered as a distinctly created racial group. Our community of

2020 will have a qualitatively different proportionate ethnic make-up than that in 1992 as the waves of immigrants from various Asian nations make their way to these shores. Our collective American experience in the number of years may be limited, but factors such as racial violence and anti-immigrant hostilities will intensify that experience. Civil rights advocates will have to harness the lessons of the past, and present the commonalities that mandate working under a common civil rights agenda.

Like other communities of color, and like the rest of the general U.S. population, our community hopes that 2020 will not be a year when the issues of racial polarization, xenophobia, and discrimination dominate the social relations of our country. The ideal that we call "United States democracy" has yet to be fully realized for the vast majority, but especially for those communities legally and socially marginalized because of their immigration status, race or national origin. Unfortunately, the years of professed belief from the federal government and from the national social agenda of the late 1960s in "full equality" and "full remedies" to address centuries of societal discrimination are still, when placed against the backdrop of United States history, an aberration and an exception to the rule. The escalation of racism throughout the 1980s and 1990s serves as a painful reminder that our work to build a nation committed to full rights and opportunity remains.

At the same time, years of common experience have provided valuable insights and produced new coalitions in the civil rights arena. It will be incumbent upon advocates for civil rights to extrapolate the lessons from history in order to articulate a more relevant and more effective agenda.

Notes

1 "Figures are far from precise—partly because of poor monitoring, partly because of illegal immigration—but 4 million to 5 million workers from South and east Asia probably work abroad." "Asia Supplies the World with Workers," *The Economist,* reprinted in *San Francisco Chronicle* (September 21, 1988).

2 U.S. Department of State, *Visa Bulletin* 7:9A (1992).

3 *Ibid.* As of January 1992, following the Philippines, the next six countries have the following registered: Mexico (466,684), India (254,049), China, mainland-born (181,143), China, Taiwan-born (122,284), Korea (118,949), and Vietnam (109,276).

4 "Immediate relatives" are defined as parents, spouses, and unmarried minor children under 21, and are exempt from the preference waiting lists.

5 For example, approximately 40,000 Filipinos (twice the number allowed under the preference system) entered as immediate relatives of U.S. citizens annually for the past three years.

6 Workers from the Philippines, Korea, Pakistan, India, Bangladesh, and Thailand already migrate all over the world. In 1985 approximately 460,000 Fil-

ipinos, 200,000 Koreans, 230,000 Pakistanis, 160,000 Indians, 80,000 Bangladeshis, and 70,000 Thais worked abroad. The United States is but one of dozens of countries to which they migrate for employment. See "Asia Supplies the World with Workers."

7 For a review of anti-Asian immigration laws and policies, see William R. Tamayo, "Asian Americans and Present U.S. Immigration Policies: A Legacy of Asian Exclusion," in *Asian Americans and the Supreme Court,* edited by Hyung-Chan Kim (Westport, Connecticut: Greenwood Press, 1992), 1105–1130.

8 It's no accident that the Civil Rights Act of 1964, the Voting Rights Act of 1965, and the Immigration Act of 1965 were enacted during a period when the U.S. economy was generally healthy, and the unemployment rate was relatively low. Many believe that the Immigration Act of 1965 was designed to increase immigration from Asian and Latin American countries. However, its proponents perceived it as a measure to increase European immigration, and assumed that Asian immigration under the act would be minimal. See Tamayo, "Asian Americans and Present U.S. Immigration Policies."

9 Mari Matusda, "We Will Not Be Used," *Asian Law Caucus Reporter* (Spring 1990).

10 The impact of the proposed North American Free Trade Agreement (Canada, United States, and Mexico) and other measures on the export of light manufacturing jobs, e.g., electronics and garment, will also have to be taken into consideration.

11 W. O'Hare and J. Felt, "Asian Americans: Fastest Growing Minority Group," Population Reference Bureau, February 1991.

12 Section 141 of the Immigration Act of 1990 provides for the establishment of a nine-member Commission on Legal Immigration Reform to review and evaluate the impact of the 1990 Act. Its first report is due on September 30, 1994, and its final annual report, including findings and recommendations with respect to legal immigration, is due September 30, 1997. Particular issues that the Commission will address include:

a. Family reunification-based immigration;
b. The impact of immigration and the implementation of the employment-based and diversity programs on labor needs, employment, and other economic and domestic conditions in the United States;
c. The social, demographic, and natural resources impact of immigration;
d. The impact of immigration on the foreign policy and national security interests of the United States;
e. The impact of per-country immigration levels on family-sponsored immigration;
f. The impact of the numerical limitation on the adjustment of status of aliens granted asylum;

g. The impact of the numerical limitations on the admission of nonimmigrants under Section 214 (g) of the Immigration and Nationality Act (H categories);
h. The impact of the diversity program including the characteristics of the individuals admitted and how such characteristics compare to the characteristics of family-sponsored immigrants and employment-based immigrants.

The nine members appointed are:

Lawrence Fuchs, Ph.D., former Executive Director of the Select Commission on Immigration & Refugee Policy (which eventually led to the passage of IRCA 1986); Professor, Brandeis University

Cardinal Bernard Law, Boston, Massachusetts

Harold Ezell, former INS Western Regional Commissioner (1981–89), former executive for Der Wienerschnitzel

Nelson Merced, member, Massachusetts legislature

Richard Estrada, the Federation for American Immigration Reform (FAIR)

Robert Hill, lawyer, Graham & James

Bruce Morrison, former member of Congress from Connecticut, former chair of House Subcommittee on Immigration, Refugees and International Law, co-author of 1990 Act

Warren Leiden, Executive Director, American Immigration Lawyers Association

Legislation is pending in the 1992 Congress to expand the Commission to 13 members (S. 3090). Thus far, no Asian Pacific Americans have been appointed.

13 For an elaboration of various immigrant rights concerns for the Asian American community, see William R. Tamayo, "Broadening the Asian Interests in United States Immigration Policy," *Asian American Policy Review,* Harvard University (Spring 1991).

14 "English-Only" rules have been implemented in the medical industry which is overwhelmingly dependent on nurses and nursing assistants from the Philippines.

Index